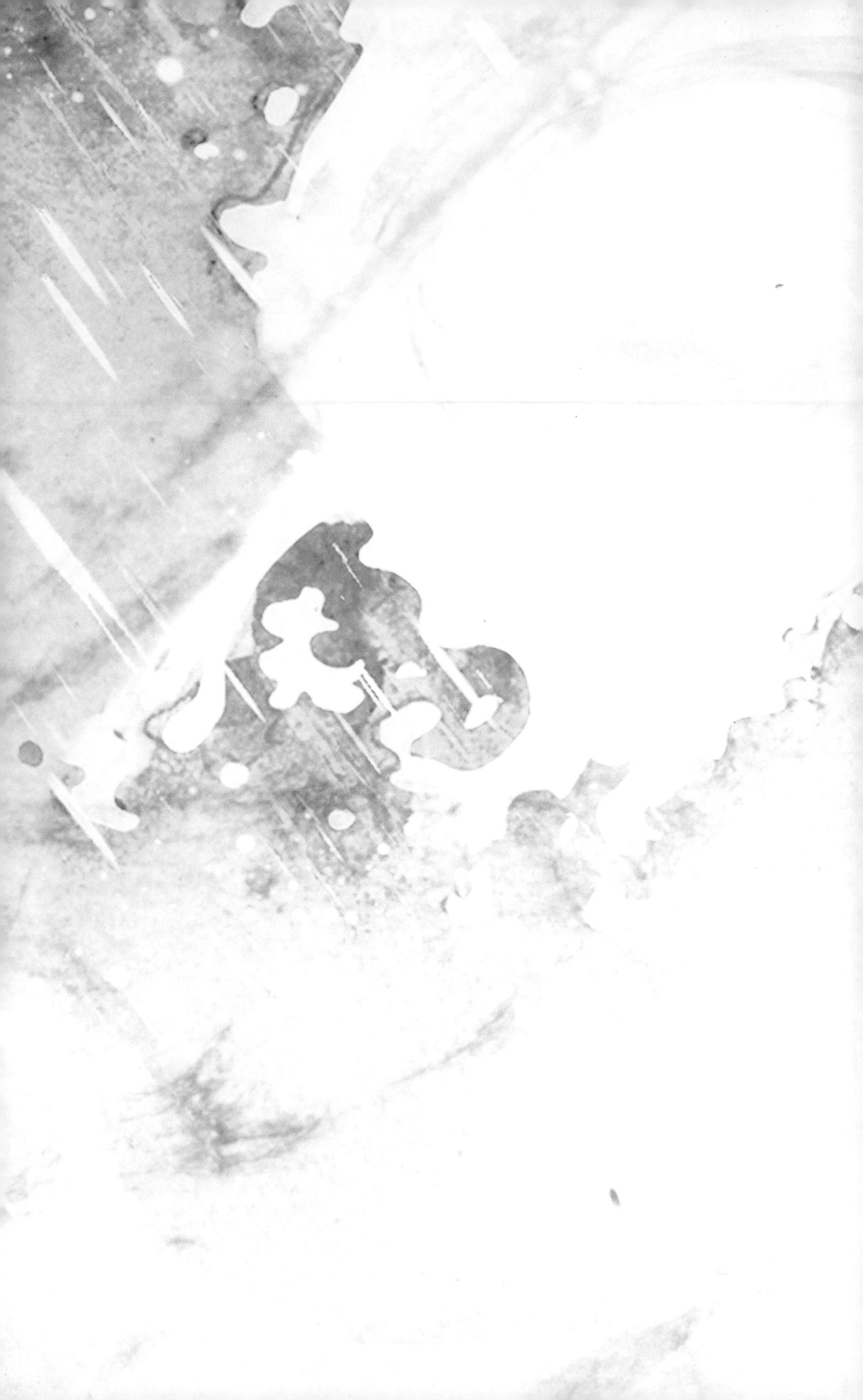

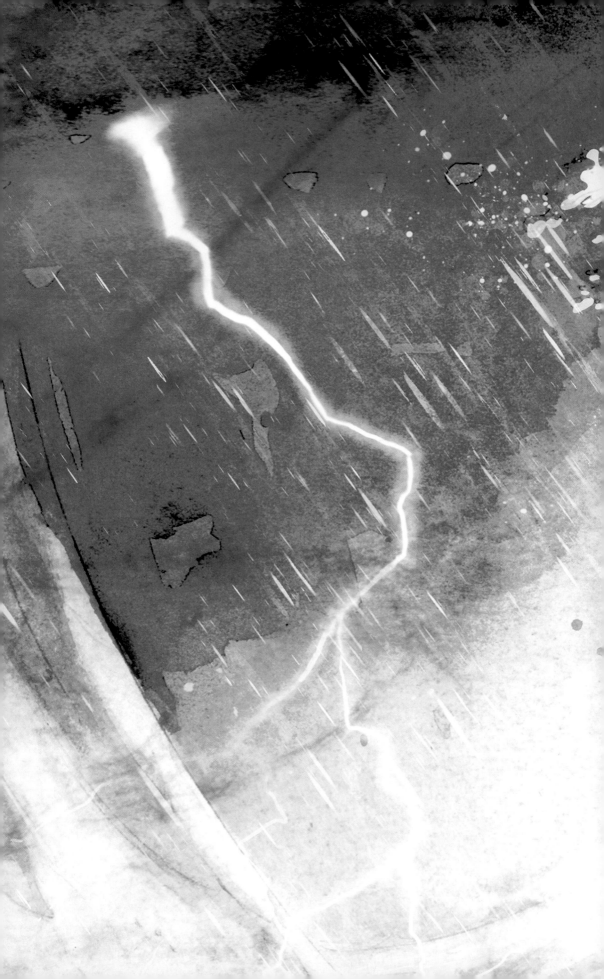

the unwritten

tommy taylor and the ship that sank twice

Mike Carey Writer/Co-Creator   **Peter Gross** Layouts/Co-Creator

Kurt Huggins, Peter Gross, Al Davison, Russ Braun,
Shawn McManus, Dean Ormston and **Gary Erskine** Finishes

Zelda Devon, Al Davison, Chris Chuckry, Eva de la Cruz and **Jeanne McGee** Colors

Yuko Shimizu Cover Art   Special thanks to **Zander Cannon** and **Barb Guttman**

THE UNWRITTEN is created by Mike Carey and Peter Gross

Pornsak Pichetshote, Shelly Bond, Gregory Lockard Editors
Robbin Brosterman Design Director – Books
Louis Prandi Publication Design

Shelly Bond Executive Editor - Vertigo
Hank Kanalz Senior VP – Vertigo & Integrated Publishing

Diane Nelson President
Dan DiDio and Jim Lee Co-Publishers
Geoff Johns Chief Creative Officer
John Rood Executive VP – Sales, Marketing & Business Development
Amy Genkins Senior VP – Business & Legal Affairs
Nairi Gardiner Senior VP – Finance
Jeff Boison VP – Publishing Planning
Mark Chiarello VP – Art Direction & Design
John Cunningham VP – Marketing
Terri Cunningham VP – Editorial Administration
Alison Gill Senior VP – Manufacturing & Operations
Jay Kogan VP – Business & Legal Affairs, Publishing
Jack Mahan VP – Business Affairs, Talent
Nick Napolitano VP – Manufacturing Administration
Sue Pohja VP – Book Sales
Courtney Simmons Senior VP – Publicity
Bob Wayne Senior VP – Sales

Library of Congress Cataloging-in-Publication Data

Carey, Mike, 1959-
  The unwritten : Tommy Taylor and the ship that sank twice / Mike Carey, Peter Gross,
Kurt Huggins, Zelda Devon.
    pages cm
  ISBN 978-1-4012-2976-4
1. Characters and characteristics in literature--Comic books, strips, etc. 2. Identity
(Philosophical concept)--Comic books, strips, etc. 3. Fiction--Comic books, strips, etc.
4. Graphic novels. I. Gross, Peter, 1958- II. Huggins, Kurt. III. Devon, Zelda. IV. Title.
  PN6727.C377U65 2013
  741.5'973--dc23
                    2013020333

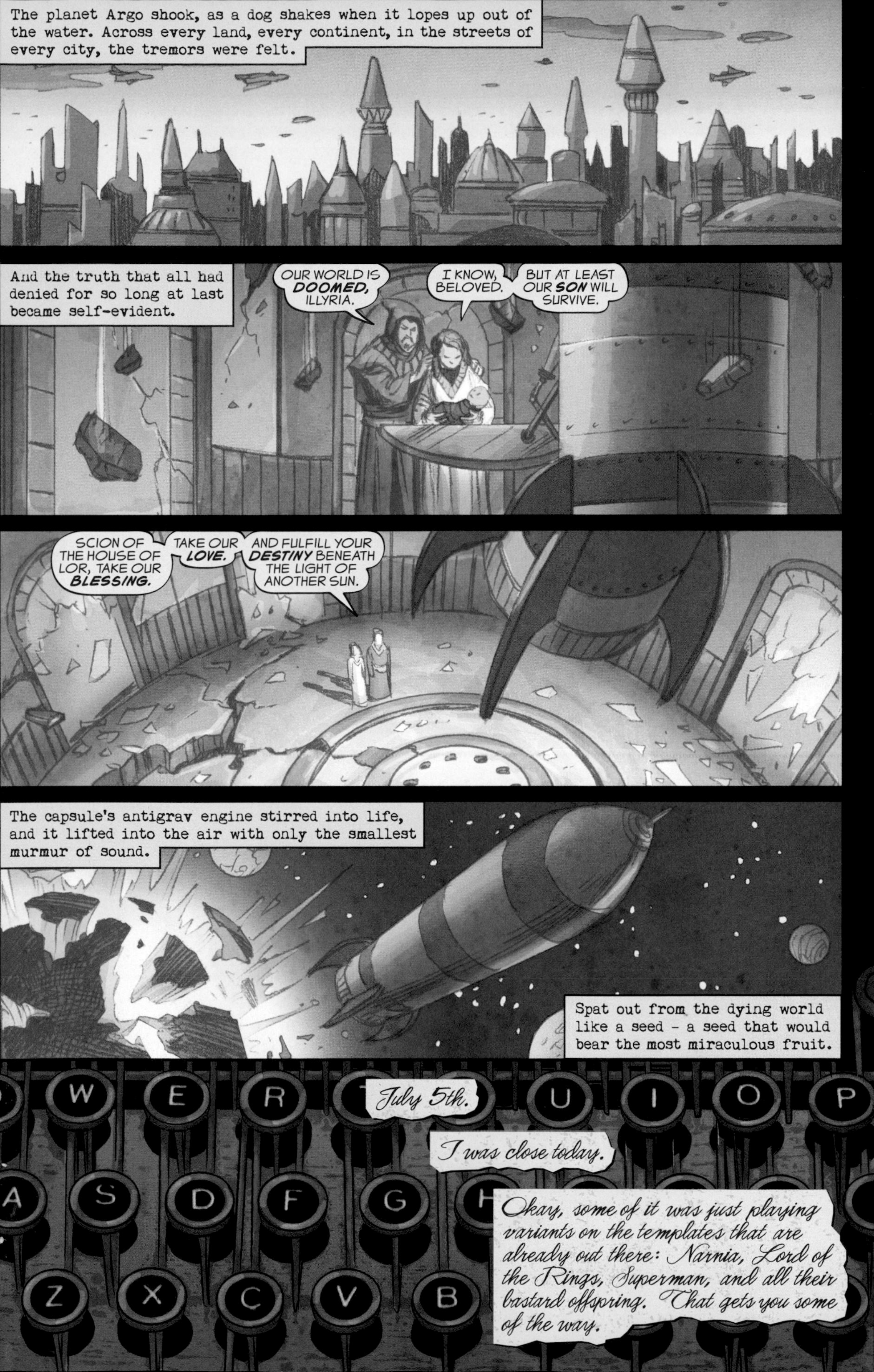

The planet Argo shook, as a dog shakes when it lopes up out of the water. Across every land, every continent, in the streets of every city, the tremors were felt.
And the truth that all had denied for so long at last became self-evident.
OUR WORLD IS DOOMED, ILLYRIA.
I KNOW, BELOVED.
BUT AT LEAST OUR SON WILL SURVIVE.
SCION OF THE HOUSE OF LOR, TAKE OUR BLESSING.
TAKE OUR LOVE.
AND FULFILL YOUR DESTINY BENEATH THE LIGHT OF ANOTHER SUN.
The capsule's antigrav engine stirred into life, and it lifted into the air with only the smallest murmur of sound.
Spat out from the dying world like a seed - a seed that would bear the most miraculous fruit.
July 5th.
I was close today.
Okay, some of it was just playing variants on the templates that are already out there: Narnia, Lord of the Rings, Superman, and all their bastard offspring. That gets you some of the way.

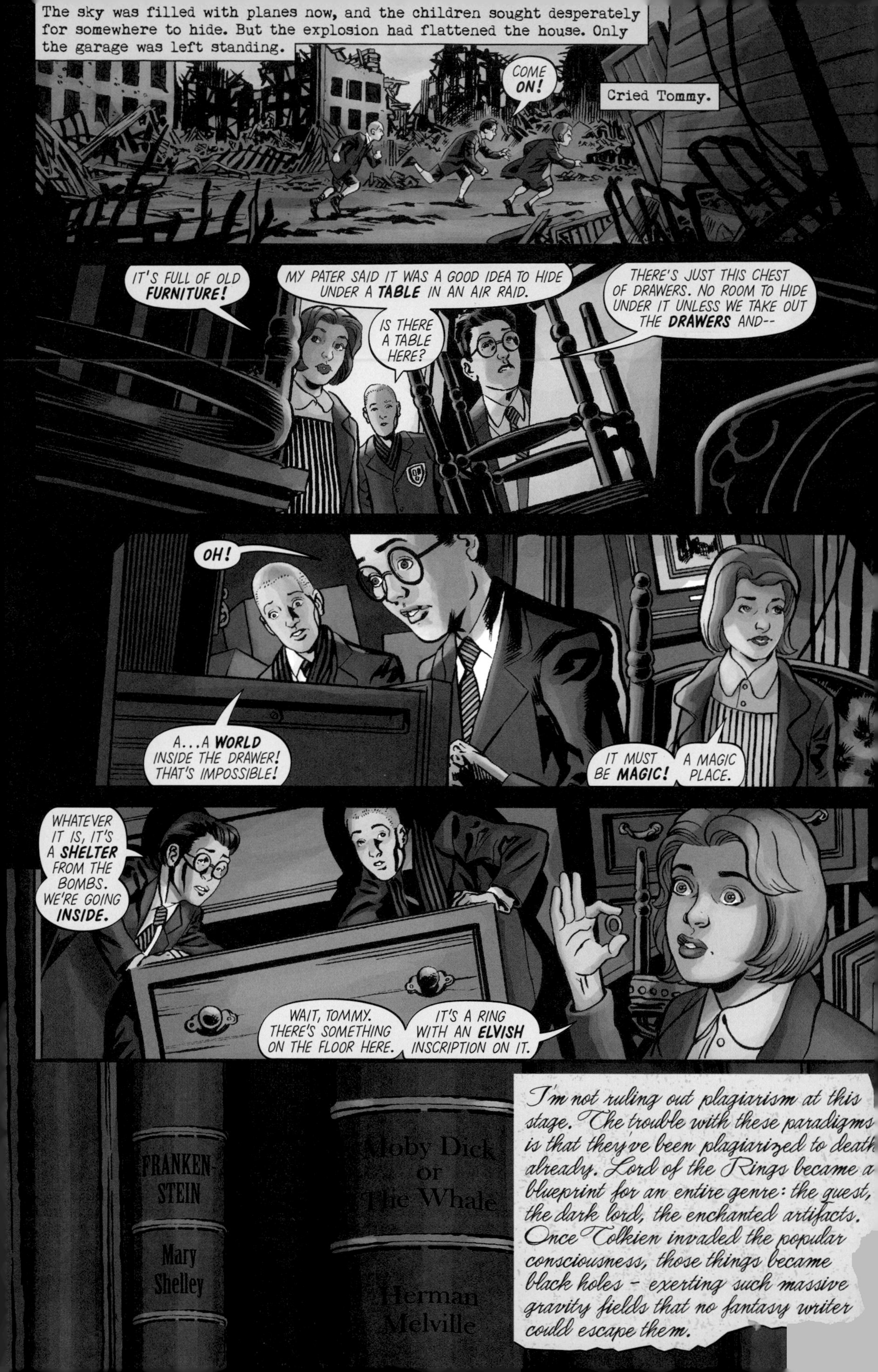
The sky was filled with planes now, and the children sought desperately for somewhere to hide. But the explosion had flattened the house. Only the garage was left standing.
COME ON!
Cried Tommy.
IT'S FULL OF OLD FURNITURE!
MY PATER SAID IT WAS A GOOD IDEA TO HIDE UNDER A TABLE IN AN AIR RAID.
IS THERE A TABLE HERE?
THERE'S JUST THIS CHEST OF DRAWERS. NO ROOM TO HIDE UNDER IT UNLESS WE TAKE OUT THE DRAWERS AND--
OH!
A...A WORLD INSIDE THE DRAWER! THAT'S IMPOSSIBLE!
IT MUST BE MAGIC!
A MAGIC PLACE.
WHATEVER IT IS, IT'S A SHELTER FROM THE BOMBS. WE'RE GOING INSIDE.
WAIT, TOMMY. THERE'S SOMETHING ON THE FLOOR HERE.
IT'S A RING WITH AN ELVISH INSCRIPTION ON IT.
FRANKEN-STEIN
Mary Shelley
Moby Dick or The Whale
Herman Melville
I'm not ruling out plagiarism at this stage. The trouble with these paradigms is that they've been plagiarized to death already. Lord of the Rings became a blueprint for an entire genre: the quest, the dark lord, the enchanted artifacts. Once Tolkien invaded the popular consciousness, those things became black holes - exerting such massive gravity fields that no fantasy writer could escape them.

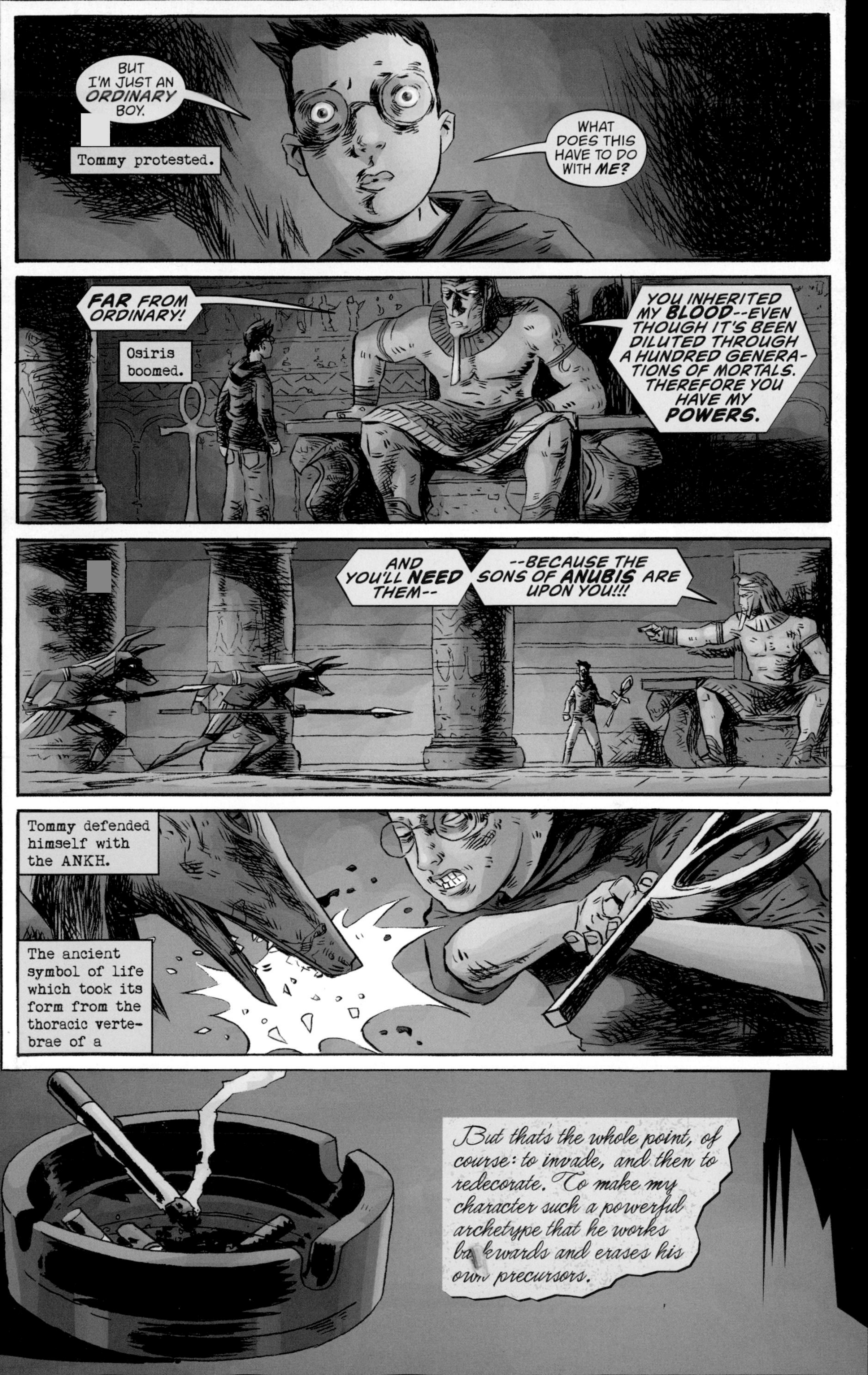

BUT I'M JUST AN ORDINARY BOY.
Tommy protested.
WHAT DOES THIS HAVE TO DO WITH ME?
FAR FROM ORDINARY!
Osiris boomed.
YOU INHERITED MY BLOOD--EVEN THOUGH IT'S BEEN DILUTED THROUGH A HUNDRED GENERATIONS OF MORTALS. THEREFORE YOU HAVE MY POWERS.
AND YOU'LL NEED THEM--
--BECAUSE THE SONS OF ANUBIS ARE UPON YOU!!!
Tommy defended himself with the ANKH.
The ancient symbol of life which took its form from the thoracic vertebrae of a
But thats the whole point, of course: to invade, and then to redecorate. To make my character such a powerful archetype that he works backwards and erases his own precursors.

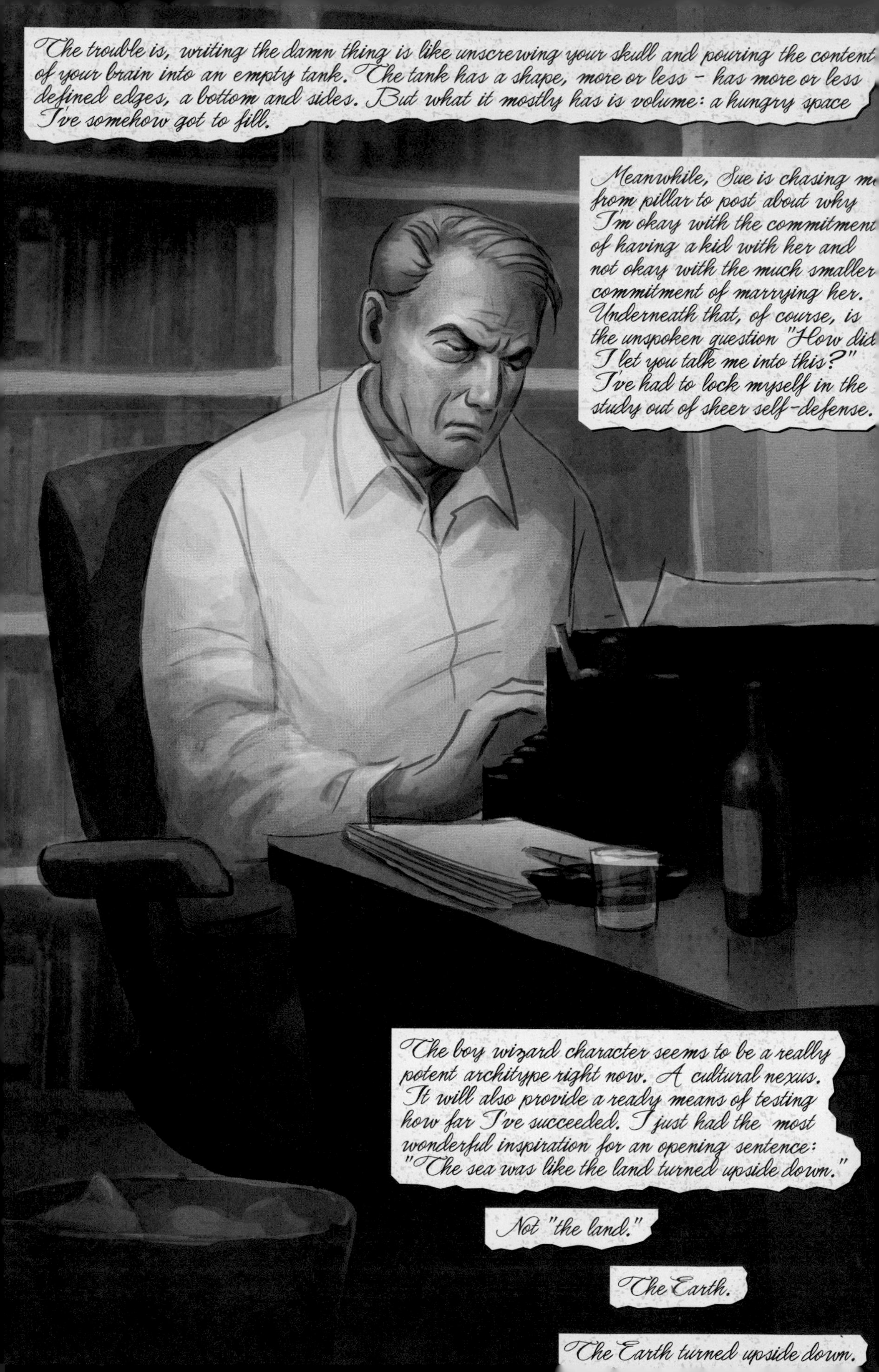
The trouble is, writing the damn thing is like unscrewing your skull and pouring the content of your brain into an empty tank. The tank has a shape, more or less - has more or less defined edges, a bottom and sides. But what it mostly has is volume: a hungry space I've somehow got to fill.
Meanwhile, Sue is chasing me from pillar to post about why I'm okay with the commitment of having a kid with her and not okay with the much smaller commitment of marrying her. Underneath that, of course, is the unspoken question "How did I let you talk me into this?" I've had to lock myself in the study out of sheer self-defense.
The boy wizard character seems to be a really potent architype right now. A cultural nexus. It will also provide a ready means of testing how far I've succeeded. I just had the most wonderful inspiration for an opening sentence: "The sea was like the land turned upside down."
Not "the land."
The Earth.
The Earth turned upside down.

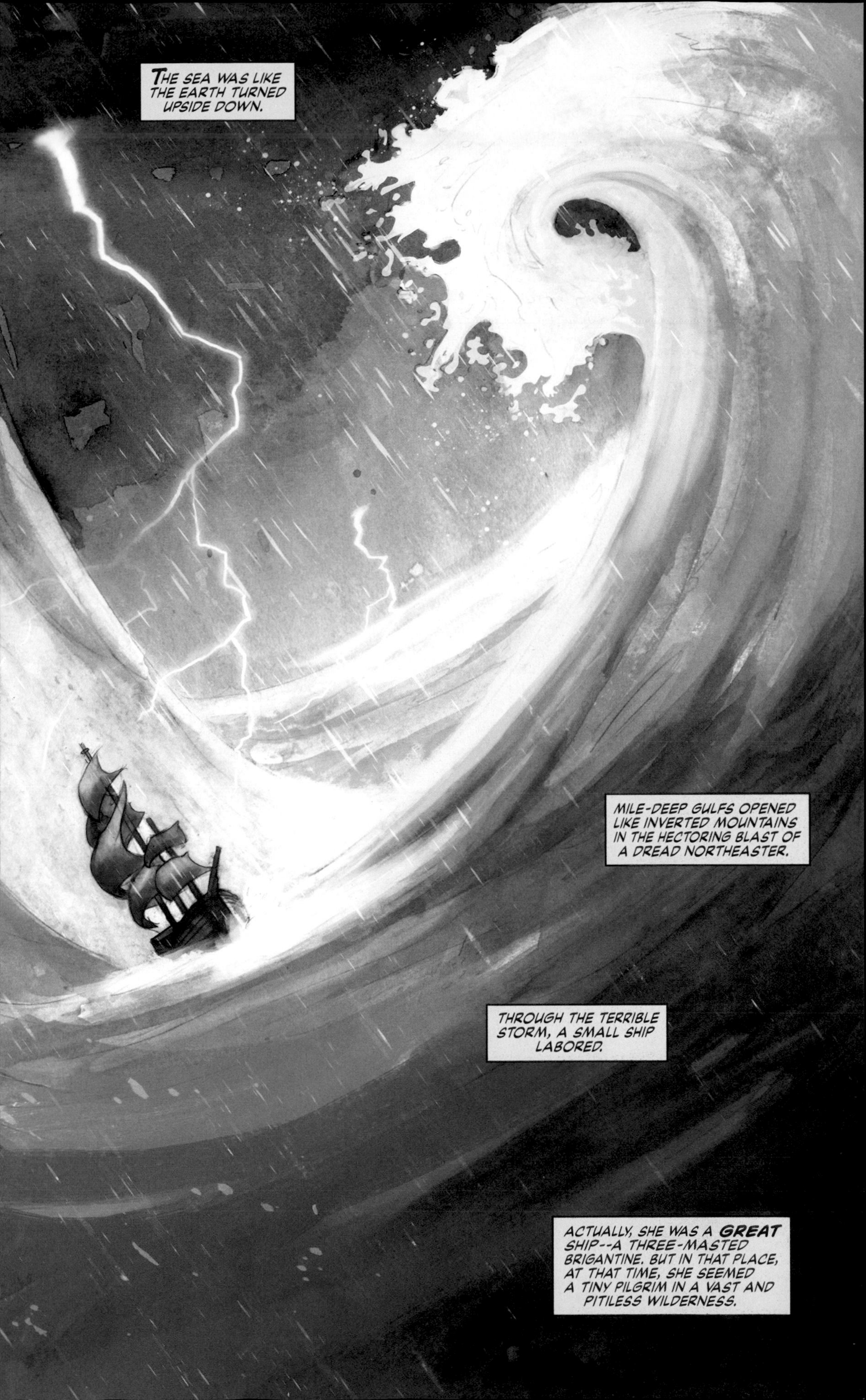
THE SEA WAS LIKE THE EARTH TURNED UPSIDE DOWN.
MILE-DEEP GULFS OPENED LIKE INVERTED MOUNTAINS IN THE HECTORING BLAST OF A DREAD NORTHEASTER.
THROUGH THE TERRIBLE STORM, A SMALL SHIP LABORED.
ACTUALLY, SHE WAS A GREAT SHIP--A THREE-MASTED BRIGANTINE. BUT IN THAT PLACE, AT THAT TIME, SHE SEEMED A TINY PILGRIM IN A VAST AND PITILESS WILDERNESS.

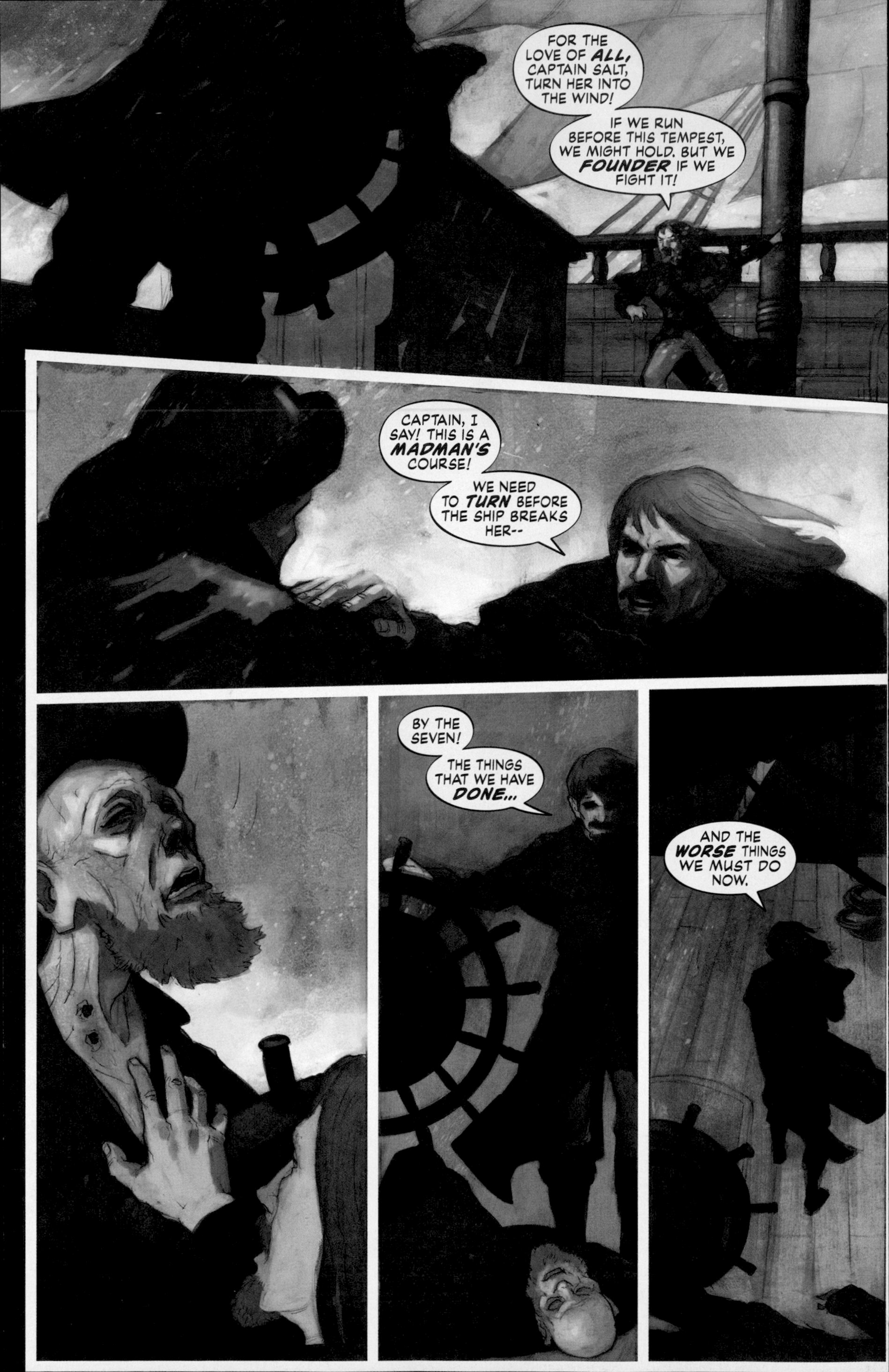
FOR THE LOVE OF ALL, CAPTAIN SALT, TURN HER INTO THE WIND!
IF WE RUN BEFORE THIS TEMPEST, WE MIGHT HOLD. BUT WE FOUNDER IF WE FIGHT IT!
CAPTAIN, I SAY! THIS IS A MADMAN'S COURSE!
WE NEED TO TURN BEFORE THE SHIP BREAKS HER--
BY THE SEVEN!
THE THINGS THAT WE HAVE DONE...
AND THE WORSE THINGS WE MUST DO NOW.

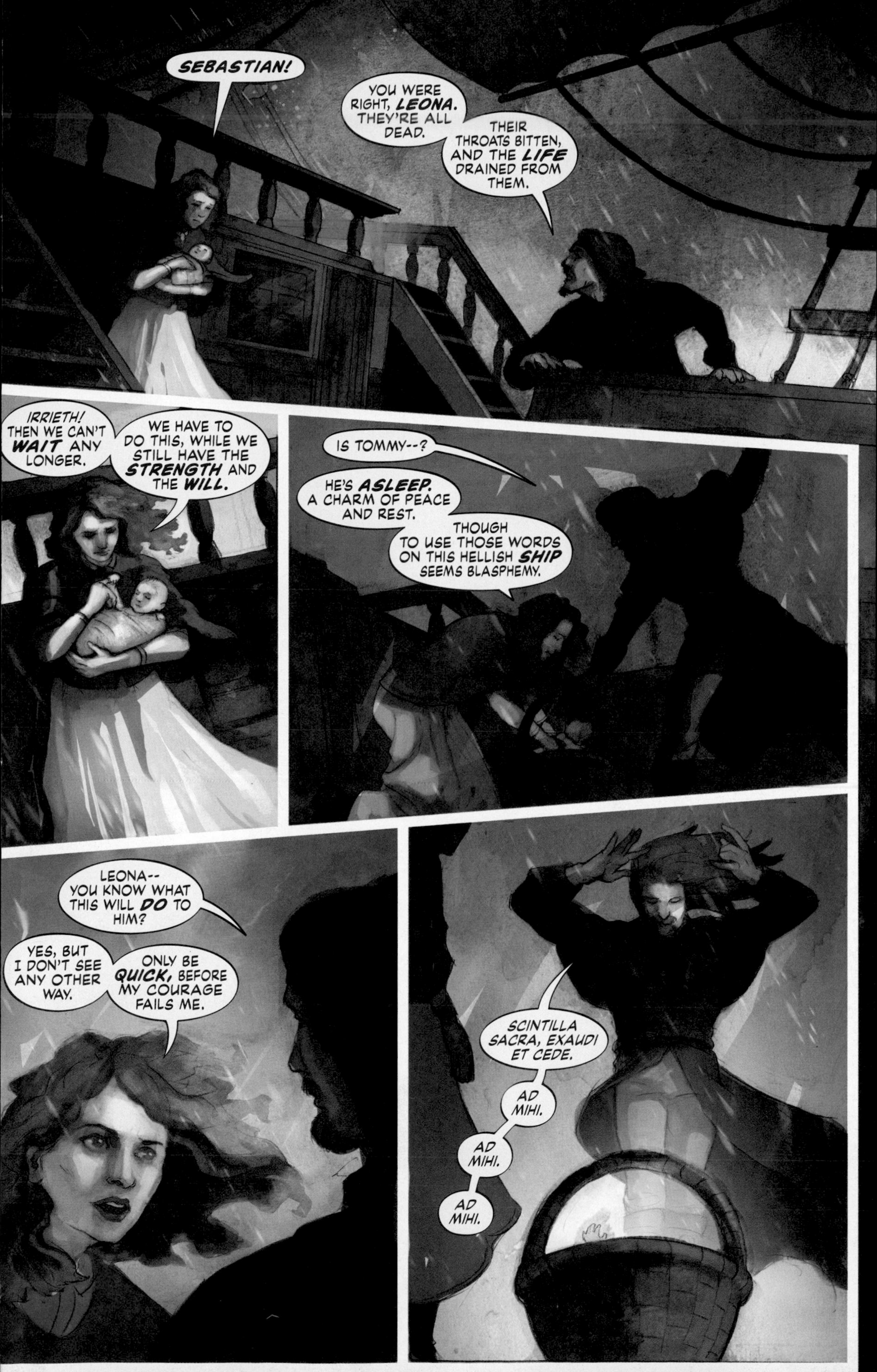
SEBASTIAN!
YOU WERE RIGHT, LEONA. THEY'RE ALL DEAD.
THEIR THROATS BITTEN, AND THE LIFE DRAINED FROM THEM.
IRRIETH! THEN WE CAN'T WAIT ANY LONGER.
WE HAVE TO DO THIS, WHILE WE STILL HAVE THE STRENGTH AND THE WILL.
IS TOMMY--?
HE'S ASLEEP. A CHARM OF PEACE AND REST.
THOUGH TO USE THOSE WORDS ON THIS HELLISH SHIP SEEMS BLASPHEMY.
LEONA-- YOU KNOW WHAT THIS WILL DO TO HIM?
YES, BUT I DON'T SEE ANY OTHER WAY.
ONLY BE QUICK, BEFORE MY COURAGE FAILS ME.
SCINTILLA SACRA, EXAUDI ET CEDE.
AD MIHI.
AD MIHI.
AD MIHI.

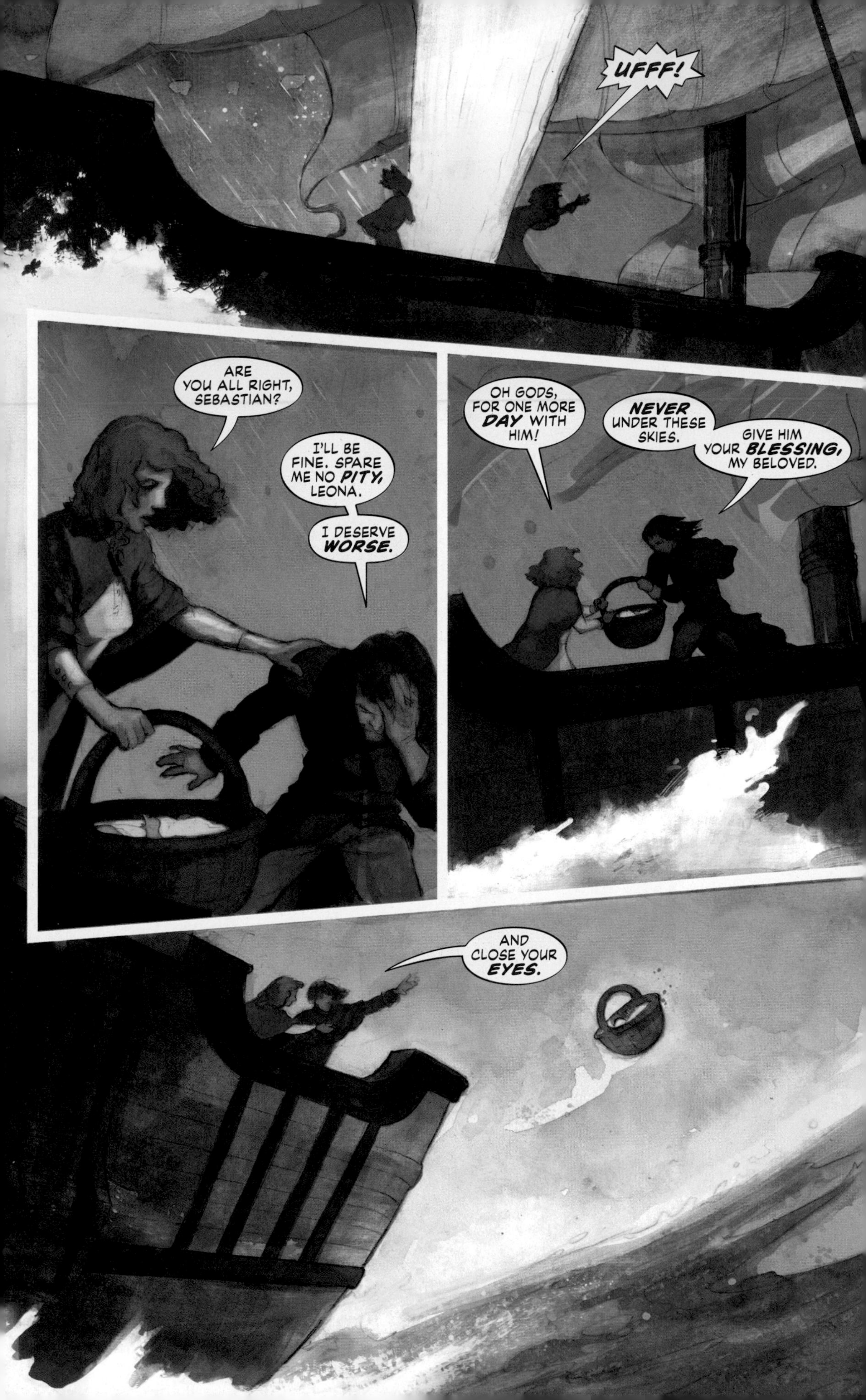
UFFF!
ARE YOU ALL RIGHT, SEBASTIAN?
I'LL BE FINE. SPARE ME NO PITY, LEONA.
I DESERVE WORSE.
OH GODS, FOR ONE MORE DAY WITH HIM!
NEVER UNDER THESE SKIES.
GIVE HIM YOUR BLESSING, MY BELOVED.
AND CLOSE YOUR EYES.

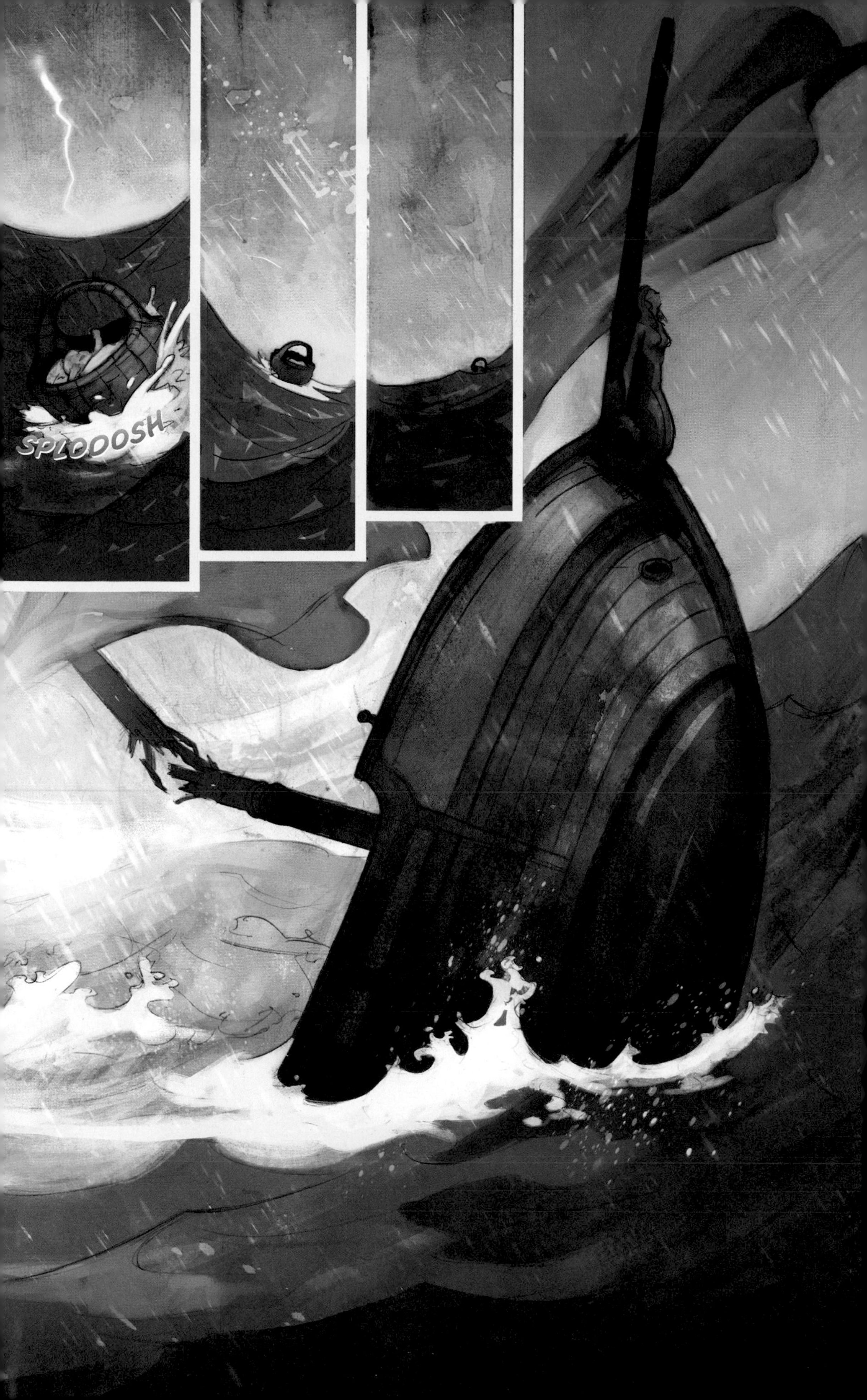
SPLOODOSH

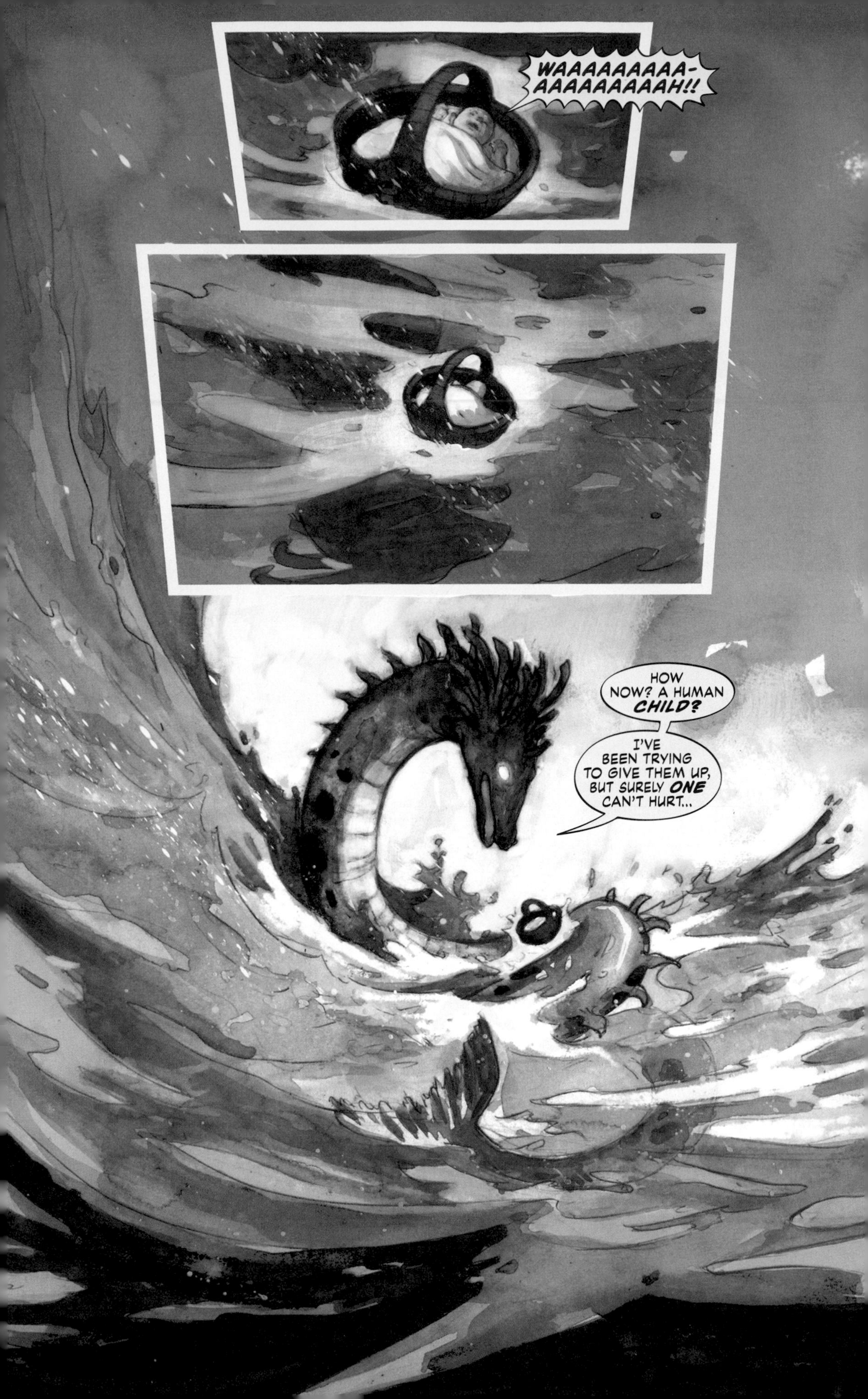
WAAAAAAAAA-AAAAAAAAAAH!!
HOW NOW? A HUMAN *CHILD?*
I'VE BEEN TRYING TO GIVE THEM UP, BUT SURELY *ONE* CAN'T HURT...

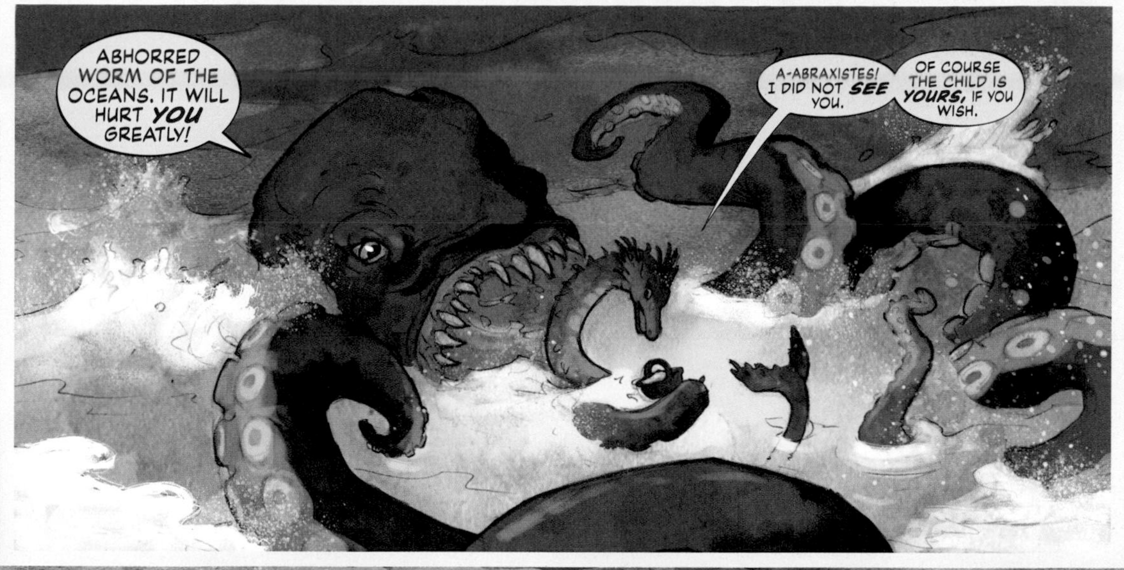
ABHORRED WORM OF THE OCEANS. IT WILL HURT YOU GREATLY!
A-ABRAXISTES! I DID NOT SEE YOU.
OF COURSE THE CHILD IS YOURS, IF YOU WISH.

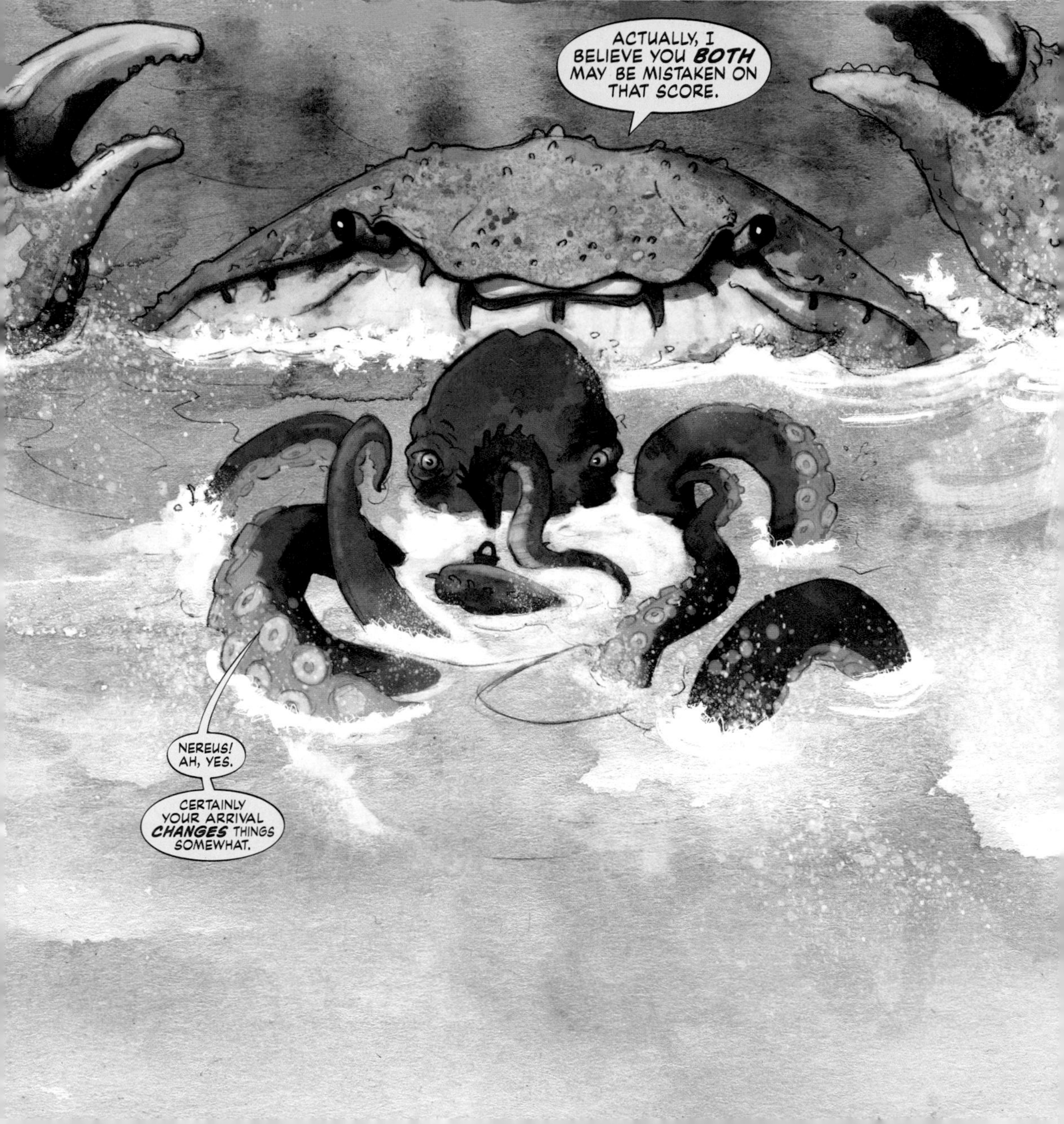
ACTUALLY, I BELIEVE YOU BOTH MAY BE MISTAKEN ON THAT SCORE.
NEREUS! AH, YES.
CERTAINLY YOUR ARRIVAL CHANGES THINGS SOMEWHAT.

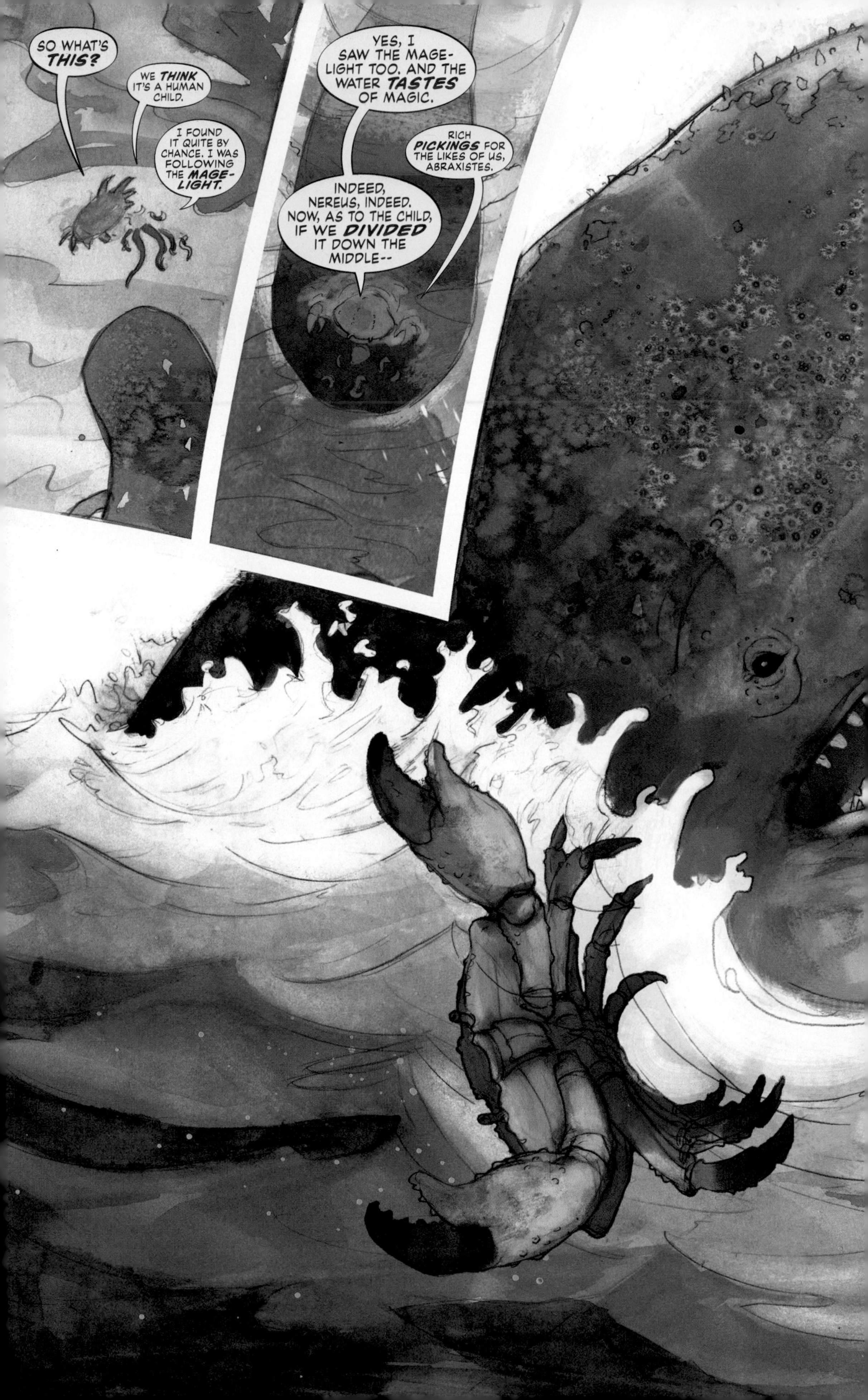

SO WHAT'S **THIS?**
WE **THINK** IT'S A HUMAN CHILD.
I FOUND IT QUITE BY CHANCE. I WAS FOLLOWING THE **MAGE-LIGHT.**
YES, I SAW THE MAGE-LIGHT TOO, AND THE WATER **TASTES** OF MAGIC.
RICH **PICKINGS** FOR THE LIKES OF US, ABRAXISTES.
INDEED, NEREUS, INDEED. NOW, AS TO THE CHILD, IF WE **DIVIDED** IT DOWN THE MIDDLE--

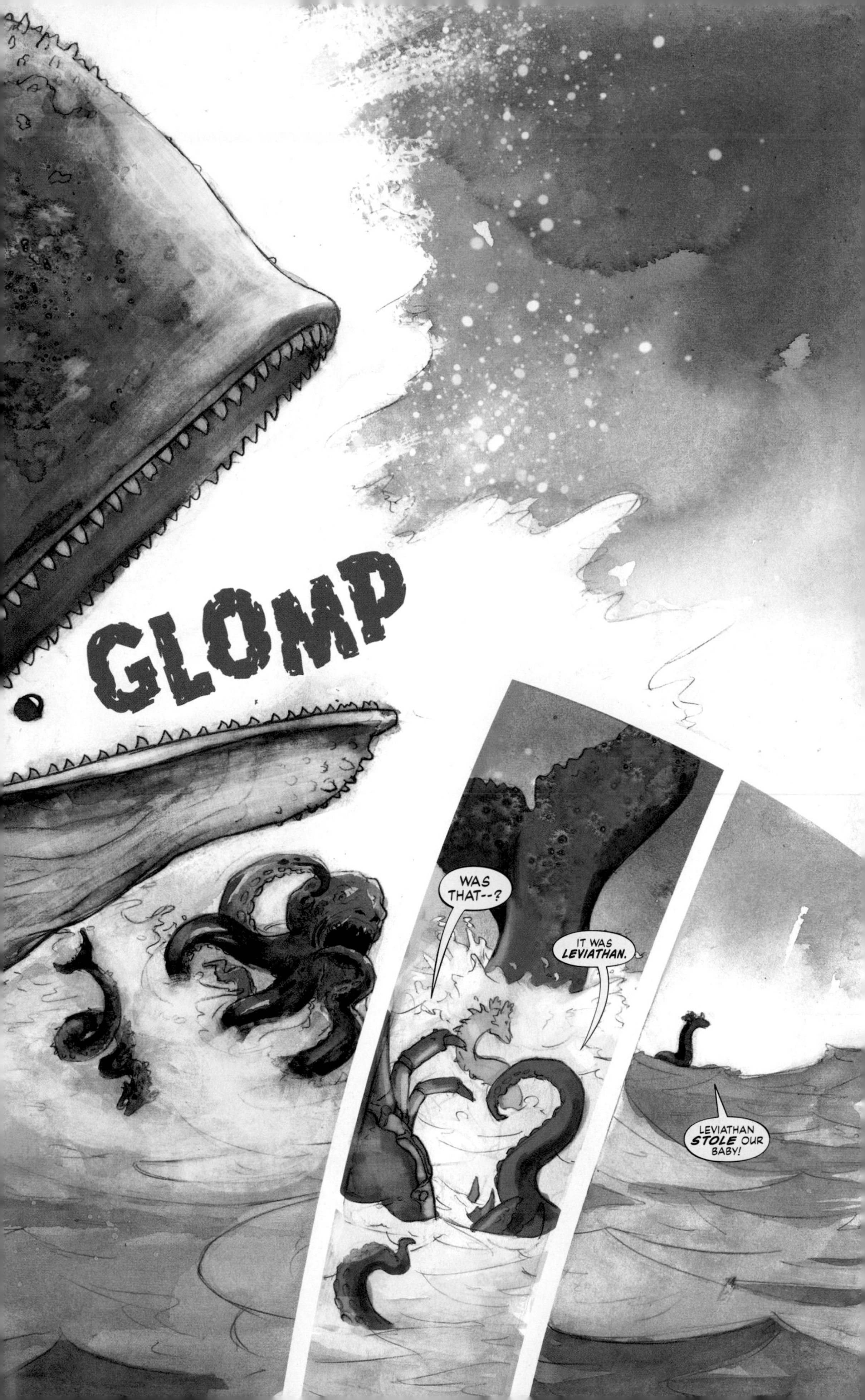
GLOMP
WAS THAT--?
IT WAS LEVIATHAN.
LEVIATHAN STOLE OUR BABY!

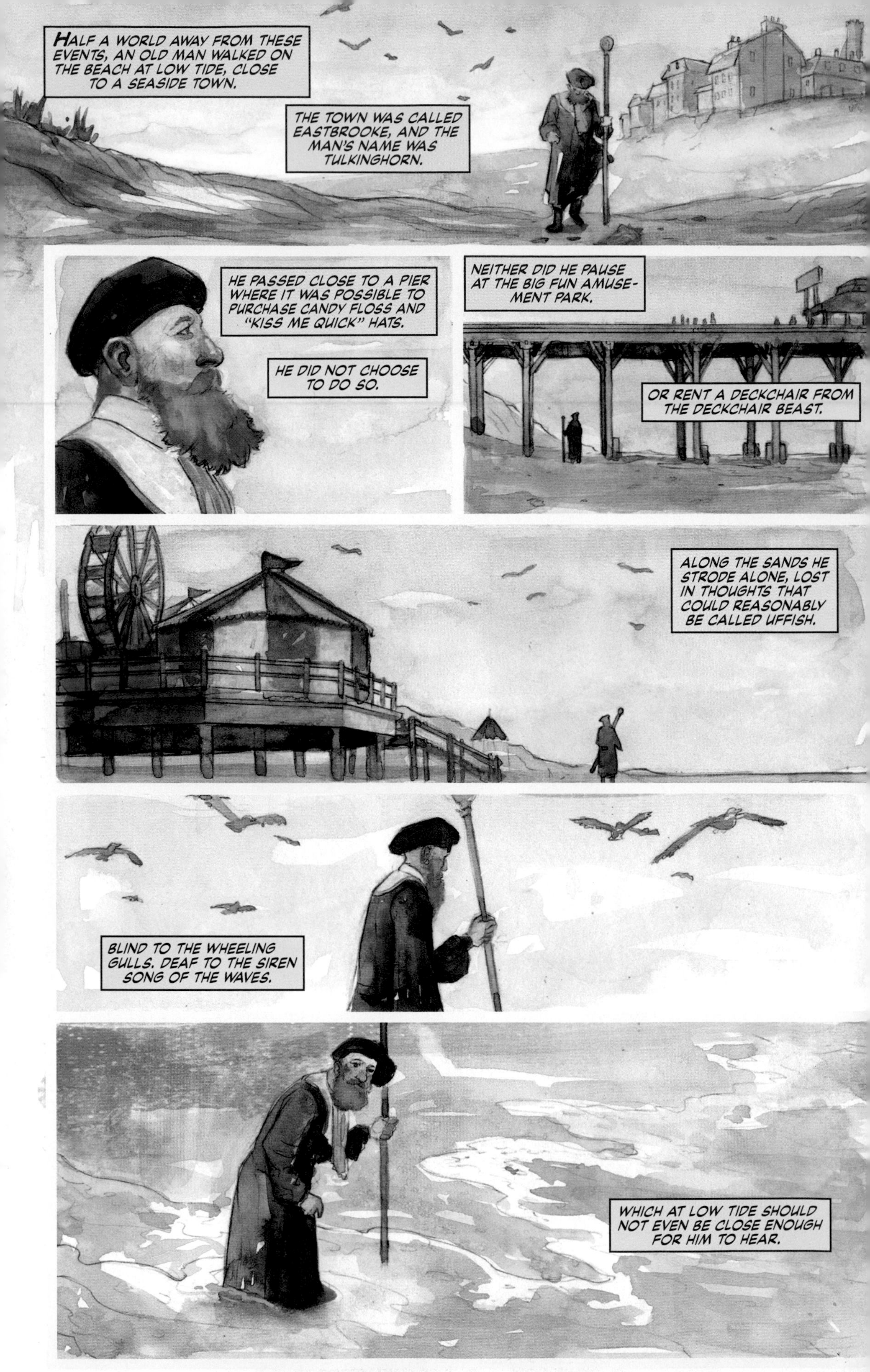
HALF A WORLD AWAY FROM THESE EVENTS, AN OLD MAN WALKED ON THE BEACH AT LOW TIDE, CLOSE TO A SEASIDE TOWN.
THE TOWN WAS CALLED EASTBROOKE, AND THE MAN'S NAME WAS TULKINGHORN.
HE PASSED CLOSE TO A PIER WHERE IT WAS POSSIBLE TO PURCHASE CANDY FLOSS AND "KISS ME QUICK" HATS.
HE DID NOT CHOOSE TO DO SO.
NEITHER DID HE PAUSE AT THE BIG FUN AMUSEMENT PARK.
OR RENT A DECKCHAIR FROM THE DECKCHAIR BEAST.
ALONG THE SANDS HE STRODE ALONE, LOST IN THOUGHTS THAT COULD REASONABLY BE CALLED UFFISH.
BLIND TO THE WHEELING GULLS. DEAF TO THE SIREN SONG OF THE WAVES.
WHICH AT LOW TIDE SHOULD NOT EVEN BE CLOSE ENOUGH FOR HIM TO HEAR.

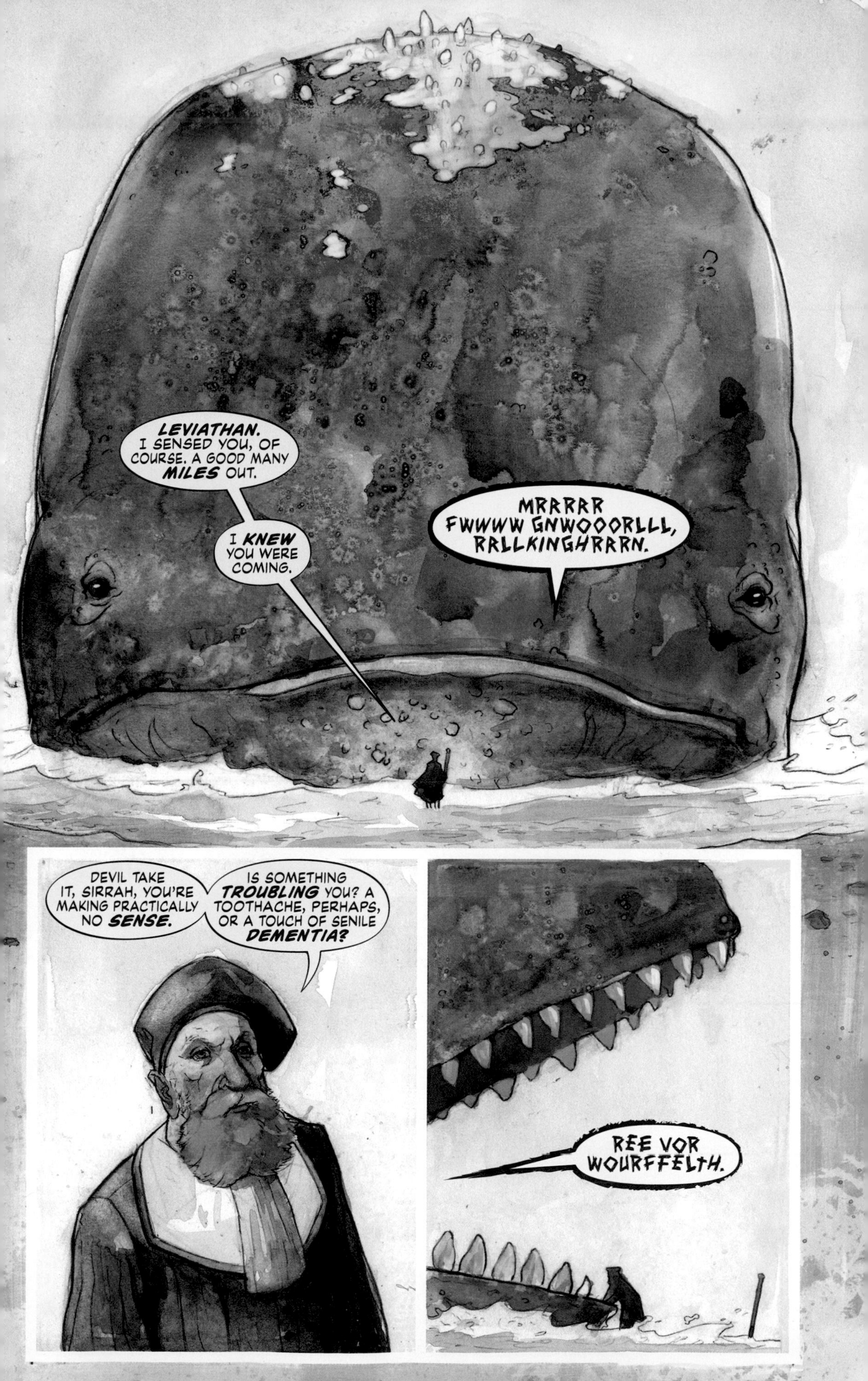

LEVIATHAN. I SENSED YOU, OF COURSE. A GOOD MANY MILES OUT.
I KNEW YOU WERE COMING.
MRRRRR FWWWW GNWOOORLLL, RRLLKINGHRRRN.
DEVIL TAKE IT, SIRRAH, YOU'RE MAKING PRACTICALLY NO SENSE.
IS SOMETHING TROUBLING YOU? A TOOTHACHE, PERHAPS, OR A TOUCH OF SENILE DEMENTIA?
REE VOR WOURFFELTH.

WELL, THERE'S A *SHOPPING TROLLEY* WRAPPED AROUND YOUR LEFT FRONT BICUSPID.

THAT MIGHT CAUSE THE ODD *TWINGE,* I'D HAVE THOUGHT. BUT SURELY--

WAAAAAAH!

... OH.

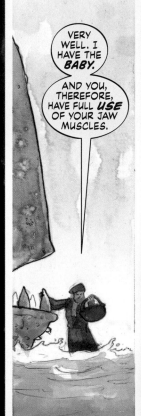

VERY WELL. I HAVE THE *BABY.*

AND YOU, THEREFORE, HAVE FULL *USE* OF YOUR JAW MUSCLES.

A CHILD. A *BOY,* IF I'M NOT MISTAKEN.

I DREAMED LAST NIGHT THAT MY FRIENDS WERE *SLEEPING* AT THE BOTTOM OF THE SEA.

THAT IS NOT SO.

NO?

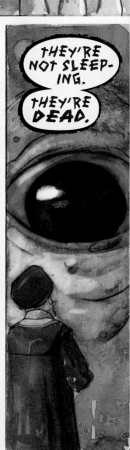

THEY'RE NOT SLEEPING.

THEY'RE *DEAD.*

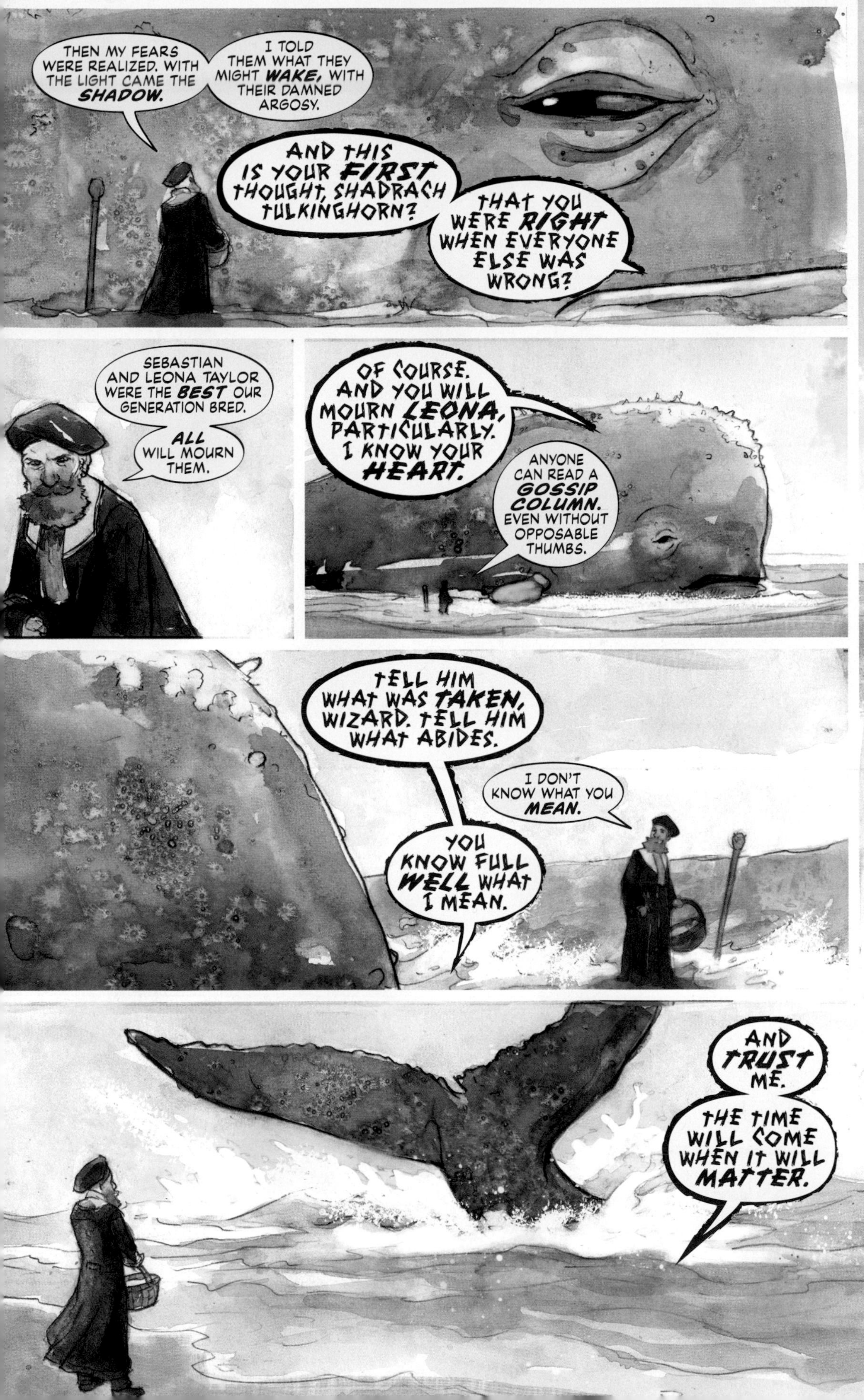
THEN MY FEARS WERE REALIZED. WITH THE LIGHT CAME THE SHADOW.
I TOLD THEM WHAT THEY MIGHT WAKE, WITH THEIR DAMNED ARGOSY.
AND THIS IS YOUR FIRST THOUGHT, SHADRACH TULKINGHORN?
THAT YOU WERE RIGHT WHEN EVERYONE ELSE WAS WRONG?
SEBASTIAN AND LEONA TAYLOR WERE THE BEST OUR GENERATION BRED.
ALL WILL MOURN THEM.
OF COURSE. AND YOU WILL MOURN LEONA, PARTICULARLY. I KNOW YOUR HEART.
ANYONE CAN READ A GOSSIP COLUMN. EVEN WITHOUT OPPOSABLE THUMBS.
TELL HIM WHAT WAS TAKEN, WIZARD. TELL HIM WHAT ABIDES.
I DON'T KNOW WHAT YOU MEAN.
YOU KNOW FULL WELL WHAT I MEAN.
AND TRUST ME.
THE TIME WILL COME WHEN IT WILL MATTER.

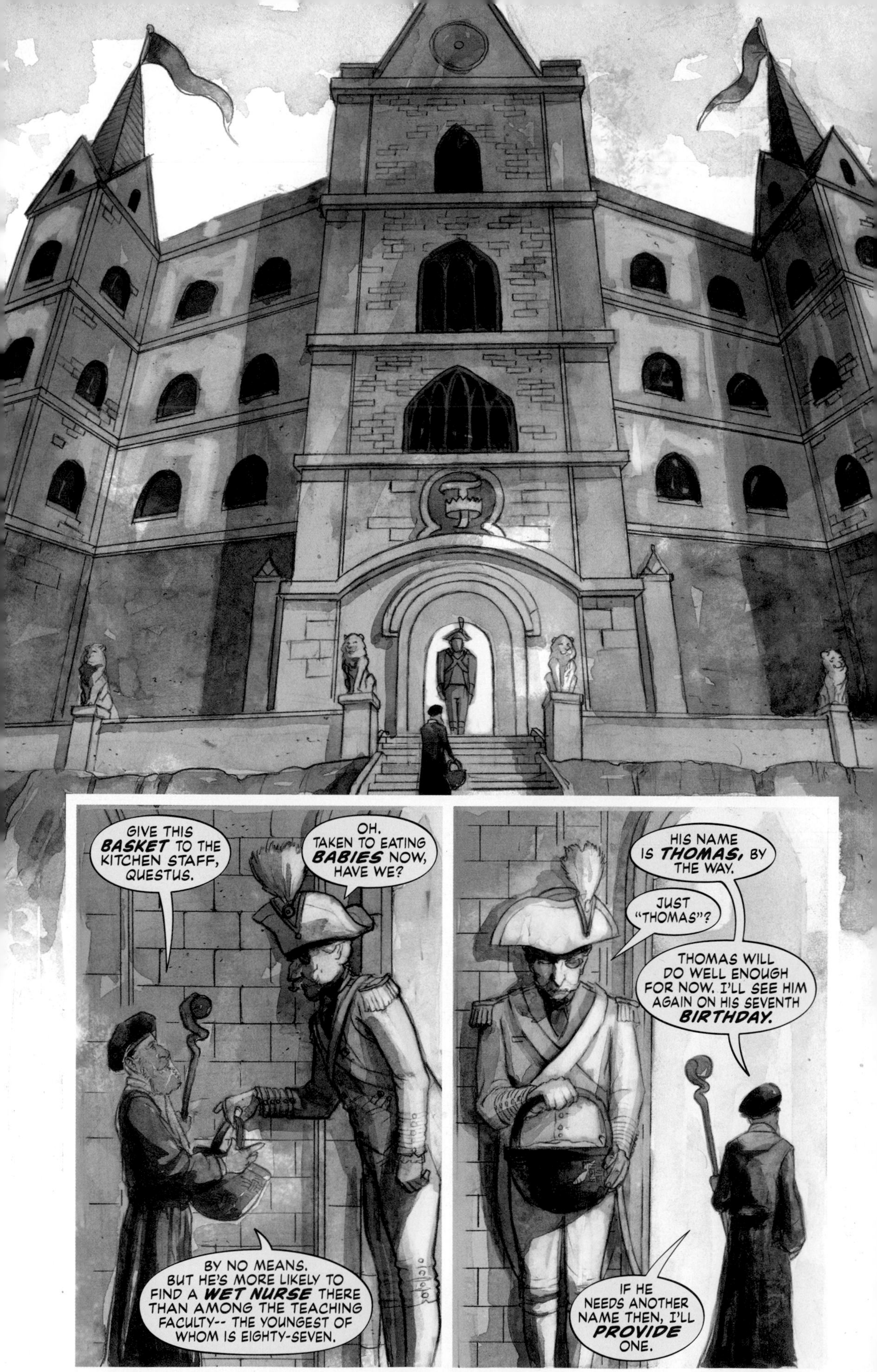
GIVE THIS **BASKET** TO THE KITCHEN STAFF, QUESTUS.
OH. TAKEN TO EATING **BABIES** NOW, HAVE WE?
BY NO MEANS. BUT HE'S MORE LIKELY TO FIND A **WET NURSE** THERE THAN AMONG THE TEACHING FACULTY-- THE YOUNGEST OF WHOM IS EIGHTY-SEVEN.
HIS NAME IS **THOMAS,** BY THE WAY.
JUST "THOMAS"?
THOMAS WILL DO WELL ENOUGH FOR NOW. I'LL SEE HIM AGAIN ON HIS SEVENTH **BIRTHDAY.**
IF HE NEEDS ANOTHER NAME THEN, I'LL **PROVIDE** ONE.

Aug 12th. Lunch with Cole at the Groucho. I showed him the completed chapters, and he was impressed. Also puzzled, I could see. He sees fantasy as a niche market, so the possibility of a fantasy bestseller - pace Tolkien - is alien to his consciousness.

I told him Sue was great with child, and he shook his head at that: he remembers her saying that time in Highgate that neither she nor I would ever do the world the disservice of breeding.

Then I told him I was pregnant too, and he just shoved his linguini way over to the side of the table where it almost tipped over the edge.

I DON'T EVEN KNOW WHAT THAT MEANS.

he said, sounding sullen and unhappy.

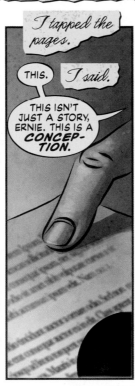

I tapped the pages.

THIS. *I said.*

THIS ISN'T JUST A STORY, ERNIE. THIS IS A **CONCEPTION**.

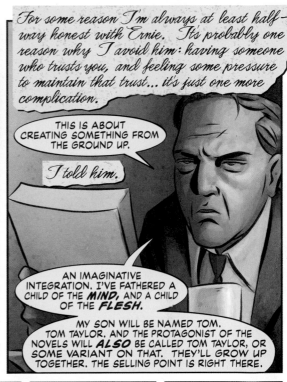

For some reason I'm always at least half-way honest with Ernie. It's probably one reason why I avoid him: having someone who trusts you, and feeling some pressure to maintain that trust... it's just one more complication.

THIS IS ABOUT CREATING SOMETHING FROM THE GROUND UP.

I told him.

AN IMAGINATIVE INTEGRATION. I'VE FATHERED A CHILD OF THE **MIND**, AND A CHILD OF THE **FLESH**.

MY SON WILL BE NAMED TOM. TOM TAYLOR. AND THE PROTAGONIST OF THE NOVELS WILL **ALSO** BE CALLED TOM TAYLOR, OR SOME VARIANT ON THAT. THEY'LL GROW UP TOGETHER. THE SELLING POINT IS RIGHT THERE.

THE SELLING POINT?

Ernie echoed.

THE **MARKETING ANGLE**, THEN. THE CONCEPTUAL TWIST THAT WILL GET US INTO THE SPOTLIGHT IN THE FIRST PLACE. AFTER THAT, IT'S GOING TO DEVELOP ITS OWN MOMENTUM.

AND WHAT MAKES YOU THINK I'LL **PUBLISH** THIS?

he demanded.

He sounded a lot angrier than I'd expected, but I know he'll come around.

I'VE ALREADY TALKED TO DARREN AT VICTOR GOLLANCZ.

I told him.

IF YOU BALK, ERNIE, I'M RIGHT THERE WITH PLAN B. JUST BE HAPPY YOU WERE **PLAN A**.

Neither of us felt like staying for dessert.

But the contracts came through by fax about an hour later. I amended the clause about the publication date, signed them, sent them back, then waited for the phone to ring.

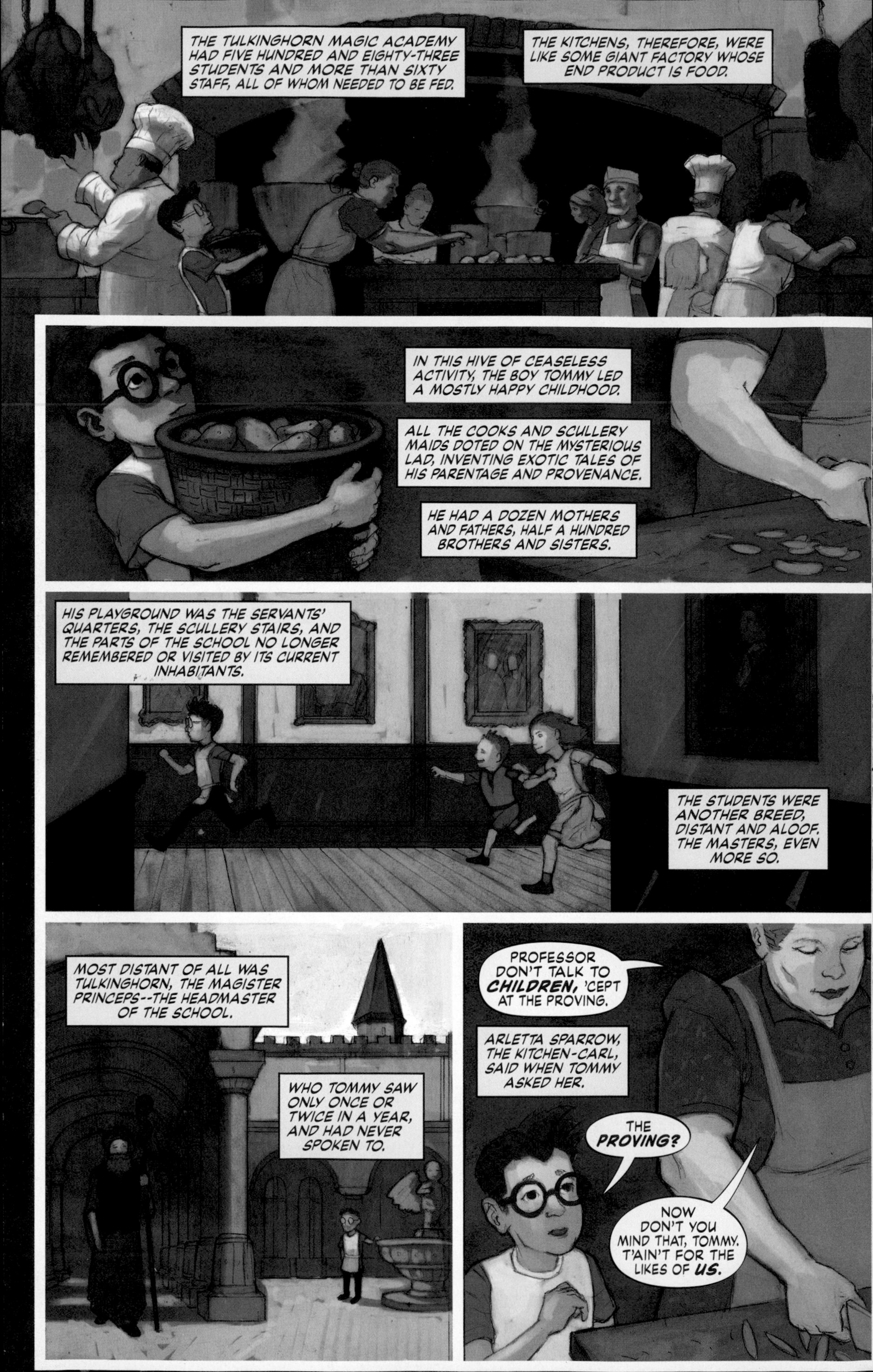
THE TULKINGHORN MAGIC ACADEMY HAD FIVE HUNDRED AND EIGHTY-THREE STUDENTS AND MORE THAN SIXTY STAFF, ALL OF WHOM NEEDED TO BE FED.
THE KITCHENS, THEREFORE, WERE LIKE SOME GIANT FACTORY WHOSE END PRODUCT IS FOOD.
IN THIS HIVE OF CEASELESS ACTIVITY, THE BOY TOMMY LED A MOSTLY HAPPY CHILDHOOD.
ALL THE COOKS AND SCULLERY MAIDS DOTED ON THE MYSTERIOUS LAD, INVENTING EXOTIC TALES OF HIS PARENTAGE AND PROVENANCE.
HE HAD A DOZEN MOTHERS AND FATHERS, HALF A HUNDRED BROTHERS AND SISTERS.
HIS PLAYGROUND WAS THE SERVANTS' QUARTERS, THE SCULLERY STAIRS, AND THE PARTS OF THE SCHOOL NO LONGER REMEMBERED OR VISITED BY ITS CURRENT INHABITANTS.
THE STUDENTS WERE ANOTHER BREED, DISTANT AND ALOOF. THE MASTERS, EVEN MORE SO.
MOST DISTANT OF ALL WAS TULKINGHORN, THE MAGISTER PRINCEPS--THE HEADMASTER OF THE SCHOOL.
WHO TOMMY SAW ONLY ONCE OR TWICE IN A YEAR, AND HAD NEVER SPOKEN TO.
PROFESSOR DON'T TALK TO **CHILDREN,** 'CEPT AT THE PROVING.
ARLETTA SPARROW, THE KITCHEN-CARL, SAID WHEN TOMMY ASKED HER.
THE ***PROVING?***
NOW DON'T YOU MIND THAT, TOMMY. T'AIN'T FOR THE LIKES OF ***US.***

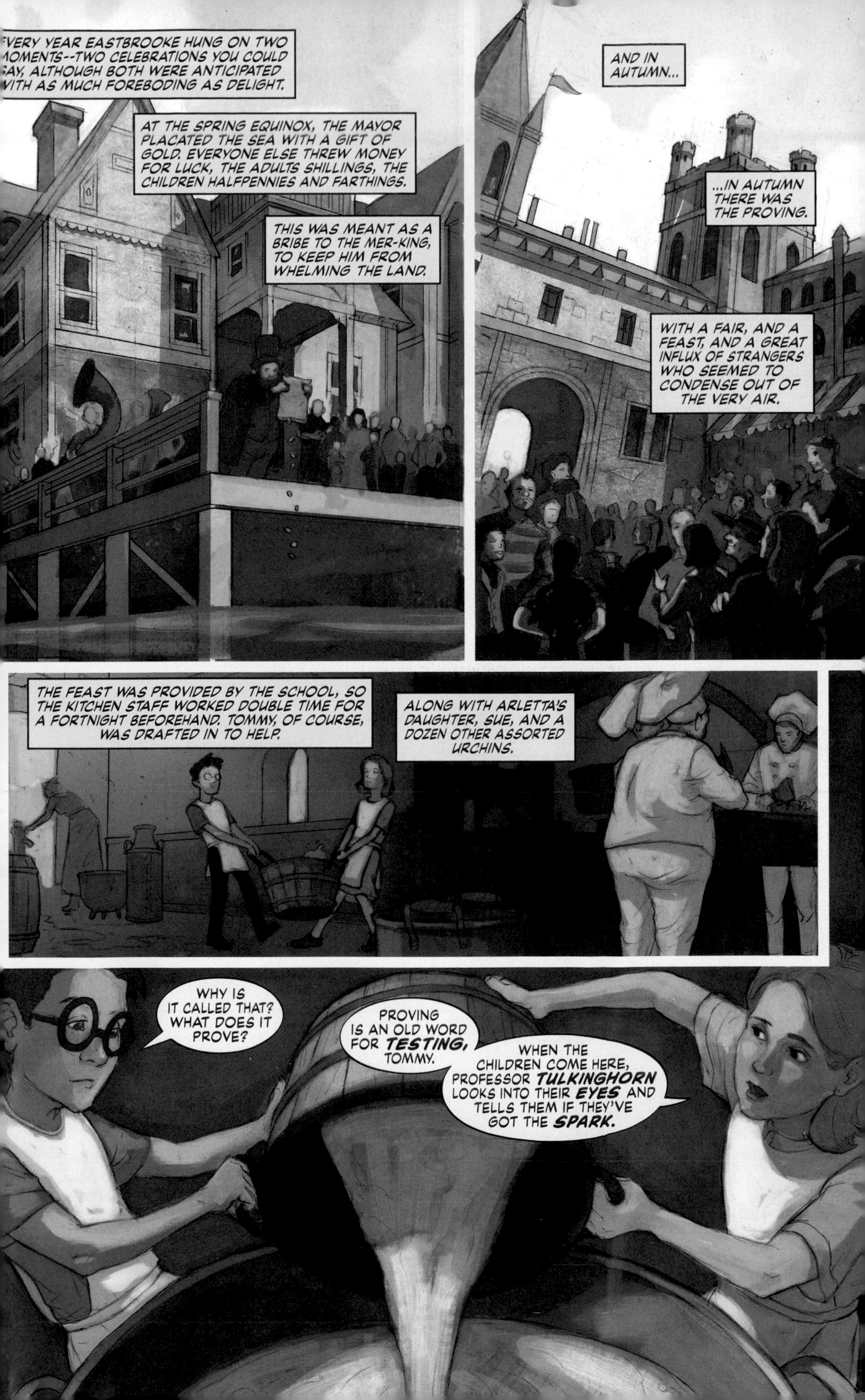
EVERY YEAR EASTBROOKE HUNG ON TWO MOMENTS--TWO CELEBRATIONS YOU COULD SAY, ALTHOUGH BOTH WERE ANTICIPATED WITH AS MUCH FOREBODING AS DELIGHT.
AT THE SPRING EQUINOX, THE MAYOR PLACATED THE SEA WITH A GIFT OF GOLD. EVERYONE ELSE THREW MONEY FOR LUCK, THE ADULTS SHILLINGS, THE CHILDREN HALFPENNIES AND FARTHINGS.
THIS WAS MEANT AS A BRIBE TO THE MER-KING, TO KEEP HIM FROM WHELMING THE LAND.
AND IN AUTUMN...
...IN AUTUMN THERE WAS THE PROVING.
WITH A FAIR, AND A FEAST, AND A GREAT INFLUX OF STRANGERS WHO SEEMED TO CONDENSE OUT OF THE VERY AIR.
THE FEAST WAS PROVIDED BY THE SCHOOL, SO THE KITCHEN STAFF WORKED DOUBLE TIME FOR A FORTNIGHT BEFOREHAND. TOMMY, OF COURSE, WAS DRAFTED IN TO HELP.
ALONG WITH ARLETTA'S DAUGHTER, SUE, AND A DOZEN OTHER ASSORTED URCHINS.
WHY IS IT CALLED THAT? WHAT DOES IT PROVE?
PROVING IS AN OLD WORD FOR TESTING, TOMMY.
WHEN THE CHILDREN COME HERE, PROFESSOR TULKINGHORN LOOKS INTO THEIR EYES AND TELLS THEM IF THEY'VE GOT THE SPARK.

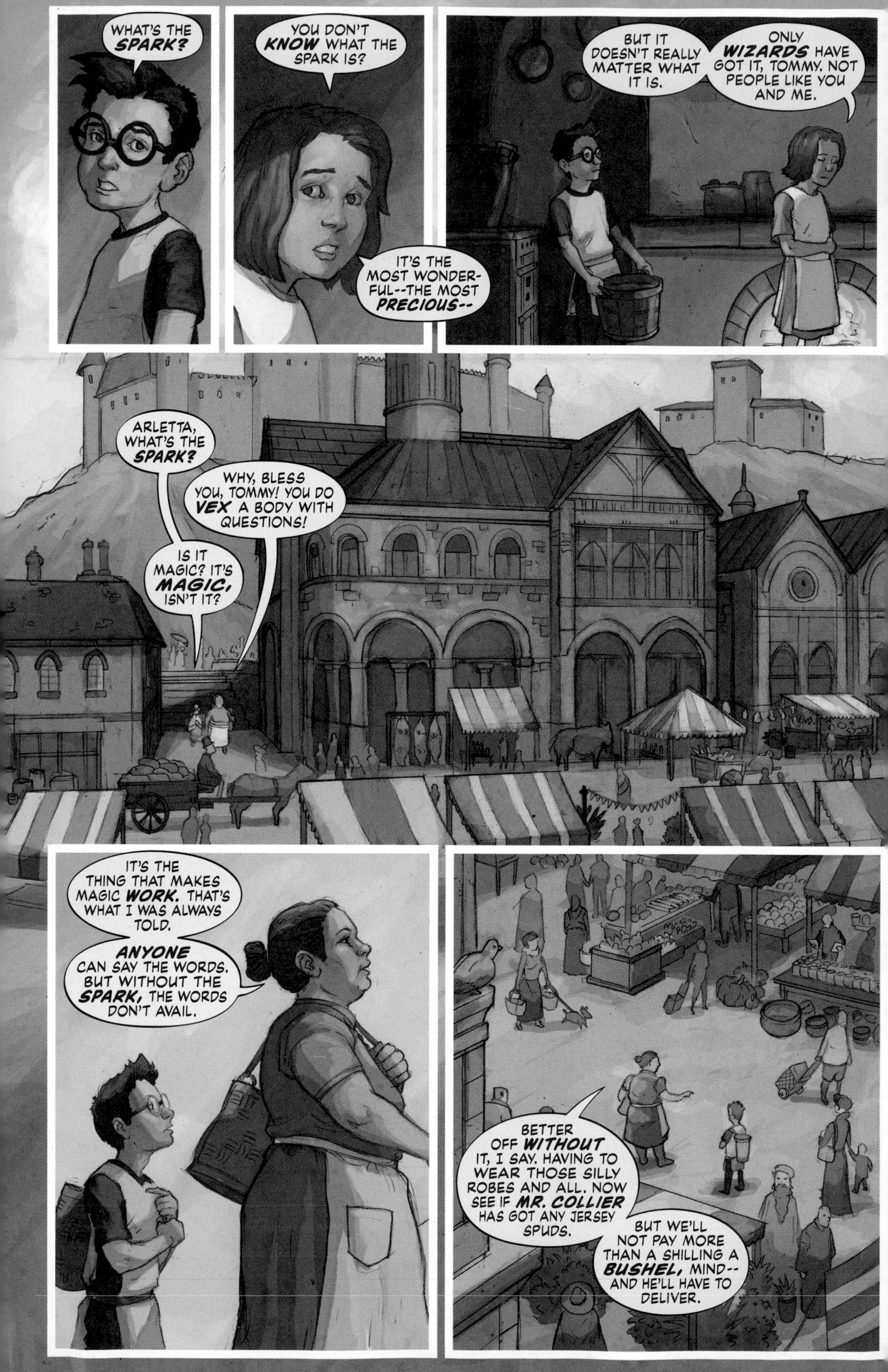
WHAT'S THE SPARK?
YOU DON'T KNOW WHAT THE SPARK IS?
IT'S THE MOST WONDER-FUL--THE MOST PRECIOUS--
BUT IT DOESN'T REALLY MATTER WHAT IT IS.
ONLY WIZARDS HAVE GOT IT, TOMMY. NOT PEOPLE LIKE YOU AND ME.
ARLETTA, WHAT'S THE SPARK?
WHY, BLESS YOU, TOMMY! YOU DO VEX A BODY WITH QUESTIONS!
IS IT MAGIC? IT'S MAGIC, ISN'T IT?
IT'S THE THING THAT MAKES MAGIC WORK. THAT'S WHAT I WAS ALWAYS TOLD.
ANYONE CAN SAY THE WORDS. BUT WITHOUT THE SPARK, THE WORDS DON'T AVAIL.
BETTER OFF WITHOUT IT, I SAY. HAVING TO WEAR THOSE SILLY ROBES AND ALL. NOW SEE IF MR. COLLIER HAS GOT ANY JERSEY SPUDS.
BUT WE'LL NOT PAY MORE THAN A SHILLING A BUSHEL, MIND-- AND HE'LL HAVE TO DELIVER.

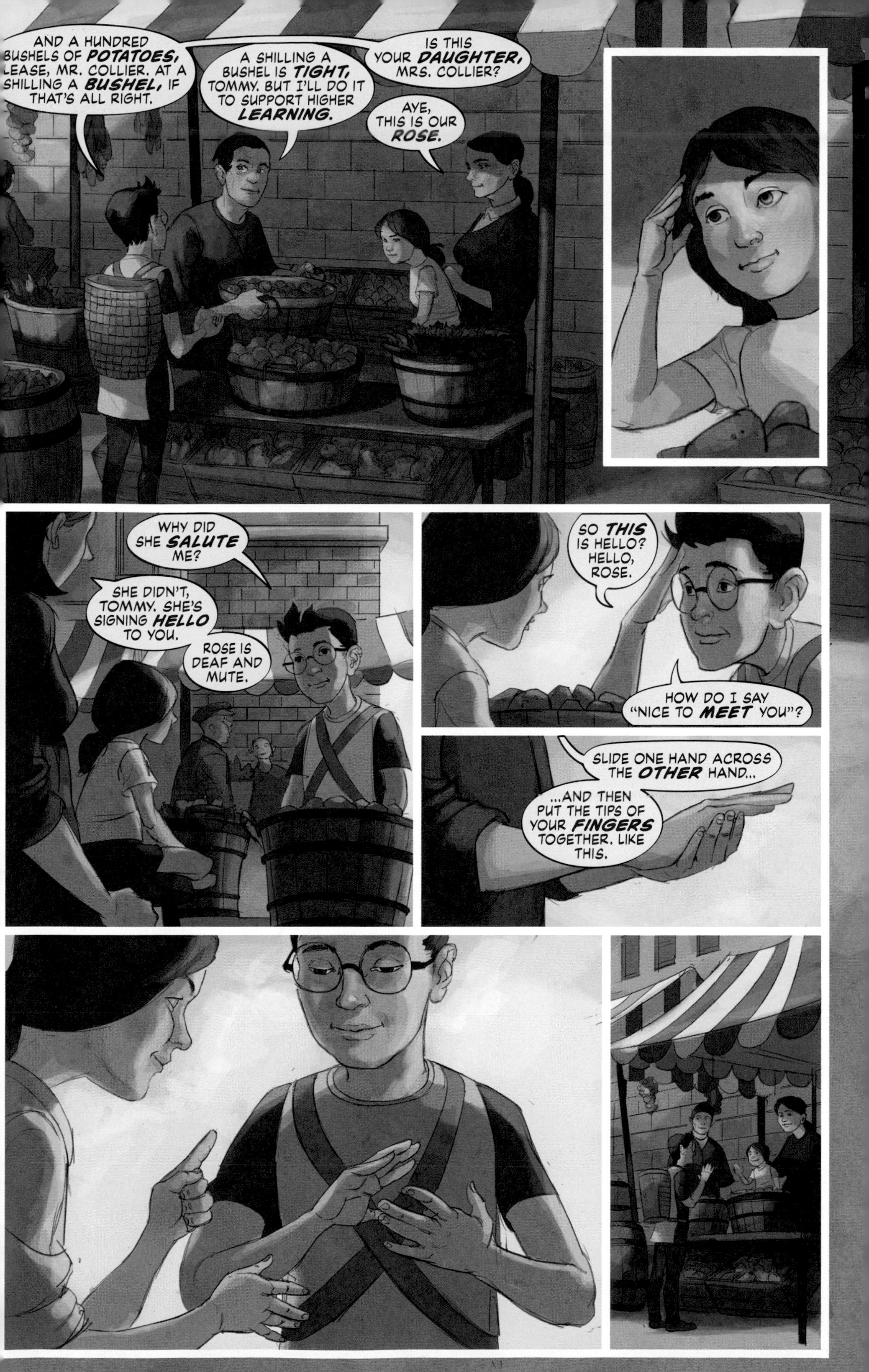
AND A HUNDRED BUSHELS OF POTATOES, LEASE, MR. COLLIER. AT A SHILLING A BUSHEL, IF THAT'S ALL RIGHT.
A SHILLING A BUSHEL IS TIGHT, TOMMY. BUT I'LL DO IT TO SUPPORT HIGHER LEARNING.
IS THIS YOUR DAUGHTER, MRS. COLLIER?
AYE, THIS IS OUR ROSE.
WHY DID SHE SALUTE ME?
SHE DIDN'T, TOMMY. SHE'S SIGNING HELLO TO YOU.
ROSE IS DEAF AND MUTE.
SO THIS IS HELLO? HELLO, ROSE.
HOW DO I SAY "NICE TO MEET YOU"?
SLIDE ONE HAND ACROSS THE OTHER HAND...
...AND THEN PUT THE TIPS OF YOUR FINGERS TOGETHER. LIKE THIS.

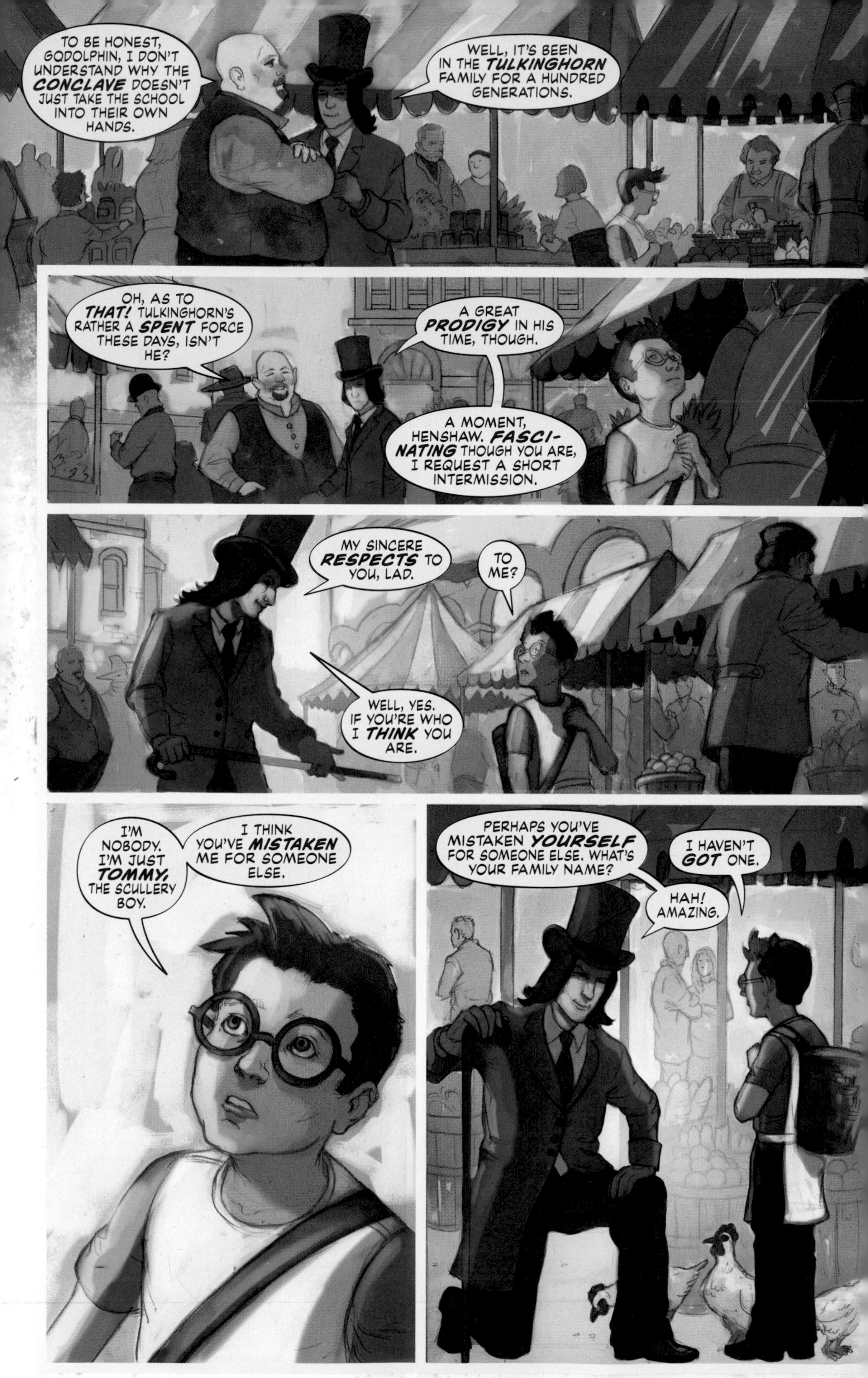
TO BE HONEST, GODOLPHIN, I DON'T UNDERSTAND WHY THE **CONCLAVE** DOESN'T JUST TAKE THE SCHOOL INTO THEIR OWN HANDS.
WELL, IT'S BEEN IN THE **TULKINGHORN** FAMILY FOR A HUNDRED GENERATIONS.
OH, AS TO **THAT!** TULKINGHORN'S RATHER A **SPENT** FORCE THESE DAYS, ISN'T HE?
A GREAT **PRODIGY** IN HIS TIME, THOUGH.
A MOMENT, HENSHAW. **FASCI-NATING** THOUGH YOU ARE, I REQUEST A SHORT INTERMISSION.
MY SINCERE **RESPECTS** TO YOU, LAD.
TO ME?
WELL, YES. IF YOU'RE WHO I **THINK** YOU ARE.
I THINK YOU'VE **MISTAKEN** ME FOR SOMEONE ELSE.
I'M NOBODY. I'M JUST **TOMMY,** THE SCULLERY BOY.
PERHAPS YOU'VE MISTAKEN **YOURSELF** FOR SOMEONE ELSE. WHAT'S YOUR FAMILY NAME?
I HAVEN'T **GOT** ONE.
HAH! AMAZING.

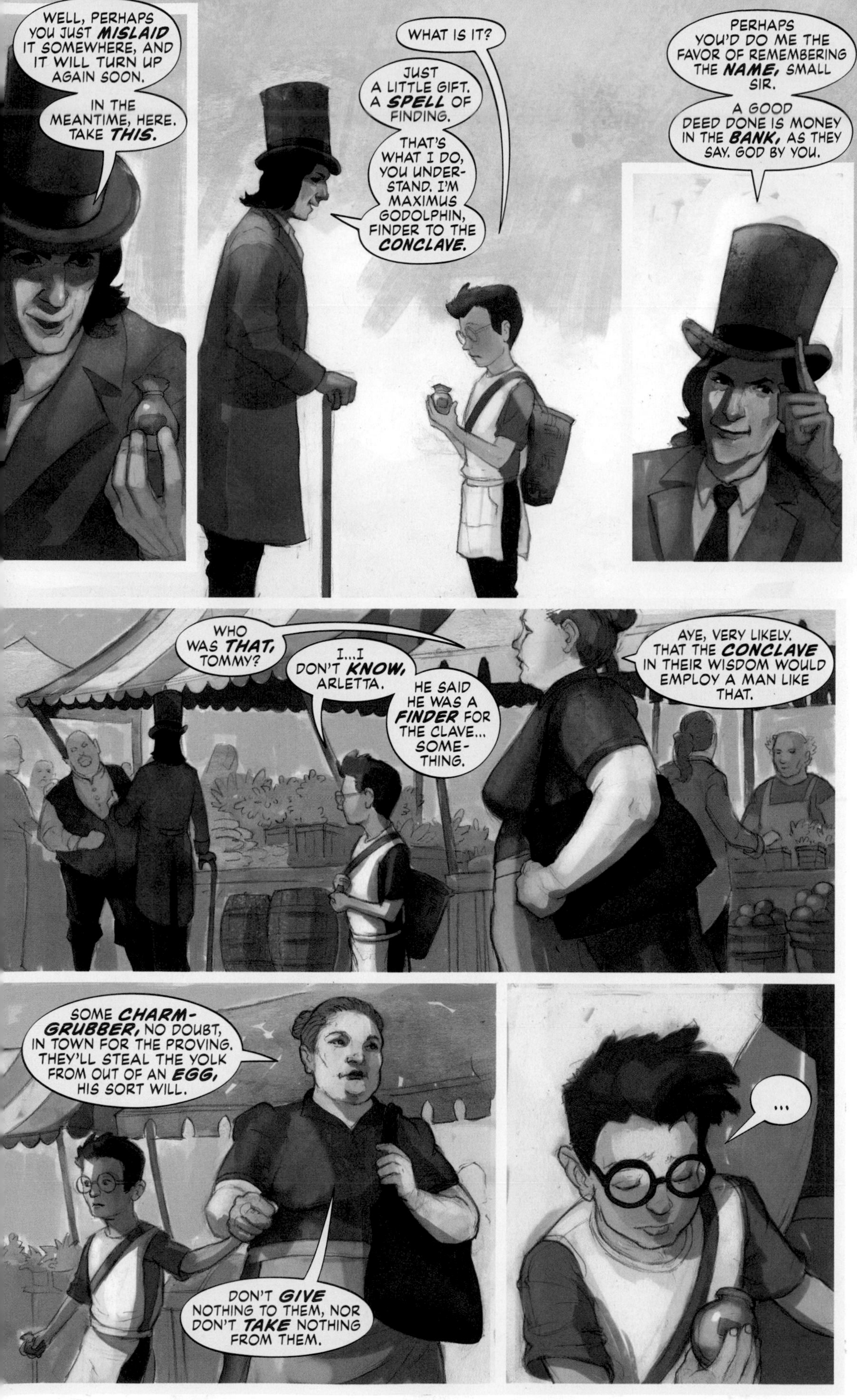
WELL, PERHAPS YOU JUST MISLAID IT SOMEWHERE, AND IT WILL TURN UP AGAIN SOON.
IN THE MEANTIME, HERE. TAKE THIS.
WHAT IS IT?
JUST A LITTLE GIFT. A SPELL OF FINDING.
THAT'S WHAT I DO, YOU UNDERSTAND. I'M MAXIMUS GODOLPHIN, FINDER TO THE CONCLAVE.
PERHAPS YOU'D DO ME THE FAVOR OF REMEMBERING THE NAME, SMALL SIR.
A GOOD DEED DONE IS MONEY IN THE BANK, AS THEY SAY. GOD BY YOU.
WHO WAS THAT, TOMMY?
I...I DON'T KNOW, ARLETTA.
HE SAID HE WAS A FINDER FOR THE CLAVE... SOME-THING.
AYE, VERY LIKELY. THAT THE CONCLAVE IN THEIR WISDOM WOULD EMPLOY A MAN LIKE THAT.
SOME CHARM-GRUBBER, NO DOUBT, IN TOWN FOR THE PROVING. THEY'LL STEAL THE YOLK FROM OUT OF AN EGG, HIS SORT WILL.
DON'T GIVE NOTHING TO THEM, NOR DON'T TAKE NOTHING FROM THEM.
...

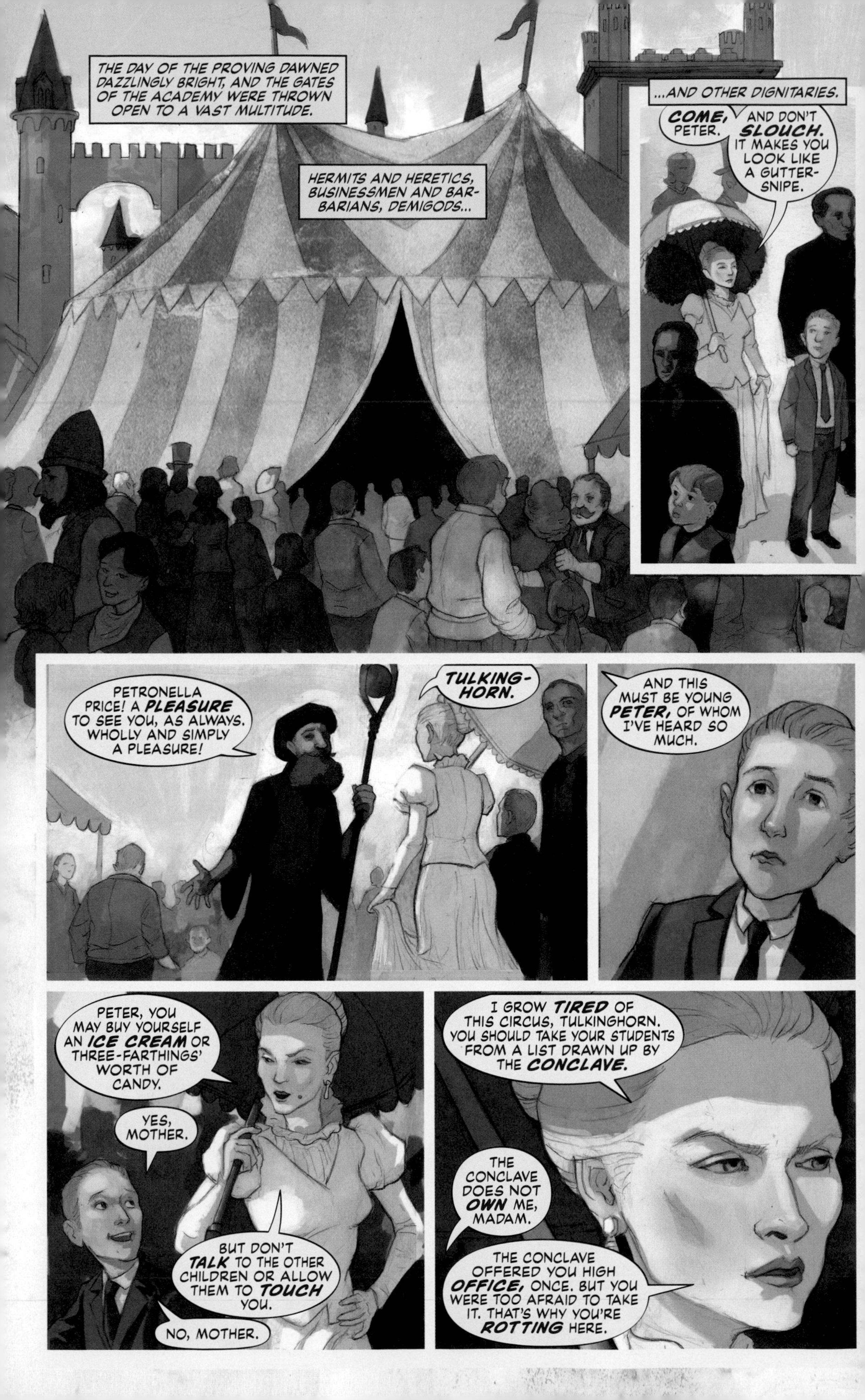
THE DAY OF THE PROVING DAWNED DAZZLINGLY BRIGHT, AND THE GATES OF THE ACADEMY WERE THROWN OPEN TO A VAST MULTITUDE.
HERMITS AND HERETICS, BUSINESSMEN AND BARBARIANS, DEMIGODS...
...AND OTHER DIGNITARIES.
COME, PETER.
AND DON'T SLOUCH. IT MAKES YOU LOOK LIKE A GUTTER-SNIPE.
PETRONELLA PRICE! A PLEASURE TO SEE YOU, AS ALWAYS. WHOLLY AND SIMPLY A PLEASURE!
TULKINGHORN.
AND THIS MUST BE YOUNG PETER, OF WHOM I'VE HEARD SO MUCH.
PETER, YOU MAY BUY YOURSELF AN ICE CREAM OR THREE-FARTHINGS' WORTH OF CANDY.
YES, MOTHER.
BUT DON'T TALK TO THE OTHER CHILDREN OR ALLOW THEM TO TOUCH YOU.
NO, MOTHER.
I GROW TIRED OF THIS CIRCUS, TULKINGHORN. YOU SHOULD TAKE YOUR STUDENTS FROM A LIST DRAWN UP BY THE CONCLAVE.
THE CONCLAVE DOES NOT OWN ME, MADAM.
THE CONCLAVE OFFERED YOU HIGH OFFICE, ONCE. BUT YOU WERE TOO AFRAID TO TAKE IT. THAT'S WHY YOU'RE ROTTING HERE.

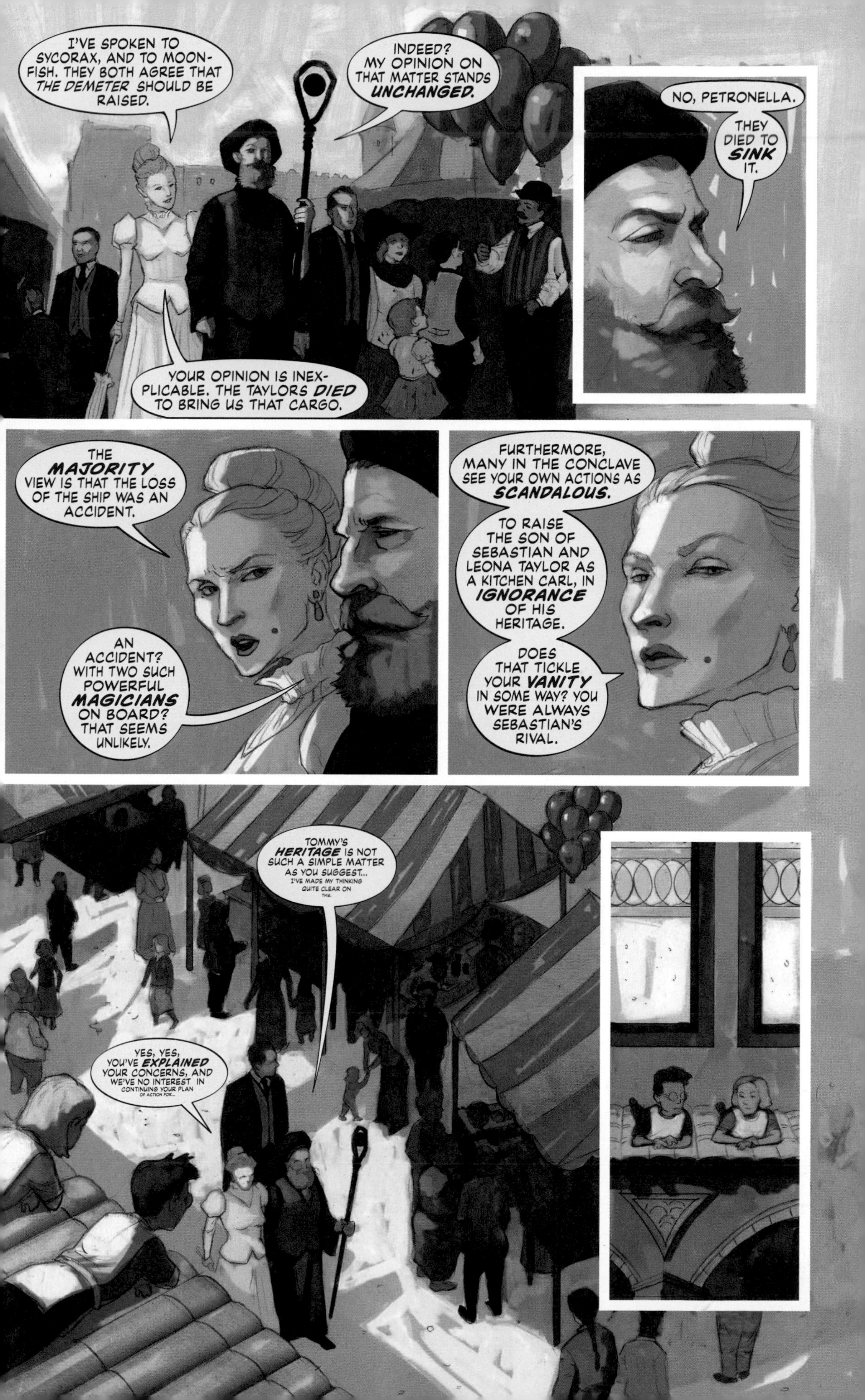
I'VE SPOKEN TO SYCORAX, AND TO MOON-FISH. THEY BOTH AGREE THAT *THE DEMETER* SHOULD BE RAISED.
INDEED? MY OPINION ON THAT MATTER STANDS **UNCHANGED.**
YOUR OPINION IS INEX-PLICABLE. THE TAYLORS ***DIED*** TO BRING US THAT CARGO.
NO, PETRONELLA.
THEY DIED TO ***SINK*** IT.
THE ***MAJORITY*** VIEW IS THAT THE LOSS OF THE SHIP WAS AN ACCIDENT.
AN ACCIDENT? WITH TWO SUCH POWERFUL ***MAGICIANS*** ON BOARD? THAT SEEMS UNLIKELY.
FURTHERMORE, MANY IN THE CONCLAVE SEE YOUR OWN ACTIONS AS ***SCANDALOUS.***
TO RAISE THE SON OF SEBASTIAN AND LEONA TAYLOR AS A KITCHEN CARL, IN ***IGNORANCE*** OF HIS HERITAGE.
DOES THAT TICKLE YOUR ***VANITY*** IN SOME WAY? YOU WERE ALWAYS SEBASTIAN'S RIVAL.
TOMMY'S ***HERITAGE*** IS NOT SUCH A SIMPLE MATTER AS YOU SUGGEST... I'VE MADE MY THINKING QUITE CLEAR ON THIS.
YES, YES, YOU'VE ***EXPLAINED*** YOUR CONCERNS, AND WE'VE NO INTEREST IN CONTINUING YOUR PLAN OF ACTION FOR...

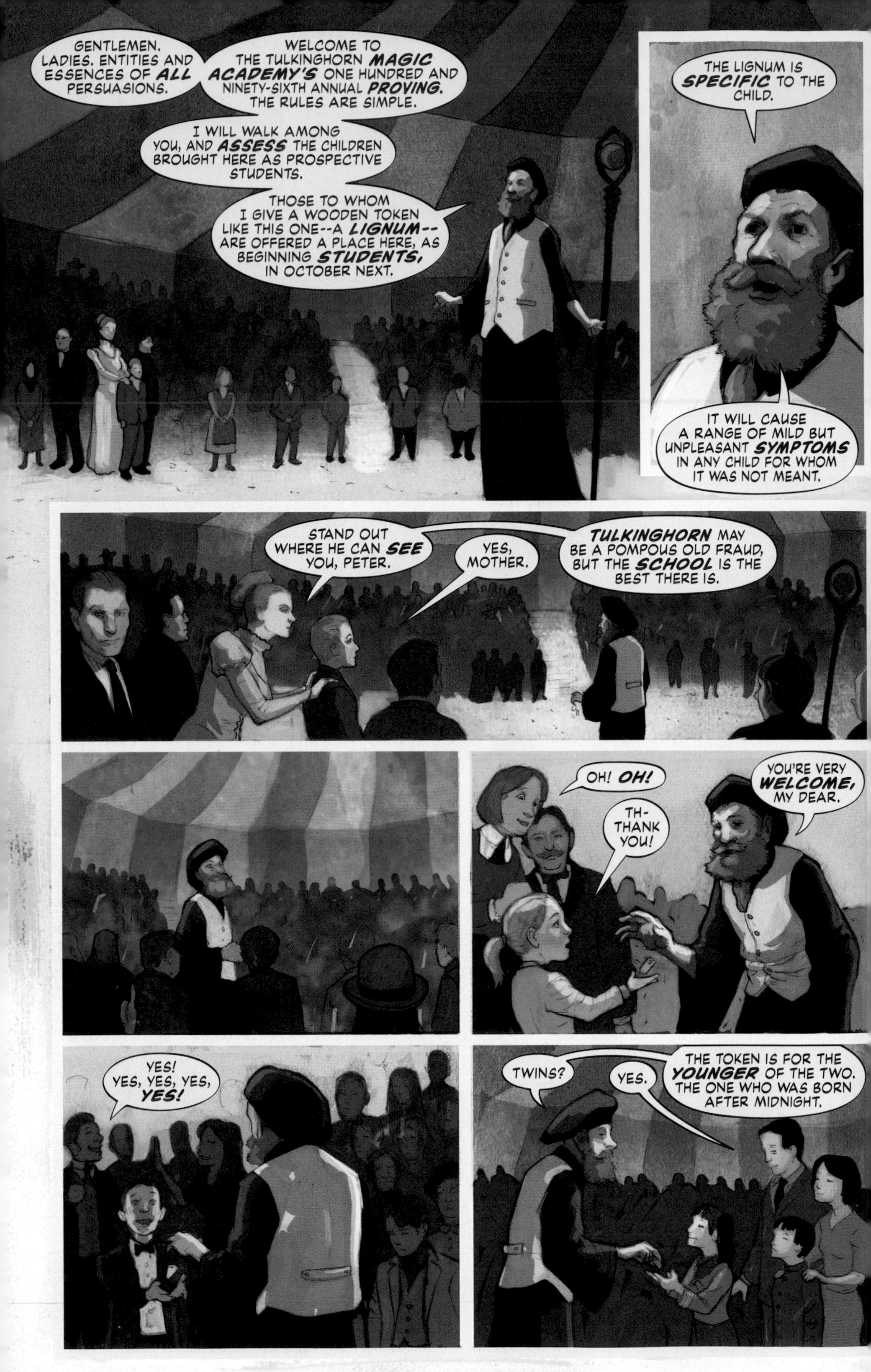
GENTLEMEN. LADIES. ENTITIES AND ESSENCES OF ALL PERSUASIONS.
WELCOME TO THE TULKINGHORN MAGIC ACADEMY'S ONE HUNDRED AND NINETY-SIXTH ANNUAL PROVING. THE RULES ARE SIMPLE.
I WILL WALK AMONG YOU, AND ASSESS THE CHILDREN BROUGHT HERE AS PROSPECTIVE STUDENTS.
THOSE TO WHOM I GIVE A WOODEN TOKEN LIKE THIS ONE--A LIGNUM--ARE OFFERED A PLACE HERE, AS BEGINNING STUDENTS, IN OCTOBER NEXT.
THE LIGNUM IS SPECIFIC TO THE CHILD.
IT WILL CAUSE A RANGE OF MILD BUT UNPLEASANT SYMPTOMS IN ANY CHILD FOR WHOM IT WAS NOT MEANT.
STAND OUT WHERE HE CAN SEE YOU, PETER.
YES, MOTHER.
TULKINGHORN MAY BE A POMPOUS OLD FRAUD, BUT THE SCHOOL IS THE BEST THERE IS.
OH! OH!
TH-THANK YOU!
YOU'RE VERY WELCOME, MY DEAR.
YES! YES, YES, YES, YES!
TWINS?
YES.
THE TOKEN IS FOR THE YOUNGER OF THE TWO. THE ONE WHO WAS BORN AFTER MIDNIGHT.

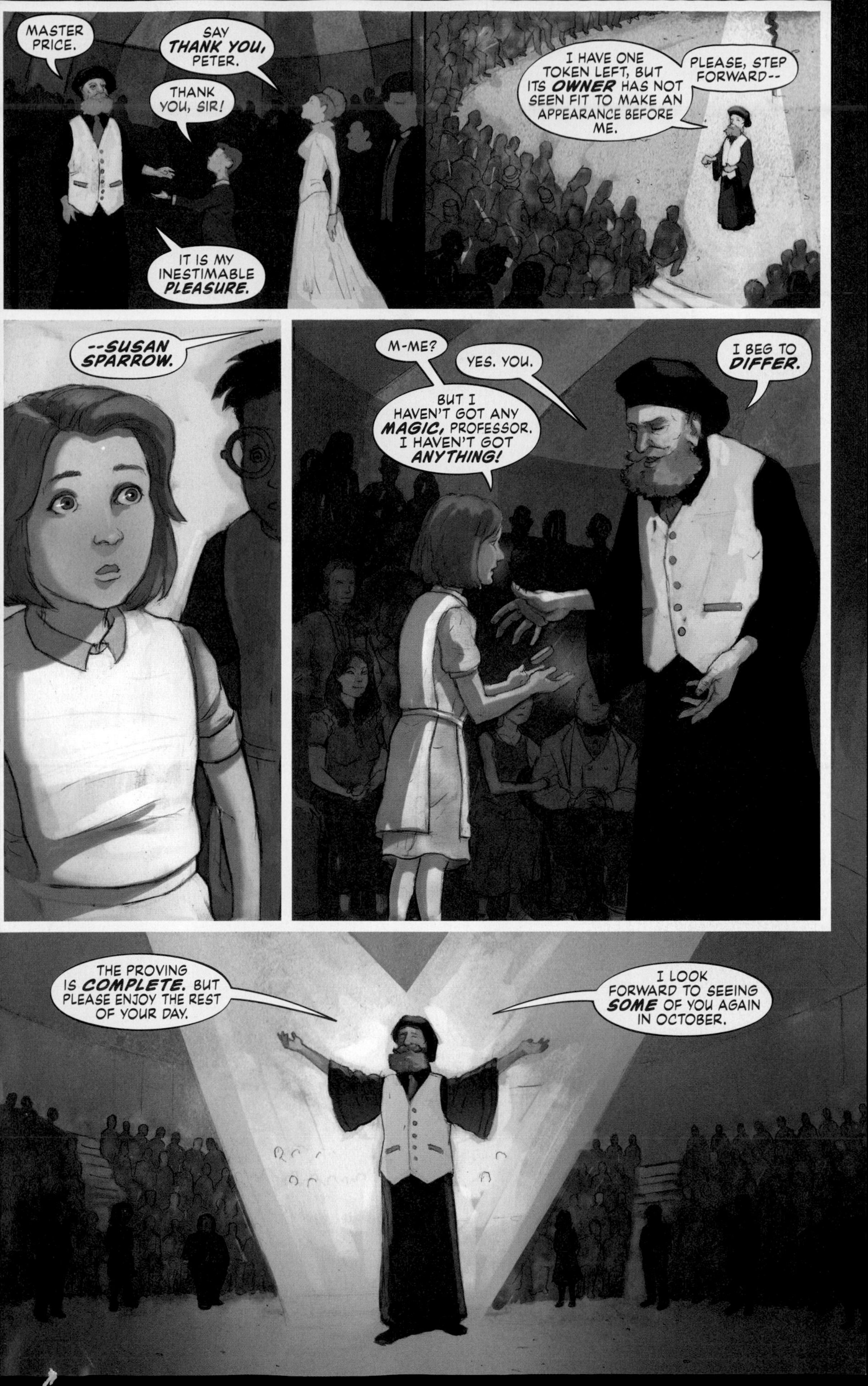
MASTER PRICE.
SAY *THANK YOU,* PETER.
THANK YOU, SIR!
IT IS MY INESTIMABLE *PLEASURE.*
I HAVE ONE TOKEN LEFT, BUT ITS *OWNER* HAS NOT SEEN FIT TO MAKE AN APPEARANCE BEFORE ME.
PLEASE, STEP FORWARD--
--*SUSAN SPARROW.*
M-ME?
YES. YOU.
BUT I HAVEN'T GOT ANY *MAGIC,* PROFESSOR. I HAVEN'T GOT *ANYTHING!*
I BEG TO *DIFFER.*
THE PROVING IS *COMPLETE.* BUT PLEASE ENJOY THE REST OF YOUR DAY.
I LOOK FORWARD TO SEEING *SOME* OF YOU AGAIN IN OCTOBER.

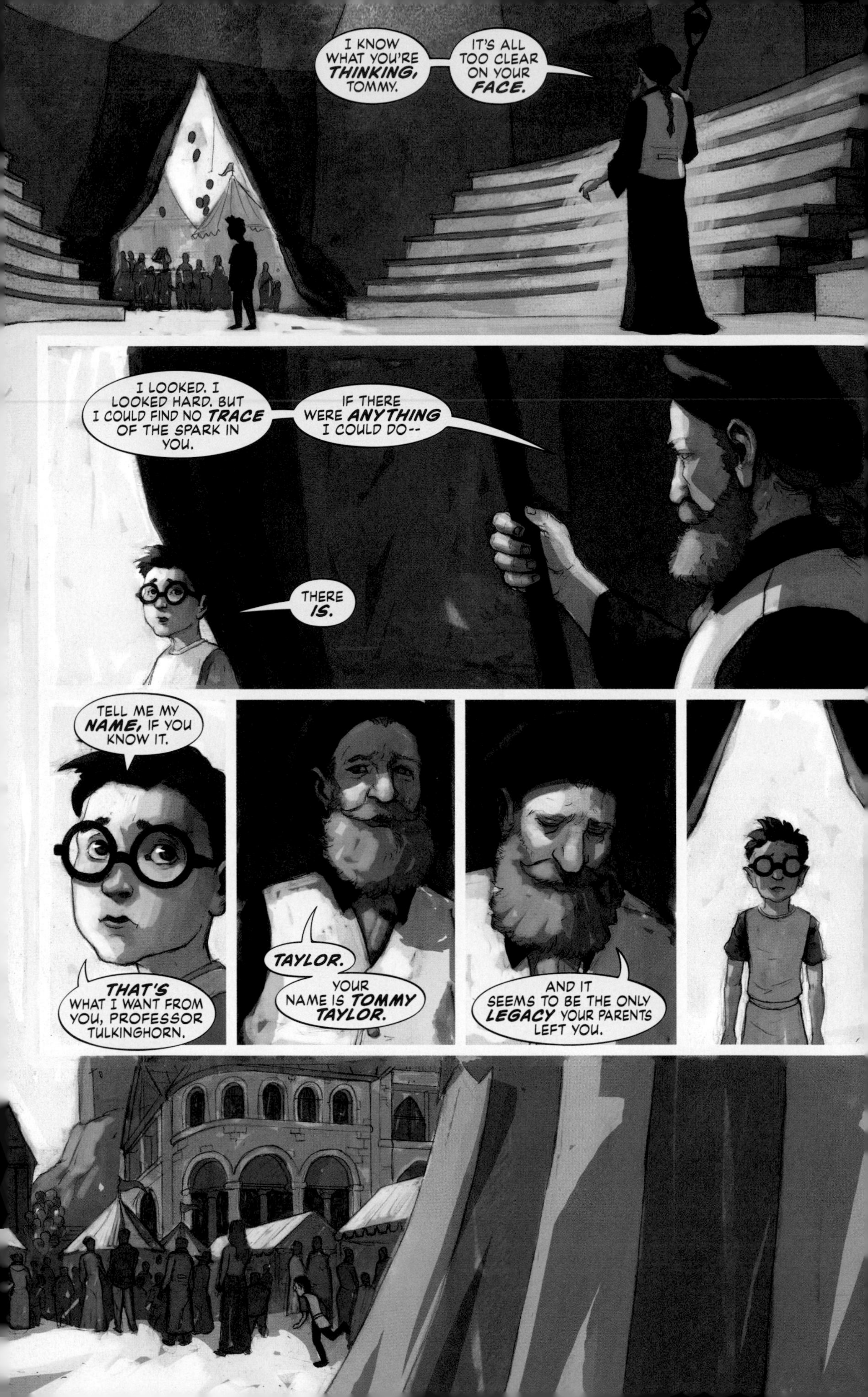
I KNOW WHAT YOU'RE THINKING, TOMMY.
IT'S ALL TOO CLEAR ON YOUR FACE.
I LOOKED. I LOOKED HARD. BUT I COULD FIND NO TRACE OF THE SPARK IN YOU.
IF THERE WERE ANYTHING I COULD DO--
THERE IS.
TELL ME MY NAME, IF YOU KNOW IT.
THAT'S WHAT I WANT FROM YOU, PROFESSOR TULKINGHORN.
TAYLOR.
YOUR NAME IS TOMMY TAYLOR.
AND IT SEEMS TO BE THE ONLY LEGACY YOUR PARENTS LEFT YOU.

Feb 19th. Writing like a maniac. It's all taking shape, now. But I'm utterly, utterly, utterly fed [up] to the teeth and eyeballs and brainpan with bloody London. I told Swope to find me a place [far] from the maddling gits who plague me here. I gave him May 5th for publication date. It's our [best] guess, for the birth.

Mar 21st. In Switzerland. Bit of a [ra]dical solution, but once Swope showed [me] the pictures, it started to grow on me. [It]'s a long way from anywhere. A very [lo]ng way. And neither of us speaks [F]rench, so the distractions wouldn't even [be] there if we went looking for them.

[S]ue was appalled. She's scared that when [it] comes to the birth, she'll be surrounded [by] people who don't speak the same [la]nguage as her. Plays into my hands, [ac]tually. I promised her a home delivery, [as] if it was a big concession, but that was [w]hat I wanted in any case. Up to us [w]hen we notify the authorities and get a [c]ertificate drawn up. No public time of [b]irth. A bit of a mystery.

Start the little guy off on the right foot. It works for me. Also, that much easier to induce the birth if we're at home and in control of the process.

April 2nd. Diodati is perfect. The middle of nowhere. Peace and calm and forty or so rooms.

This far into the third trimester, Sue's not very limber, so in a space as big as this, I don't have to meet her at all if I don't want to.

May 5th. "My waters have broken," Sue announced.

And that was a day's writing lost right there. But in the circumstances I can hardly complain.

So I'm a father now. That part of the deal was easy.

No need to induce, as it turned out. And no need to tell Sue that was ever part of the plan.

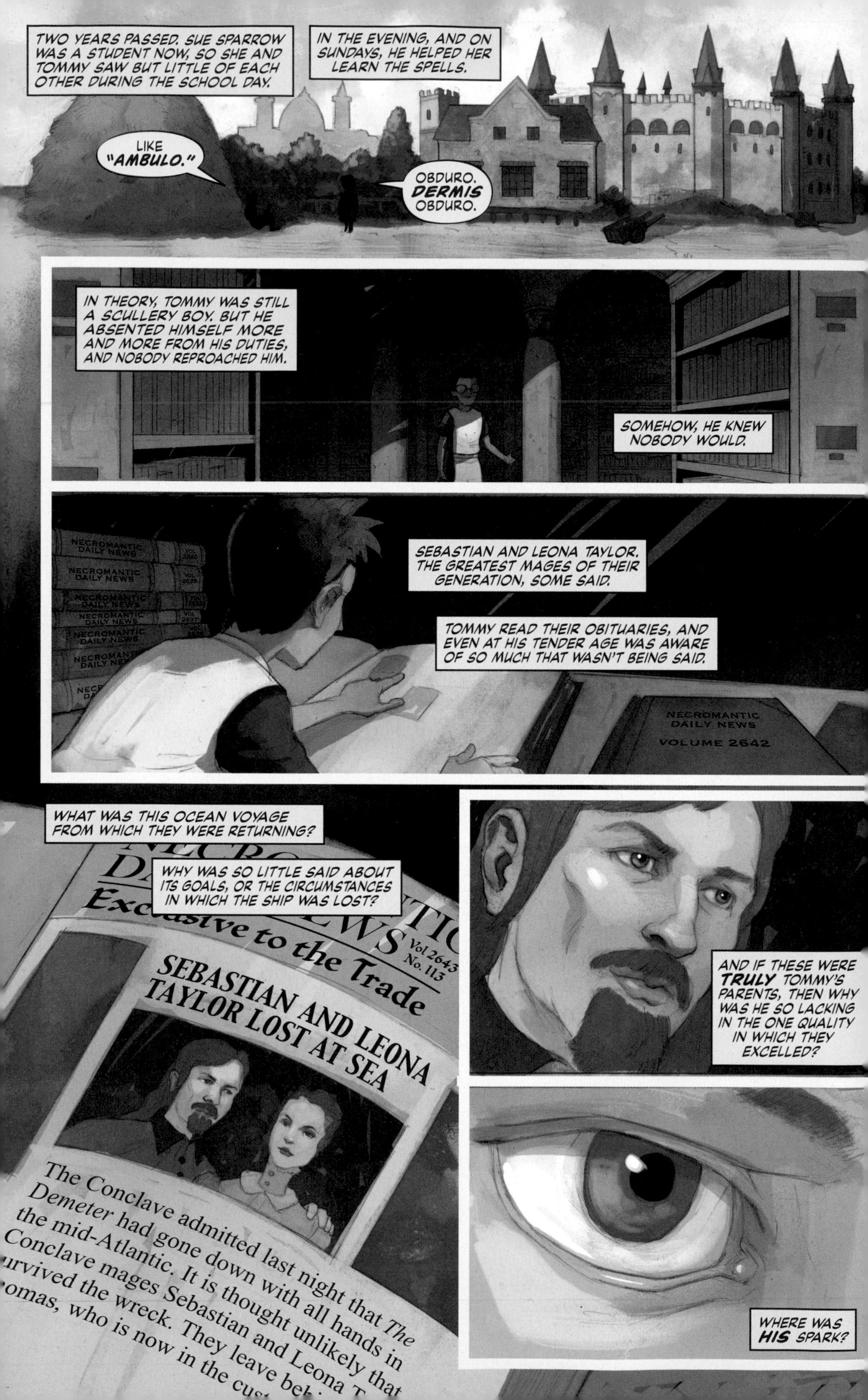

TWO YEARS PASSED. SUE SPARROW WAS A STUDENT NOW, SO SHE AND TOMMY SAW BUT LITTLE OF EACH OTHER DURING THE SCHOOL DAY.
IN THE EVENING, AND ON SUNDAYS, HE HELPED HER LEARN THE SPELLS.
LIKE "AMBULO."
OBDURO. DERMIS OBDURO.
IN THEORY, TOMMY WAS STILL A SCULLERY BOY. BUT HE ABSENTED HIMSELF MORE AND MORE FROM HIS DUTIES, AND NOBODY REPROACHED HIM.
SOMEHOW, HE KNEW NOBODY WOULD.
SEBASTIAN AND LEONA TAYLOR. THE GREATEST MAGES OF THEIR GENERATION, SOME SAID.
TOMMY READ THEIR OBITUARIES, AND EVEN AT HIS TENDER AGE WAS AWARE OF SO MUCH THAT WASN'T BEING SAID.
NECROMANTIC DAILY NEWS
VOLUME 2642
WHAT WAS THIS OCEAN VOYAGE FROM WHICH THEY WERE RETURNING?
WHY WAS SO LITTLE SAID ABOUT ITS GOALS, OR THE CIRCUMSTANCES IN WHICH THE SHIP WAS LOST?
Exclusive to the Trade
Vol 2643 No. 113
SEBASTIAN AND LEONA TAYLOR LOST AT SEA
The Conclave admitted last night that The Demeter had gone down with all hands in the mid-Atlantic. It is thought unlikely that Conclave mages Sebastian and Leona
urvived the wreck. They leave
omas, who is now in the
AND IF THESE WERE TRULY TOMMY'S PARENTS, THEN WHY WAS HE SO LACKING IN THE ONE QUALITY IN WHICH THEY EXCELLED?
WHERE WAS HIS SPARK?

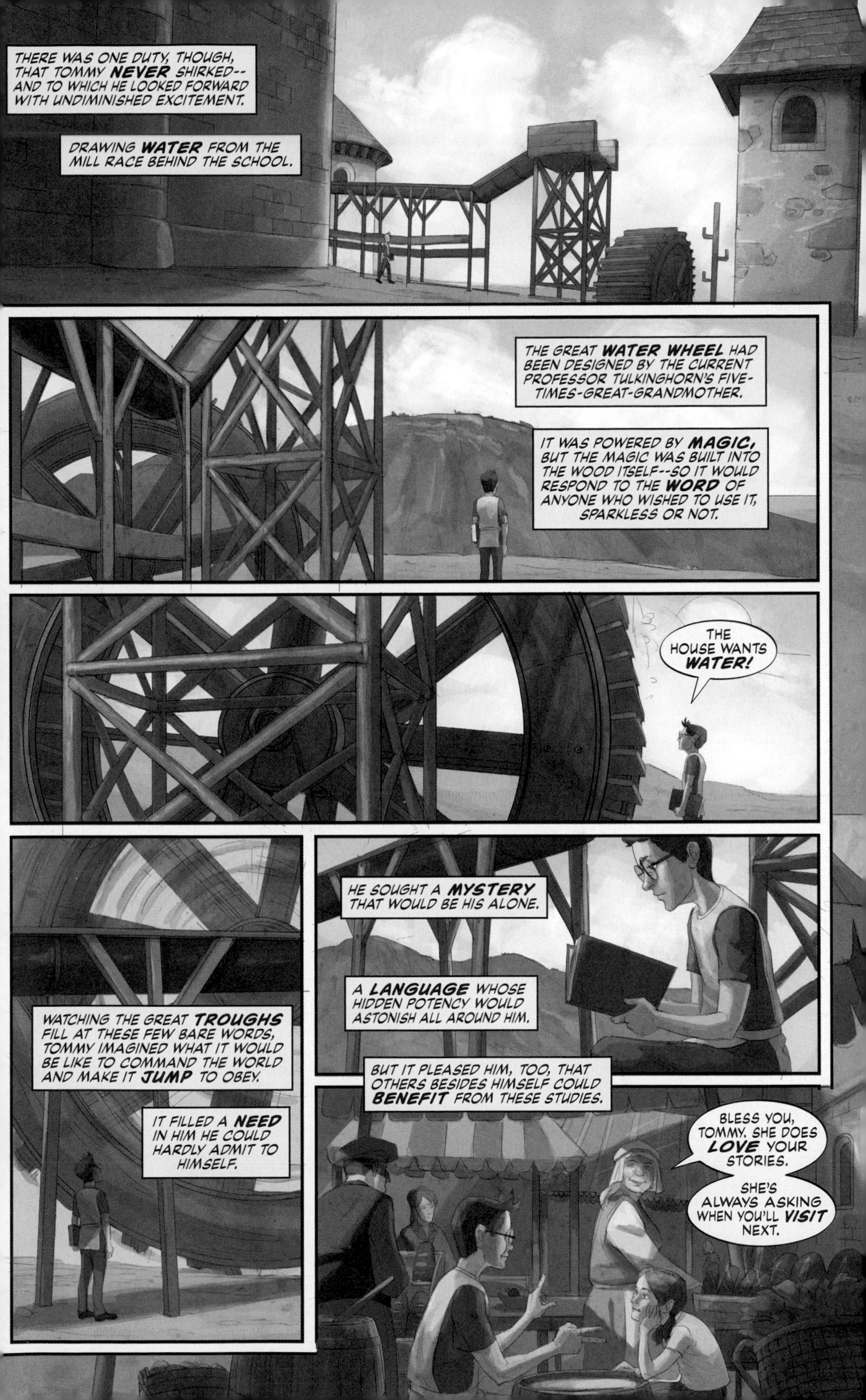
THERE WAS ONE DUTY, THOUGH, THAT TOMMY NEVER SHIRKED-- AND TO WHICH HE LOOKED FORWARD WITH UNDIMINISHED EXCITEMENT.
DRAWING WATER FROM THE MILL RACE BEHIND THE SCHOOL.
THE GREAT WATER WHEEL HAD BEEN DESIGNED BY THE CURRENT PROFESSOR TULKINGHORN'S FIVE-TIMES-GREAT-GRANDMOTHER.
IT WAS POWERED BY MAGIC, BUT THE MAGIC WAS BUILT INTO THE WOOD ITSELF--SO IT WOULD RESPOND TO THE WORD OF ANYONE WHO WISHED TO USE IT, SPARKLESS OR NOT.
THE HOUSE WANTS WATER!
WATCHING THE GREAT TROUGHS FILL AT THESE FEW BARE WORDS, TOMMY IMAGINED WHAT IT WOULD BE LIKE TO COMMAND THE WORLD AND MAKE IT JUMP TO OBEY.
IT FILLED A NEED IN HIM HE COULD HARDLY ADMIT TO HIMSELF.
HE SOUGHT A MYSTERY THAT WOULD BE HIS ALONE.
A LANGUAGE WHOSE HIDDEN POTENCY WOULD ASTONISH ALL AROUND HIM.
BUT IT PLEASED HIM, TOO, THAT OTHERS BESIDES HIMSELF COULD BENEFIT FROM THESE STUDIES.
BLESS YOU, TOMMY. SHE DOES LOVE YOUR STORIES.
SHE'S ALWAYS ASKING WHEN YOU'LL VISIT NEXT.

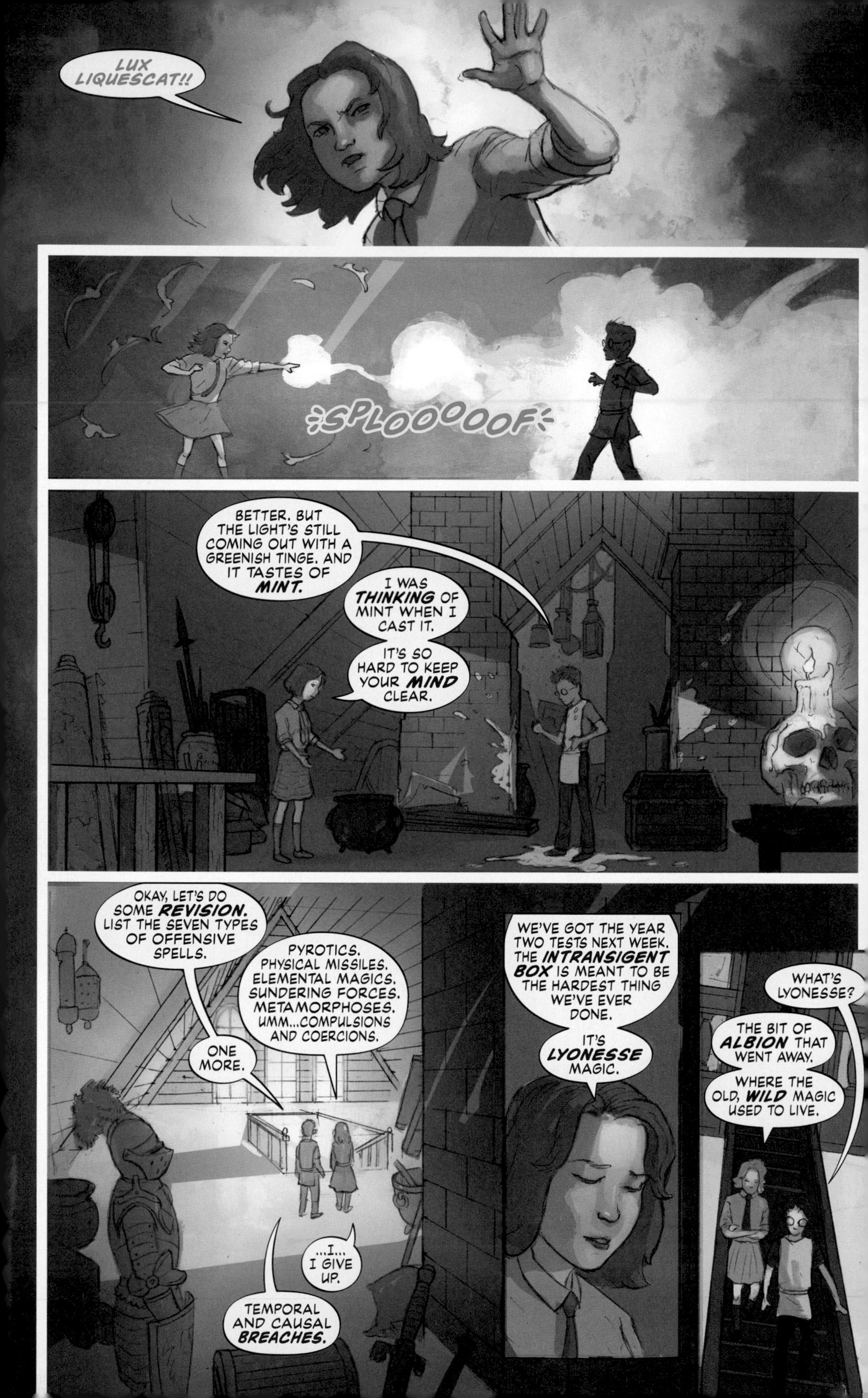
LUX LIQUESCAT!!
SPLOOOOOOF
BETTER. BUT THE LIGHT'S STILL COMING OUT WITH A GREENISH TINGE. AND IT TASTES OF MINT.
I WAS THINKING OF MINT WHEN I CAST IT.
IT'S SO HARD TO KEEP YOUR MIND CLEAR.
OKAY, LET'S DO SOME REVISION. LIST THE SEVEN TYPES OF OFFENSIVE SPELLS.
PYROTICS. PHYSICAL MISSILES. ELEMENTAL MAGICS. SUNDERING FORCES. METAMORPHOSES. UMM...COMPULSIONS AND COERCIONS.
ONE MORE.
...I... I GIVE UP.
TEMPORAL AND CAUSAL BREACHES.
WE'VE GOT THE YEAR TWO TESTS NEXT WEEK. THE INTRANSIGENT BOX IS MEANT TO BE THE HARDEST THING WE'VE EVER DONE.
IT'S LYONESSE MAGIC.
WHAT'S LYONESSE?
THE BIT OF ALBION THAT WENT AWAY.
WHERE THE OLD, WILD MAGIC USED TO LIVE.

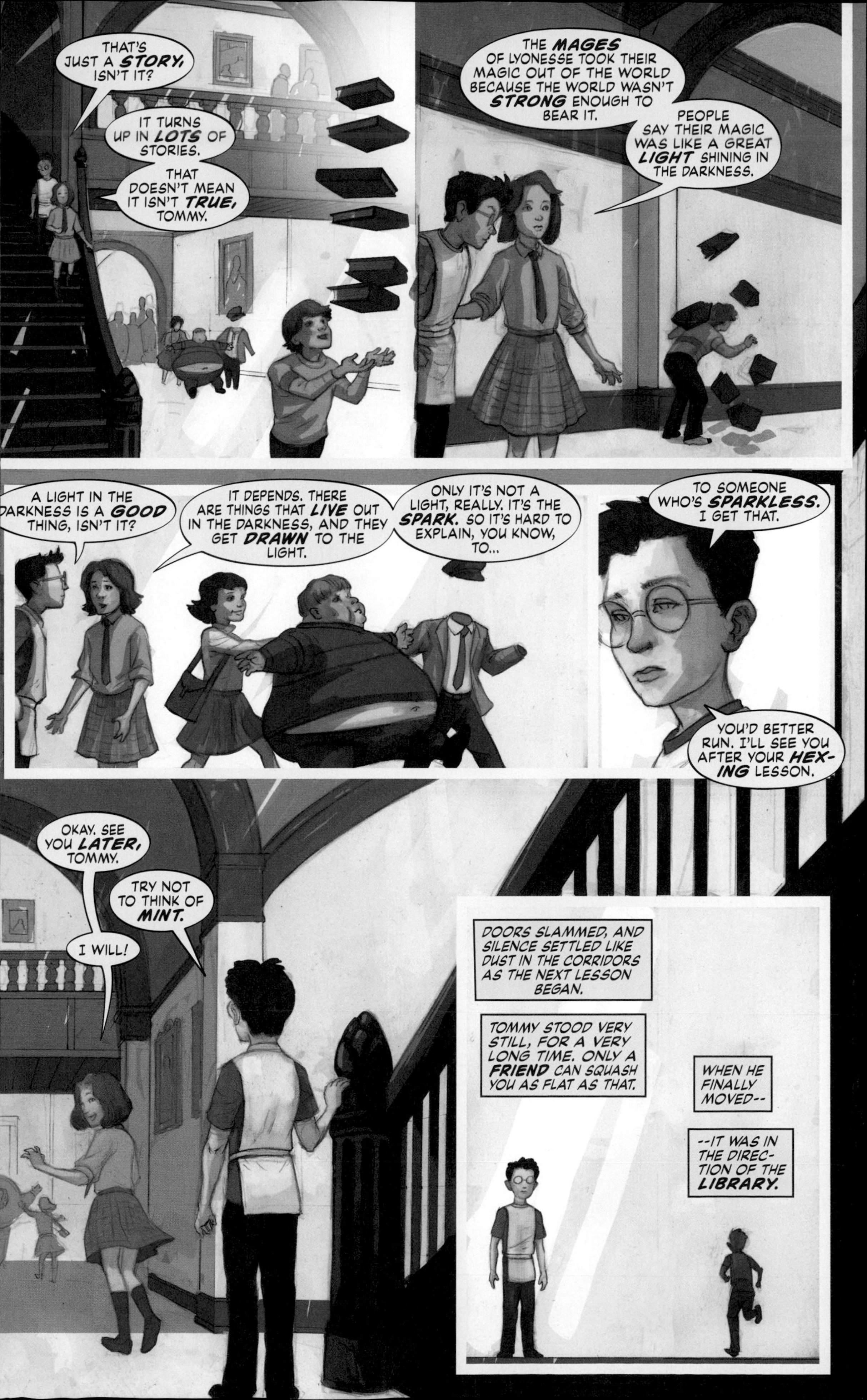
THAT'S JUST A STORY, ISN'T IT?
IT TURNS UP IN LOTS OF STORIES.
THAT DOESN'T MEAN IT ISN'T TRUE, TOMMY.
THE MAGES OF LYONESSE TOOK THEIR MAGIC OUT OF THE WORLD BECAUSE THE WORLD WASN'T STRONG ENOUGH TO BEAR IT.
PEOPLE SAY THEIR MAGIC WAS LIKE A GREAT LIGHT SHINING IN THE DARKNESS.
A LIGHT IN THE DARKNESS IS A GOOD THING, ISN'T IT?
IT DEPENDS. THERE ARE THINGS THAT LIVE OUT IN THE DARKNESS, AND THEY GET DRAWN TO THE LIGHT.
ONLY IT'S NOT A LIGHT, REALLY. IT'S THE SPARK. SO IT'S HARD TO EXPLAIN, YOU KNOW, TO...
TO SOMEONE WHO'S SPARKLESS. I GET THAT.
YOU'D BETTER RUN. I'LL SEE YOU AFTER YOUR HEX-ING LESSON.
OKAY. SEE YOU LATER, TOMMY.
TRY NOT TO THINK OF MINT.
I WILL!
DOORS SLAMMED, AND SILENCE SETTLED LIKE DUST IN THE CORRIDORS AS THE NEXT LESSON BEGAN.
TOMMY STOOD VERY STILL, FOR A VERY LONG TIME. ONLY A FRIEND CAN SQUASH YOU AS FLAT AS THAT.
WHEN HE FINALLY MOVED--
--IT WAS IN THE DIREC-TION OF THE LIBRARY.

In times long past (see Antediluvian Age, Saturna Regna) the kingdom of Lyonesse was a part of Albion, to the South and West of where Cornwall is now located. It covered an area of some fourteen hundred square miles, and its capital city, Keris, was populated in equal measure by humans and people of the aes sidhe.

The history of Lyonesse is inextricably entwined with that of the "old, wild magic," a thaumaturgical system of interwoven energies which has now vanished from the Earth, and whose theoretical basis and internal logic are no longer known.

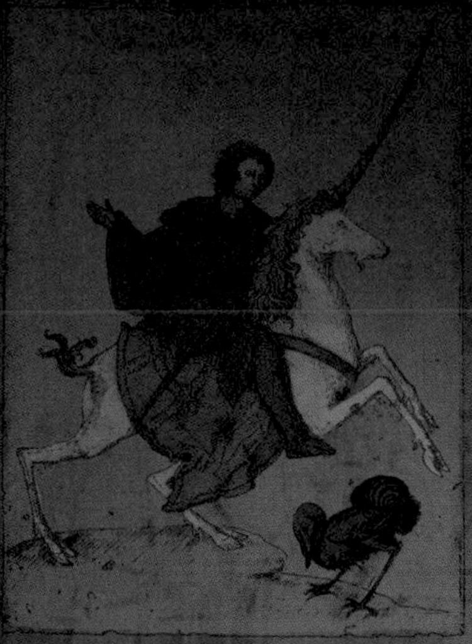

The old, wild magic is commonly thought to have been many thousands of times stronger than the thaumaturgy of the modern era. The mages of Lyonesse are reputed to have been able to make the sun move in the sky to have added entire dimensions to physical space, to have conquered and turned back time (and therefore achieved immortality) and so on. While some of these stories have grown in the telling, the few Lyonesse artifacts still extant do display remarkable properties, which modern mages can neither copy nor explain.

Where modern magic depends mostly on the spoken word as thaumatic focus, Lyonesse magic could subsist in engraved runes, music, patterns of light on water, or any other patterned or inscaped totality. Its endurance — without fading or weakening — in the places where it was formerly used is indeed one of its most striking characteristics.

At some point in the past, before the rising of our current civilization, the mages of Lyonesse moved their entire land away from Albion to a far distant place — the distance in question being one that is not strictly measurable in three dimensions, since it subtends across the magical hyperplanes of Taractul and Phrax, as well as across the trans-temporal

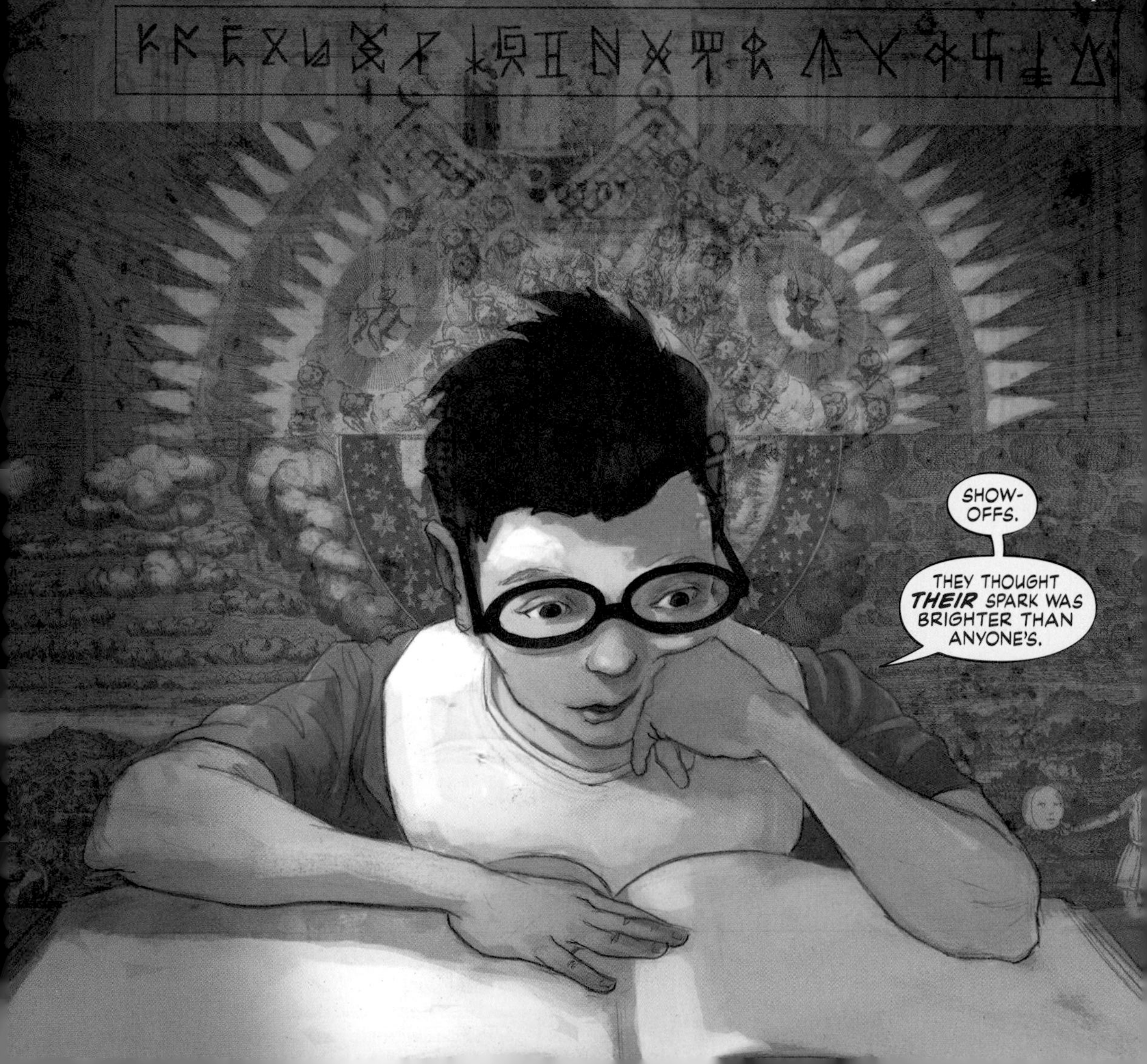

SHOW-OFFS.
THEY THOUGHT ***THEIR*** SPARK WAS BRIGHTER THAN ANYONE'S.

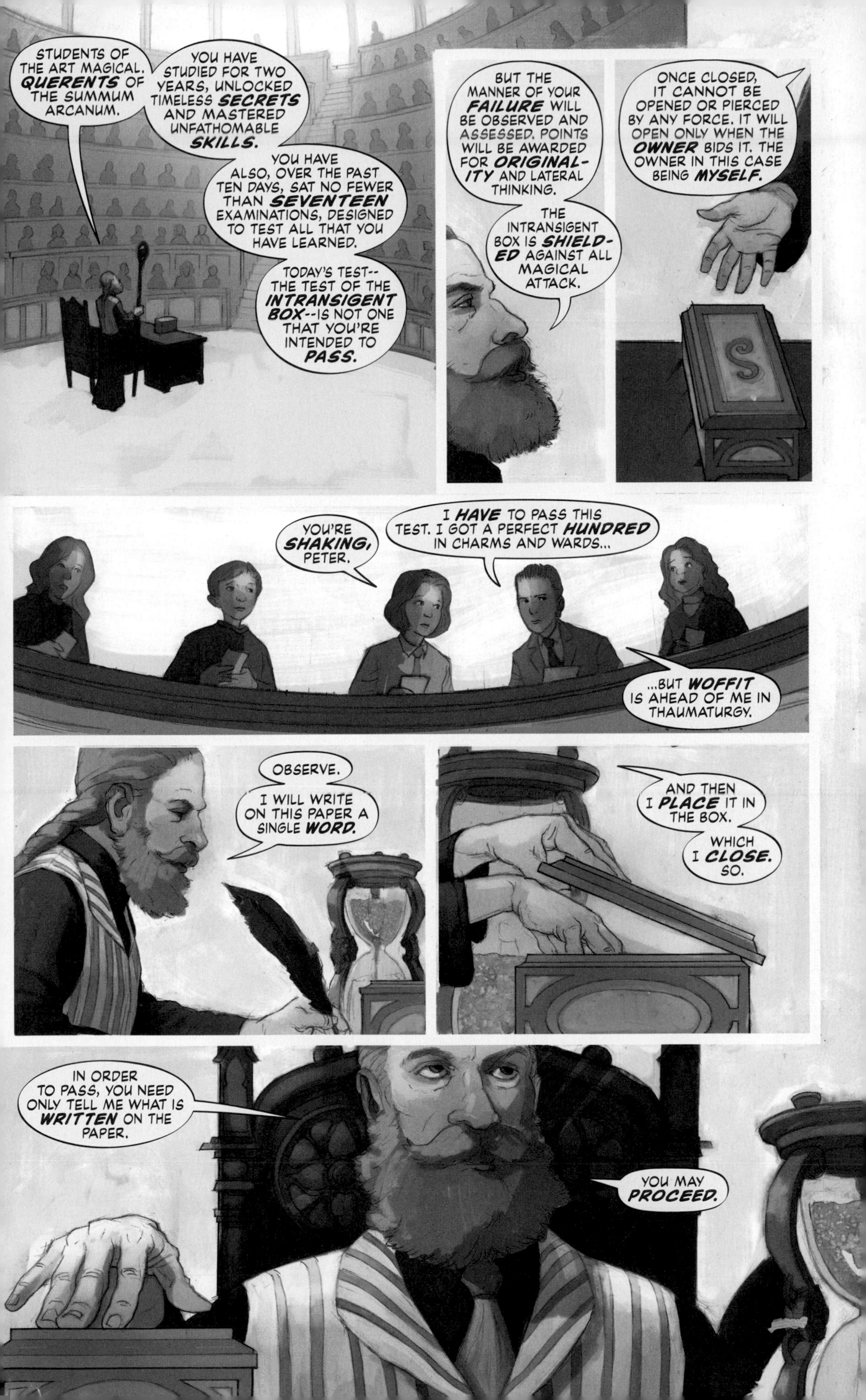

STUDENTS OF THE ART MAGICAL. QUERENTS OF THE SUMMUM ARCANUM.
YOU HAVE STUDIED FOR TWO YEARS, UNLOCKED TIMELESS SECRETS AND MASTERED UNFATHOMABLE SKILLS.
YOU HAVE ALSO, OVER THE PAST TEN DAYS, SAT NO FEWER THAN SEVENTEEN EXAMINATIONS, DESIGNED TO TEST ALL THAT YOU HAVE LEARNED.
TODAY'S TEST-- THE TEST OF THE INTRANSIGENT BOX--IS NOT ONE THAT YOU'RE INTENDED TO PASS.
BUT THE MANNER OF YOUR FAILURE WILL BE OBSERVED AND ASSESSED. POINTS WILL BE AWARDED FOR ORIGINAL-ITY AND LATERAL THINKING.
THE INTRANSIGENT BOX IS SHIELD-ED AGAINST ALL MAGICAL ATTACK.
ONCE CLOSED, IT CANNOT BE OPENED OR PIERCED BY ANY FORCE. IT WILL OPEN ONLY WHEN THE OWNER BIDS IT. THE OWNER IN THIS CASE BEING MYSELF.
YOU'RE SHAKING, PETER.
I HAVE TO PASS THIS TEST. I GOT A PERFECT HUNDRED IN CHARMS AND WARDS...
...BUT WOFFIT IS AHEAD OF ME IN THAUMATURGY.
OBSERVE.
I WILL WRITE ON THIS PAPER A SINGLE WORD.
AND THEN I PLACE IT IN THE BOX.
WHICH I CLOSE. SO.
IN ORDER TO PASS, YOU NEED ONLY TELL ME WHAT IS WRITTEN ON THE PAPER.
YOU MAY PROCEED.

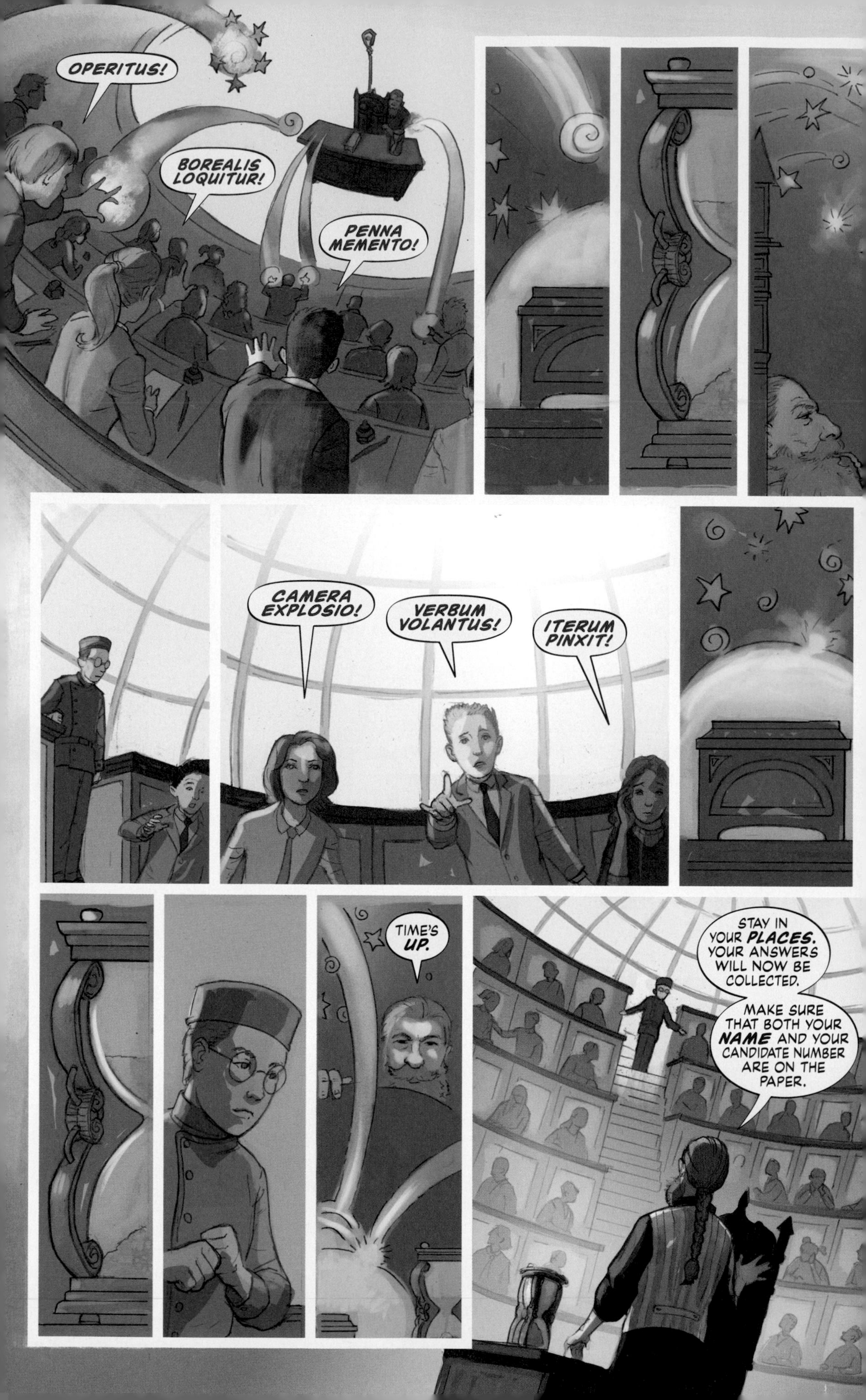
OPERITUS!
BOREALIS LOQUITUR!
PENNA MEMENTO!
CAMERA EXPLOSIO!
VERBUM VOLANTUS!
ITERUM PINXIT!
TIME'S **UP.**
STAY IN YOUR **PLACES.** YOUR ANSWERS WILL NOW BE COLLECTED.
MAKE SURE THAT BOTH YOUR **NAME** AND YOUR CANDIDATE NUMBER ARE ON THE PAPER.

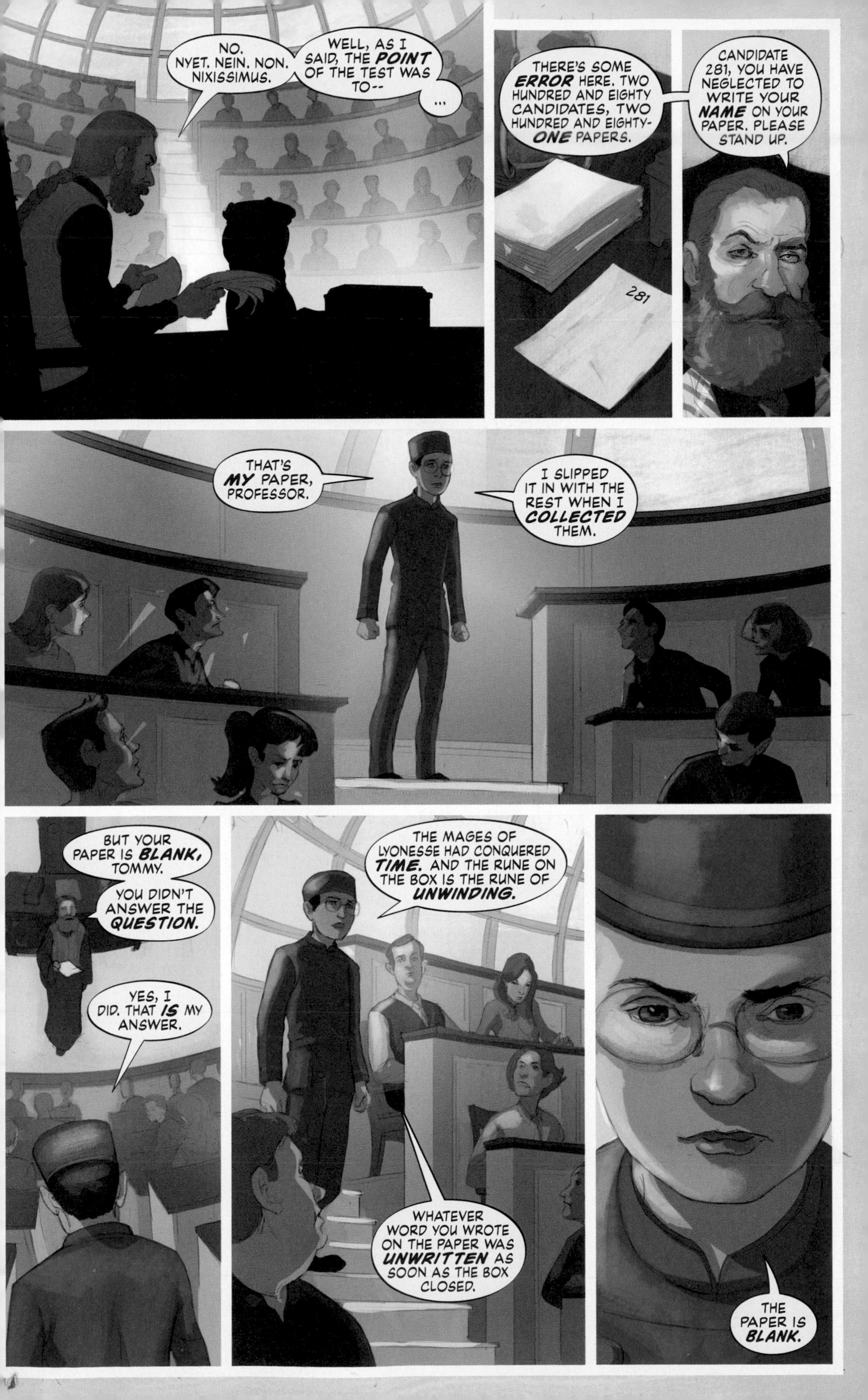
NO. NYET. NEIN. NON. NIXISSIMUS.
WELL, AS I SAID, THE **POINT** OF THE TEST WAS TO--
...
THERE'S SOME **ERROR** HERE. TWO HUNDRED AND EIGHTY CANDIDATES, TWO HUNDRED AND EIGHTY-**ONE** PAPERS.
281
CANDIDATE 281, YOU HAVE NEGLECTED TO WRITE YOUR **NAME** ON YOUR PAPER. PLEASE STAND UP.
THAT'S **MY** PAPER, PROFESSOR.
I SLIPPED IT IN WITH THE REST WHEN I **COLLECTED** THEM.
BUT YOUR PAPER IS **BLANK,** TOMMY.
YOU DIDN'T ANSWER THE **QUESTION.**
YES, I DID. THAT **IS** MY ANSWER.
THE MAGES OF LYONESSE HAD CONQUERED **TIME.** AND THE RUNE ON THE BOX IS THE RUNE OF **UNWINDING.**
WHATEVER WORD YOU WROTE ON THE PAPER WAS **UNWRITTEN** AS SOON AS THE BOX CLOSED.
THE PAPER IS **BLANK.**

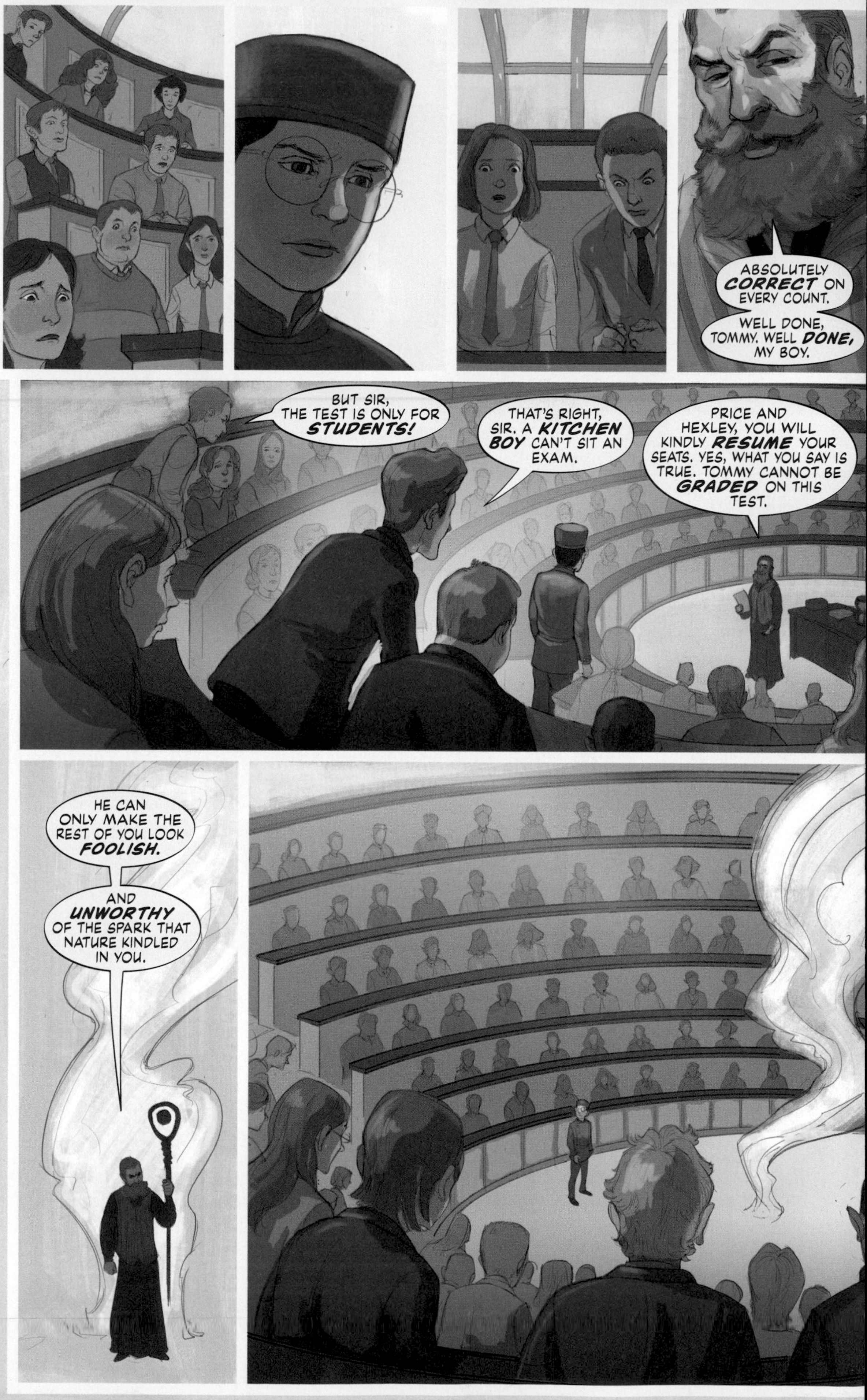
ABSOLUTELY CORRECT ON EVERY COUNT.
WELL DONE, TOMMY. WELL DONE, MY BOY.
BUT SIR, THE TEST IS ONLY FOR STUDENTS!
THAT'S RIGHT, SIR. A KITCHEN BOY CAN'T SIT AN EXAM.
PRICE AND HEXLEY, YOU WILL KINDLY RESUME YOUR SEATS. YES, WHAT YOU SAY IS TRUE. TOMMY CANNOT BE GRADED ON THIS TEST.
HE CAN ONLY MAKE THE REST OF YOU LOOK FOOLISH.
AND UNWORTHY OF THE SPARK THAT NATURE KINDLED IN YOU.

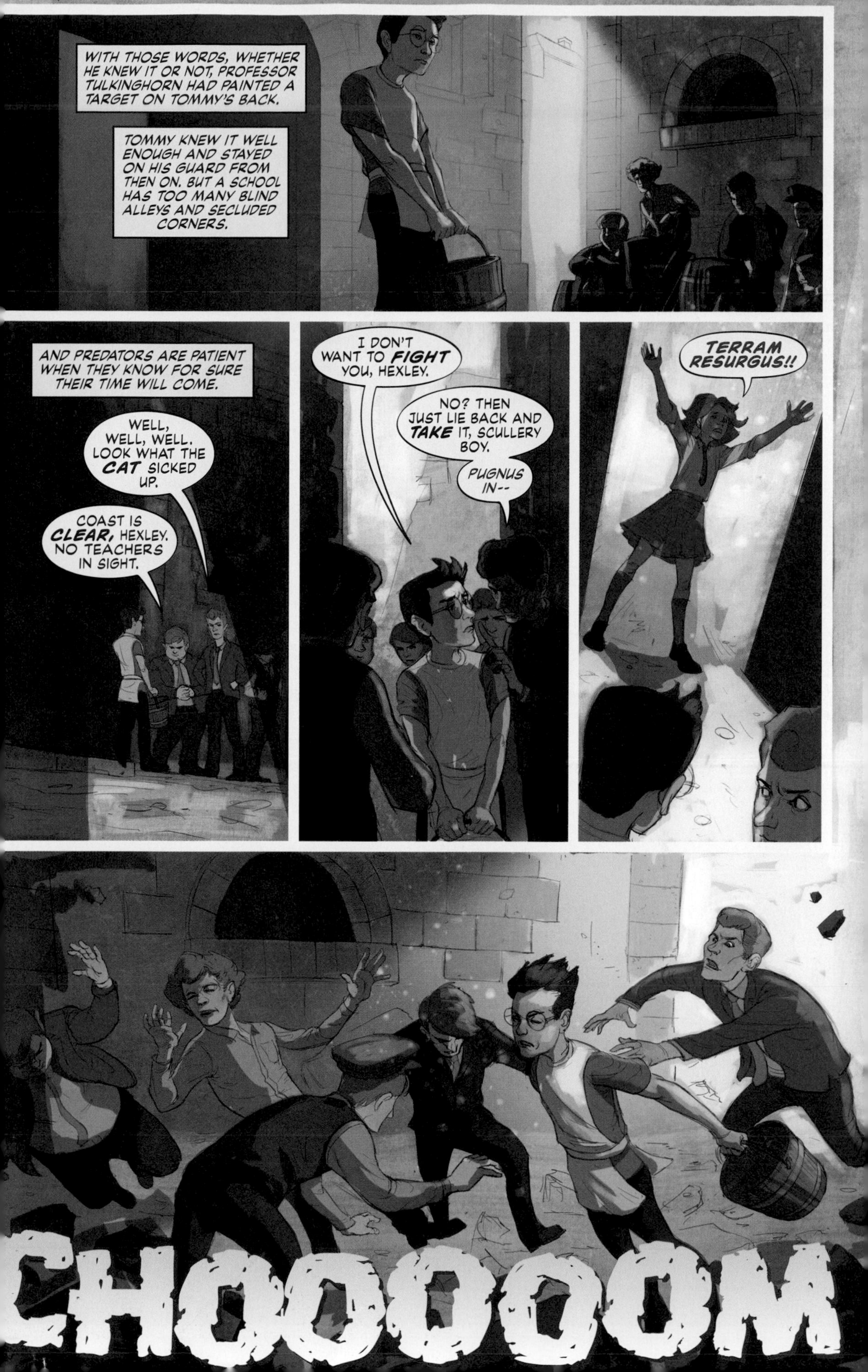
WITH THOSE WORDS, WHETHER HE KNEW IT OR NOT, PROFESSOR TULKINGHORN HAD PAINTED A TARGET ON TOMMY'S BACK.
TOMMY KNEW IT WELL ENOUGH AND STAYED ON HIS GUARD FROM THEN ON. BUT A SCHOOL HAS TOO MANY BLIND ALLEYS AND SECLUDED CORNERS.
AND PREDATORS ARE PATIENT WHEN THEY KNOW FOR SURE THEIR TIME WILL COME.
WELL, WELL, WELL. LOOK WHAT THE CAT SICKED UP.
COAST IS CLEAR, HEXLEY. NO TEACHERS IN SIGHT.
I DON'T WANT TO FIGHT YOU, HEXLEY.
NO? THEN JUST LIE BACK AND TAKE IT, SCULLERY BOY.
PUGNUS IN--
TERRAM RESURGUS!!
CHOOOOOM

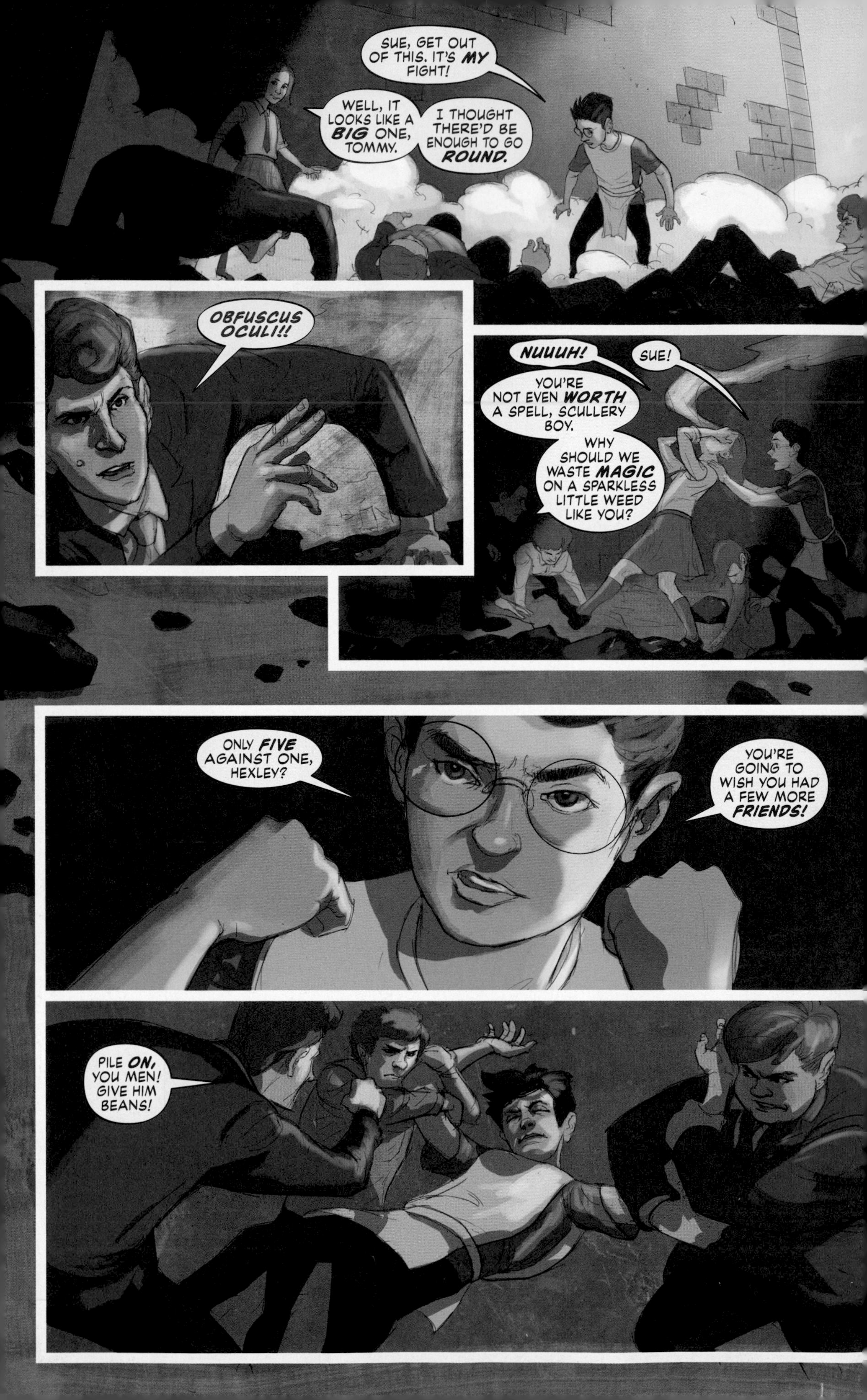

SUE, GET OUT OF THIS. IT'S MY FIGHT!
WELL, IT LOOKS LIKE A BIG ONE, TOMMY.
I THOUGHT THERE'D BE ENOUGH TO GO ROUND.
OBFUSCUS OCULI!!
NUUUH!
SUE!
YOU'RE NOT EVEN WORTH A SPELL, SCULLERY BOY.
WHY SHOULD WE WASTE MAGIC ON A SPARKLESS LITTLE WEED LIKE YOU?
ONLY FIVE AGAINST ONE, HEXLEY?
YOU'RE GOING TO WISH YOU HAD A FEW MORE FRIENDS!
PILE ON, YOU MEN! GIVE HIM BEANS!

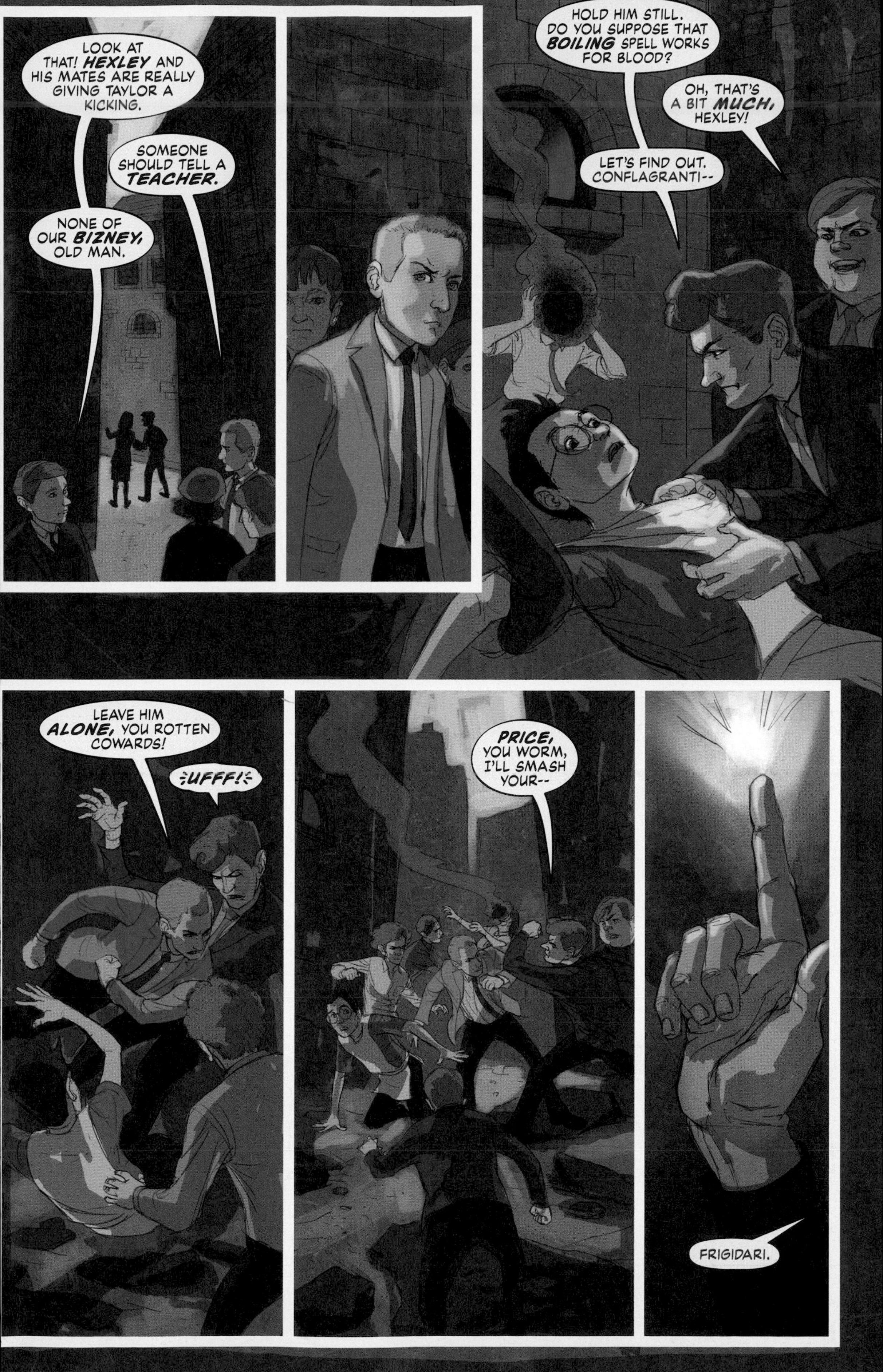
LOOK AT THAT! HEXLEY AND HIS MATES ARE REALLY GIVING TAYLOR A KICKING.
SOMEONE SHOULD TELL A TEACHER.
NONE OF OUR BIZNEY, OLD MAN.
HOLD HIM STILL. DO YOU SUPPOSE THAT BOILING SPELL WORKS FOR BLOOD?
OH, THAT'S A BIT MUCH, HEXLEY!
LET'S FIND OUT. CONFLAGRANTI--
LEAVE HIM ALONE, YOU ROTTEN COWARDS!
UFFF!
PRICE, YOU WORM, I'LL SMASH YOUR--
FRIGIDARI.

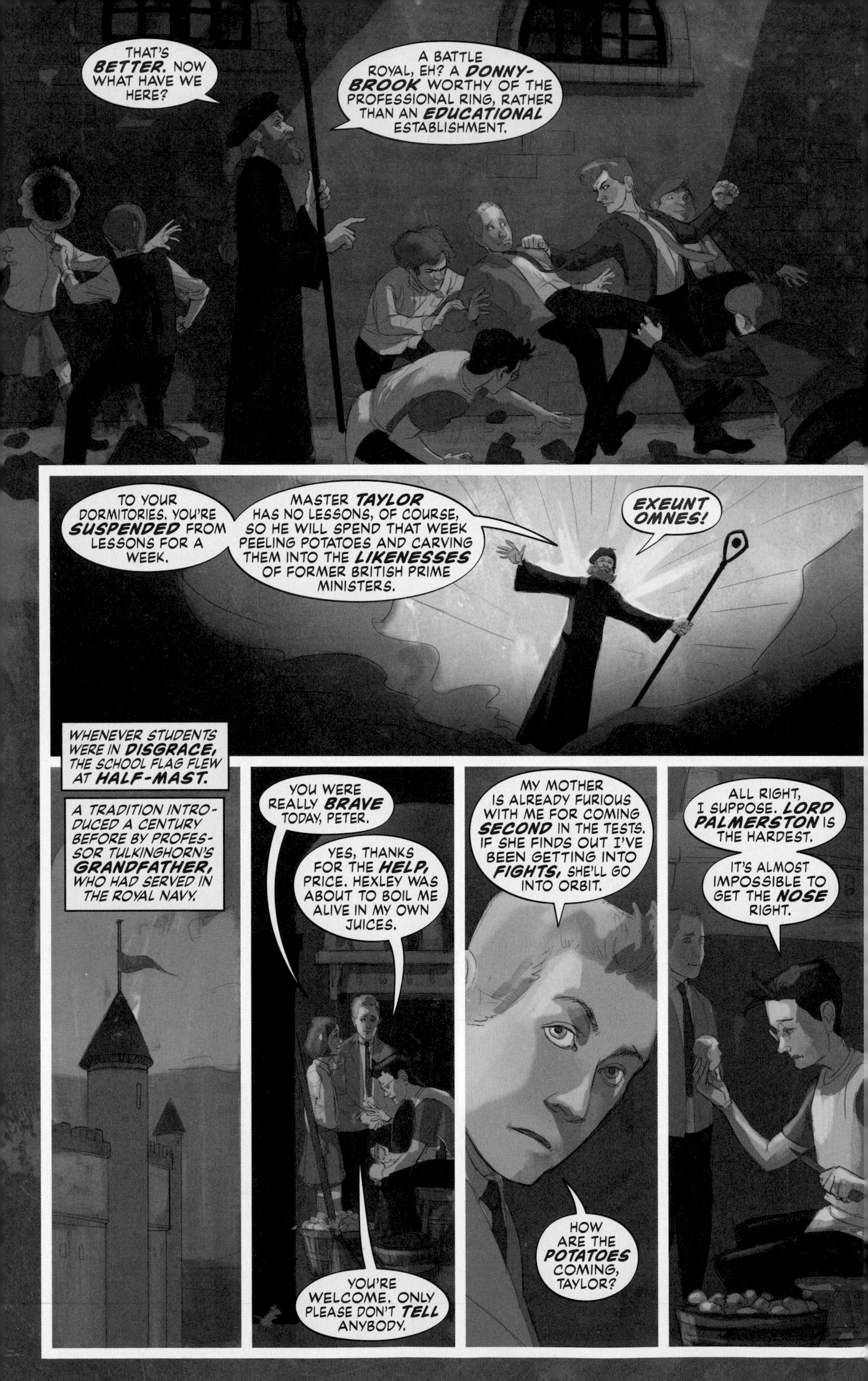
THAT'S BETTER. NOW WHAT HAVE WE HERE?
A BATTLE ROYAL, EH? A DONNY-BROOK WORTHY OF THE PROFESSIONAL RING, RATHER THAN AN EDUCATIONAL ESTABLISHMENT.
TO YOUR DORMITORIES. YOU'RE SUSPENDED FROM LESSONS FOR A WEEK.
MASTER TAYLOR HAS NO LESSONS, OF COURSE, SO HE WILL SPEND THAT WEEK PEELING POTATOES AND CARVING THEM INTO THE LIKENESSES OF FORMER BRITISH PRIME MINISTERS.
EXEUNT OMNES!
WHENEVER STUDENTS WERE IN DISGRACE, THE SCHOOL FLAG FLEW AT HALF-MAST.
A TRADITION INTRODUCED A CENTURY BEFORE BY PROFESSOR TULKINGHORN'S GRANDFATHER, WHO HAD SERVED IN THE ROYAL NAVY.
YOU WERE REALLY BRAVE TODAY, PETER.
YES, THANKS FOR THE HELP, PRICE. HEXLEY WAS ABOUT TO BOIL ME ALIVE IN MY OWN JUICES.
YOU'RE WELCOME. ONLY PLEASE DON'T TELL ANYBODY.
MY MOTHER IS ALREADY FURIOUS WITH ME FOR COMING SECOND IN THE TESTS. IF SHE FINDS OUT I'VE BEEN GETTING INTO FIGHTS, SHE'LL GO INTO ORBIT.
HOW ARE THE POTATOES COMING, TAYLOR?
ALL RIGHT, I SUPPOSE. LORD PALMERSTON IS THE HARDEST.
IT'S ALMOST IMPOSSIBLE TO GET THE NOSE RIGHT.

May 15th. Sue was wrecked by the birth, and now she seems to be wrecked by everything else, too. But I planned for this, and I think on some level it was my preferred option.

Enter Calliope Madigan.

'Calliope's a false trail, an outrageous PR McGuffin (if you can have McGuffins in PR), but my God she's a wizard wheeze. She's my wife, and Tom's mother, and the fact that she doesn't even exist doesn't seem to be much of a barrier to that.

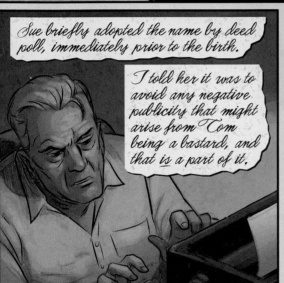

Sue briefly adopted the name by deed poll, immediately prior to the birth.

I told her it was to avoid any negative publicity that might arise from Tom being a bastard, and that is a part of it.

So the mother's name as per the birth certificate is Calliope Madigan, and since Sue then took her own name again a week later, the paper trail from Calliope leads nowhere.

No photos of Calliope.

No public utterances from Calliope, except the ones I write myself.

No danger of Calliope going off-message.

And no need to put Sue in front of a camera even once, thank God.

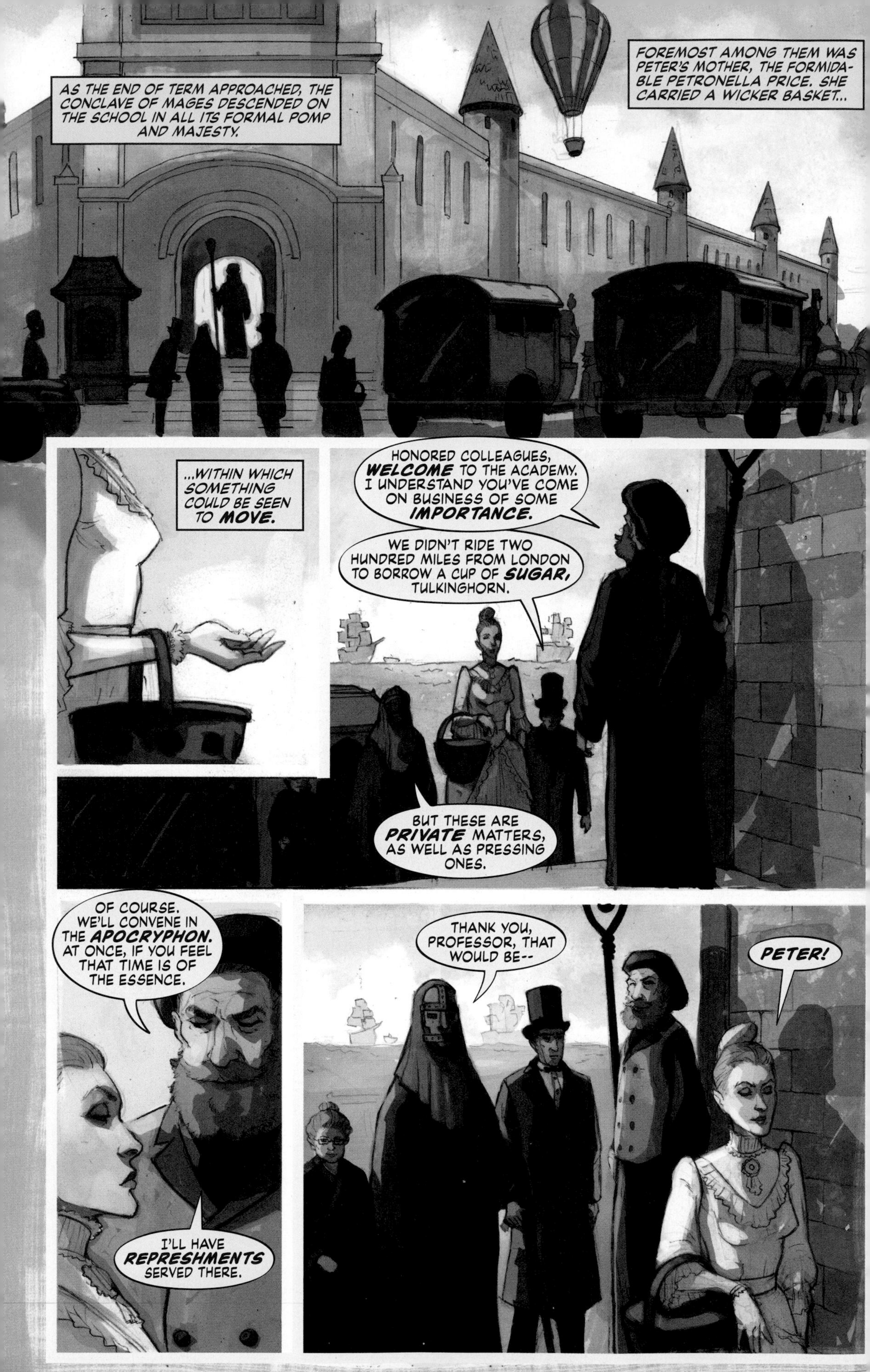
AS THE END OF TERM APPROACHED, THE CONCLAVE OF MAGES DESCENDED ON THE SCHOOL IN ALL ITS FORMAL POMP AND MAJESTY.
FOREMOST AMONG THEM WAS PETER'S MOTHER, THE FORMIDABLE PETRONELLA PRICE. SHE CARRIED A WICKER BASKET...
...WITHIN WHICH SOMETHING COULD BE SEEN TO MOVE.
HONORED COLLEAGUES, WELCOME TO THE ACADEMY. I UNDERSTAND YOU'VE COME ON BUSINESS OF SOME IMPORTANCE.
WE DIDN'T RIDE TWO HUNDRED MILES FROM LONDON TO BORROW A CUP OF SUGAR, TULKINGHORN.
BUT THESE ARE PRIVATE MATTERS, AS WELL AS PRESSING ONES.
OF COURSE. WE'LL CONVENE IN THE APOCRYPHON. AT ONCE, IF YOU FEEL THAT TIME IS OF THE ESSENCE.
I'LL HAVE REFRESHMENTS SERVED THERE.
THANK YOU, PROFESSOR, THAT WOULD BE--
PETER!

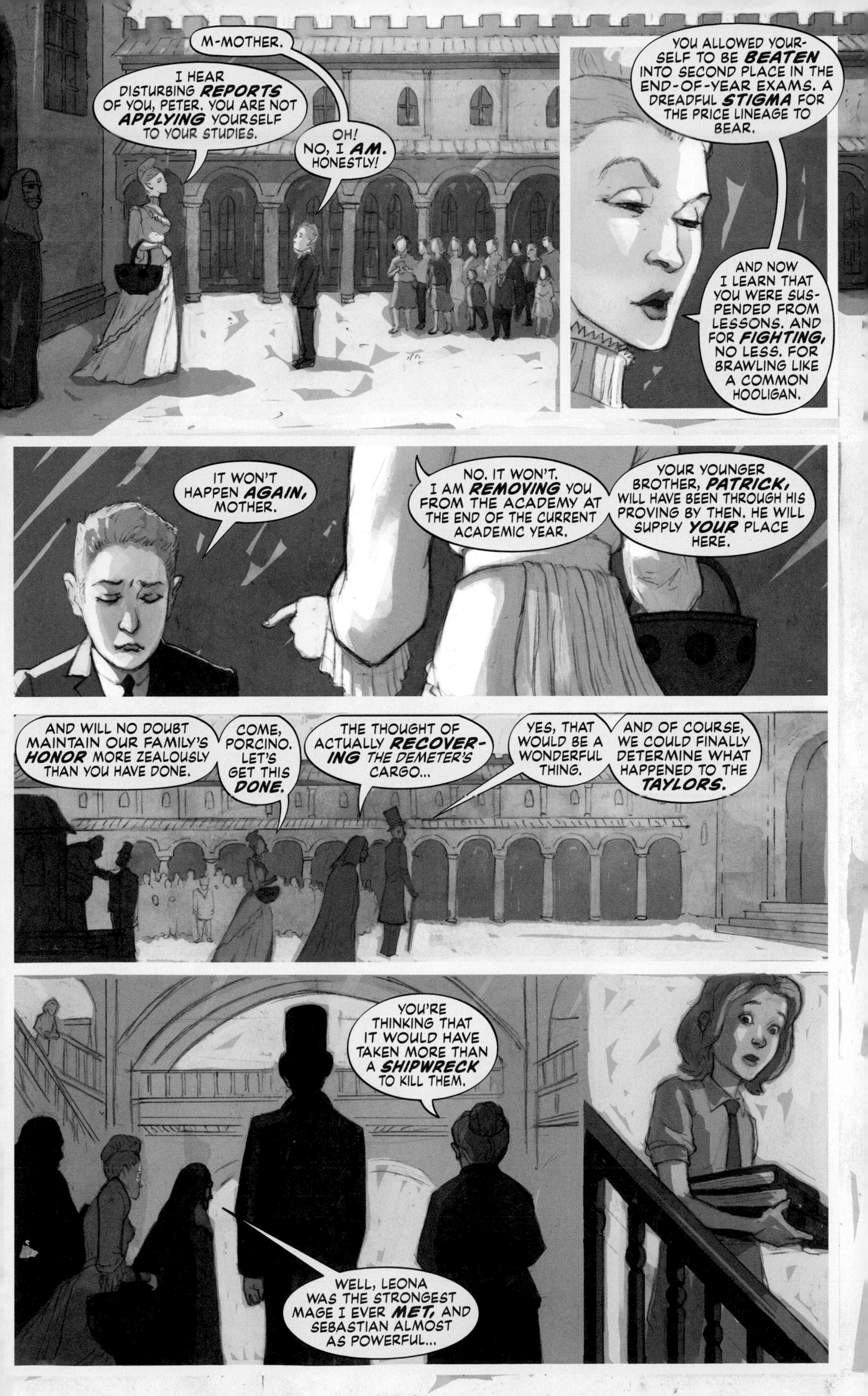
M-MOTHER.
I HEAR DISTURBING REPORTS OF YOU, PETER. YOU ARE NOT APPLYING YOURSELF TO YOUR STUDIES.
OH! NO, I AM. HONESTLY!
YOU ALLOWED YOURSELF TO BE BEATEN INTO SECOND PLACE IN THE END-OF-YEAR EXAMS. A DREADFUL STIGMA FOR THE PRICE LINEAGE TO BEAR.
AND NOW I LEARN THAT YOU WERE SUSPENDED FROM LESSONS. AND FOR FIGHTING, NO LESS. FOR BRAWLING LIKE A COMMON HOOLIGAN.
IT WON'T HAPPEN AGAIN, MOTHER.
NO. IT WON'T. I AM REMOVING YOU FROM THE ACADEMY AT THE END OF THE CURRENT ACADEMIC YEAR.
YOUR YOUNGER BROTHER, PATRICK, WILL HAVE BEEN THROUGH HIS PROVING BY THEN. HE WILL SUPPLY YOUR PLACE HERE.
AND WILL NO DOUBT MAINTAIN OUR FAMILY'S HONOR MORE ZEALOUSLY THAN YOU HAVE DONE.
COME, PORCINO. LET'S GET THIS DONE.
THE THOUGHT OF ACTUALLY RECOVERING THE DEMETER'S CARGO...
YES, THAT WOULD BE A WONDERFUL THING.
AND OF COURSE, WE COULD FINALLY DETERMINE WHAT HAPPENED TO THE TAYLORS.
YOU'RE THINKING THAT IT WOULD HAVE TAKEN MORE THAN A SHIPWRECK TO KILL THEM.
WELL, LEONA WAS THE STRONGEST MAGE I EVER MET, AND SEBASTIAN ALMOST AS POWERFUL...

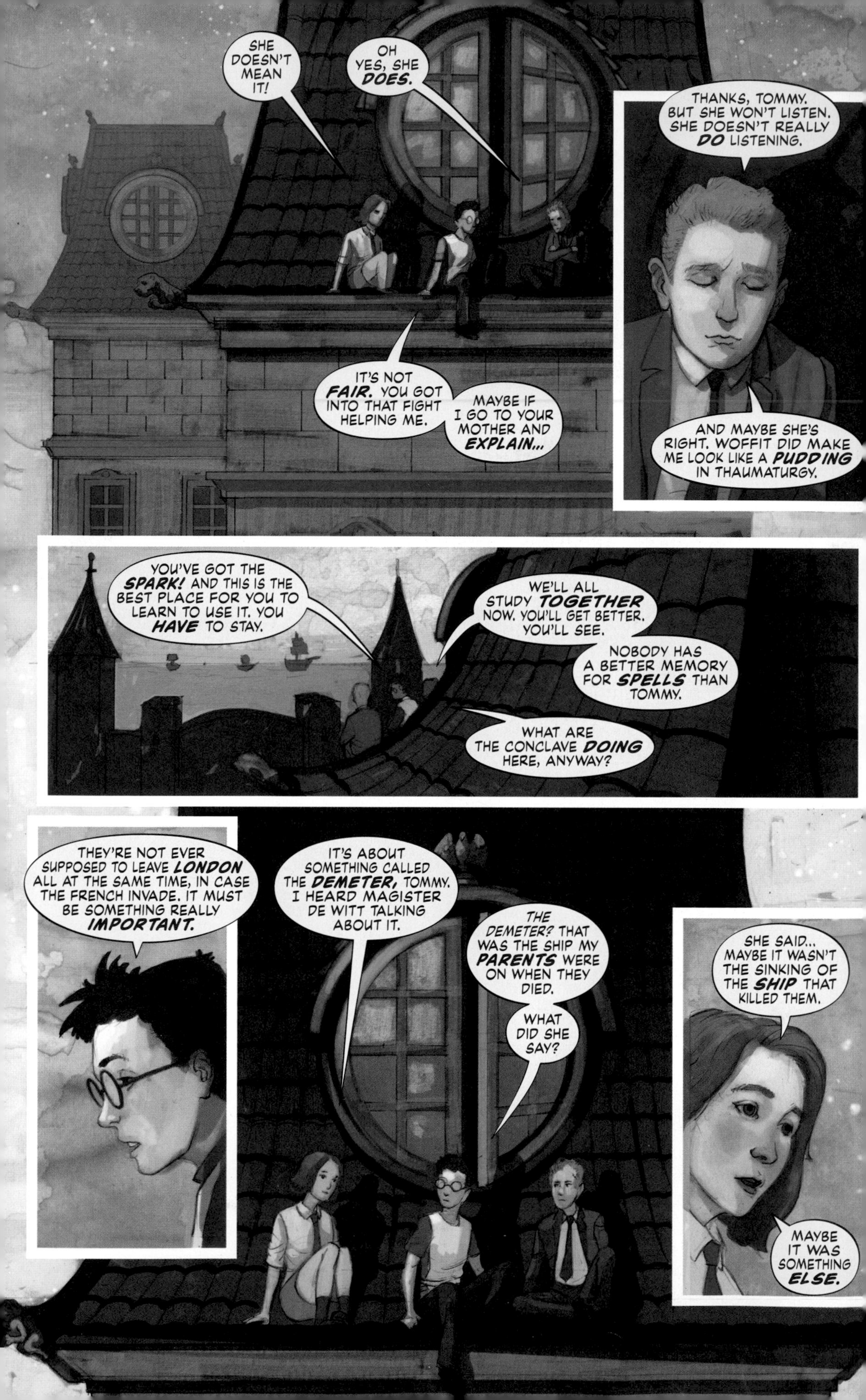
SHE DOESN'T MEAN IT!
OH YES, SHE DOES.
THANKS, TOMMY. BUT SHE WON'T LISTEN. SHE DOESN'T REALLY DO LISTENING.
IT'S NOT FAIR. YOU GOT INTO THAT FIGHT HELPING ME.
MAYBE IF I GO TO YOUR MOTHER AND EXPLAIN...
AND MAYBE SHE'S RIGHT. WOFFIT DID MAKE ME LOOK LIKE A PUDDING IN THAUMATURGY.
YOU'VE GOT THE SPARK! AND THIS IS THE BEST PLACE FOR YOU TO LEARN TO USE IT. YOU HAVE TO STAY.
WE'LL ALL STUDY TOGETHER NOW. YOU'LL GET BETTER. YOU'LL SEE.
NOBODY HAS A BETTER MEMORY FOR SPELLS THAN TOMMY.
WHAT ARE THE CONCLAVE DOING HERE, ANYWAY?
THEY'RE NOT EVER SUPPOSED TO LEAVE LONDON ALL AT THE SAME TIME, IN CASE THE FRENCH INVADE. IT MUST BE SOMETHING REALLY IMPORTANT.
IT'S ABOUT SOMETHING CALLED THE DEMETER, TOMMY. I HEARD MAGISTER DE WITT TALKING ABOUT IT.
THE DEMETER? THAT WAS THE SHIP MY PARENTS WERE ON WHEN THEY DIED.
WHAT DID SHE SAY?
SHE SAID... MAYBE IT WASN'T THE SINKING OF THE SHIP THAT KILLED THEM.
MAYBE IT WAS SOMETHING ELSE.

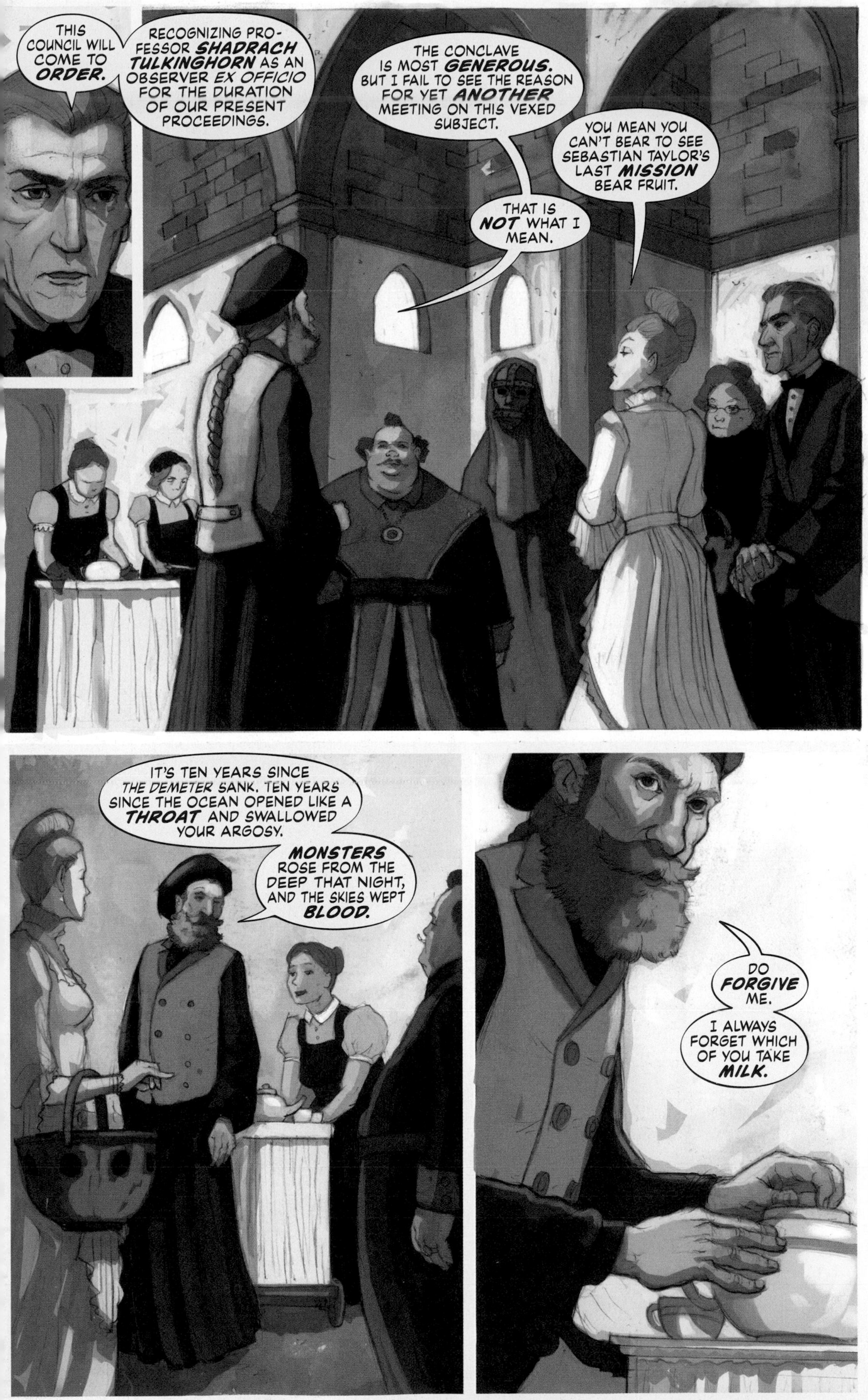
THIS COUNCIL WILL COME TO ORDER.
RECOGNIZING PROFESSOR SHADRACH TULKINGHORN AS AN OBSERVER EX OFFICIO FOR THE DURATION OF OUR PRESENT PROCEEDINGS.
THE CONCLAVE IS MOST GENEROUS. BUT I FAIL TO SEE THE REASON FOR YET ANOTHER MEETING ON THIS VEXED SUBJECT.
YOU MEAN YOU CAN'T BEAR TO SEE SEBASTIAN TAYLOR'S LAST MISSION BEAR FRUIT.
THAT IS NOT WHAT I MEAN.
IT'S TEN YEARS SINCE THE DEMETER SANK. TEN YEARS SINCE THE OCEAN OPENED LIKE A THROAT AND SWALLOWED YOUR ARGOSY.
MONSTERS ROSE FROM THE DEEP THAT NIGHT, AND THE SKIES WEPT BLOOD.
DO FORGIVE ME.
I ALWAYS FORGET WHICH OF YOU TAKE MILK.

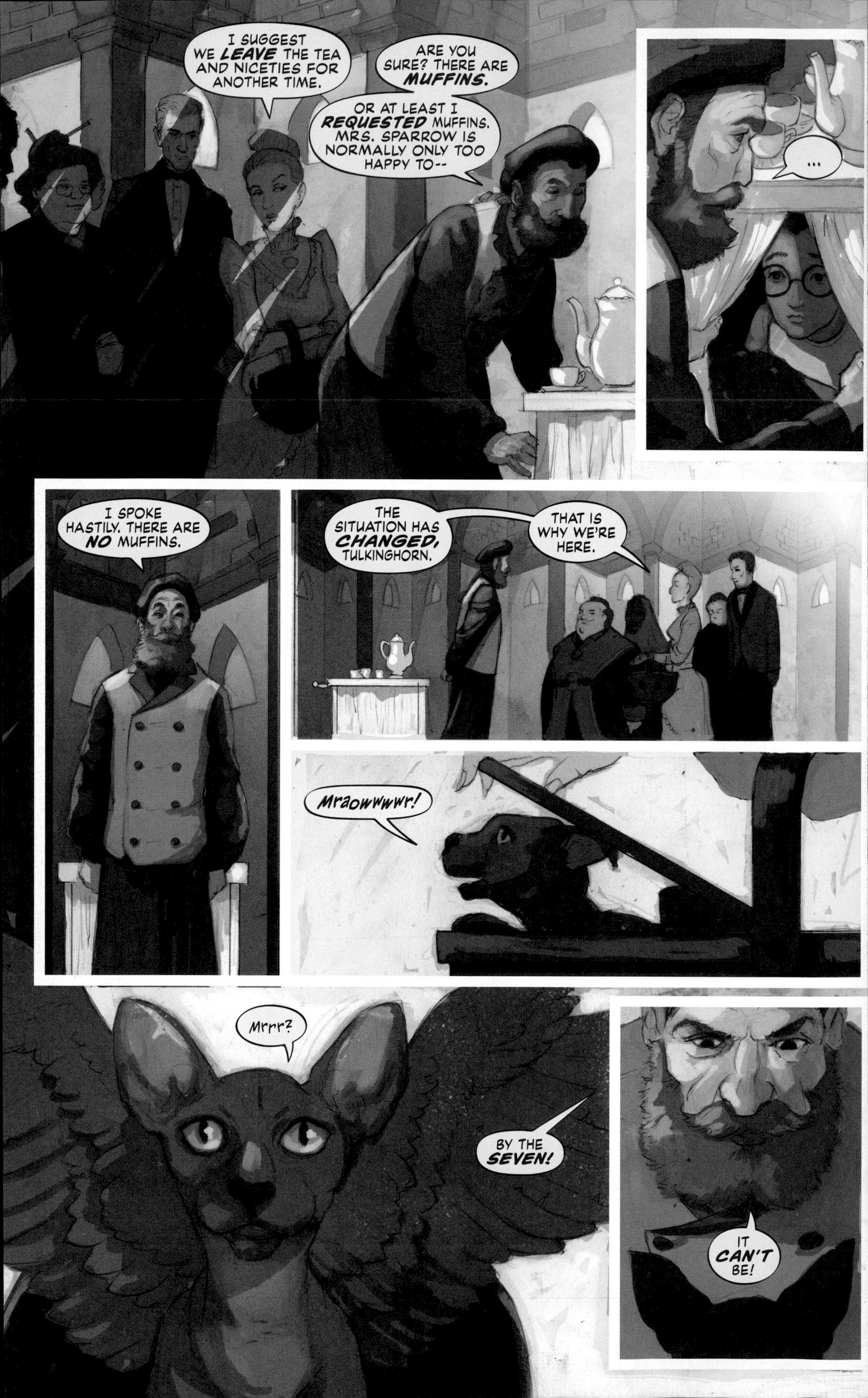

I SUGGEST WE **LEAVE** THE TEA AND NICETIES FOR ANOTHER TIME.
ARE YOU SURE? THERE ARE **MUFFINS.**
OR AT LEAST I **REQUESTED** MUFFINS. MRS. SPARROW IS NORMALLY ONLY TOO HAPPY TO--
...
I SPOKE HASTILY. THERE ARE **NO** MUFFINS.
THE SITUATION HAS **CHANGED,** TULKINGHORN.
THAT IS WHY WE'RE HERE.
Mraowwwwr!
Mrrr?
BY THE **SEVEN!**
IT **CAN'T** BE!

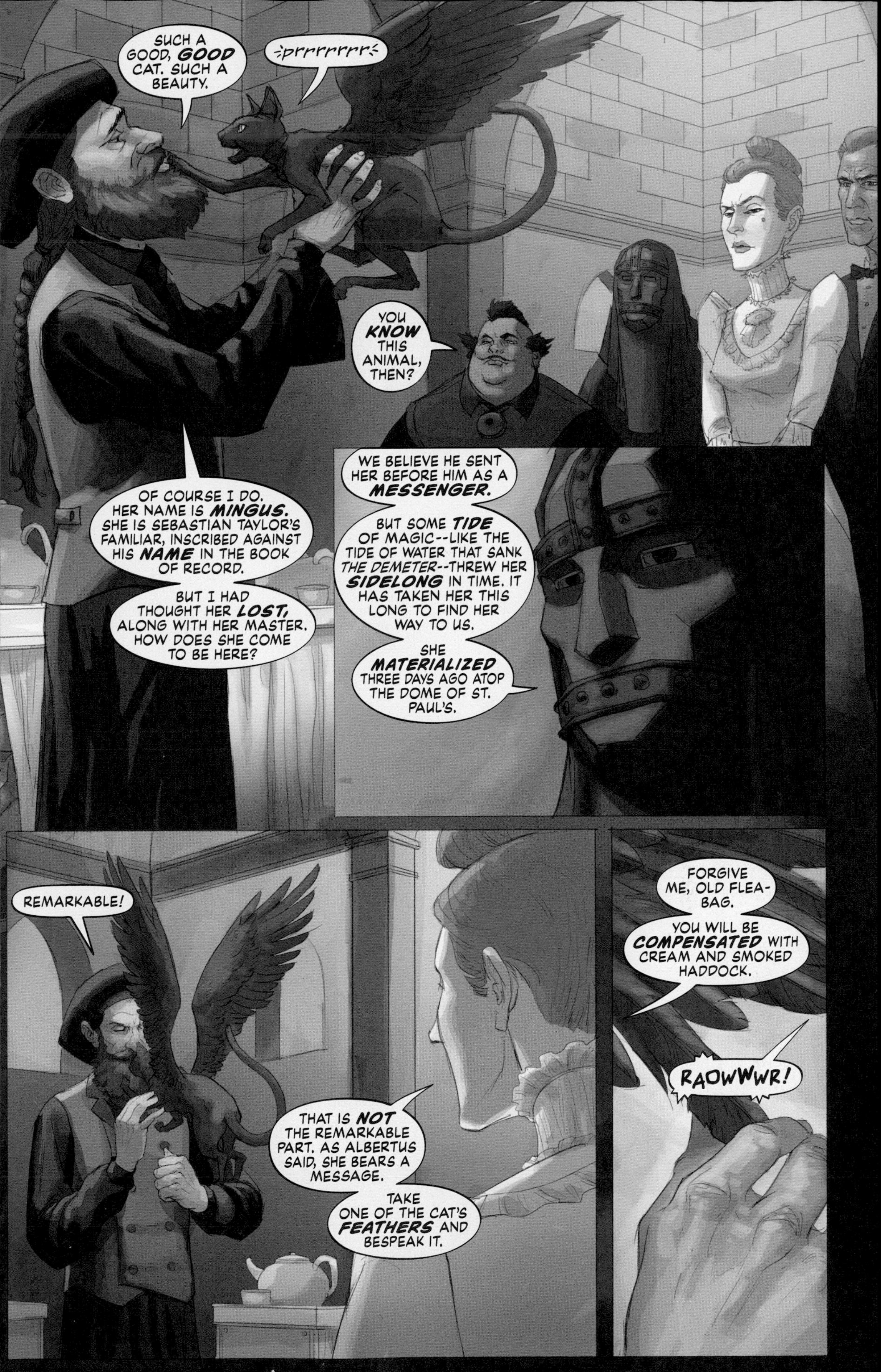
SUCH A GOOD, **GOOD** CAT. SUCH A BEAUTY.
prrrrrrrr
YOU **KNOW** THIS ANIMAL, THEN?
OF COURSE I DO. HER NAME IS **MINGUS.** SHE IS SEBASTIAN TAYLOR'S FAMILIAR, INSCRIBED AGAINST HIS **NAME** IN THE BOOK OF RECORD.
BUT I HAD THOUGHT HER **LOST,** ALONG WITH HER MASTER. HOW DOES SHE COME TO BE HERE?
WE BELIEVE HE SENT HER BEFORE HIM AS A **MESSENGER.**
BUT SOME **TIDE** OF MAGIC--LIKE THE TIDE OF WATER THAT SANK *THE DEMETER*--THREW HER **SIDELONG** IN TIME. IT HAS TAKEN HER THIS LONG TO FIND HER WAY TO US.
SHE **MATERIALIZED** THREE DAYS AGO ATOP THE DOME OF ST. PAUL'S.
REMARKABLE!
THAT IS **NOT** THE REMARKABLE PART. AS ALBERTUS SAID, SHE BEARS A MESSAGE.
TAKE ONE OF THE CAT'S **FEATHERS** AND BESPEAK IT.
FORGIVE ME, OLD FLEA-BAG.
YOU WILL BE **COMPENSATED** WITH CREAM AND SMOKED HADDOCK.
RAOWWWR!

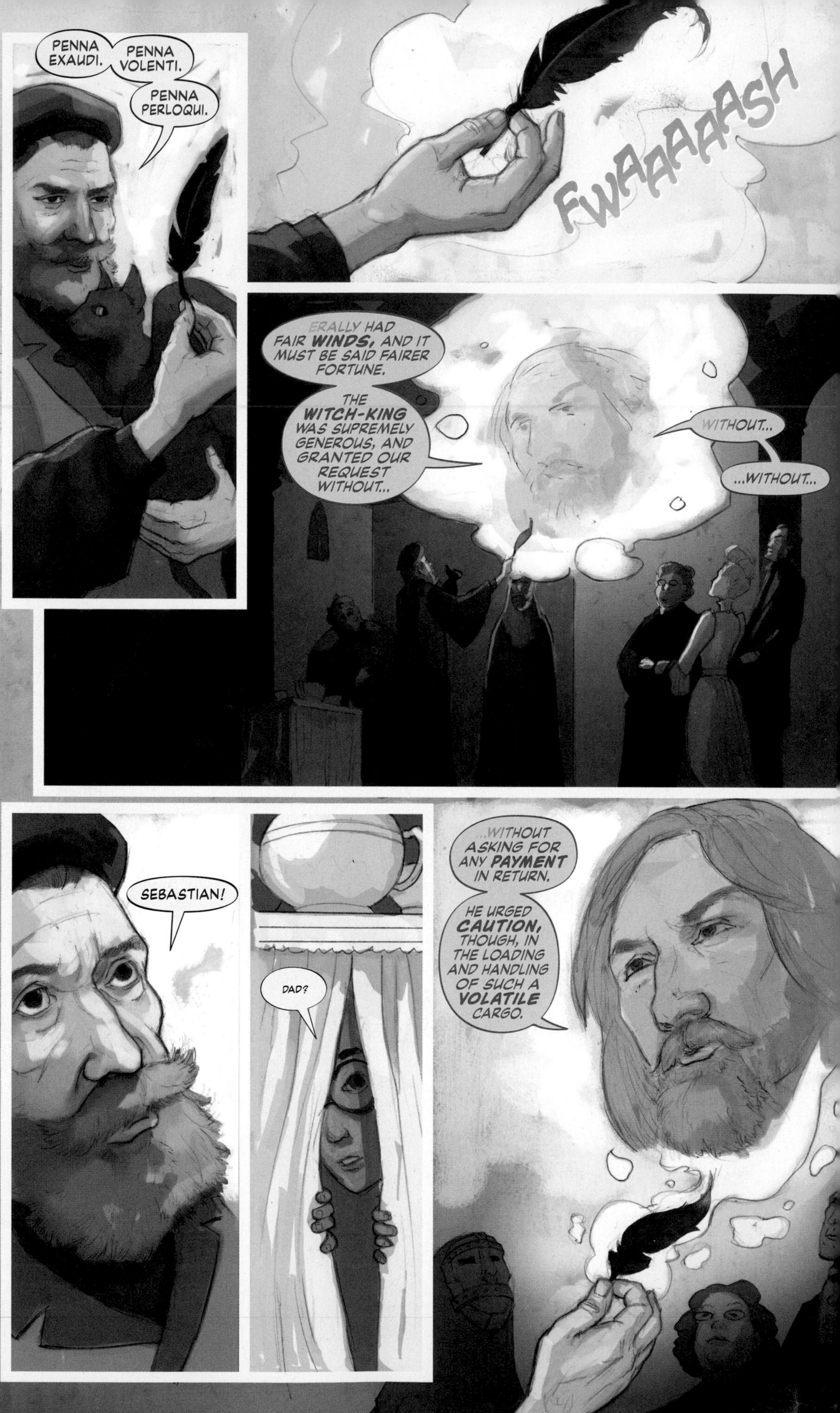
PENNA EXAUDI.
PENNA VOLENTI.
PENNA PERLOQUI.
FWAAAAASH
ERALLY HAD FAIR WINDS, AND IT MUST BE SAID FAIRER FORTUNE.
THE WITCH-KING WAS SUPREMELY GENEROUS, AND GRANTED OUR REQUEST WITHOUT...
WITHOUT...
...WITHOUT...
SEBASTIAN!
DAD?
...WITHOUT ASKING FOR ANY PAYMENT IN RETURN.
HE URGED CAUTION, THOUGH, IN THE LOADING AND HANDLING OF SUCH A VOLATILE CARGO.

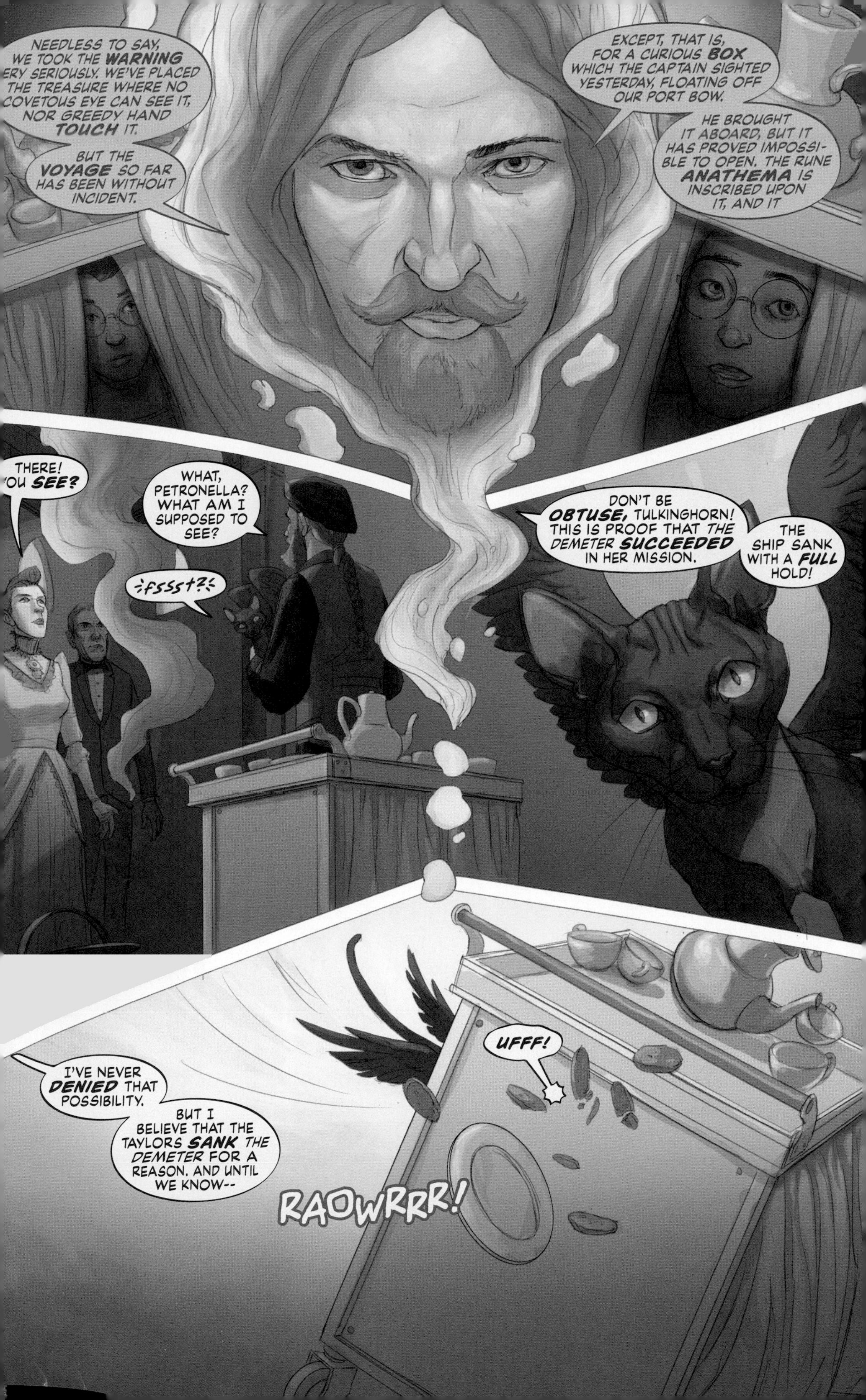
NEEDLESS TO SAY, WE TOOK THE **WARNING** ERY SERIOUSLY. WE'VE PLACED THE TREASURE WHERE NO COVETOUS EYE CAN SEE IT, NOR GREEDY HAND **TOUCH** IT.
BUT THE **VOYAGE** SO FAR HAS BEEN WITHOUT INCIDENT.
EXCEPT, THAT IS, FOR A CURIOUS **BOX** WHICH THE CAPTAIN SIGHTED YESTERDAY, FLOATING OFF OUR PORT BOW.
HE BROUGHT IT ABOARD, BUT IT HAS PROVED IMPOSSIBLE TO OPEN. THE RUNE **ANATHEMA** IS INSCRIBED UPON IT, AND IT
THERE! OU **SEE?**
WHAT, PETRONELLA? WHAT AM I SUPPOSED TO SEE?
FSSST?
DON'T BE **OBTUSE,** TULKINGHORN! THIS IS PROOF THAT *THE DEMETER* **SUCCEEDED** IN HER MISSION.
THE SHIP SANK WITH A **FULL** HOLD!
I'VE NEVER **DENIED** THAT POSSIBILITY.
BUT I BELIEVE THAT THE TAYLORS **SANK** *THE DEMETER* FOR A REASON. AND UNTIL WE KNOW--
UFFF!
RAOWRRR!

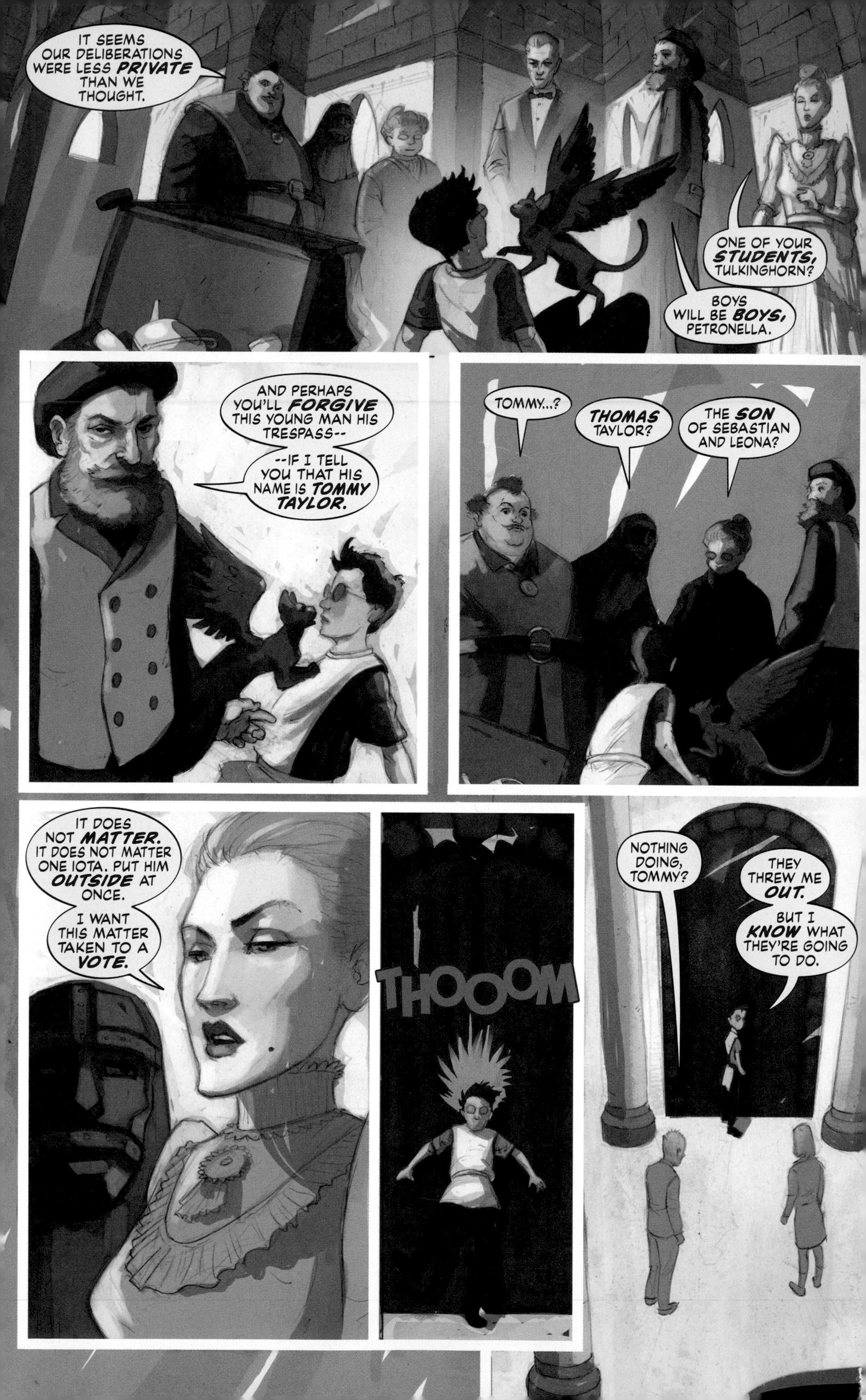
IT SEEMS OUR DELIBERATIONS WERE LESS PRIVATE THAN WE THOUGHT.
ONE OF YOUR STUDENTS, TULKINGHORN?
BOYS WILL BE BOYS, PETRONELLA.
AND PERHAPS YOU'LL FORGIVE THIS YOUNG MAN HIS TRESPASS--
--IF I TELL YOU THAT HIS NAME IS TOMMY TAYLOR.
TOMMY...?
THOMAS TAYLOR?
THE SON OF SEBASTIAN AND LEONA?
IT DOES NOT MATTER. IT DOES NOT MATTER ONE IOTA. PUT HIM OUTSIDE AT ONCE.
I WANT THIS MATTER TAKEN TO A VOTE.
THOOOM
NOTHING DOING, TOMMY?
THEY THREW ME OUT.
BUT I KNOW WHAT THEY'RE GOING TO DO.

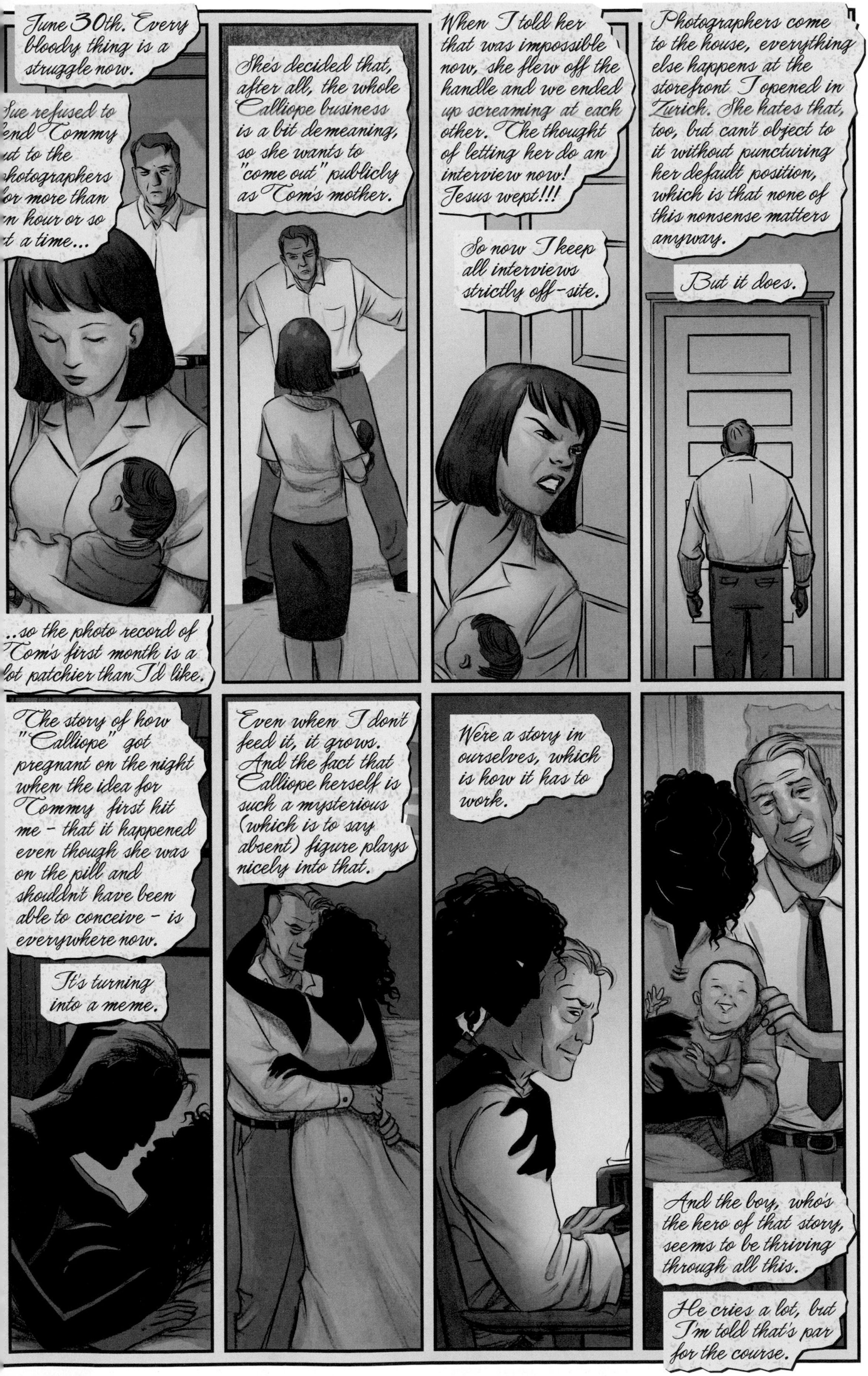
June 30th. Every bloody thing is a struggle now.
Sue refused to send Tommy out to the photographers for more than an hour or so at a time...
...so the photo record of Tom's first month is a lot patchier than I'd like.
She's decided that, after all, the whole Calliope business is a bit demeaning, so she wants to "come out" publicly as Tom's mother.
When I told her that was impossible now, she flew off the handle and we ended up screaming at each other. The thought of letting her do an interview now! Jesus wept!!!
So now I keep all interviews strictly off-site.
Photographers come to the house, everything else happens at the storefront I opened in Zurich. She hates that, too, but can't object to it without puncturing her default position, which is that none of this nonsense matters anyway.
But it does.
The story of how "Calliope" got pregnant on the night when the idea for Tommy first hit me - that it happened even though she was on the pill and shouldn't have been able to conceive - is everywhere now.
It's turning into a meme.
Even when I don't feed it, it grows. And the fact that Calliope herself is such a mysterious (which is to say absent) figure plays nicely into that.
We're a story in ourselves, which is how it has to work.
And the boy, who's the hero of that story, seems to be thriving through all this.
He cries a lot, but I'm told that's par for the course.

Aug 1st. Book went into its ninth printing. Ernie's overjoyed, and slightly shell-shocked. He's a comic turn these days – like a man who got his jacket caught in the door of a tube train and is being dragged along the platform with his arms flailing. He's never moved at zeitgeist speeds before.

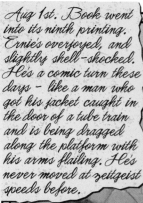

Speed of zeit. Can I use that somewhere? Not in Tommy, obviously, but in an interview.

I'm making good headway on book two. Strike while the iron's white-hot.

9.00pm. Had to stop there to put Tom to bed. With Sue out of commission most of the time, I'm having a lot more contact with him than I expected.

It's kind of astonishing, really. On the one hand, I don't have the time and I'm mostly thinking about the story when I'm with him, itching to get back to it and hammer out a few more pages.

On the other... well, Jesus.

I know it makes no biological sense, but I find myself thinking, because he's a boy, there must be more of me in him than of her. That he's a small seed from which a new me is visibly growing.

I wonder if he'll ever come to understand what I'm doing for him. To him.

If he'll be grateful.

If he'll forgive.

He is the crux of a vast enterprise, which has to have one foot in the real world and one in the books.

Back in Oxford, Barfield used to talk about how, when humanity first learned to speak, the literal and metaphorical levels of language were one and the same. Spiritus meant breath, and wind, and soul – all three, simultaneously and without ambiguity.

Tom will mean Tommy, and Tommy will mean Tom. The real world will point to the fiction, the fiction back to the reality and so on, like particles circling in a super-collider until they impact each other and something new is born.

But I wish the little bugger would sleep through the night.

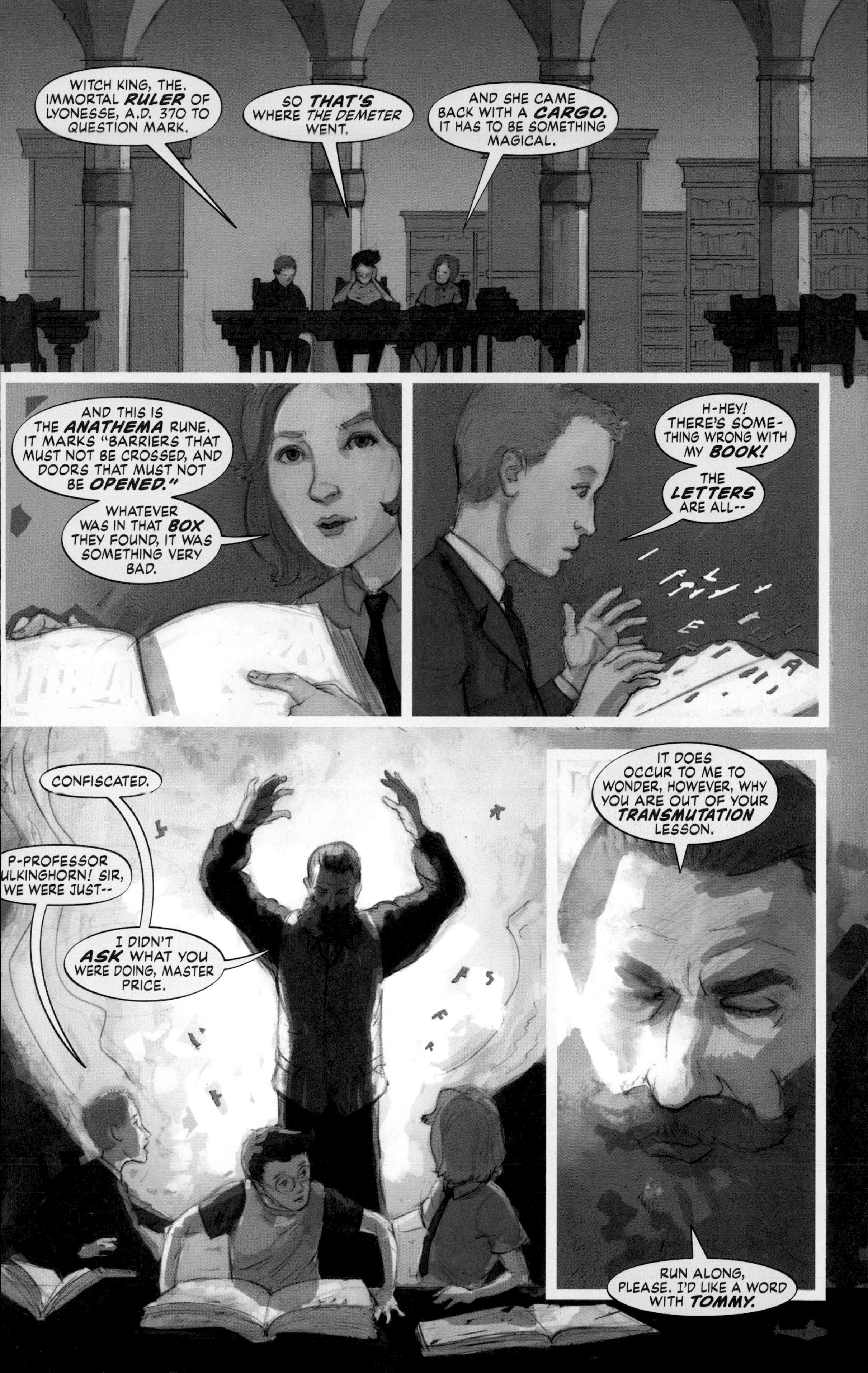
WITCH KING, THE. IMMORTAL RULER OF LYONESSE, A.D. 370 TO QUESTION MARK.
SO THAT'S WHERE THE DEMETER WENT.
AND SHE CAME BACK WITH A CARGO. IT HAS TO BE SOMETHING MAGICAL.
AND THIS IS THE ANATHEMA RUNE. IT MARKS "BARRIERS THAT MUST NOT BE CROSSED, AND DOORS THAT MUST NOT BE OPENED."
WHATEVER WAS IN THAT BOX THEY FOUND, IT WAS SOMETHING VERY BAD.
H-HEY! THERE'S SOMETHING WRONG WITH MY BOOK!
THE LETTERS ARE ALL--
CONFISCATED.
P-PROFESSOR ULKINGHORN! SIR, WE WERE JUST--
I DIDN'T ASK WHAT YOU WERE DOING, MASTER PRICE.
IT DOES OCCUR TO ME TO WONDER, HOWEVER, WHY YOU ARE OUT OF YOUR TRANSMUTATION LESSON.
RUN ALONG, PLEASE. I'D LIKE A WORD WITH TOMMY.

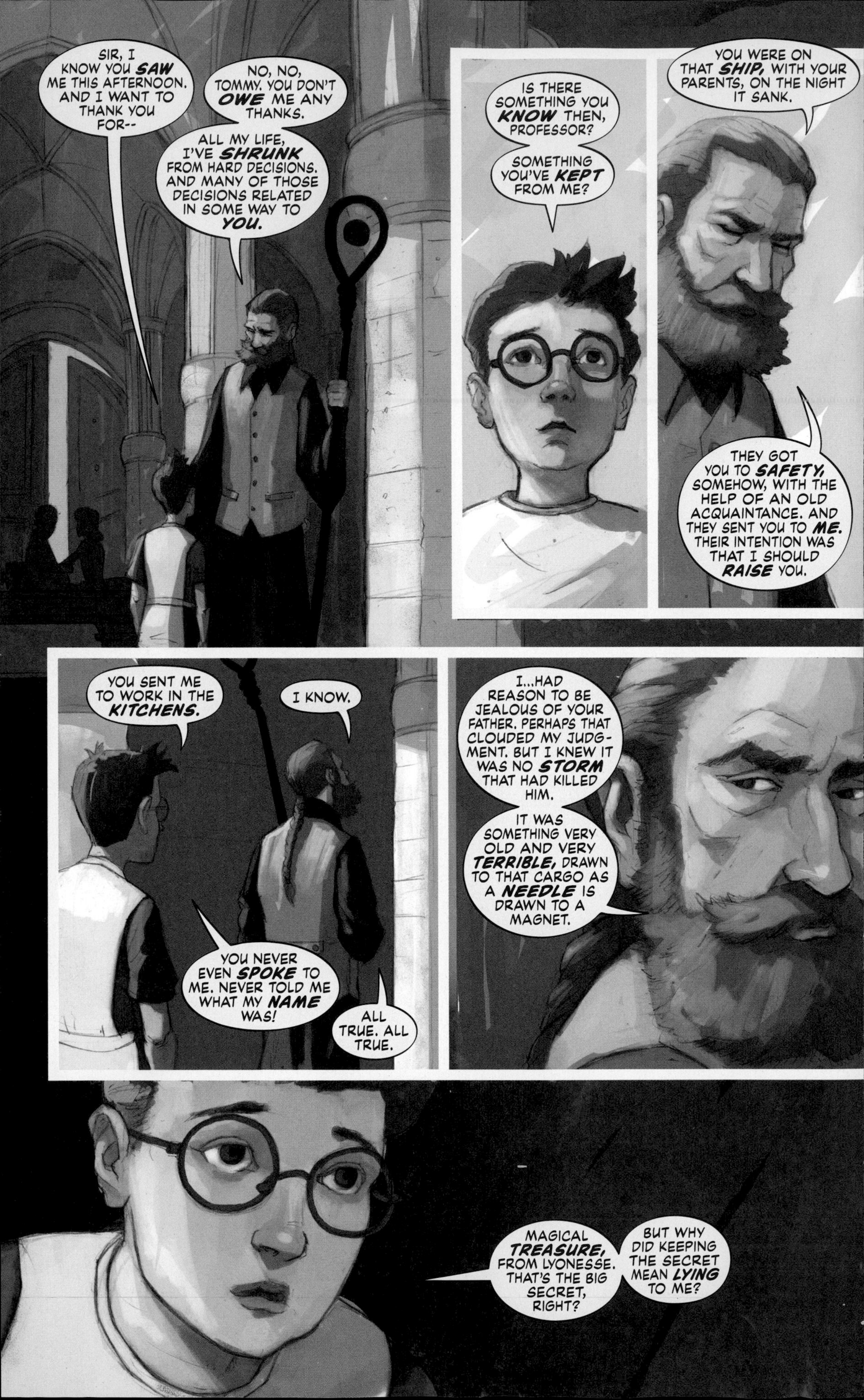
SIR, I KNOW YOU SAW ME THIS AFTERNOON. AND I WANT TO THANK YOU FOR--
NO, NO, TOMMY. YOU DON'T OWE ME ANY THANKS.
ALL MY LIFE, I'VE SHRUNK FROM HARD DECISIONS. AND MANY OF THOSE DECISIONS RELATED IN SOME WAY TO YOU.
IS THERE SOMETHING YOU KNOW THEN, PROFESSOR?
SOMETHING YOU'VE KEPT FROM ME?
YOU WERE ON THAT SHIP, WITH YOUR PARENTS, ON THE NIGHT IT SANK.
THEY GOT YOU TO SAFETY, SOMEHOW, WITH THE HELP OF AN OLD ACQUAINTANCE. AND THEY SENT YOU TO ME. THEIR INTENTION WAS THAT I SHOULD RAISE YOU.
YOU SENT ME TO WORK IN THE KITCHENS.
I KNOW.
YOU NEVER EVEN SPOKE TO ME. NEVER TOLD ME WHAT MY NAME WAS!
ALL TRUE. ALL TRUE.
I...HAD REASON TO BE JEALOUS OF YOUR FATHER. PERHAPS THAT CLOUDED MY JUDGMENT. BUT I KNEW IT WAS NO STORM THAT HAD KILLED HIM.
IT WAS SOMETHING VERY OLD AND VERY TERRIBLE, DRAWN TO THAT CARGO AS A NEEDLE IS DRAWN TO A MAGNET.
MAGICAL TREASURE, FROM LYONESSE. THAT'S THE BIG SECRET, RIGHT?
BUT WHY DID KEEPING THE SECRET MEAN LYING TO ME?

IT'S NOT "MAGICAL TREASURE," TOMMY. IT'S PURE **MAGIC.** THE WILD MAGIC OF LYONESSE.

AND I NEVER LIED TO YOU. I ONLY KEPT YOU IN **IGNORANCE.**

WHY?

BECAUSE I KNEW, BEING YOUR FATHER'S SON AND YOUR MOTHER'S SON, WHAT **METTLE** YOU WERE MADE OF.

SPARK OR NO SPARK, I KNEW YOU'D WANT TO **GO** THERE. TO GET YOUR ANSWERS, AND TO **FACE** WHATEVER KILLED THEM.

SO YOU **DO** KNOW WHAT HAPPENED. TELL ME, PROFESSOR. PLEASE!

I KNOW **NOTHING,** TOMMY. ALL I HAVE IS CONJECTURE. IN THE **MUNDANE** WORLD, OBJECTS CAST SHADOWS.

IN OUR WORLD, **LIGHT** ITSELF CASTS A SHADOW. THE MAGES OF LYONESSE **KNEW** THIS. THAT'S WHY THEY WENT AWAY.

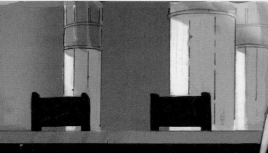

THE DEMETER WAS A **CANDLE** IN THE DARK. SOMETHING SAW THE LIGHT.

SOMETHING I **PRAY** WE NEVER MEET.

I UNDERSTAND. YOU THOUGHT YOU WERE **PROTECTING** ME.

BUT IT WAS **MY** CHOICE TO MAKE, PROFESSOR. AND I WISH YOU'D LET ME **MAKE** IT.

YOU'LL NEED TO MAKE IT **NOW,** MY BOY.

THE CONCLAVE HAS VOTED TO **RAISE** THE DEMETER.

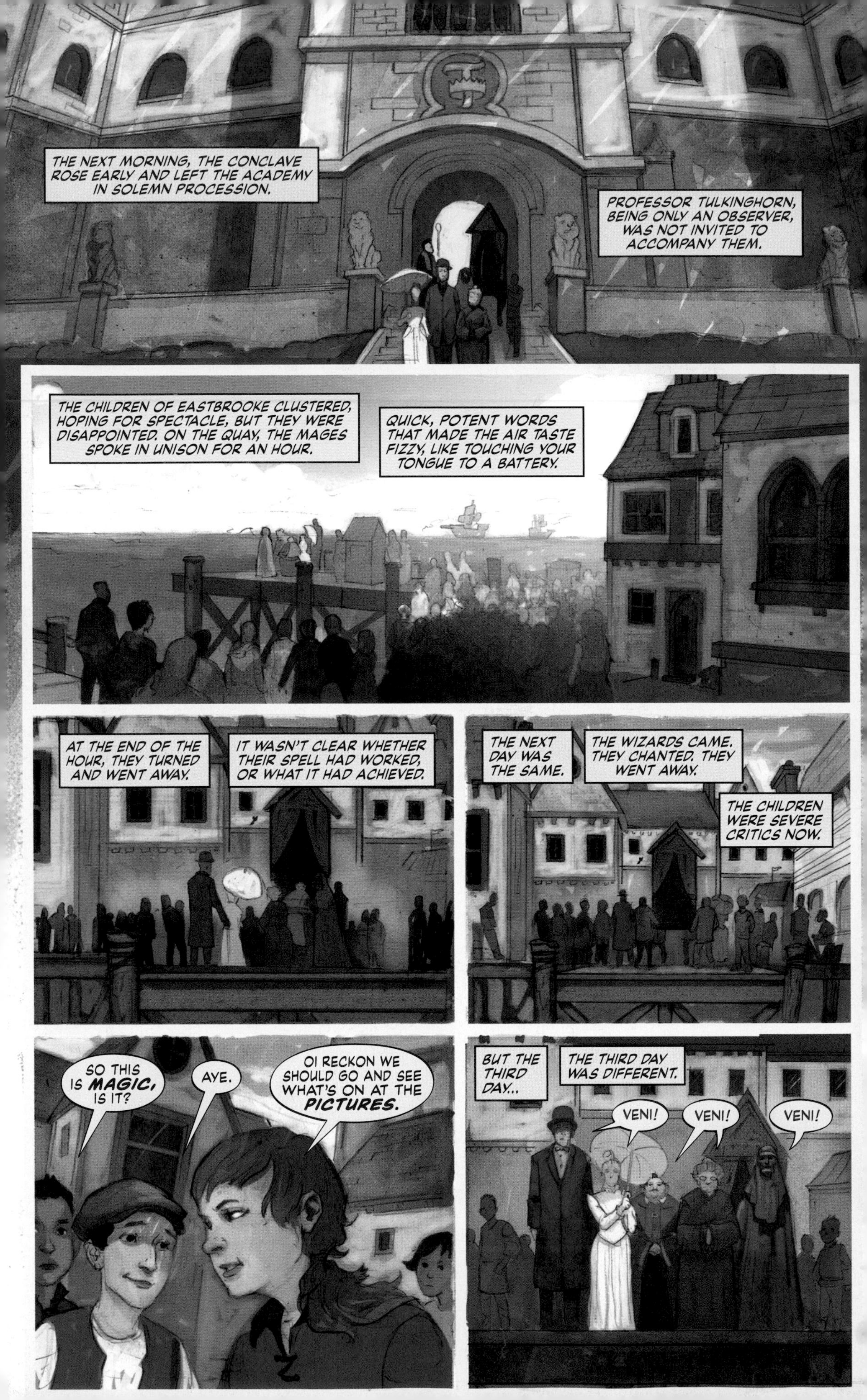
THE NEXT MORNING, THE CONCLAVE ROSE EARLY AND LEFT THE ACADEMY IN SOLEMN PROCESSION.
PROFESSOR TULKINGHORN, BEING ONLY AN OBSERVER, WAS NOT INVITED TO ACCOMPANY THEM.
THE CHILDREN OF EASTBROOKE CLUSTERED, HOPING FOR SPECTACLE, BUT THEY WERE DISAPPOINTED. ON THE QUAY, THE MAGES SPOKE IN UNISON FOR AN HOUR.
QUICK, POTENT WORDS THAT MADE THE AIR TASTE FIZZY, LIKE TOUCHING YOUR TONGUE TO A BATTERY.
AT THE END OF THE HOUR, THEY TURNED AND WENT AWAY.
IT WASN'T CLEAR WHETHER THEIR SPELL HAD WORKED, OR WHAT IT HAD ACHIEVED.
THE NEXT DAY WAS THE SAME.
THE WIZARDS CAME. THEY CHANTED. THEY WENT AWAY.
THE CHILDREN WERE SEVERE CRITICS NOW.
SO THIS IS **MAGIC,** IS IT?
AYE.
OI RECKON WE SHOULD GO AND SEE WHAT'S ON AT THE **PICTURES.**
BUT THE THIRD DAY...
THE THIRD DAY WAS DIFFERENT.
VENI!
VENI!
VENI!

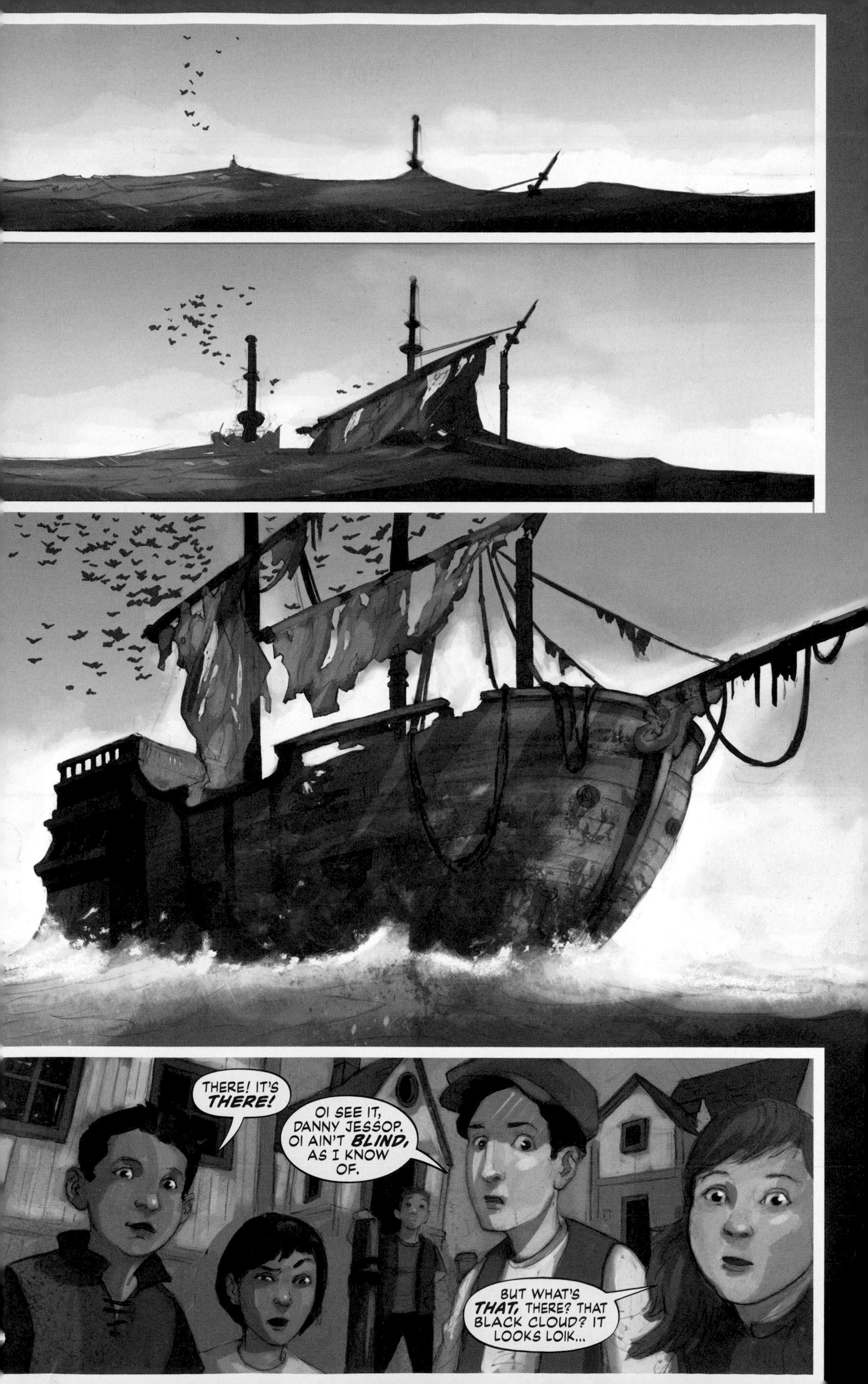
THERE! IT'S *THERE!*
OI SEE IT, DANNY JESSOP. OI AIN'T *BLIND,* AS I KNOW OF.
BUT WHAT'S *THAT,* THERE? THAT BLACK CLOUD? IT LOOKS LOIK...

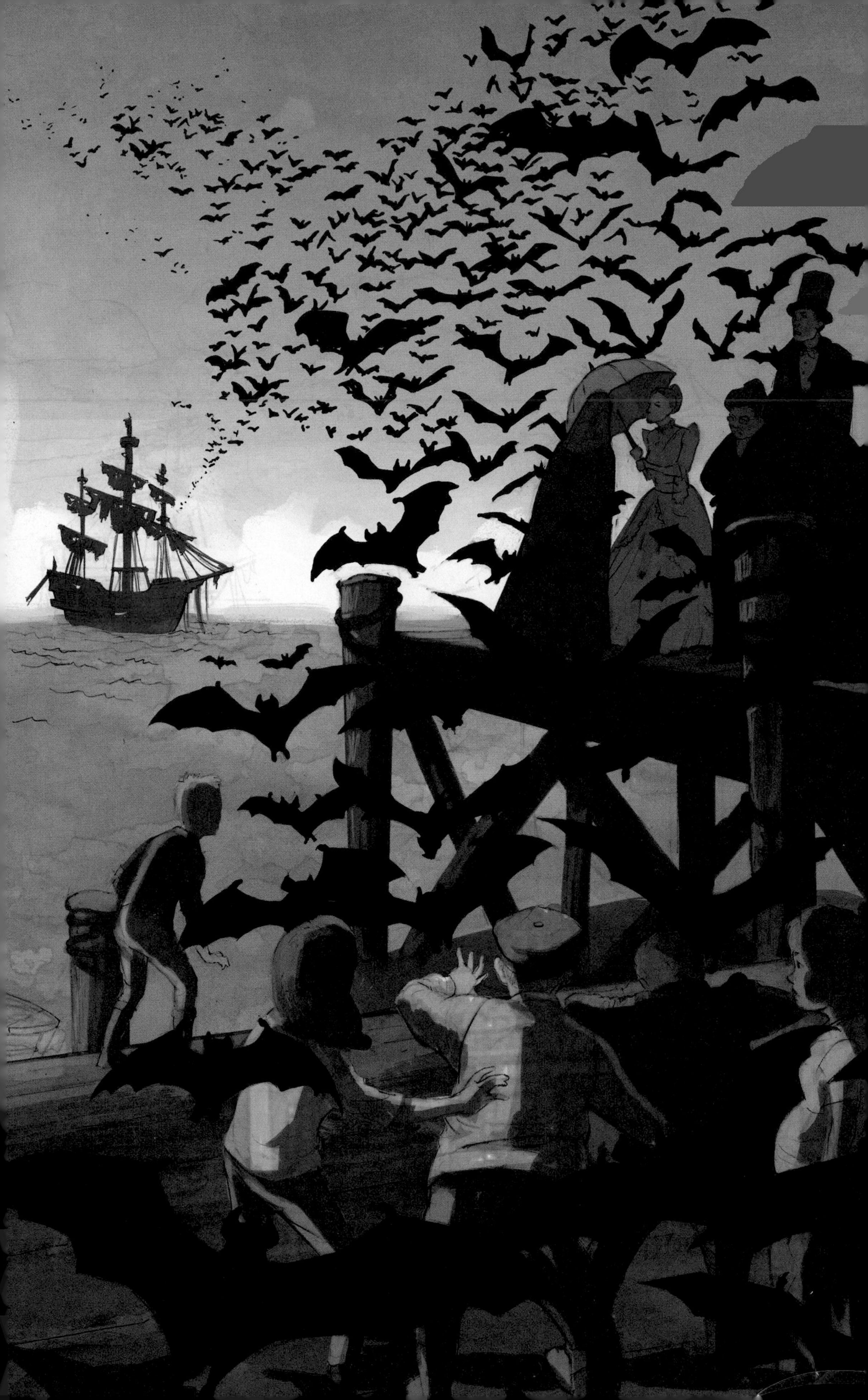

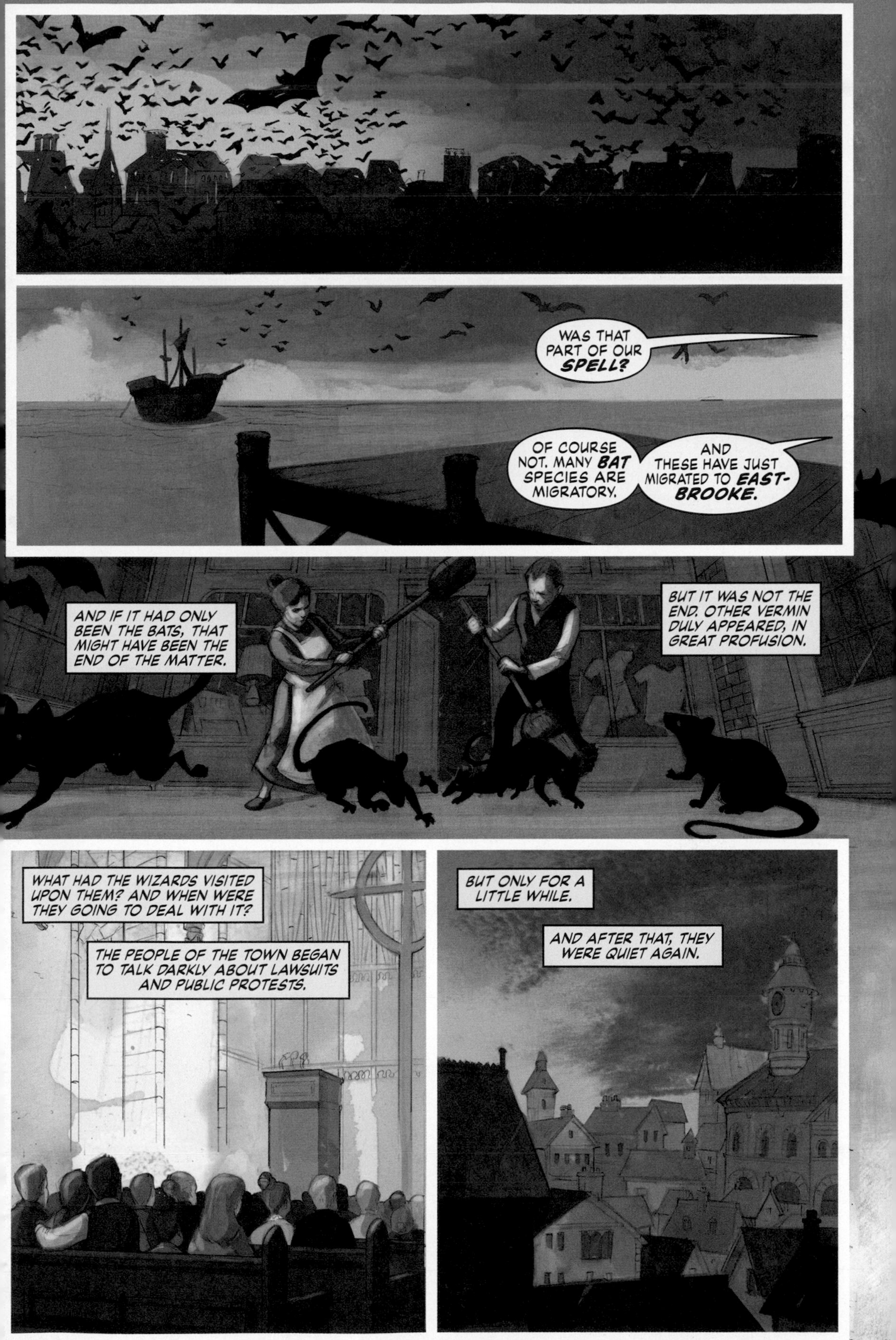
WAS THAT PART OF OUR SPELL?
OF COURSE NOT. MANY BAT SPECIES ARE MIGRATORY.
AND THESE HAVE JUST MIGRATED TO EAST-BROOKE.
AND IF IT HAD ONLY BEEN THE BATS, THAT MIGHT HAVE BEEN THE END OF THE MATTER.
BUT IT WAS NOT THE END. OTHER VERMIN DULY APPEARED, IN GREAT PROFUSION.
WHAT HAD THE WIZARDS VISITED UPON THEM? AND WHEN WERE THEY GOING TO DEAL WITH IT?
THE PEOPLE OF THE TOWN BEGAN TO TALK DARKLY ABOUT LAWSUITS AND PUBLIC PROTESTS.
BUT ONLY FOR A LITTLE WHILE.
AND AFTER THAT, THEY WERE QUIET AGAIN.

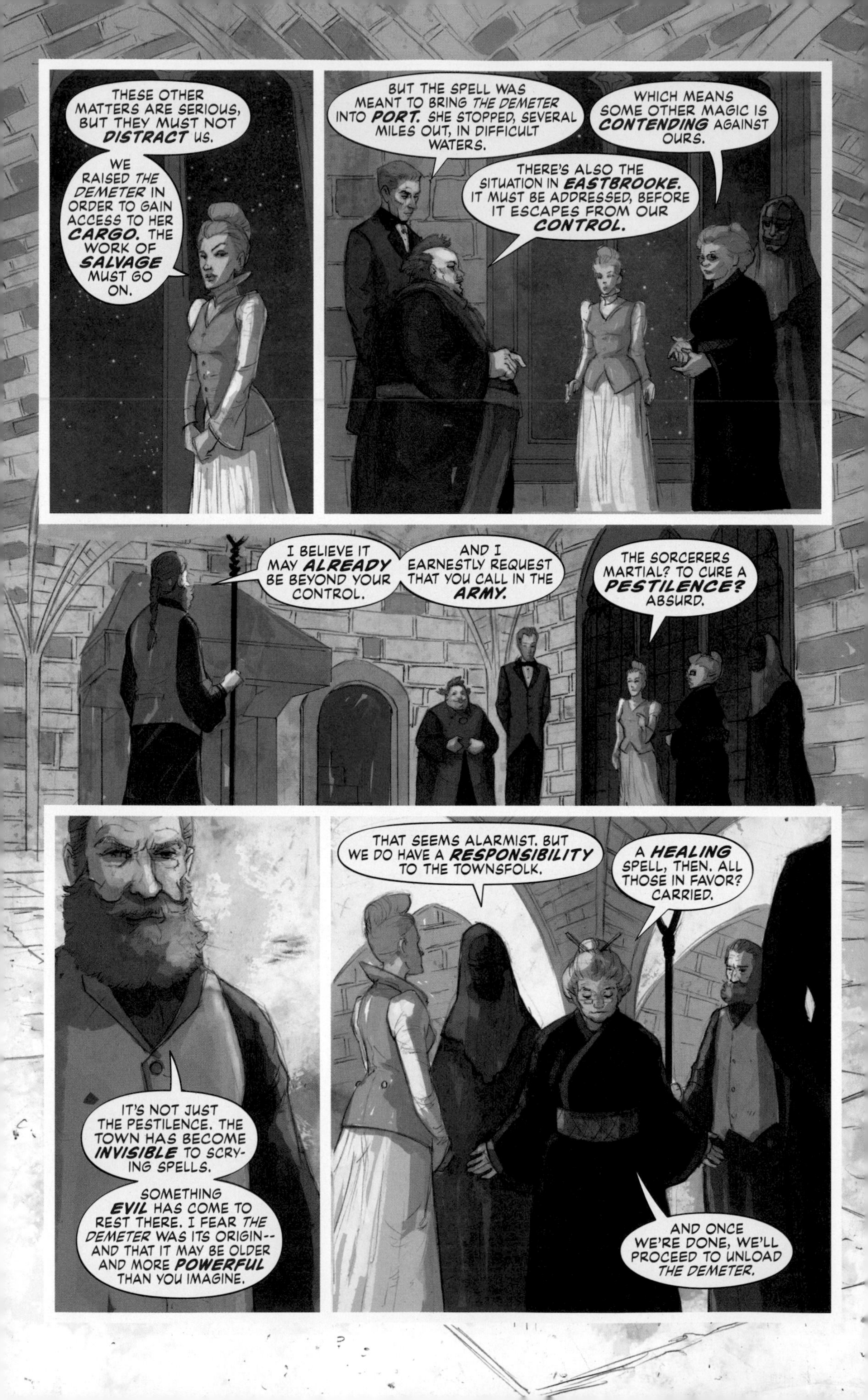

THESE OTHER MATTERS ARE SERIOUS, BUT THEY MUST NOT DISTRACT US.
WE RAISED THE DEMETER IN ORDER TO GAIN ACCESS TO HER CARGO. THE WORK OF SALVAGE MUST GO ON.
BUT THE SPELL WAS MEANT TO BRING THE DEMETER INTO PORT. SHE STOPPED, SEVERAL MILES OUT, IN DIFFICULT WATERS.
WHICH MEANS SOME OTHER MAGIC IS CONTENDING AGAINST OURS.
THERE'S ALSO THE SITUATION IN EASTBROOKE. IT MUST BE ADDRESSED, BEFORE IT ESCAPES FROM OUR CONTROL.
I BELIEVE IT MAY ALREADY BE BEYOND YOUR CONTROL.
AND I EARNESTLY REQUEST THAT YOU CALL IN THE ARMY.
THE SORCERERS MARTIAL? TO CURE A PESTILENCE? ABSURD.
IT'S NOT JUST THE PESTILENCE. THE TOWN HAS BECOME INVISIBLE TO SCRYING SPELLS.
SOMETHING EVIL HAS COME TO REST THERE. I FEAR THE DEMETER WAS ITS ORIGIN-- AND THAT IT MAY BE OLDER AND MORE POWERFUL THAN YOU IMAGINE.
THAT SEEMS ALARMIST. BUT WE DO HAVE A RESPONSIBILITY TO THE TOWNSFOLK.
A HEALING SPELL, THEN. ALL THOSE IN FAVOR? CARRIED.
AND ONCE WE'RE DONE, WE'LL PROCEED TO UNLOAD THE DEMETER.

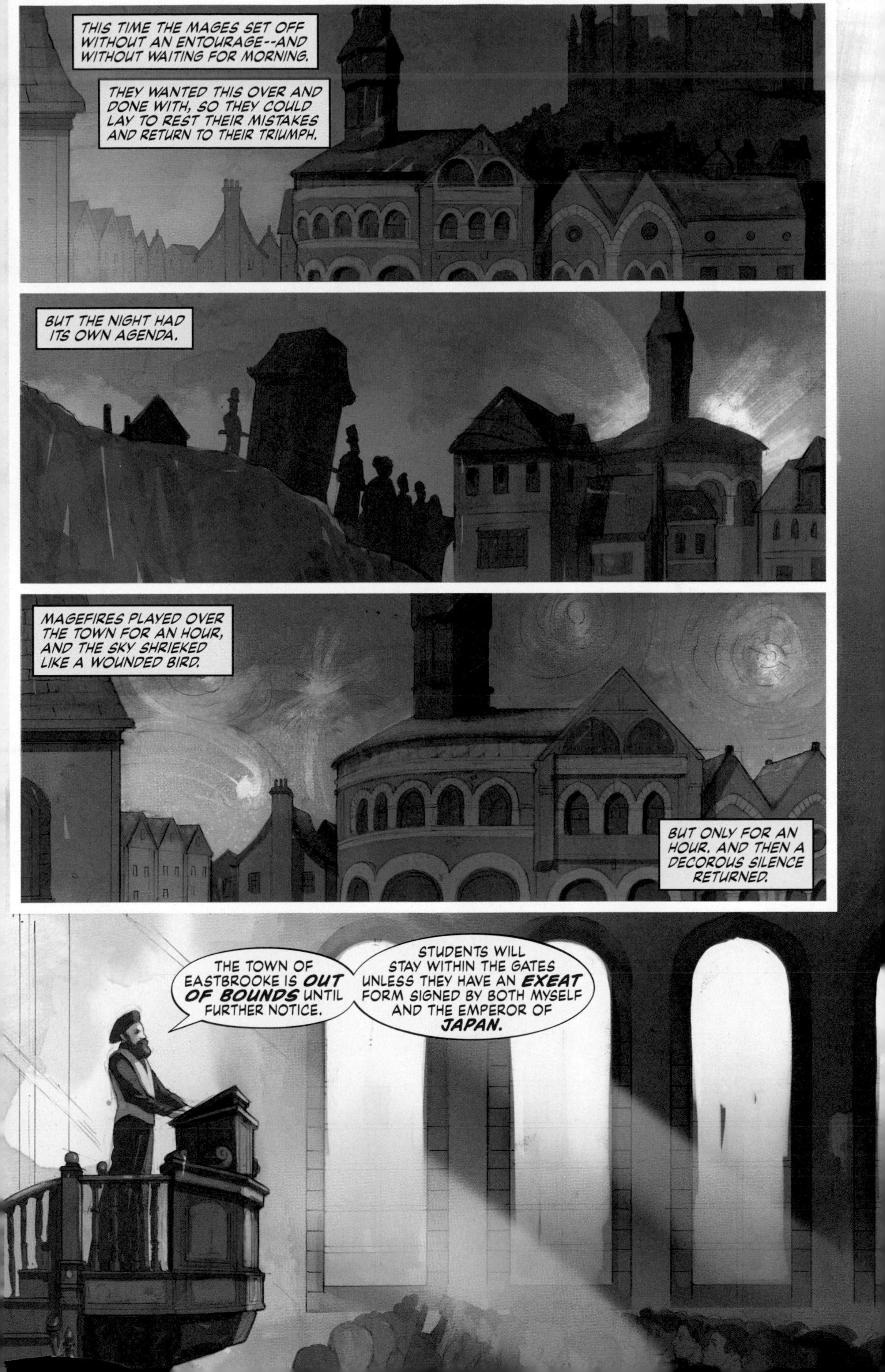
THIS TIME THE MAGES SET OFF WITHOUT AN ENTOURAGE--AND WITHOUT WAITING FOR MORNING.
THEY WANTED THIS OVER AND DONE WITH, SO THEY COULD LAY TO REST THEIR MISTAKES AND RETURN TO THEIR TRIUMPH.
BUT THE NIGHT HAD ITS OWN AGENDA.
MAGEFIRES PLAYED OVER THE TOWN FOR AN HOUR, AND THE SKY SHRIEKED LIKE A WOUNDED BIRD.
BUT ONLY FOR AN HOUR. AND THEN A DECOROUS SILENCE RETURNED.
THE TOWN OF EASTBROOKE IS **OUT OF BOUNDS** UNTIL FURTHER NOTICE.
STUDENTS WILL STAY WITHIN THE GATES UNLESS THEY HAVE AN **EXEAT** FORM SIGNED BY BOTH MYSELF AND THE EMPEROR OF **JAPAN**.

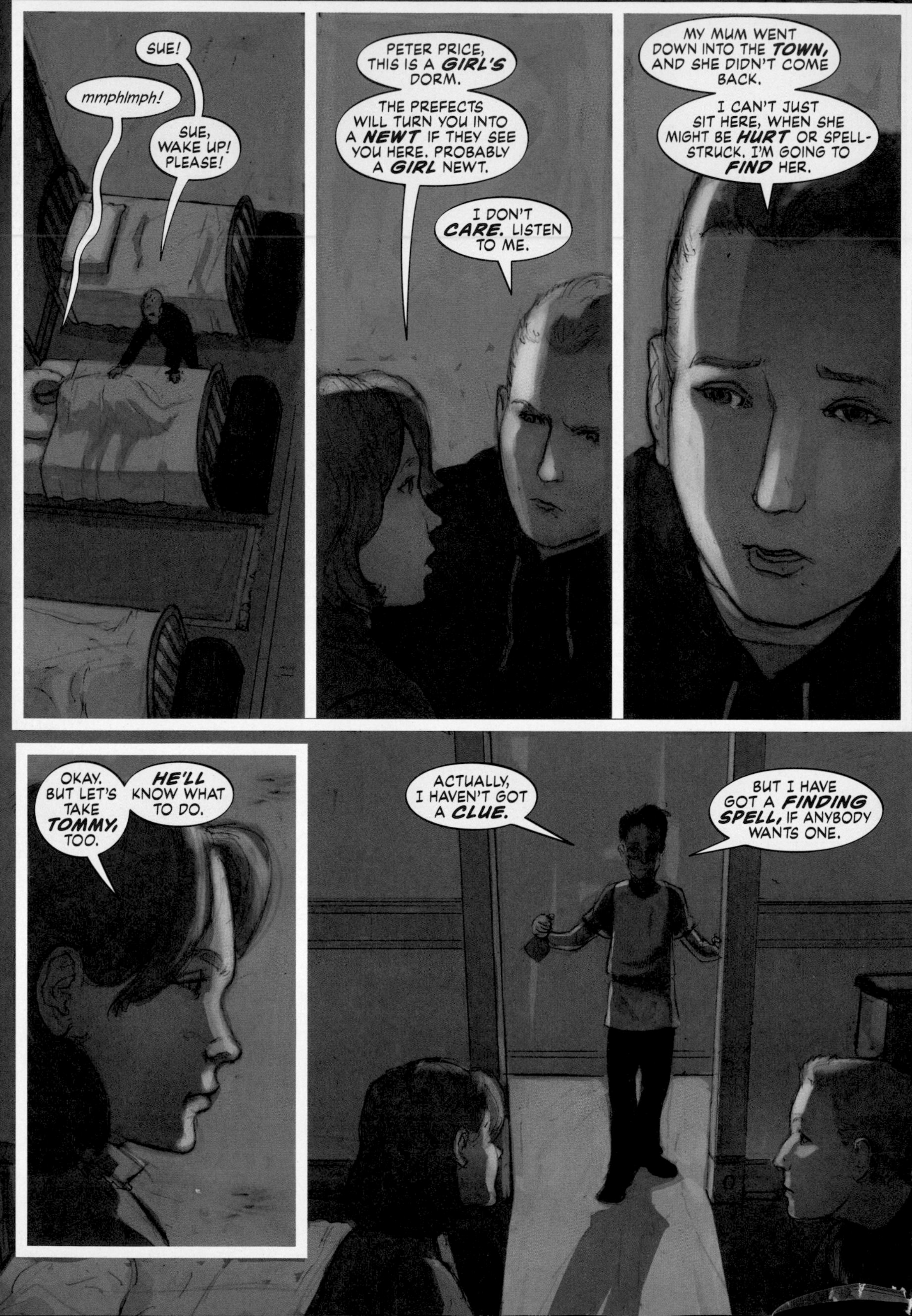
SUE!
mmphlmph!
SUE, WAKE UP! PLEASE!
PETER PRICE, THIS IS A GIRL'S DORM.
THE PREFECTS WILL TURN YOU INTO A NEWT IF THEY SEE YOU HERE. PROBABLY A GIRL NEWT.
I DON'T CARE. LISTEN TO ME.
MY MUM WENT DOWN INTO THE TOWN, AND SHE DIDN'T COME BACK.
I CAN'T JUST SIT HERE, WHEN SHE MIGHT BE HURT OR SPELL-STRUCK. I'M GOING TO FIND HER.
OKAY. BUT LET'S TAKE TOMMY, TOO.
HE'LL KNOW WHAT TO DO.
ACTUALLY, I HAVEN'T GOT A CLUE.
BUT I HAVE GOT A FINDING SPELL, IF ANYBODY WANTS ONE.

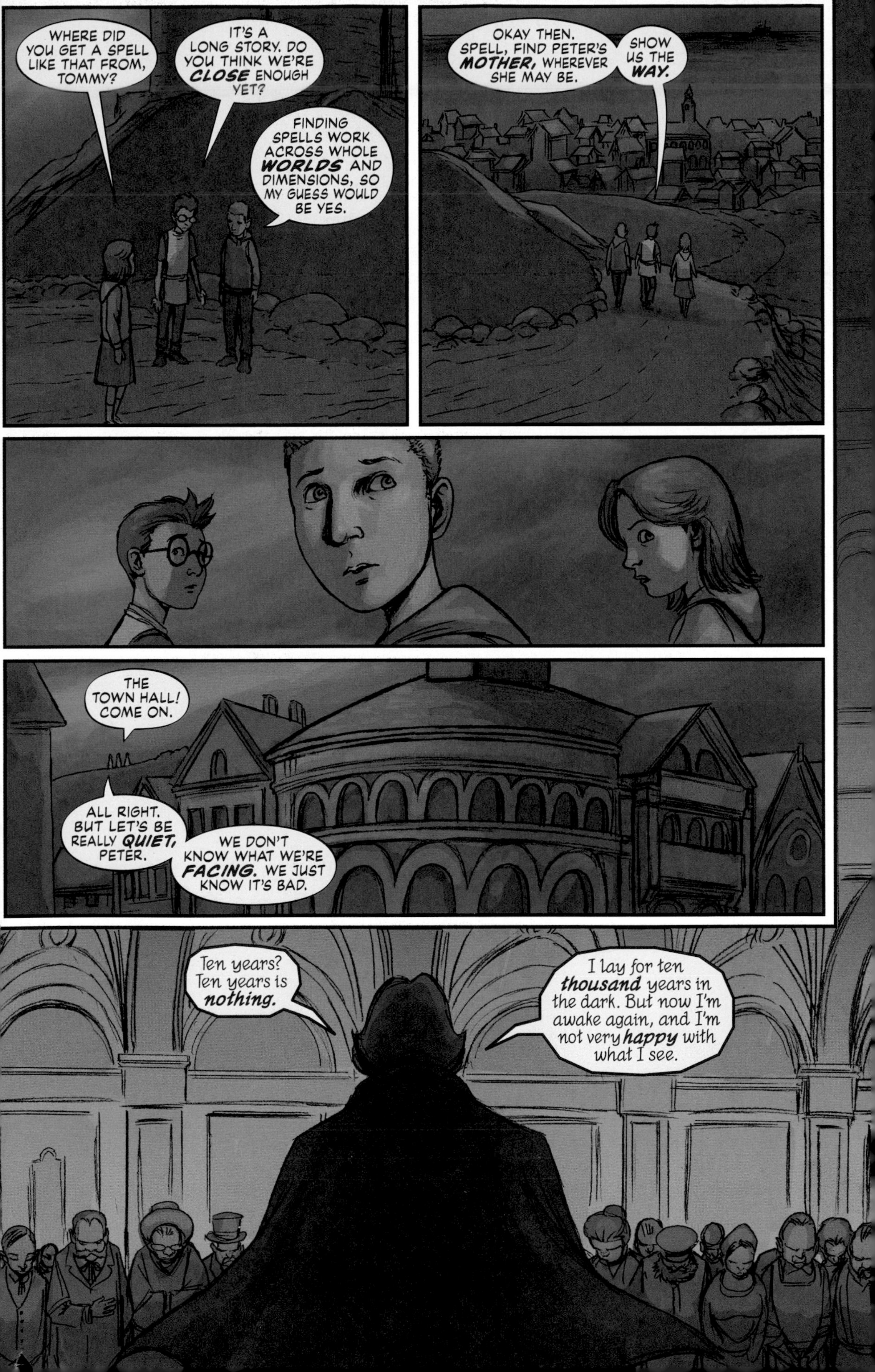
WHERE DID YOU GET A SPELL LIKE THAT FROM, TOMMY?
IT'S A LONG STORY. DO YOU THINK WE'RE CLOSE ENOUGH YET?
FINDING SPELLS WORK ACROSS WHOLE WORLDS AND DIMENSIONS, SO MY GUESS WOULD BE YES.
OKAY THEN. SPELL, FIND PETER'S MOTHER, WHEREVER SHE MAY BE.
SHOW US THE WAY.
THE TOWN HALL! COME ON.
ALL RIGHT. BUT LET'S BE REALLY QUIET, PETER.
WE DON'T KNOW WHAT WE'RE FACING. WE JUST KNOW IT'S BAD.
Ten years? Ten years is nothing.
I lay for ten thousand years in the dark. But now I'm awake again, and I'm not very happy with what I see.

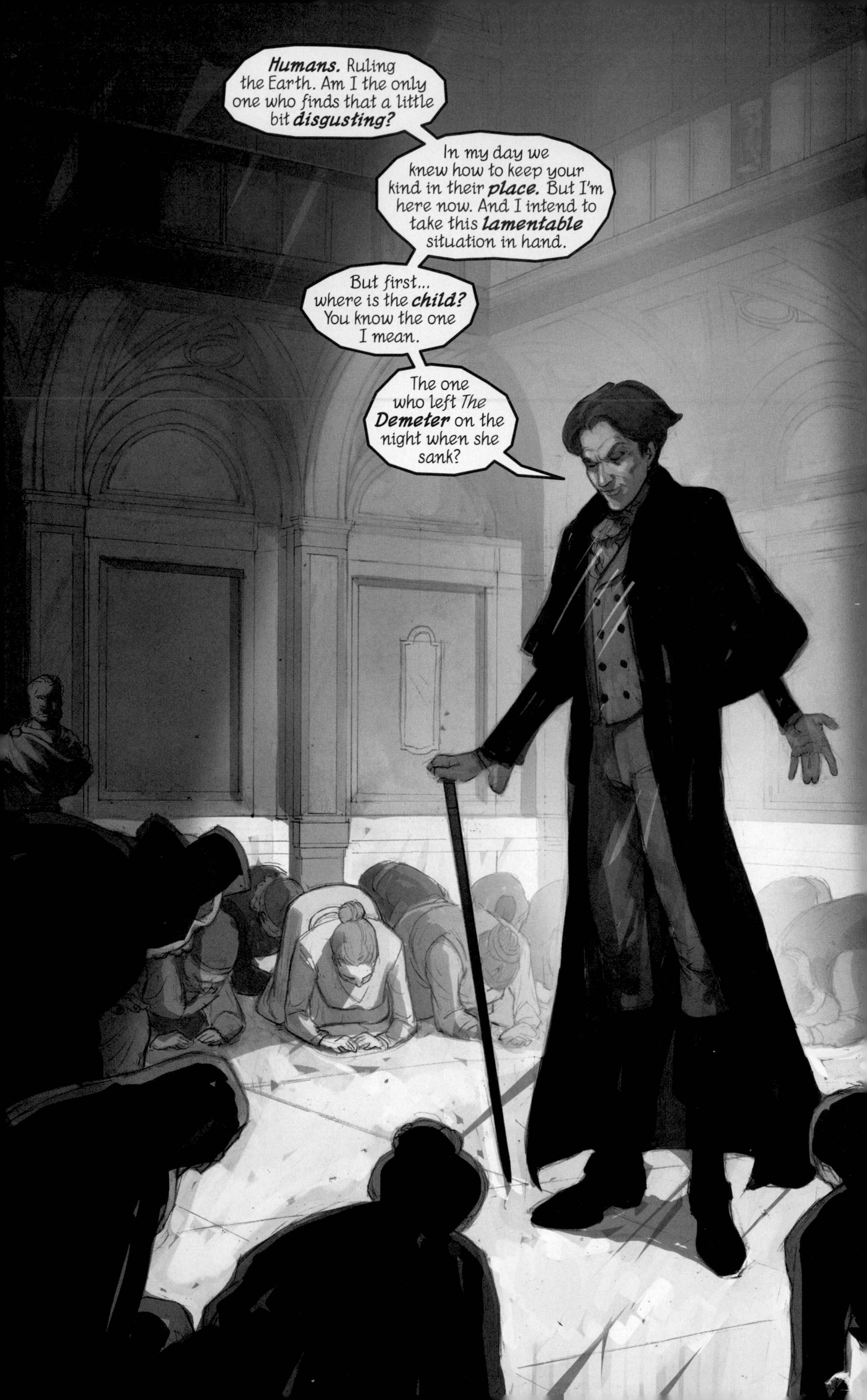
Humans. Ruling the Earth. Am I the only one who finds that a little bit **disgusting?**
In my day we knew how to keep your kind in their **place.** But I'm here now. And I intend to take this **lamentable** situation in hand.
But first... where is the **child?** You know the one I mean.
The one who left *The* **Demeter** on the night when she sank?

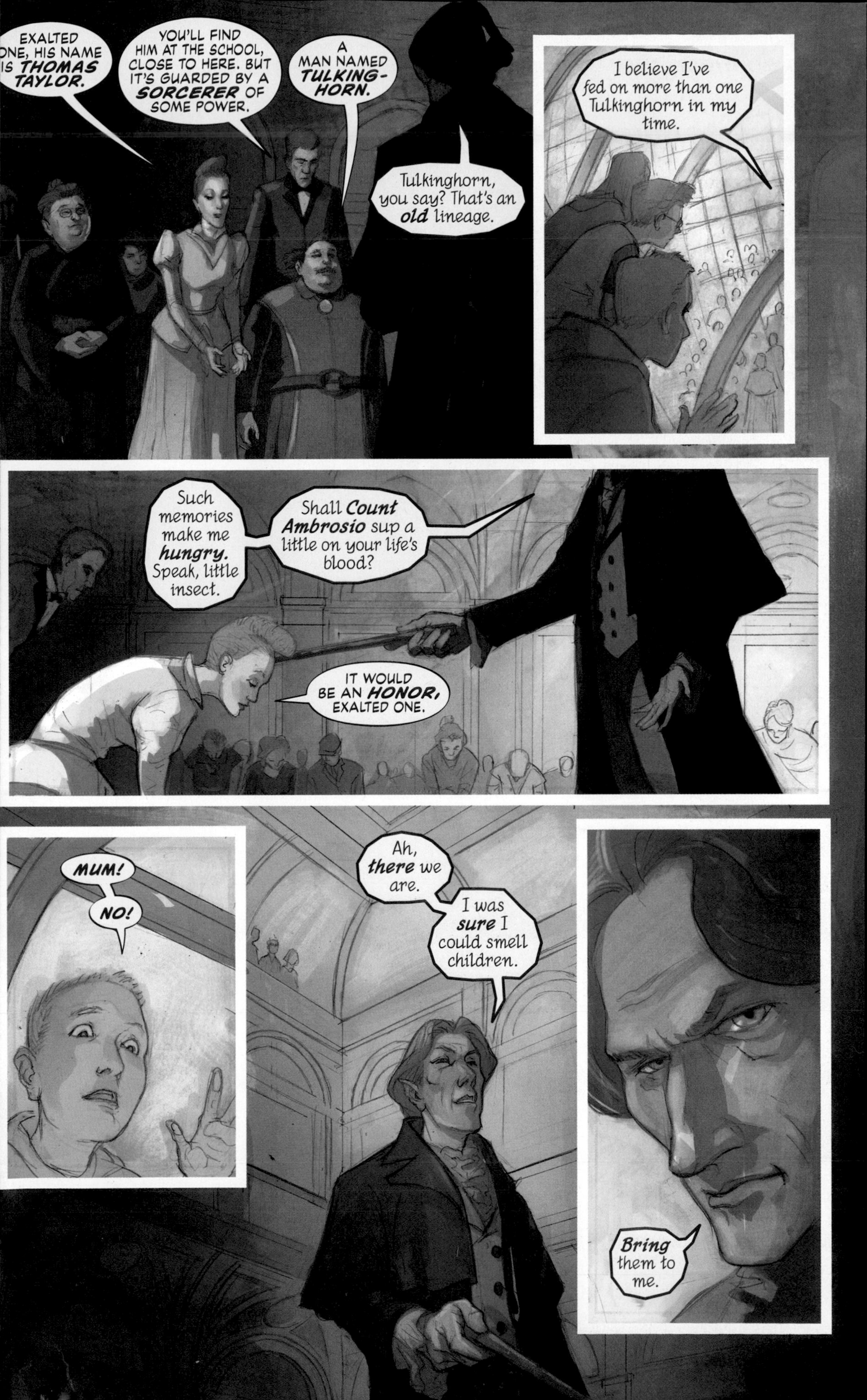
EXALTED ONE, HIS NAME IS THOMAS TAYLOR.
YOU'LL FIND HIM AT THE SCHOOL, CLOSE TO HERE. BUT IT'S GUARDED BY A SORCERER OF SOME POWER.
A MAN NAMED TULKING-HORN.
Tulkinghorn, you say? That's an old lineage.
I believe I've fed on more than one Tulkinghorn in my time.
Such memories make me hungry. Speak, little insect.
Shall Count Ambrosio sup a little on your life's blood?
IT WOULD BE AN HONOR, EXALTED ONE.
MUM!
NO!
Ah, there we are.
I was sure I could smell children.
Bring them to me.

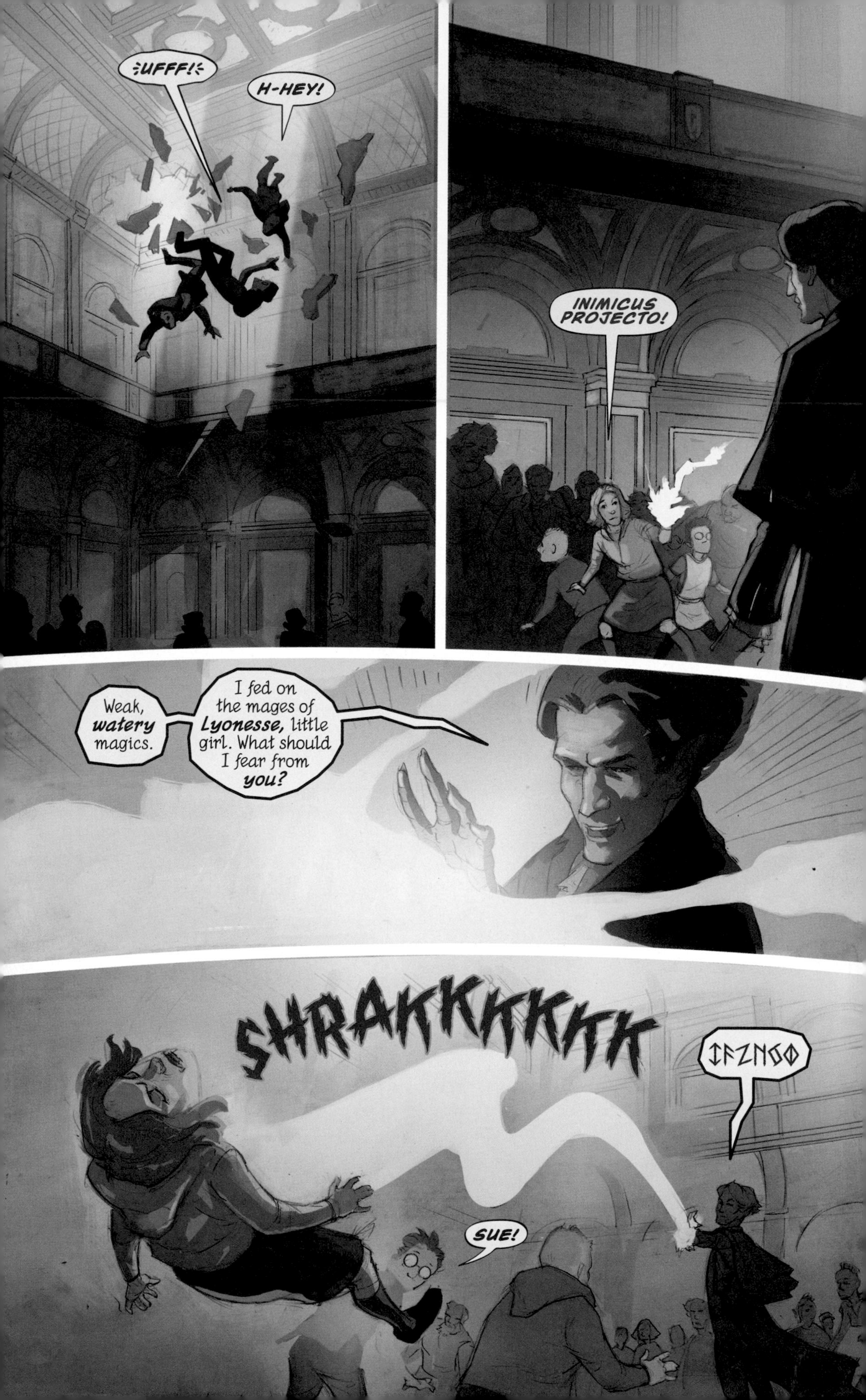
UFFF!
H-HEY!
INIMICUS PROJECTO!
Weak, watery magics.
I fed on the mages of Lyonesse, little girl. What should I fear from you?
SHRAKKKKKK
SUE!

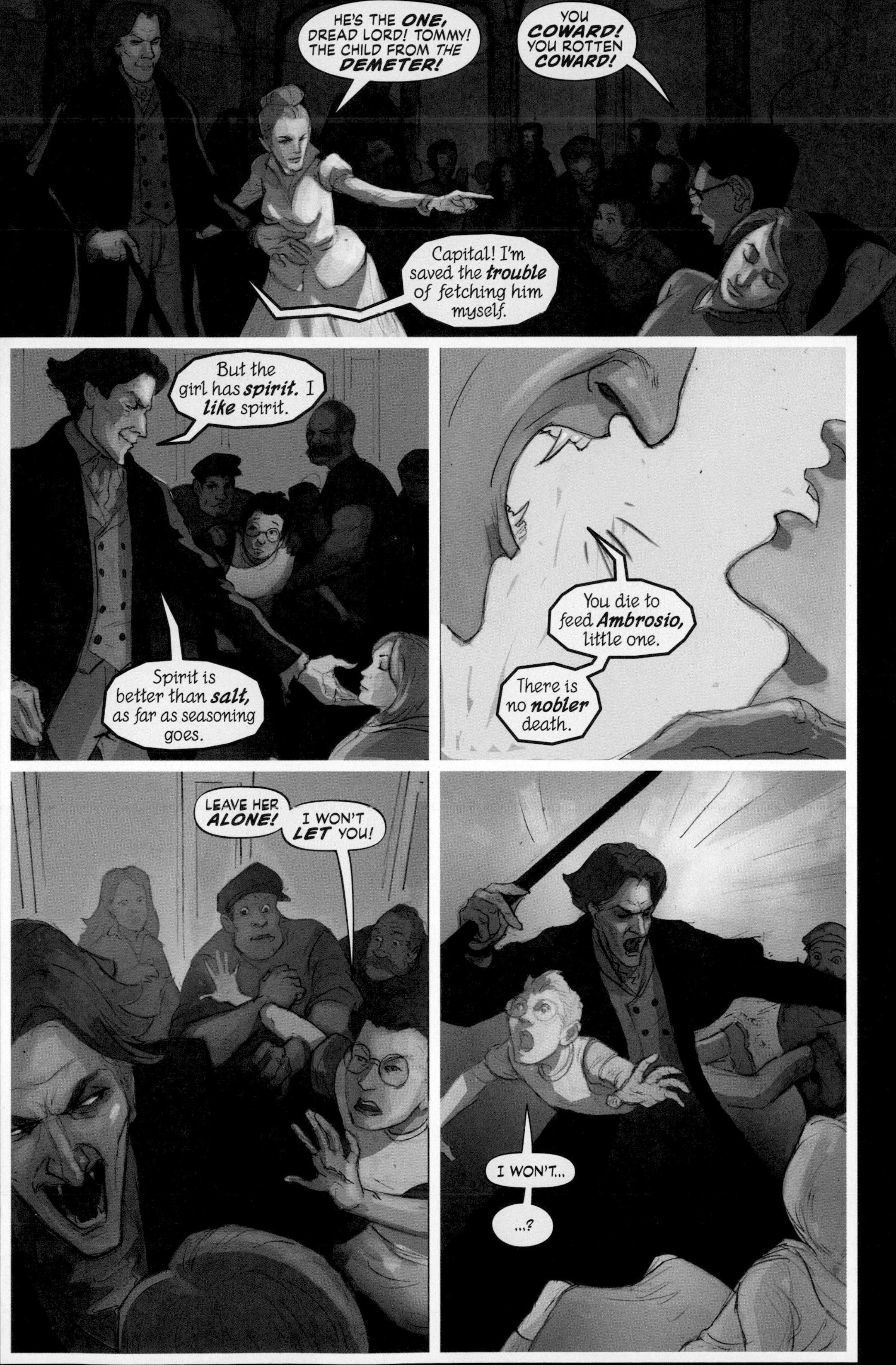
HE'S THE ONE, DREAD LORD! TOMMY! THE CHILD FROM THE DEMETER!
YOU COWARD! YOU ROTTEN COWARD!
Capital! I'm saved the trouble of fetching him myself.
But the girl has spirit. I like spirit.
Spirit is better than salt, as far as seasoning goes.
You die to feed Ambrosio, little one.
There is no nobler death.
LEAVE HER ALONE!
I WON'T LET YOU!
I WON'T...
...?

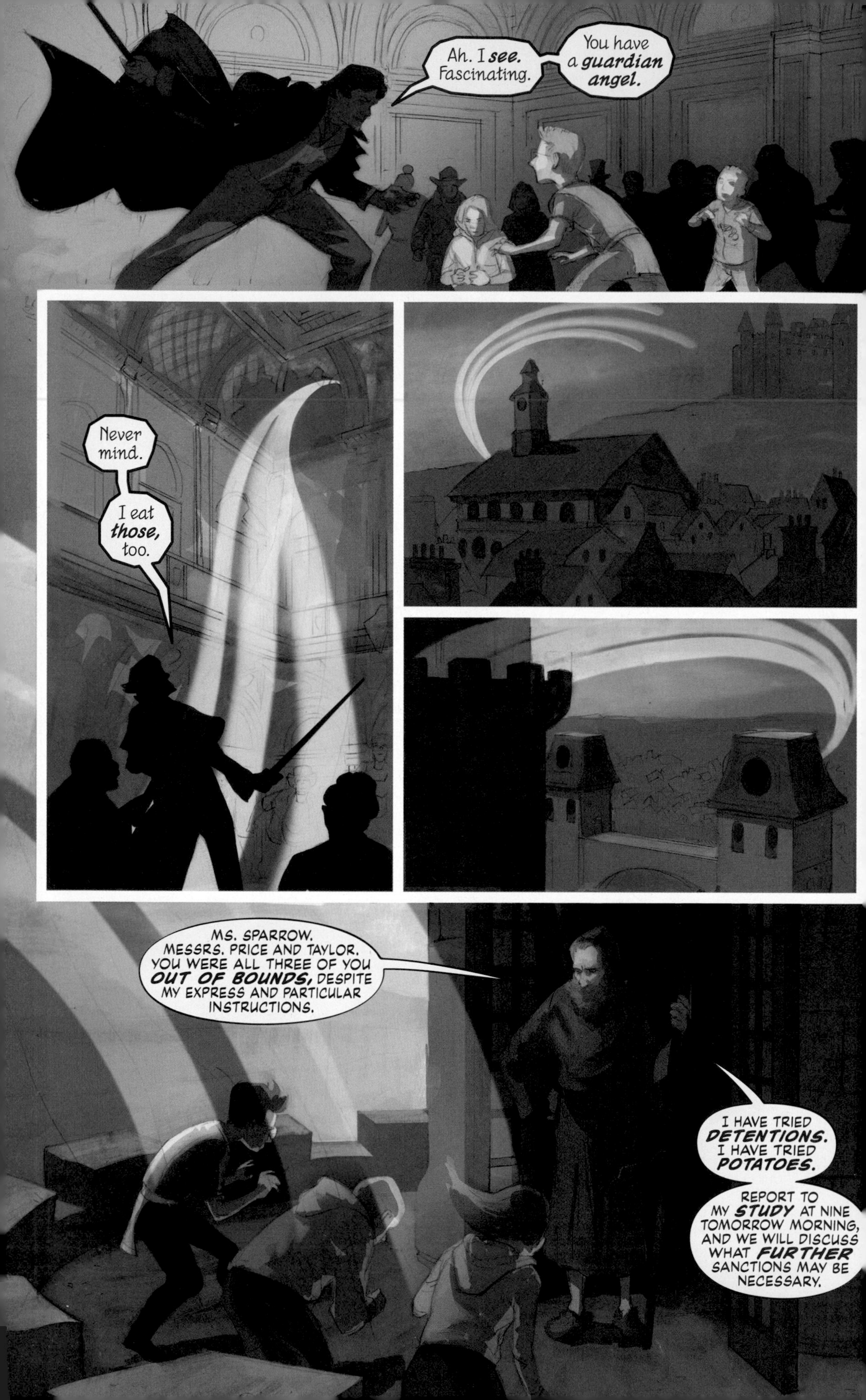
Ah. I see. Fascinating.
You have a guardian angel.
Never mind.
I eat those, too.
MS. SPARROW. MESSRS. PRICE AND TAYLOR. YOU WERE ALL THREE OF YOU OUT OF BOUNDS, DESPITE MY EXPRESS AND PARTICULAR INSTRUCTIONS.
I HAVE TRIED DETENTIONS. I HAVE TRIED POTATOES.
REPORT TO MY STUDY AT NINE TOMORROW MORNING, AND WE WILL DISCUSS WHAT FURTHER SANCTIONS MAY BE NECESSARY.

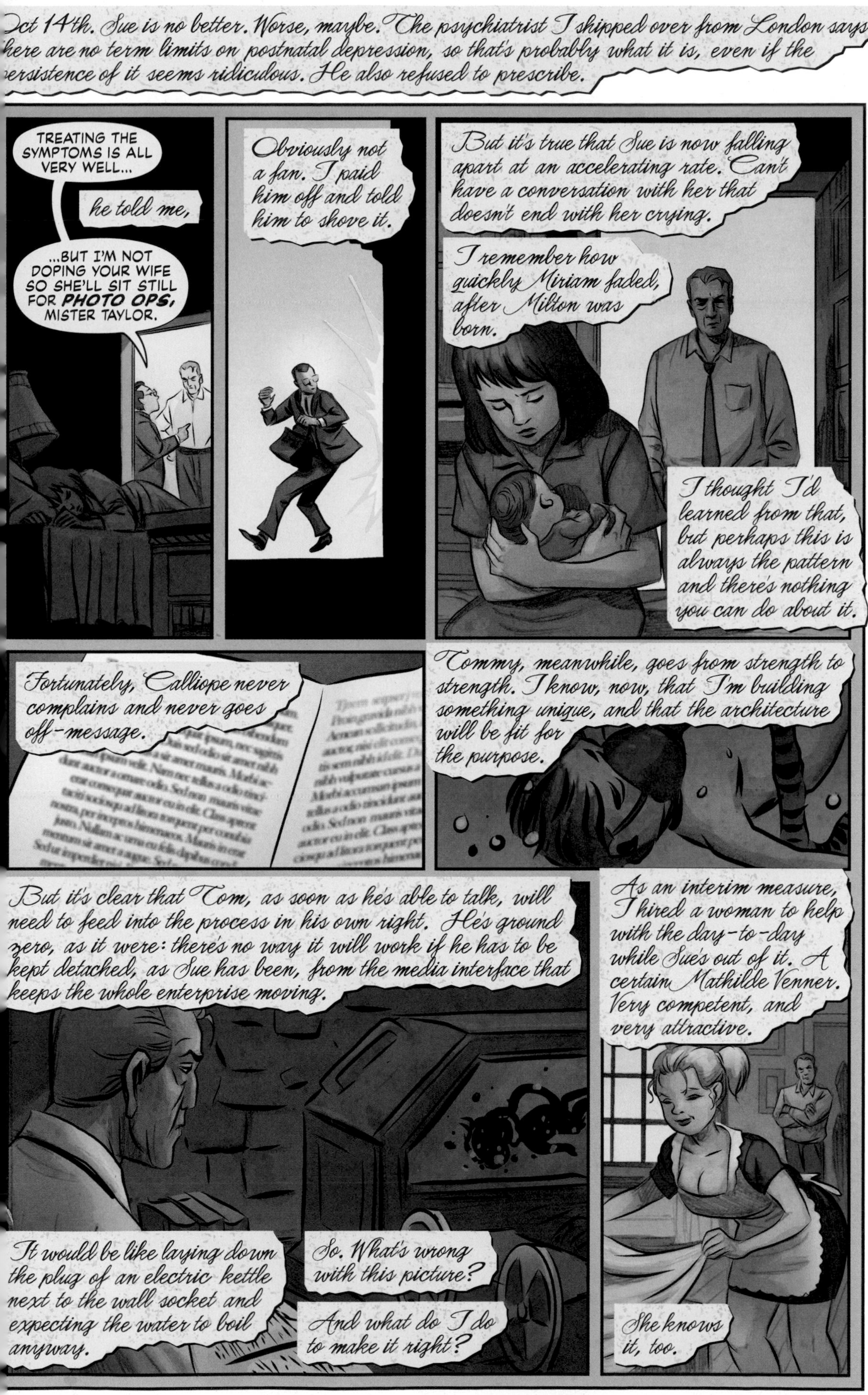
Oct 14th. Sue is no better. Worse, maybe. The psychiatrist I shipped over from London says here are no term limits on postnatal depression, so that's probably what it is, even if the ersistence of it seems ridiculous. He also refused to prescribe.
TREATING THE SYMPTOMS IS ALL VERY WELL...
he told me,
...BUT I'M NOT DOPING YOUR WIFE SO SHE'LL SIT STILL FOR PHOTO OPS, MISTER TAYLOR.
Obviously not a fan. I paid him off and told him to shove it.
But it's true that Sue is now falling apart at an accelerating rate. Can't have a conversation with her that doesn't end with her crying.
I remember how quickly Miriam faded, after Milton was born.
I thought I'd learned from that, but perhaps this is always the pattern and there's nothing you can do about it.
Fortunately, Calliope never complains and never goes off-message.
Tommy, meanwhile, goes from strength to strength. I know, now, that I'm building something unique, and that the architecture will be fit for the purpose.
But it's clear that Tom, as soon as he's able to talk, will need to feed into the process in his own right. He's ground zero, as it were: there's no way it will work if he has to be kept detached, as Sue has been, from the media interface that keeps the whole enterprise moving.
It would be like laying down the plug of an electric kettle next to the wall socket and expecting the water to boil anyway.
So. What's wrong with this picture?
And what do I do to make it right?
As an interim measure, I hired a woman to help with the day-to-day while Sue's out of it. A certain Mathilde Venner. Very competent, and very attractive.
She knows it, too.

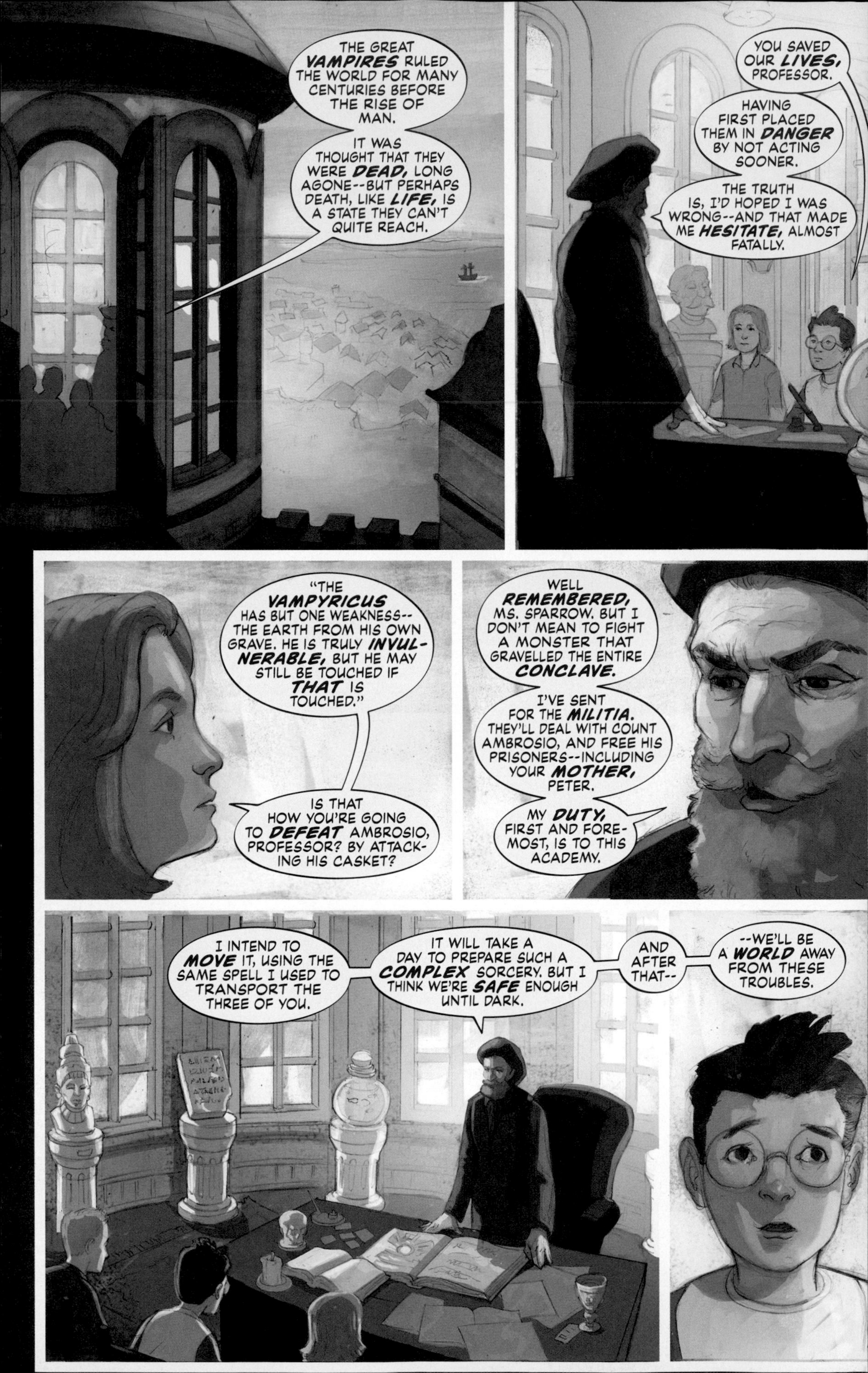
THE GREAT VAMPIRES RULED THE WORLD FOR MANY CENTURIES BEFORE THE RISE OF MAN.
IT WAS THOUGHT THAT THEY WERE DEAD, LONG AGONE--BUT PERHAPS DEATH, LIKE LIFE, IS A STATE THEY CAN'T QUITE REACH.
YOU SAVED OUR LIVES, PROFESSOR.
HAVING FIRST PLACED THEM IN DANGER BY NOT ACTING SOONER.
THE TRUTH IS, I'D HOPED I WAS WRONG--AND THAT MADE ME HESITATE, ALMOST FATALLY.
"THE VAMPYRICUS HAS BUT ONE WEAKNESS--THE EARTH FROM HIS OWN GRAVE. HE IS TRULY INVULNERABLE, BUT HE MAY STILL BE TOUCHED IF THAT IS TOUCHED."
IS THAT HOW YOU'RE GOING TO DEFEAT AMBROSIO, PROFESSOR? BY ATTACKING HIS CASKET?
WELL REMEMBERED, MS. SPARROW. BUT I DON'T MEAN TO FIGHT A MONSTER THAT GRAVELLED THE ENTIRE CONCLAVE.
I'VE SENT FOR THE MILITIA. THEY'LL DEAL WITH COUNT AMBROSIO, AND FREE HIS PRISONERS--INCLUDING YOUR MOTHER, PETER.
MY DUTY, FIRST AND FOREMOST, IS TO THIS ACADEMY.
I INTEND TO MOVE IT, USING THE SAME SPELL I USED TO TRANSPORT THE THREE OF YOU.
IT WILL TAKE A DAY TO PREPARE SUCH A COMPLEX SORCERY. BUT I THINK WE'RE SAFE ENOUGH UNTIL DARK.
AND AFTER THAT--
--WE'LL BE A WORLD AWAY FROM THESE TROUBLES.

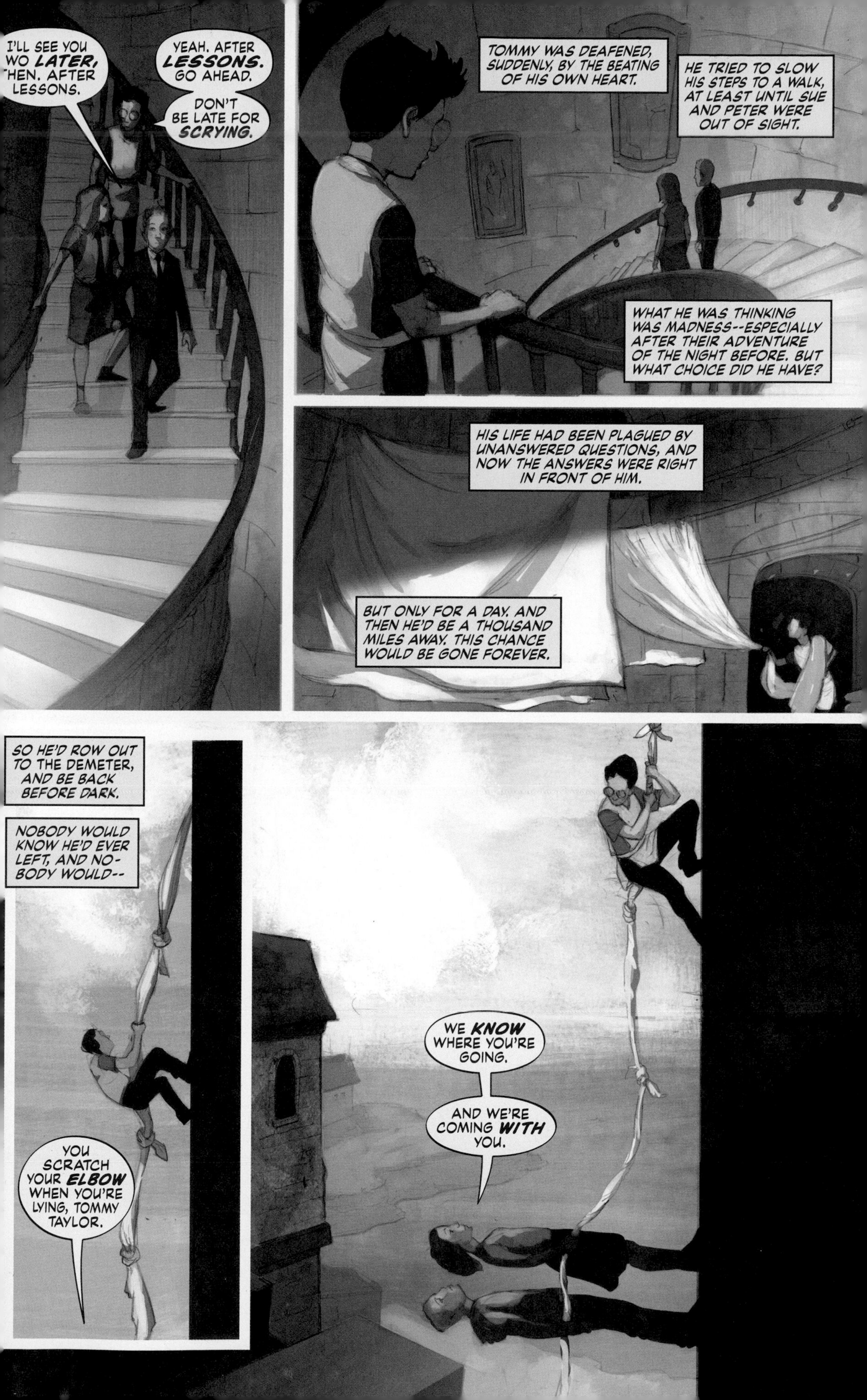
I'LL SEE YOU
WO LATER,
HEN. AFTER
LESSONS.
YEAH. AFTER LESSONS. GO AHEAD.
DON'T BE LATE FOR SCRYING.
TOMMY WAS DEAFENED, SUDDENLY, BY THE BEATING OF HIS OWN HEART.
HE TRIED TO SLOW HIS STEPS TO A WALK, AT LEAST UNTIL SUE AND PETER WERE OUT OF SIGHT.
WHAT HE WAS THINKING WAS MADNESS--ESPECIALLY AFTER THEIR ADVENTURE OF THE NIGHT BEFORE. BUT WHAT CHOICE DID HE HAVE?
HIS LIFE HAD BEEN PLAGUED BY UNANSWERED QUESTIONS, AND NOW THE ANSWERS WERE RIGHT IN FRONT OF HIM.
BUT ONLY FOR A DAY. AND THEN HE'D BE A THOUSAND MILES AWAY. THIS CHANCE WOULD BE GONE FOREVER.
SO HE'D ROW OUT TO THE DEMETER, AND BE BACK BEFORE DARK.
NOBODY WOULD KNOW HE'D EVER LEFT, AND NOBODY WOULD--
YOU SCRATCH YOUR ELBOW WHEN YOU'RE LYING, TOMMY TAYLOR.
WE KNOW WHERE YOU'RE GOING.
AND WE'RE COMING WITH YOU.

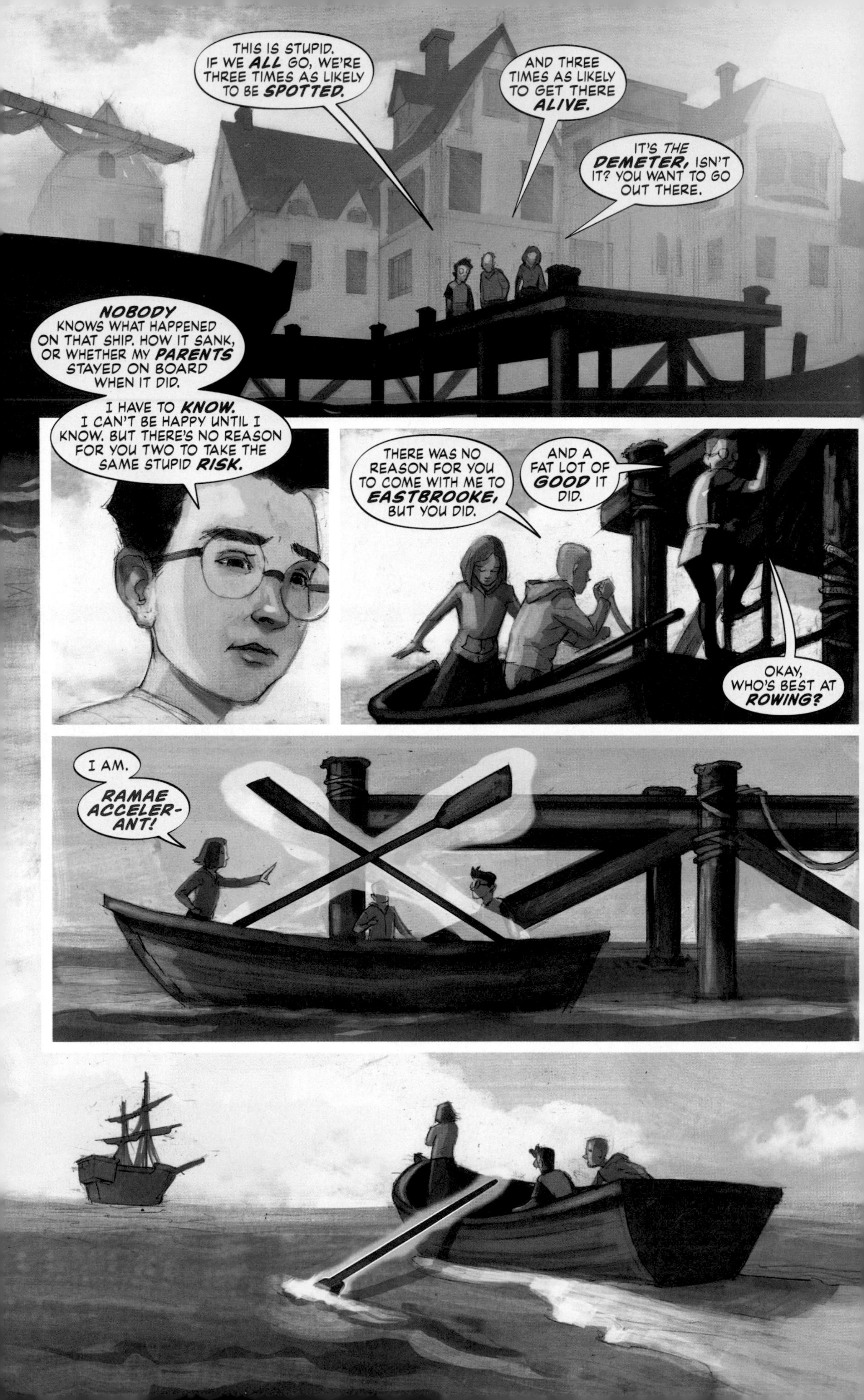
THIS IS STUPID. IF WE ALL GO, WE'RE THREE TIMES AS LIKELY TO BE SPOTTED.
AND THREE TIMES AS LIKELY TO GET THERE ALIVE.
IT'S THE DEMETER, ISN'T IT? YOU WANT TO GO OUT THERE.
NOBODY KNOWS WHAT HAPPENED ON THAT SHIP. HOW IT SANK, OR WHETHER MY PARENTS STAYED ON BOARD WHEN IT DID.
I HAVE TO KNOW. I CAN'T BE HAPPY UNTIL I KNOW. BUT THERE'S NO REASON FOR YOU TWO TO TAKE THE SAME STUPID RISK.
THERE WAS NO REASON FOR YOU TO COME WITH ME TO EASTBROOKE, BUT YOU DID.
AND A FAT LOT OF GOOD IT DID.
OKAY, WHO'S BEST AT ROWING?
I AM.
RAMAE ACCELER-ANT!

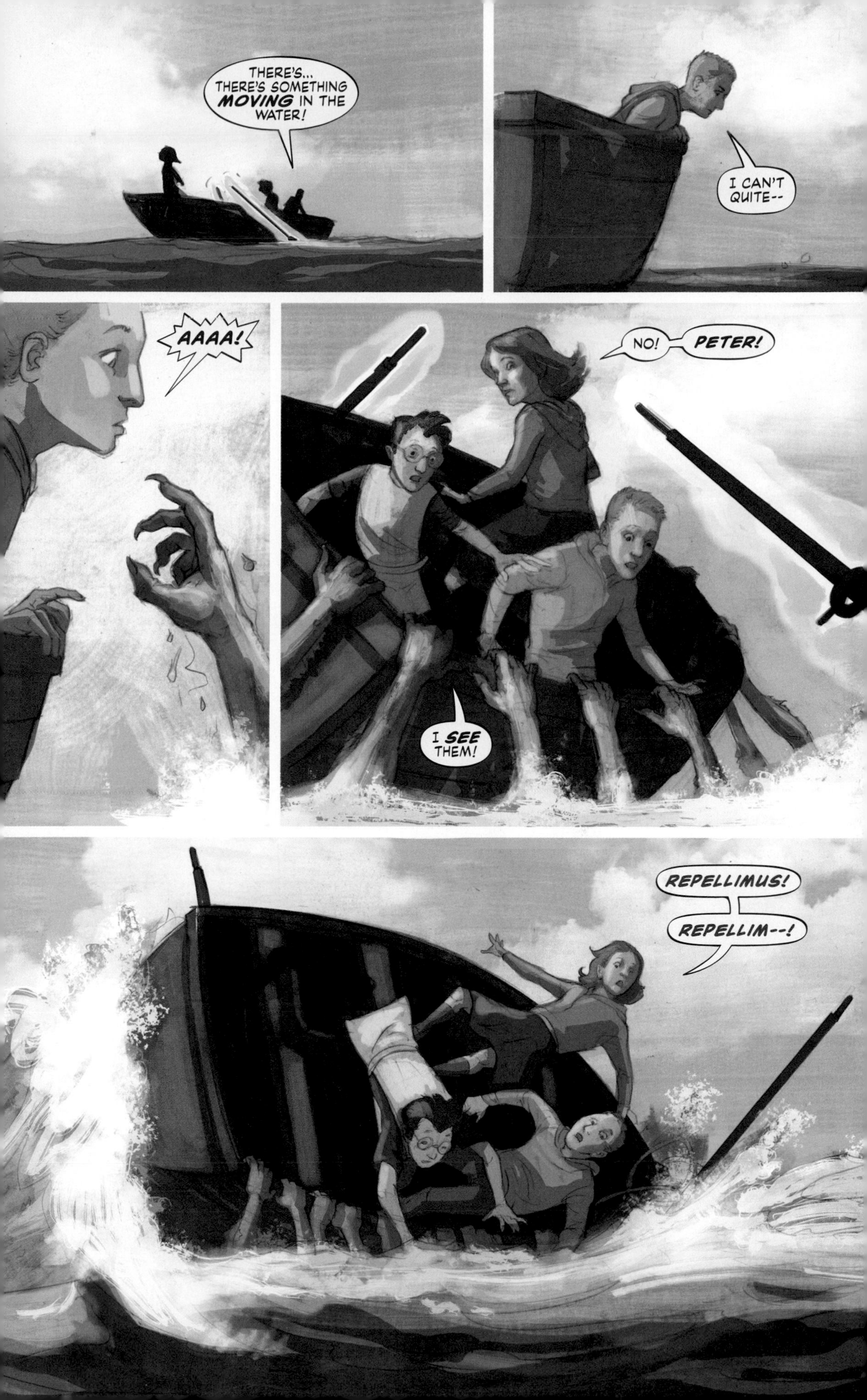
THERE'S... THERE'S SOMETHING **MOVING** IN THE WATER!
I CAN'T QUITE--
AAAA!
NO!
PETER!
I **SEE** THEM!
REPELLIMUS!
REPELLIM--!

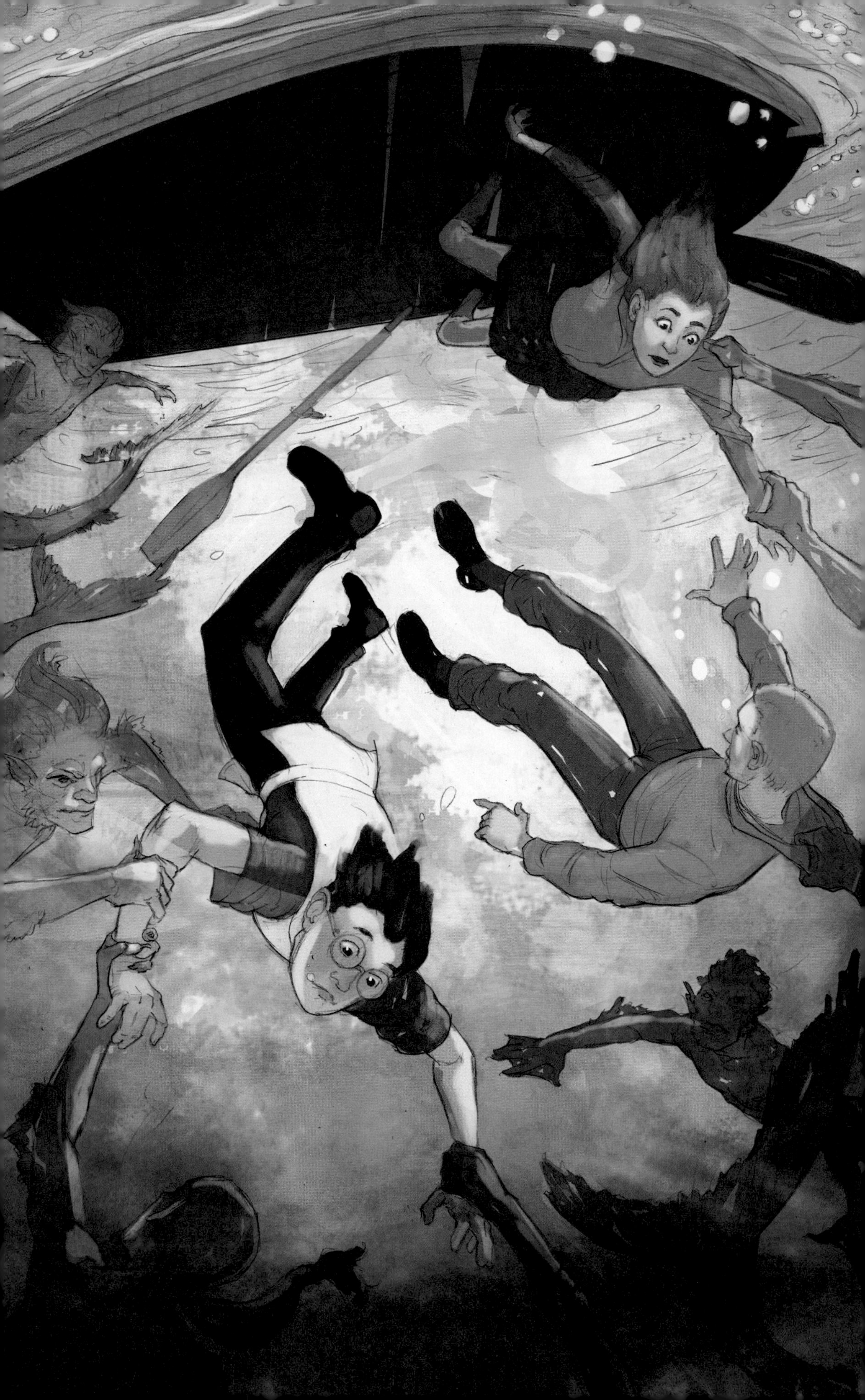

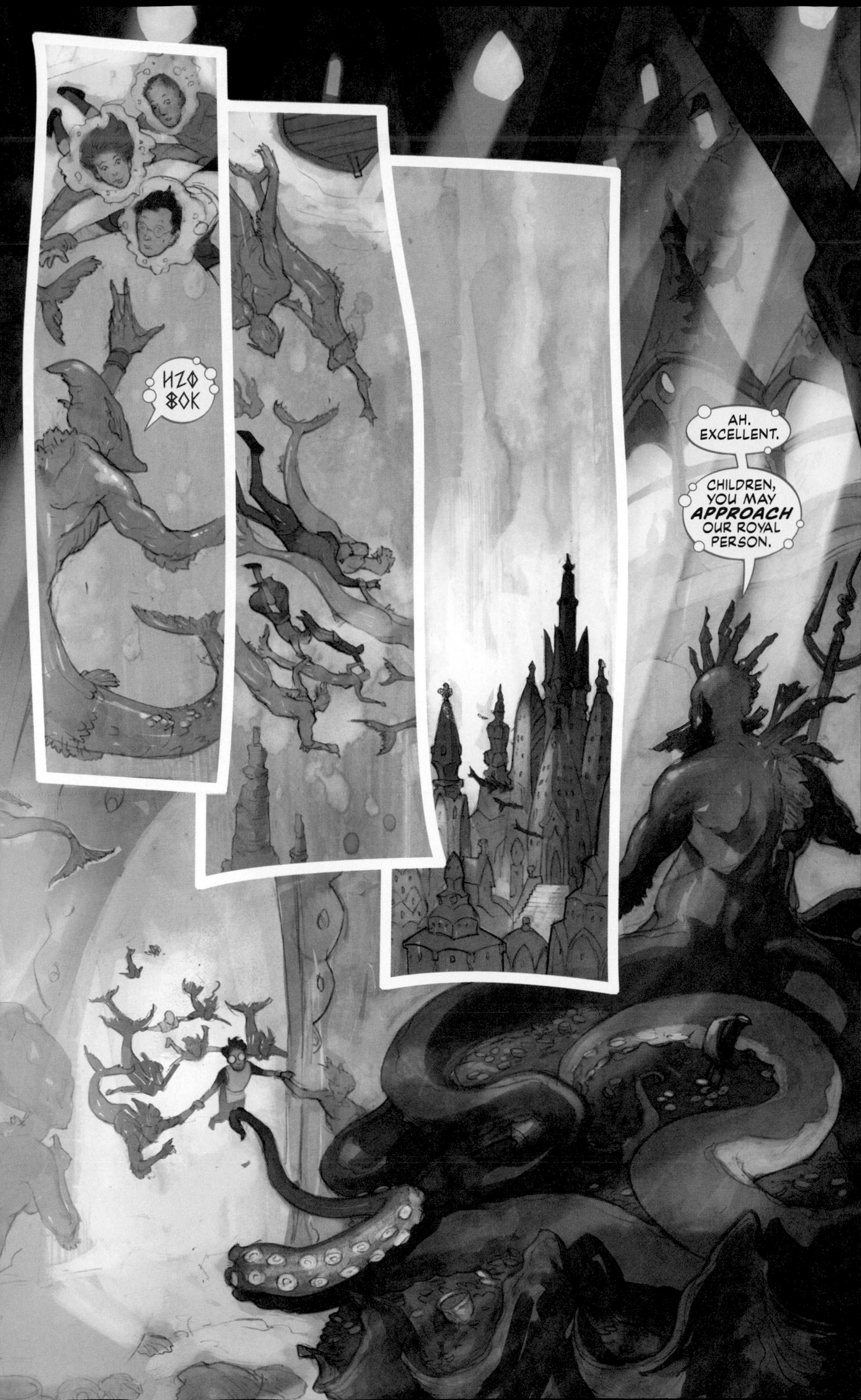
AH. EXCELLENT.
CHILDREN, YOU MAY **APPROACH** OUR ROYAL PERSON.

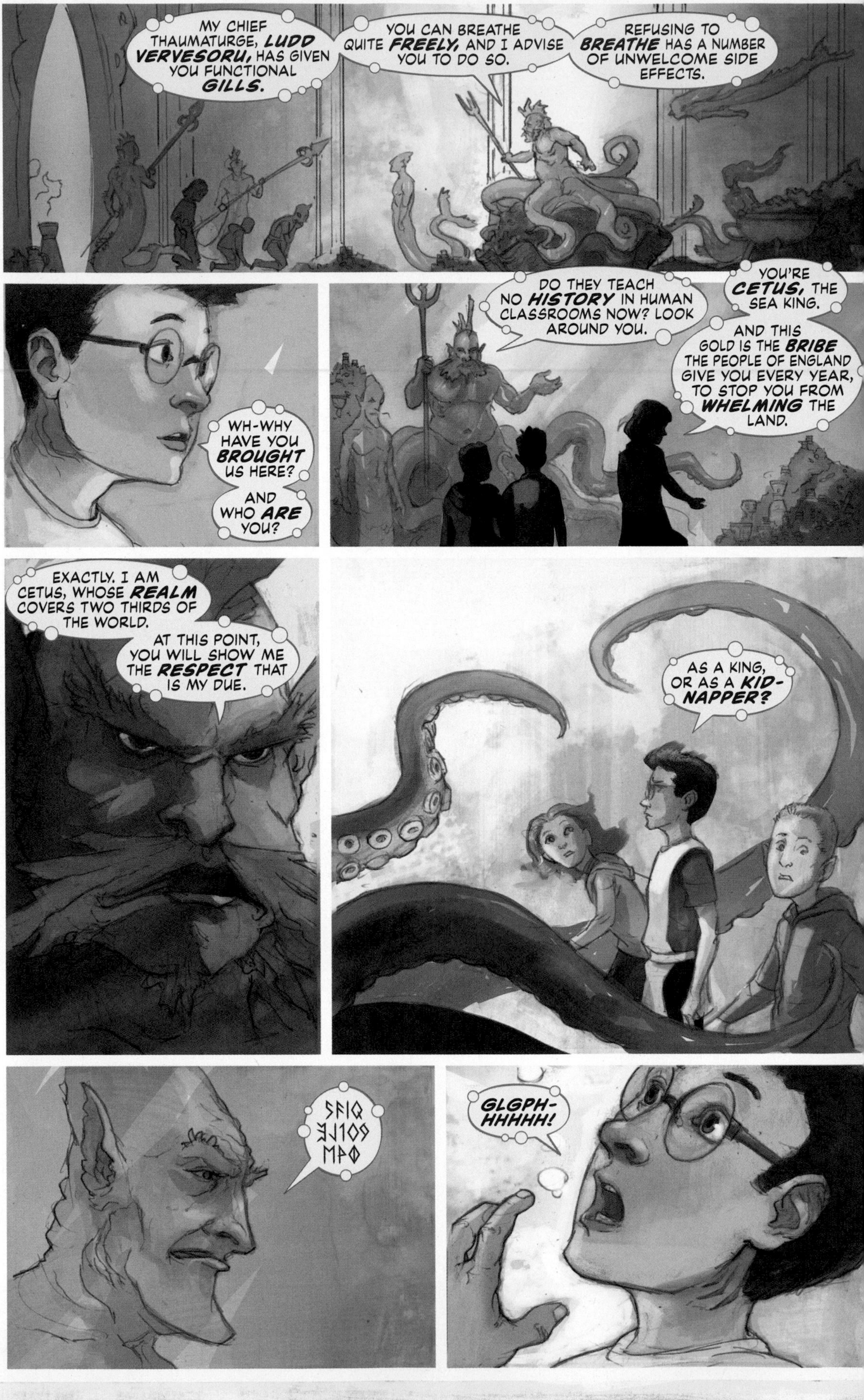
MY CHIEF THAUMATURGE, LUDD VERVESORU, HAS GIVEN YOU FUNCTIONAL GILLS.
YOU CAN BREATHE QUITE FREELY, AND I ADVISE YOU TO DO SO.
REFUSING TO BREATHE HAS A NUMBER OF UNWELCOME SIDE EFFECTS.
WH-WHY HAVE YOU BROUGHT US HERE?
AND WHO ARE YOU?
DO THEY TEACH NO HISTORY IN HUMAN CLASSROOMS NOW? LOOK AROUND YOU.
YOU'RE CETUS, THE SEA KING.
AND THIS GOLD IS THE BRIBE THE PEOPLE OF ENGLAND GIVE YOU EVERY YEAR, TO STOP YOU FROM WHELMING THE LAND.
EXACTLY. I AM CETUS, WHOSE REALM COVERS TWO THIRDS OF THE WORLD.
AT THIS POINT, YOU WILL SHOW ME THE RESPECT THAT IS MY DUE.
AS A KING, OR AS A KID-NAPPER?
GLGPH-HHHHH!

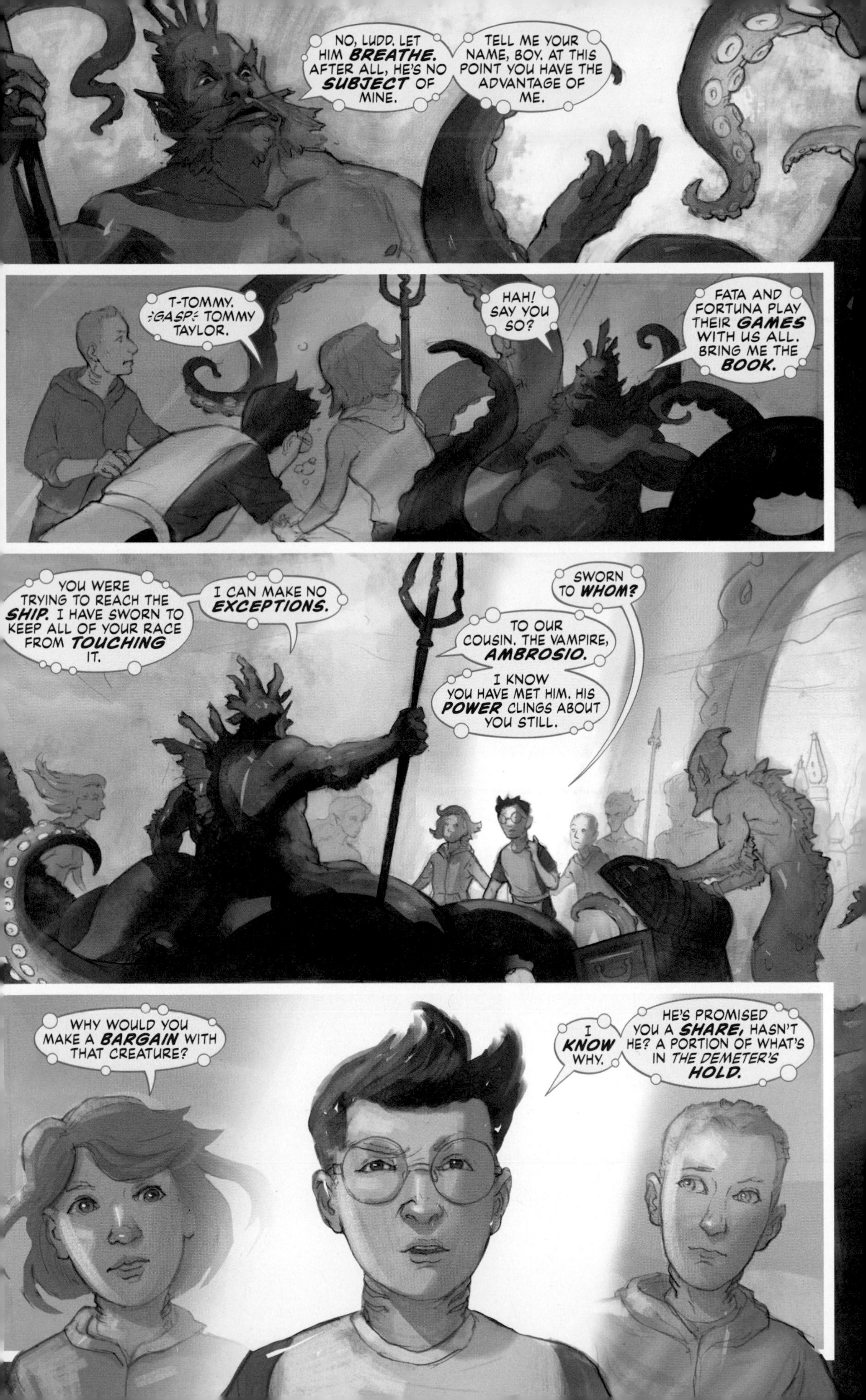
NO, LUDD. LET HIM BREATHE. AFTER ALL, HE'S NO SUBJECT OF MINE.
TELL ME YOUR NAME, BOY. AT THIS POINT YOU HAVE THE ADVANTAGE OF ME.
T-TOMMY. ÷GASP÷ TOMMY TAYLOR.
HAH! SAY YOU SO?
FATA AND FORTUNA PLAY THEIR GAMES WITH US ALL. BRING ME THE BOOK.
YOU WERE TRYING TO REACH THE SHIP. I HAVE SWORN TO KEEP ALL OF YOUR RACE FROM TOUCHING IT.
I CAN MAKE NO EXCEPTIONS.
SWORN TO WHOM?
TO OUR COUSIN. THE VAMPIRE, AMBROSIO.
I KNOW YOU HAVE MET HIM. HIS POWER CLINGS ABOUT YOU STILL.
WHY WOULD YOU MAKE A BARGAIN WITH THAT CREATURE?
I KNOW WHY.
HE'S PROMISED YOU A SHARE, HASN'T HE? A PORTION OF WHAT'S IN THE DEMETER'S HOLD.

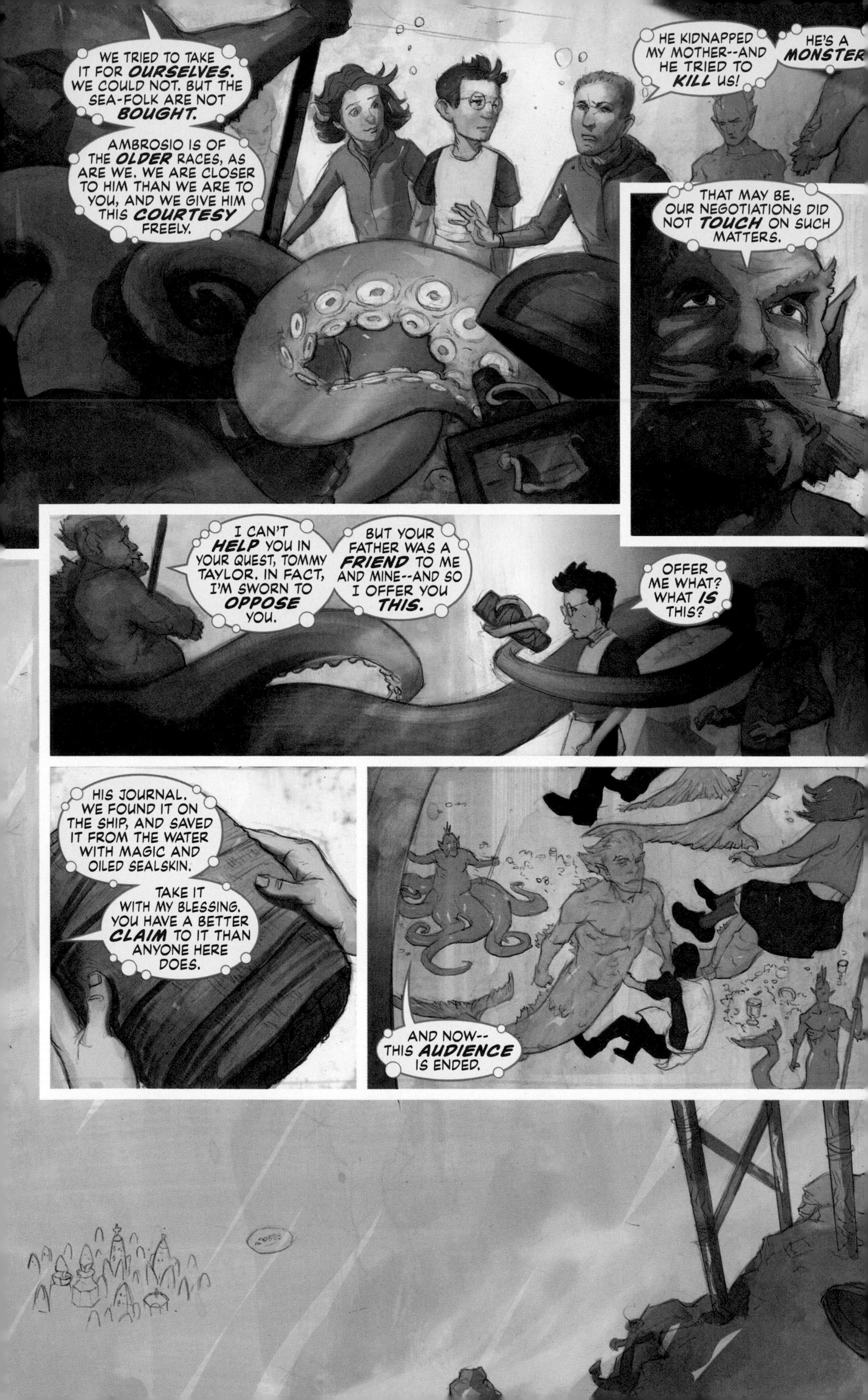
WE TRIED TO TAKE IT FOR OURSELVES. WE COULD NOT. BUT THE SEA-FOLK ARE NOT BOUGHT.
AMBROSIO IS OF THE OLDER RACES, AS ARE WE. WE ARE CLOSER TO HIM THAN WE ARE TO YOU, AND WE GIVE HIM THIS COURTESY FREELY.
HE KIDNAPPED MY MOTHER--AND HE TRIED TO KILL US!
HE'S A MONSTER
THAT MAY BE. OUR NEGOTIATIONS DID NOT TOUCH ON SUCH MATTERS.
I CAN'T HELP YOU IN YOUR QUEST, TOMMY TAYLOR. IN FACT, I'M SWORN TO OPPOSE YOU.
BUT YOUR FATHER WAS A FRIEND TO ME AND MINE--AND SO I OFFER YOU THIS.
OFFER ME WHAT? WHAT IS THIS?
HIS JOURNAL. WE FOUND IT ON THE SHIP, AND SAVED IT FROM THE WATER WITH MAGIC AND OILED SEALSKIN.
TAKE IT WITH MY BLESSING. YOU HAVE A BETTER CLAIM TO IT THAN ANYONE HERE DOES.
AND NOW--THIS AUDIENCE IS ENDED.

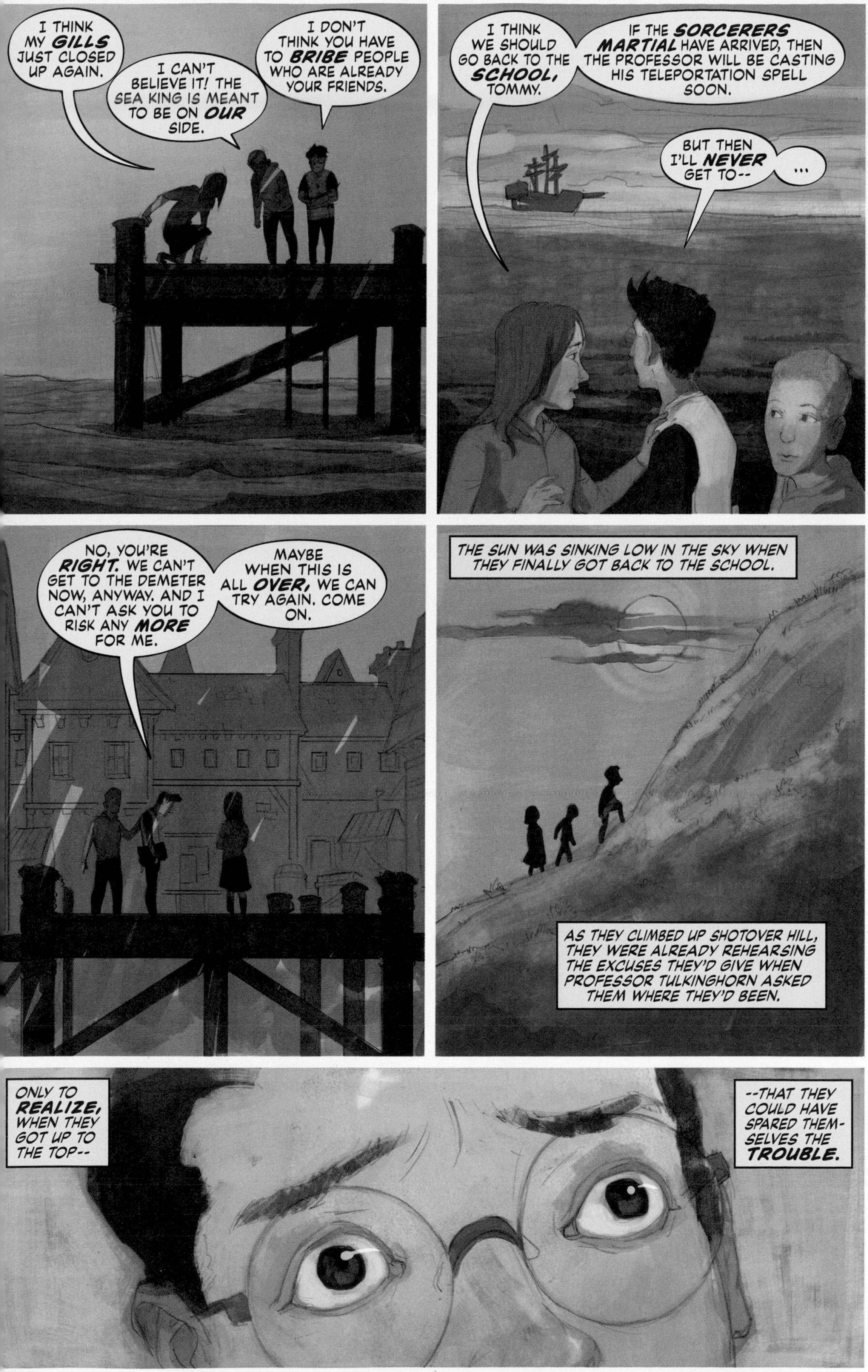
I THINK MY GILLS JUST CLOSED UP AGAIN.
I CAN'T BELIEVE IT! THE SEA KING IS MEANT TO BE ON OUR SIDE.
I DON'T THINK YOU HAVE TO BRIBE PEOPLE WHO ARE ALREADY YOUR FRIENDS.
I THINK WE SHOULD GO BACK TO THE SCHOOL, TOMMY.
IF THE SORCERERS MARTIAL HAVE ARRIVED, THEN THE PROFESSOR WILL BE CASTING HIS TELEPORTATION SPELL SOON.
BUT THEN I'LL NEVER GET TO--
...
NO, YOU'RE RIGHT. WE CAN'T GET TO THE DEMETER NOW, ANYWAY. AND I CAN'T ASK YOU TO RISK ANY MORE FOR ME.
MAYBE WHEN THIS IS ALL OVER, WE CAN TRY AGAIN. COME ON.
THE SUN WAS SINKING LOW IN THE SKY WHEN THEY FINALLY GOT BACK TO THE SCHOOL.
AS THEY CLIMBED UP SHOTOVER HILL, THEY WERE ALREADY REHEARSING THE EXCUSES THEY'D GIVE WHEN PROFESSOR TULKINGHORN ASKED THEM WHERE THEY'D BEEN.
ONLY TO REALIZE, WHEN THEY GOT UP TO THE TOP--
--THAT THEY COULD HAVE SPARED THEM-SELVES THE TROUBLE.

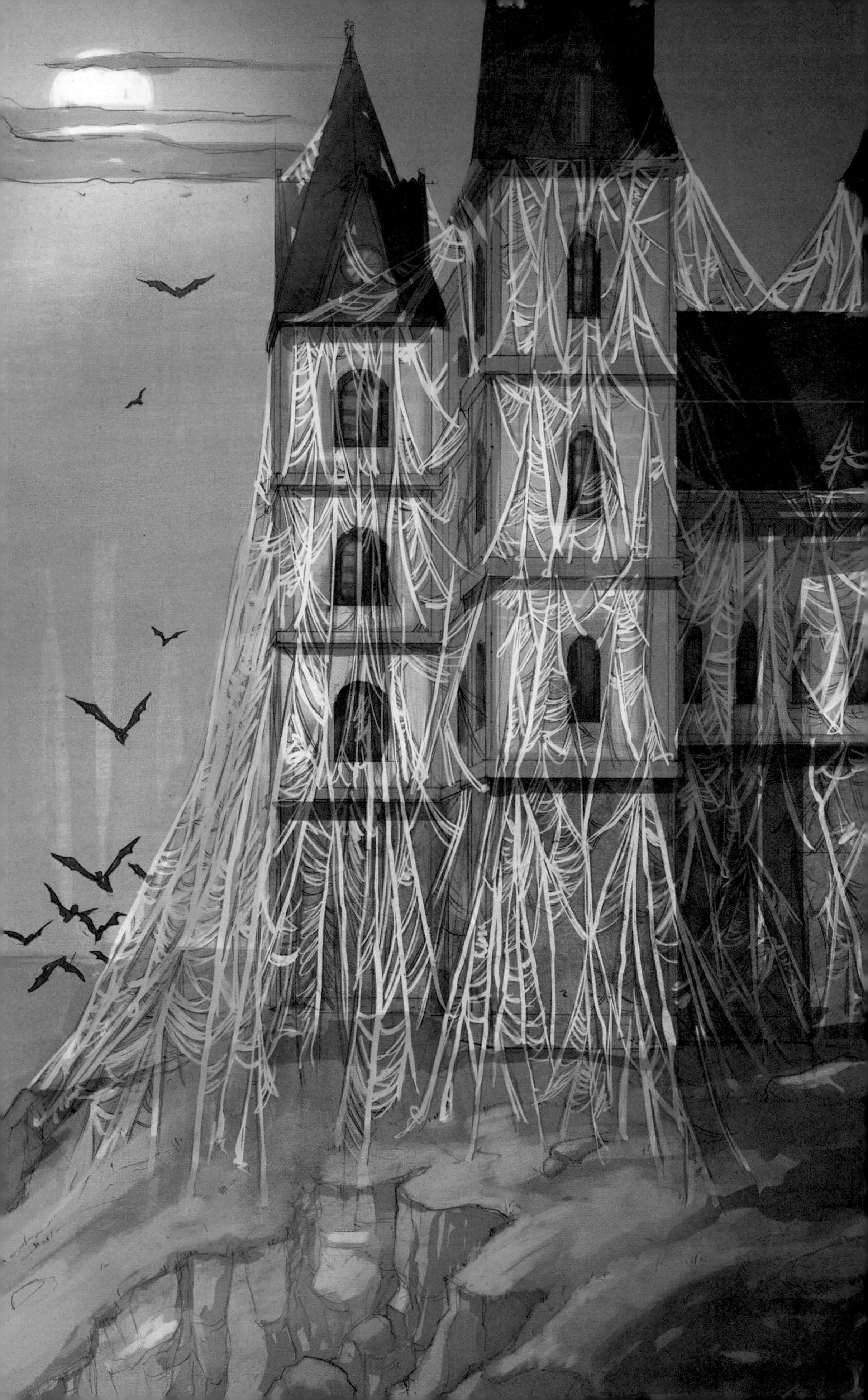

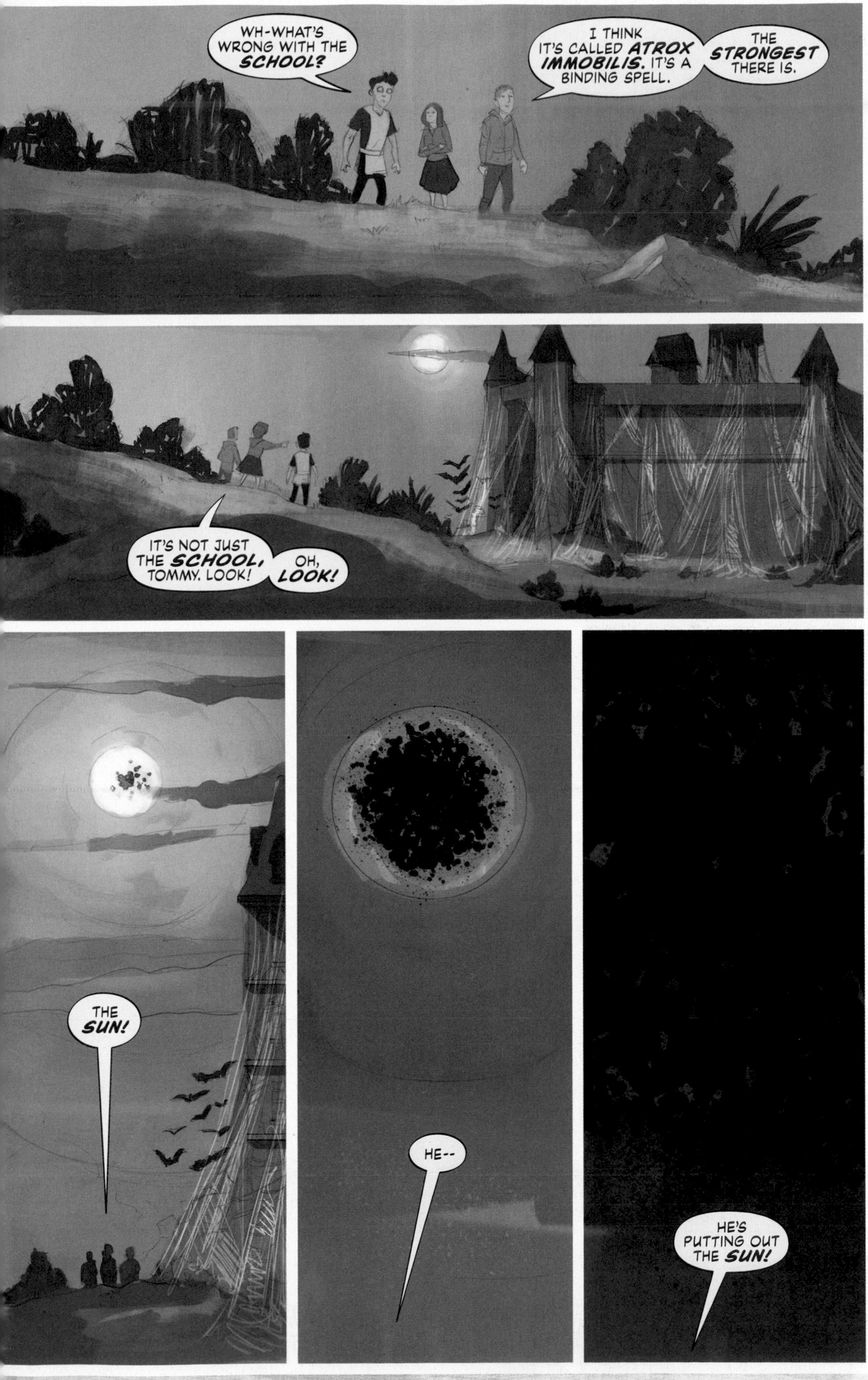
WH-WHAT'S WRONG WITH THE SCHOOL?
I THINK IT'S CALLED ATROX IMMOBILIS. IT'S A BINDING SPELL.
THE STRONGEST THERE IS.
IT'S NOT JUST THE SCHOOL, TOMMY. LOOK!
OH, LOOK!
THE SUN!
HE--
HE'S PUTTING OUT THE SUN!

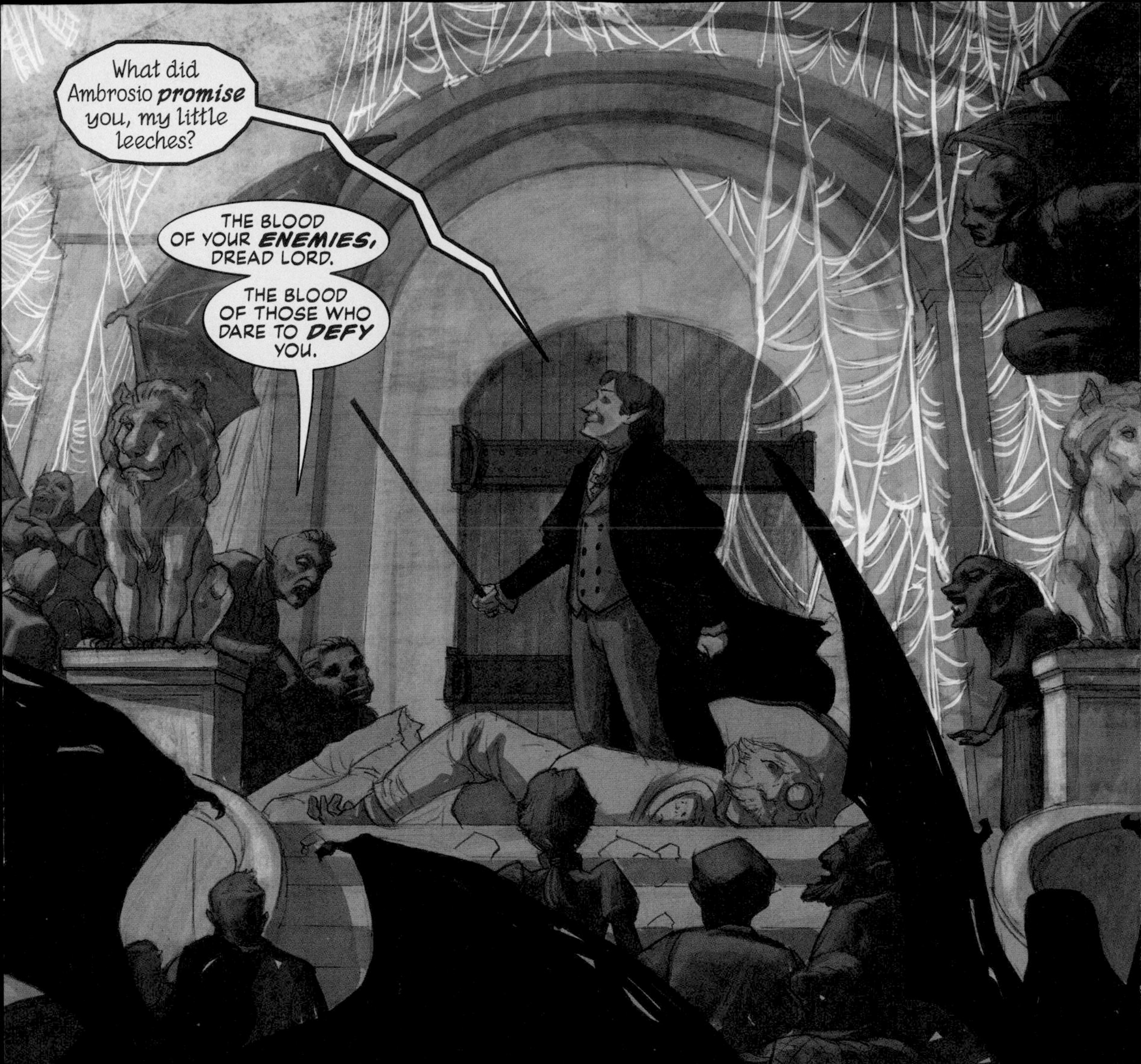
What did Ambrosio **promise** you, my little leeches?
THE BLOOD OF YOUR **ENEMIES,** DREAD LORD.
THE BLOOD OF THOSE WHO DARE TO **DEFY** YOU.

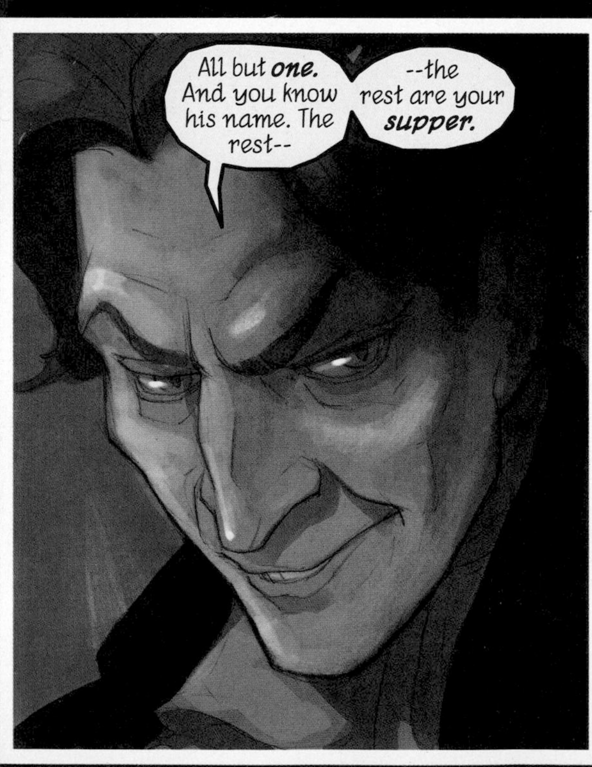
All but **one.** And you know his name. The rest--
--the rest are your **supper.**

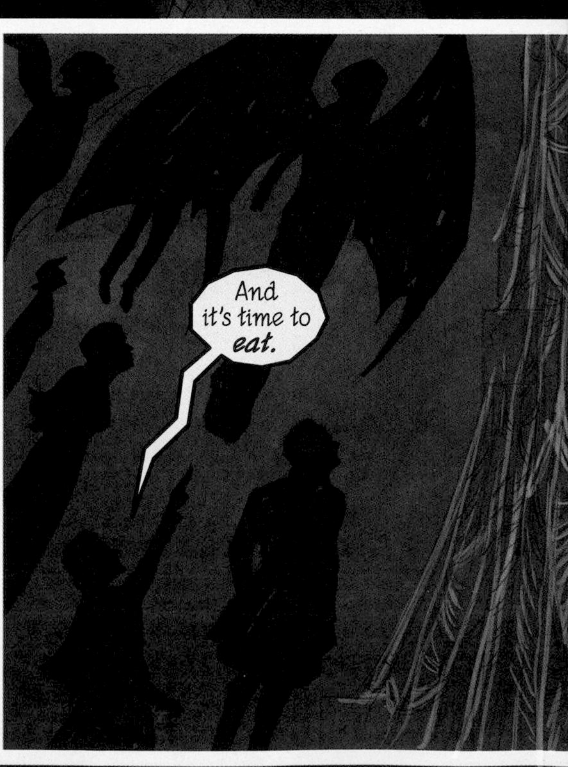
And it's time to **eat.**

Nov 5th.

"Build a bonfire, build a bonfire,
Put [insert name of someone you hate] on the top.
Put [insert another name] in the middle
And then burn the bloody lot."

That's what we used to sing, on Guy Fawkes night, when we were children — a very long time ago, now. And today, that's what I did. I built a bonfire, put Sue on top of it. The middle, for the sake of argument, was what was left of my human decency. And then I applied the match, and watched it burn.

Metaphors aside, I took advantage of her fragile emotional state and bought her out. I suggested she should just walk away from this kid that wasn't even her idea, and go back to the life she knew before — to youth, and freedom, and irresponsibility. She was grateful. It was all she wanted.

There was money in the deal, too, because freedom without money is a very abstract kind of freedom indeed. But mostly I was saying "pretend this never happened," and she was saying "Oh yes! Oh yes, please!"

I felt a little ashamed, after she'd gone, but there's no denying that this simplifies the whole situation.

And if you look at it another way I'm doing her a favor. Miriam burned out so quickly it was like something was eating her from the inside out.

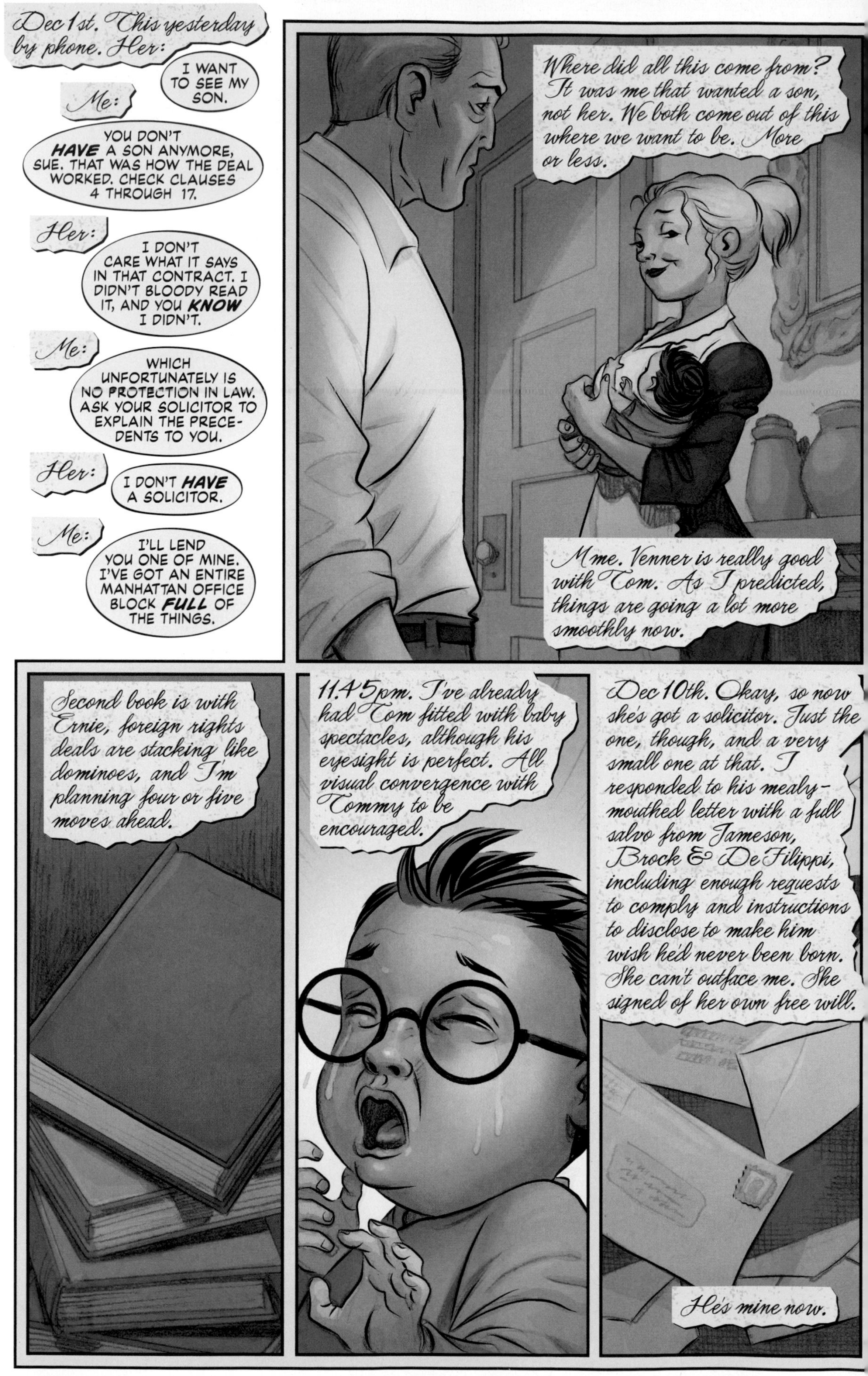
Dec 1st. This yesterday by phone. Her:
I WANT TO SEE MY SON.
Me:
YOU DON'T HAVE A SON ANYMORE, SUE. THAT WAS HOW THE DEAL WORKED. CHECK CLAUSES 4 THROUGH 17.
Her:
I DON'T CARE WHAT IT SAYS IN THAT CONTRACT. I DIDN'T BLOODY READ IT, AND YOU KNOW I DIDN'T.
Me:
WHICH UNFORTUNATELY IS NO PROTECTION IN LAW. ASK YOUR SOLICITOR TO EXPLAIN THE PRECE-DENTS TO YOU.
Her:
I DON'T HAVE A SOLICITOR.
Me:
I'LL LEND YOU ONE OF MINE. I'VE GOT AN ENTIRE MANHATTAN OFFICE BLOCK FULL OF THE THINGS.
Where did all this come from? It was me that wanted a son, not her. We both come out of this where we want to be. More or less.
Mme. Venner is really good with Tom. As I predicted, things are going a lot more smoothly now.
Second book is with Ernie, foreign rights deals are stacking like dominoes, and I'm planning four or five moves ahead.
11.45pm. I've already had Tom fitted with baby spectacles, although his eyesight is perfect. All visual convergence with Tommy to be encouraged.
Dec 10th. Okay, so now she's got a solicitor. Just the one, though, and a very small one at that. I responded to his mealy-mouthed letter with a full salvo from Jameson, Brock & De Filippi, including enough requests to comply and instructions to disclose to make him wish he'd never been born. She can't outface me. She signed of her own free will.
He's mine now.

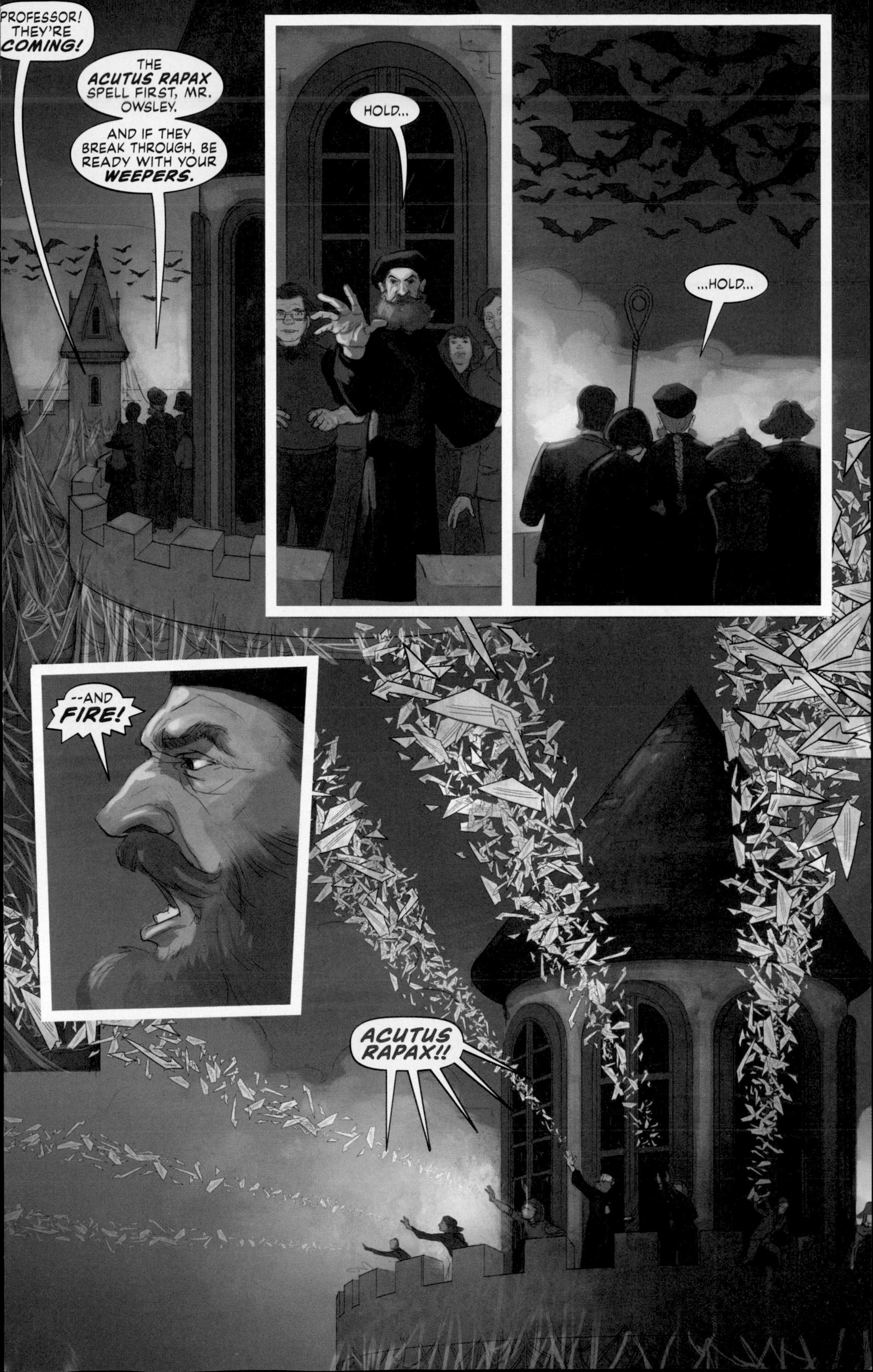
PROFESSOR! THEY'RE COMING!
THE ACUTUS RAPAX SPELL FIRST, MR. OWSLEY.
AND IF THEY BREAK THROUGH, BE READY WITH YOUR WEEPERS.
HOLD...
...HOLD...
--AND FIRE!
ACUTUS RAPAX!!

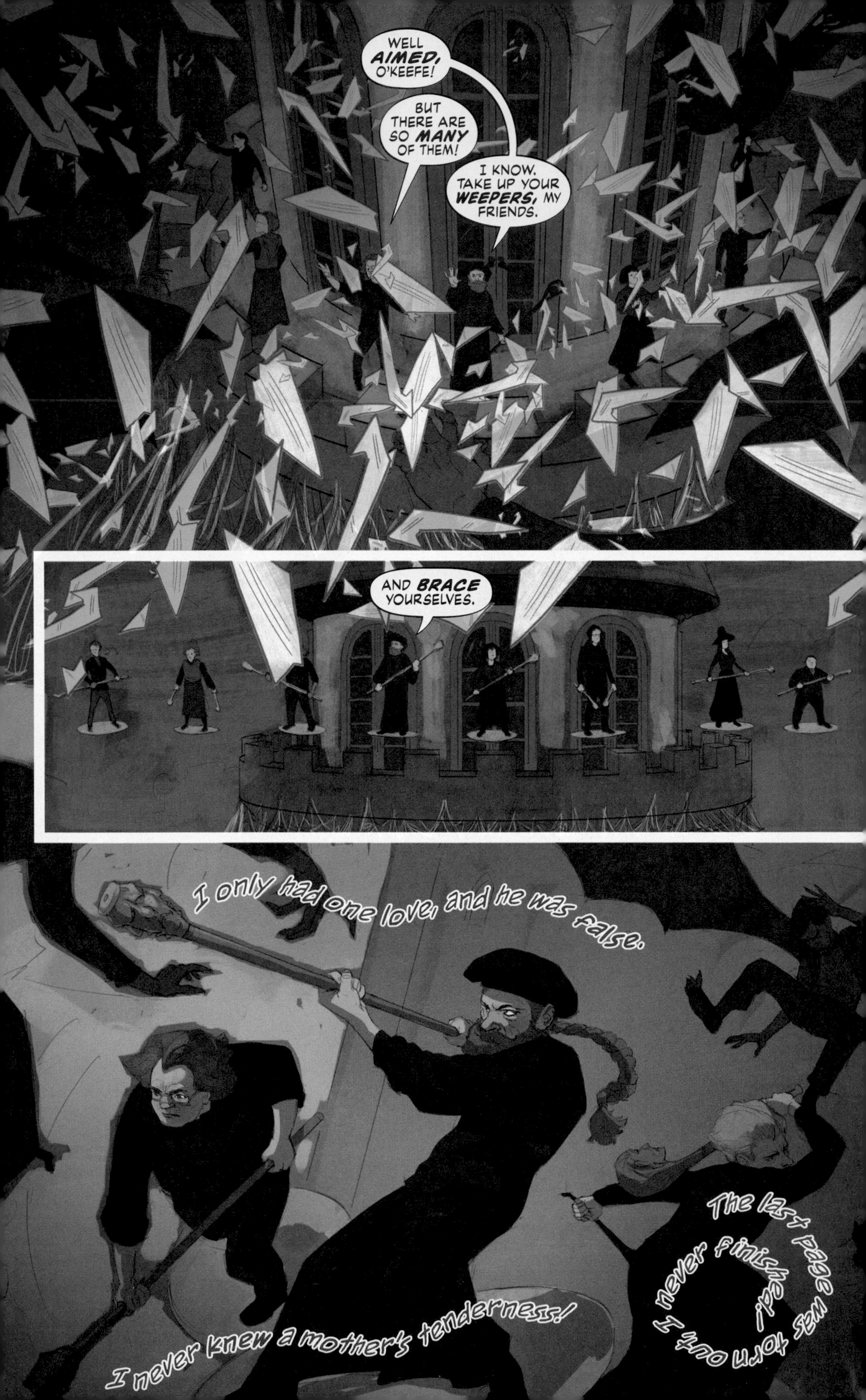
WELL AIMED, O'KEEFE!
BUT THERE ARE SO MANY OF THEM!
I KNOW. TAKE UP YOUR WEEPERS, MY FRIENDS.
AND BRACE YOURSELVES.
I only had one love, and he was false.
I never knew a mother's tenderness!
The last page was torn out; I never finished!

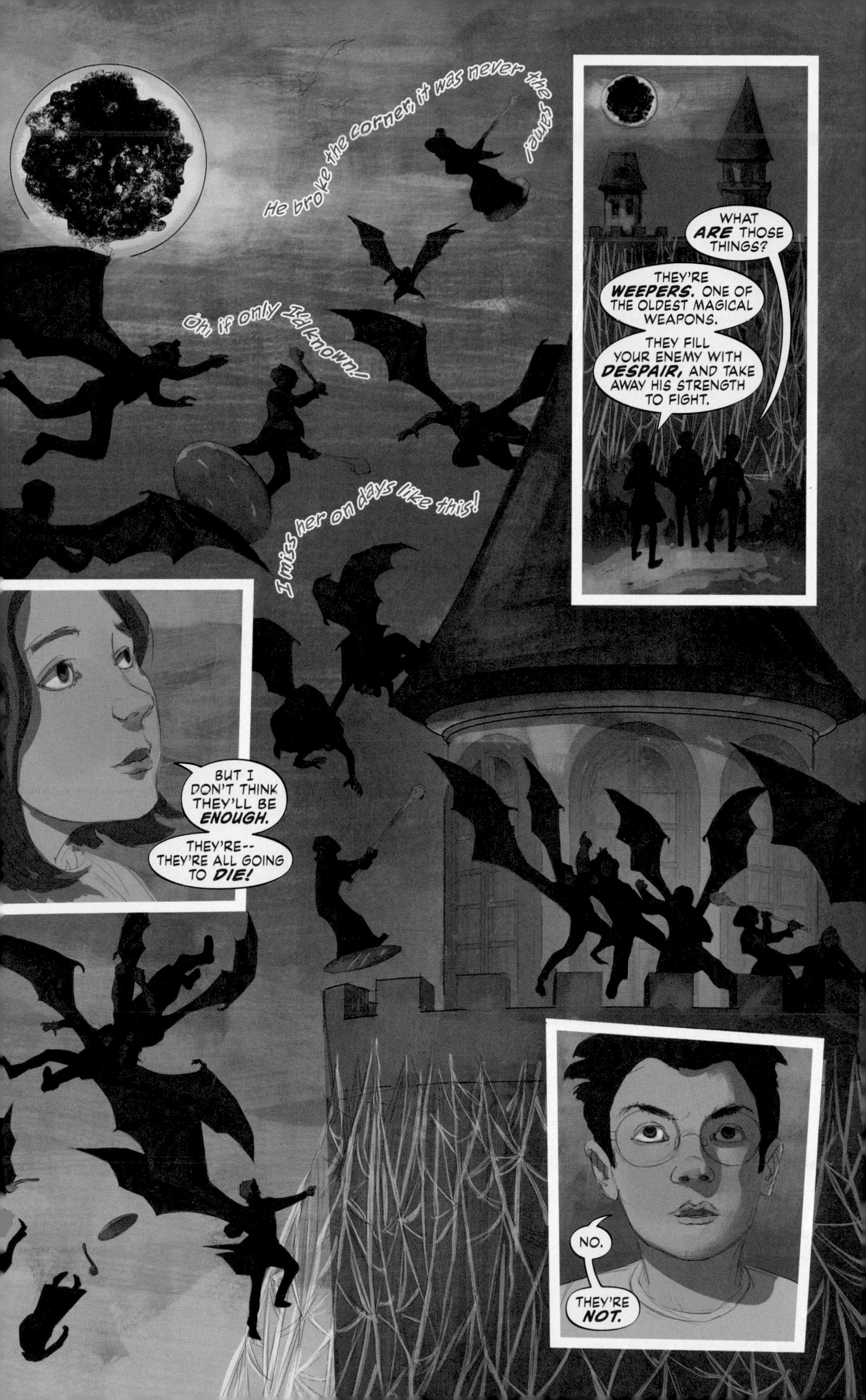He broke the corner, it was never the same!
Oh, if only I'd known!
I miss her on days like this!
WHAT ARE THOSE THINGS?
THEY'RE WEEPERS. ONE OF THE OLDEST MAGICAL WEAPONS.
THEY FILL YOUR ENEMY WITH DESPAIR, AND TAKE AWAY HIS STRENGTH TO FIGHT.
BUT I DON'T THINK THEY'LL BE ENOUGH.
THEY'RE-- THEY'RE ALL GOING TO DIE!
NO.
THEY'RE NOT.

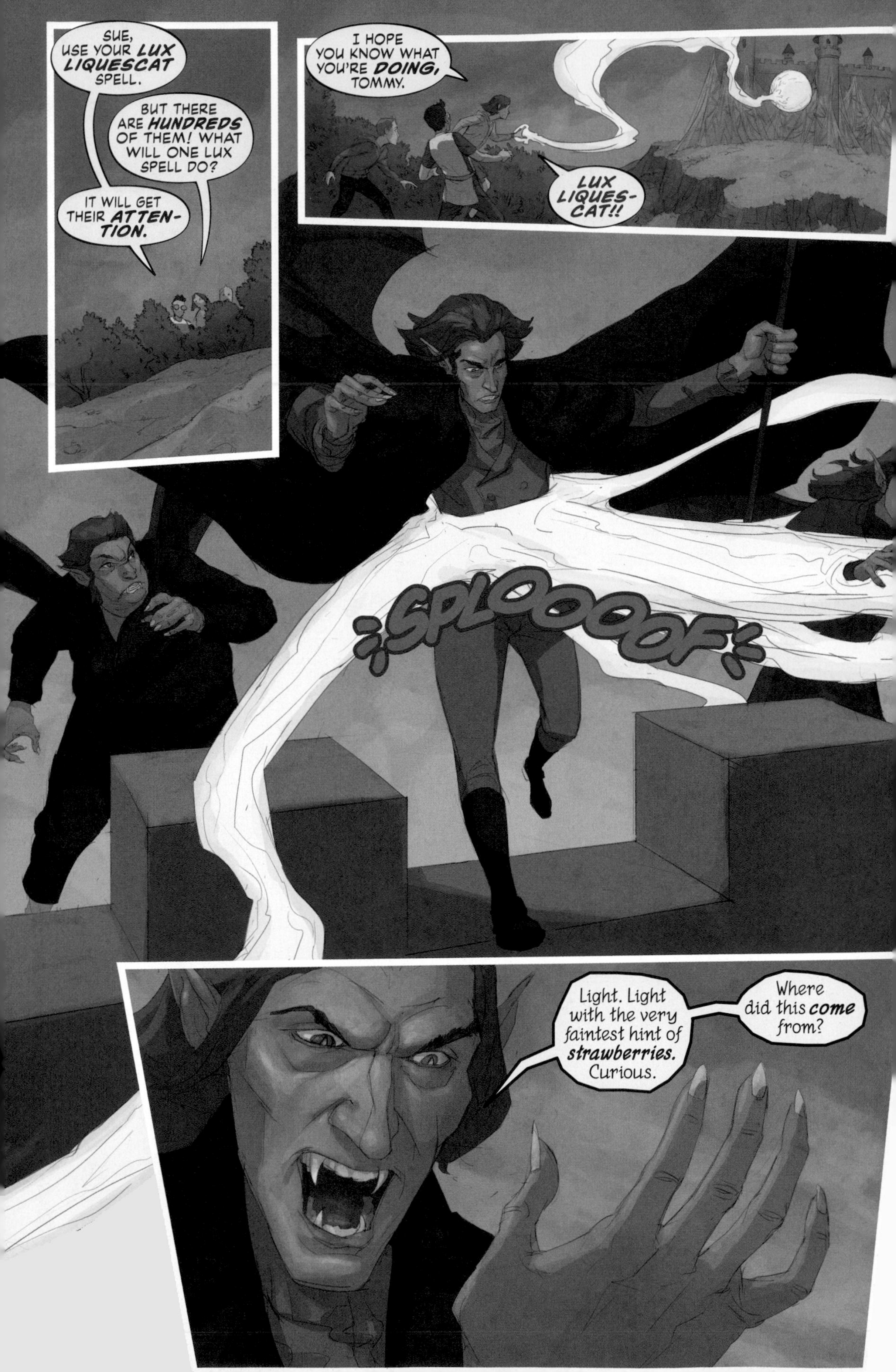
SUE, USE YOUR LUX LIQUESCAT SPELL.
BUT THERE ARE HUNDREDS OF THEM! WHAT WILL ONE LUX SPELL DO?
IT WILL GET THEIR ATTENTION.
I HOPE YOU KNOW WHAT YOU'RE DOING, TOMMY.
LUX LIQUESCAT!!
SPLOOOOOF
Light. Light with the very faintest hint of strawberries. Curious.
Where did this come from?

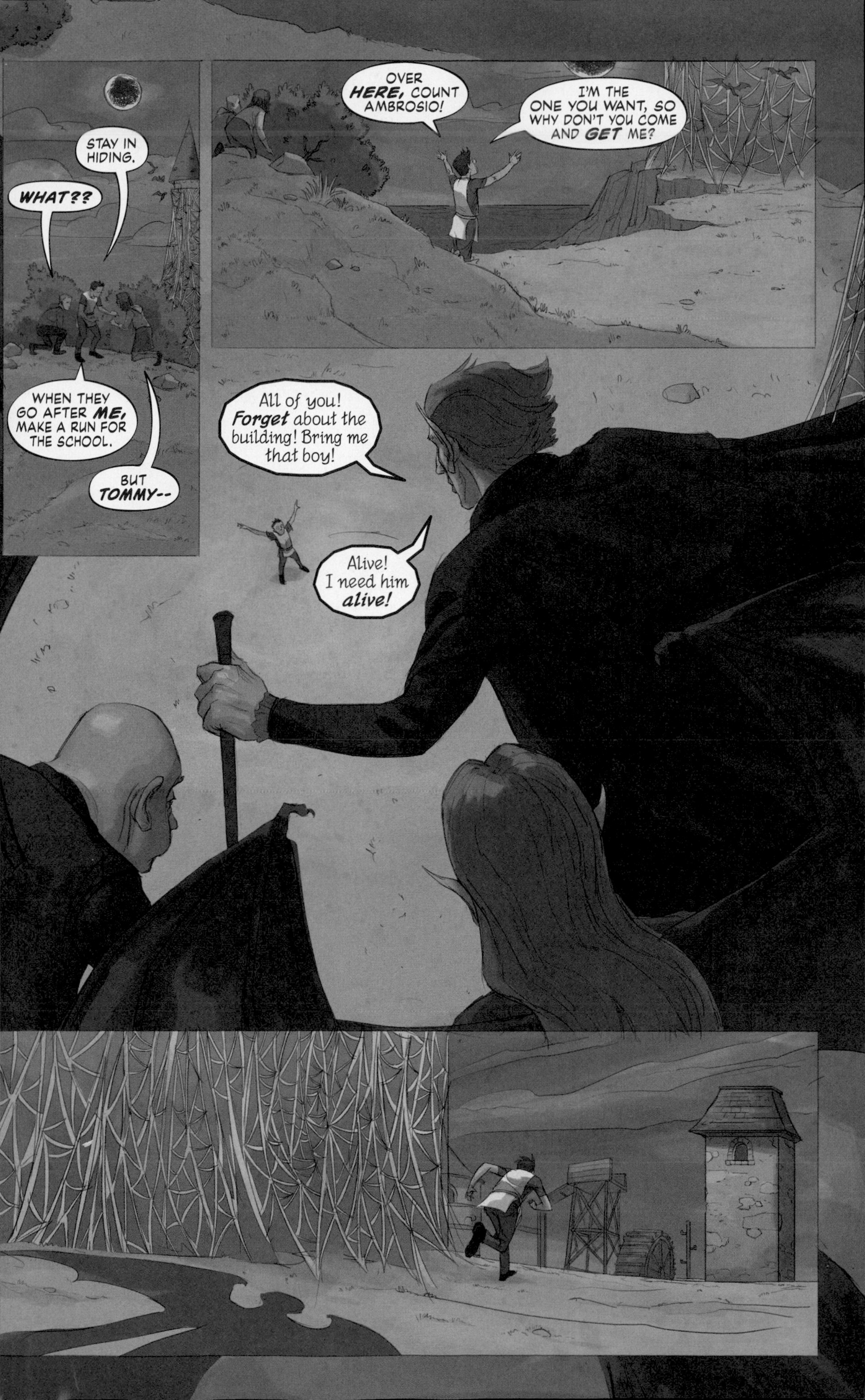

STAY IN HIDING.
WHAT??
WHEN THEY GO AFTER ME, MAKE A RUN FOR THE SCHOOL.
BUT TOMMY--
OVER HERE, COUNT AMBROSIO!
I'M THE ONE YOU WANT, SO WHY DON'T YOU COME AND GET ME?
All of you! Forget about the building! Bring me that boy!
Alive! I need him alive!

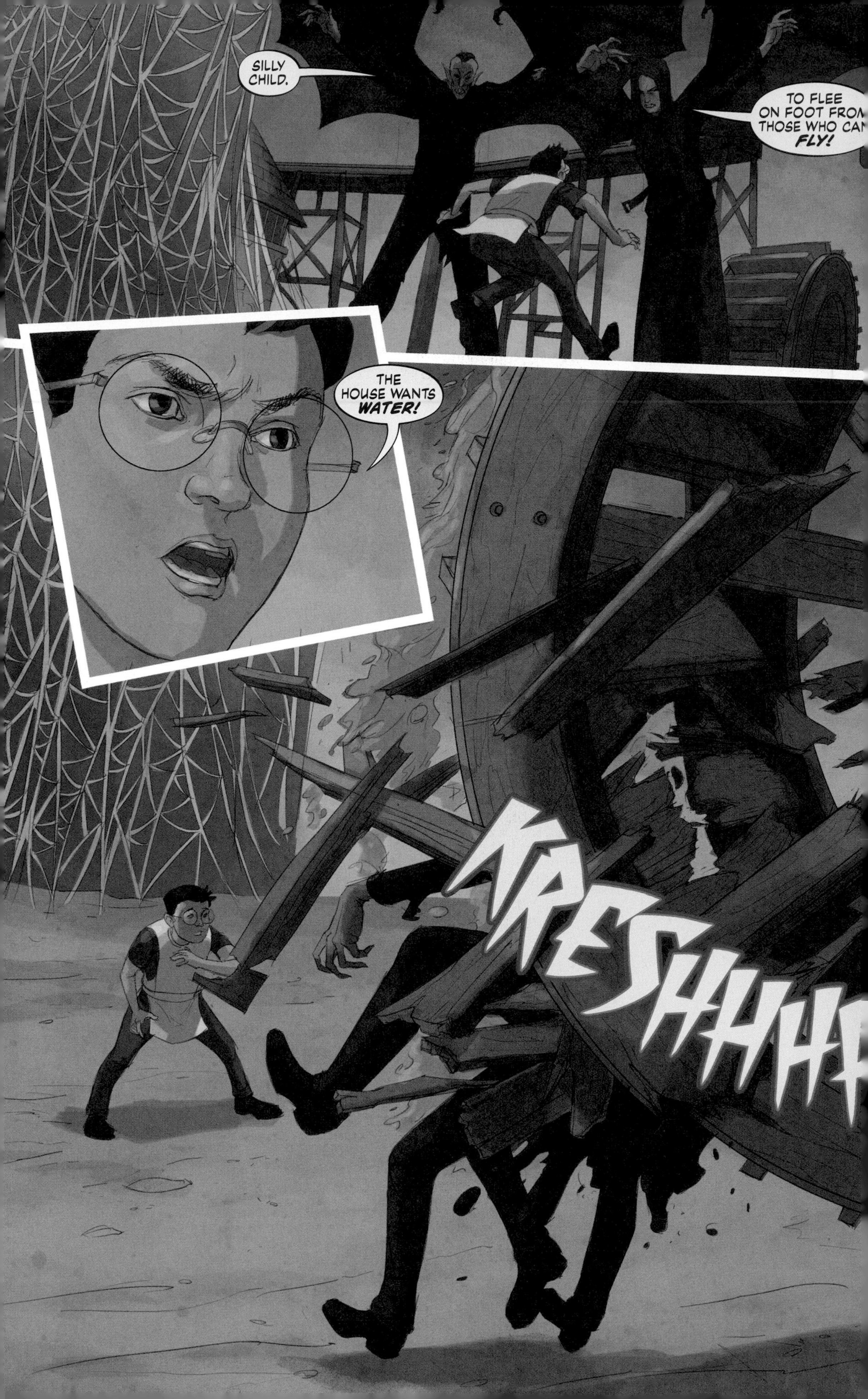

SILLY CHILD.
TO FLEE ON FOOT FROM THOSE WHO CAN FLY!
THE HOUSE WANTS WATER!
KRESHHHH

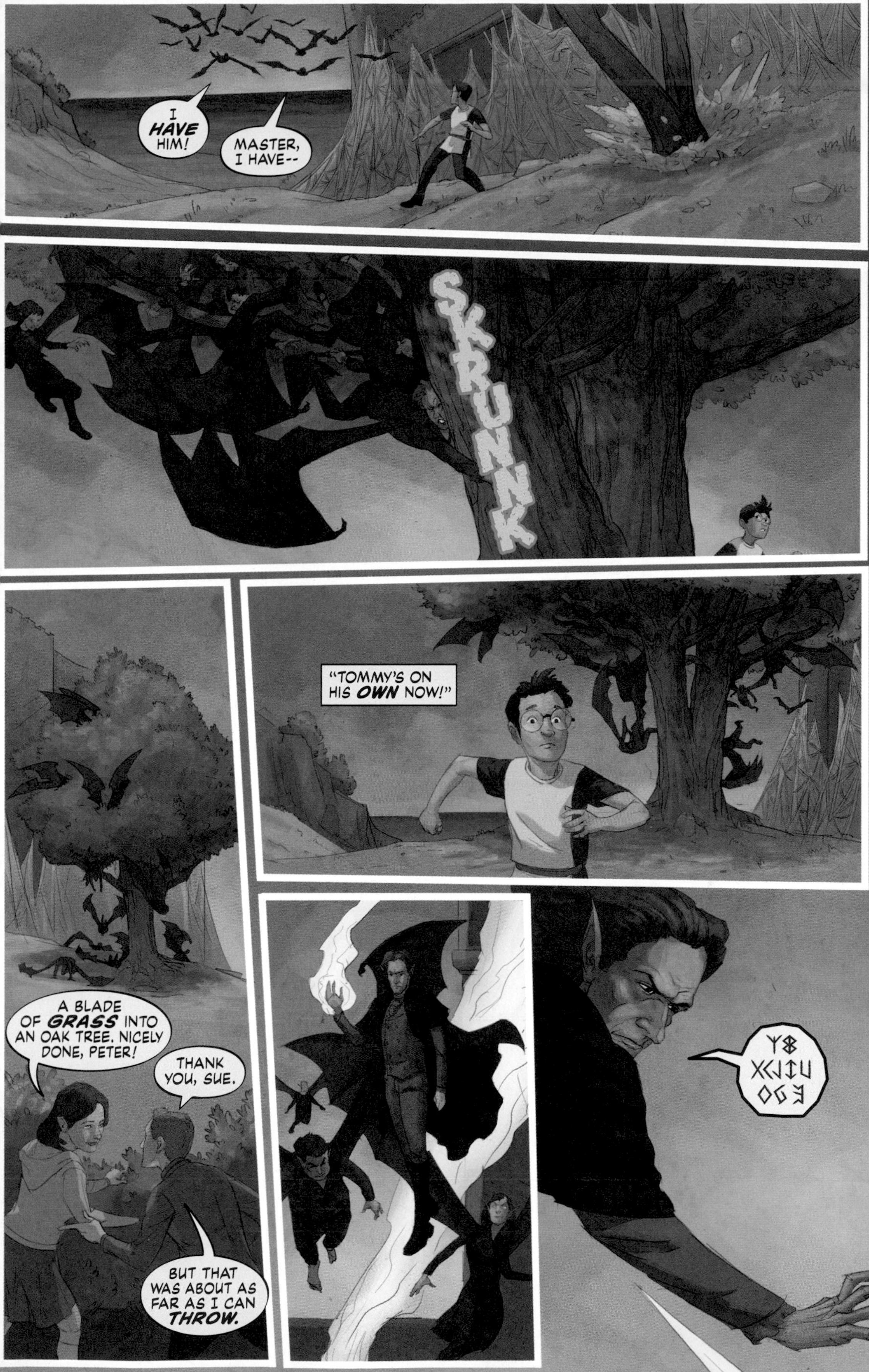
I HAVE HIM!
MASTER, I HAVE--
SKRUNNK
"TOMMY'S ON HIS OWN NOW!"
A BLADE OF GRASS INTO AN OAK TREE. NICELY DONE, PETER!
THANK YOU, SUE.
BUT THAT WAS ABOUT AS FAR AS I CAN THROW.

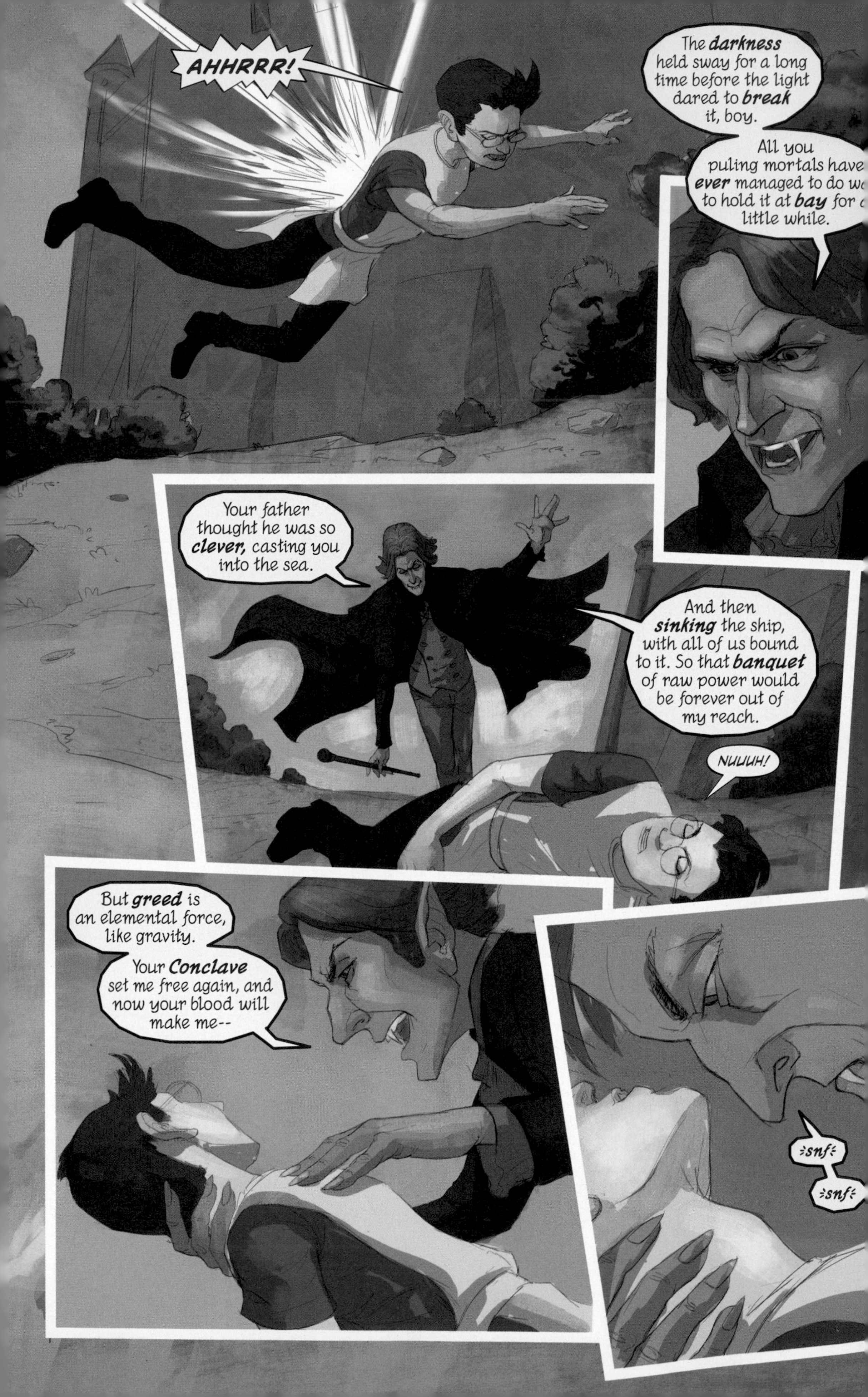

AHHRRR!
The darkness held sway for a long time before the light dared to break it, boy.
All you puling mortals have ever managed to do w to hold it at bay for little while.
Your father thought he was so clever, casting you into the sea.
And then sinking the ship, with all of us bound to it. So that banquet of raw power would be forever out of my reach.
NUUUH!
But greed is an elemental force, like gravity.
Your Conclave set me free again, and now your blood will make me--
snf
snf

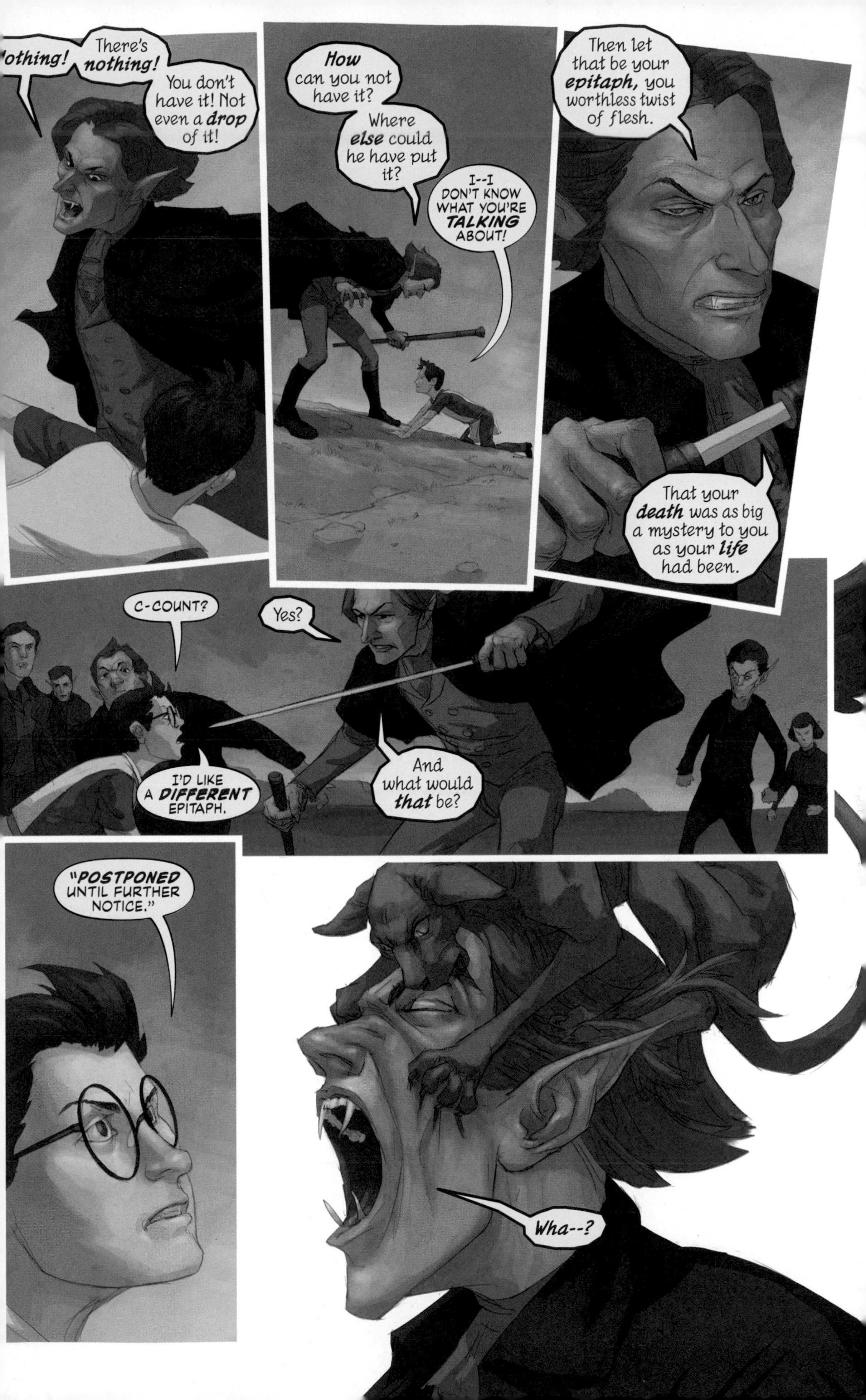

othing!
There's nothing!
You don't have it! Not even a drop of it!
How can you not have it?
Where else could he have put it?
I--I DON'T KNOW WHAT YOU'RE TALKING ABOUT!
Then let that be your epitaph, you worthless twist of flesh.
That your death was as big a mystery to you as your life had been.
C-COUNT?
Yes?
I'D LIKE A DIFFERENT EPITAPH.
And what would that be?
"POSTPONED UNTIL FURTHER NOTICE."
Wha--?

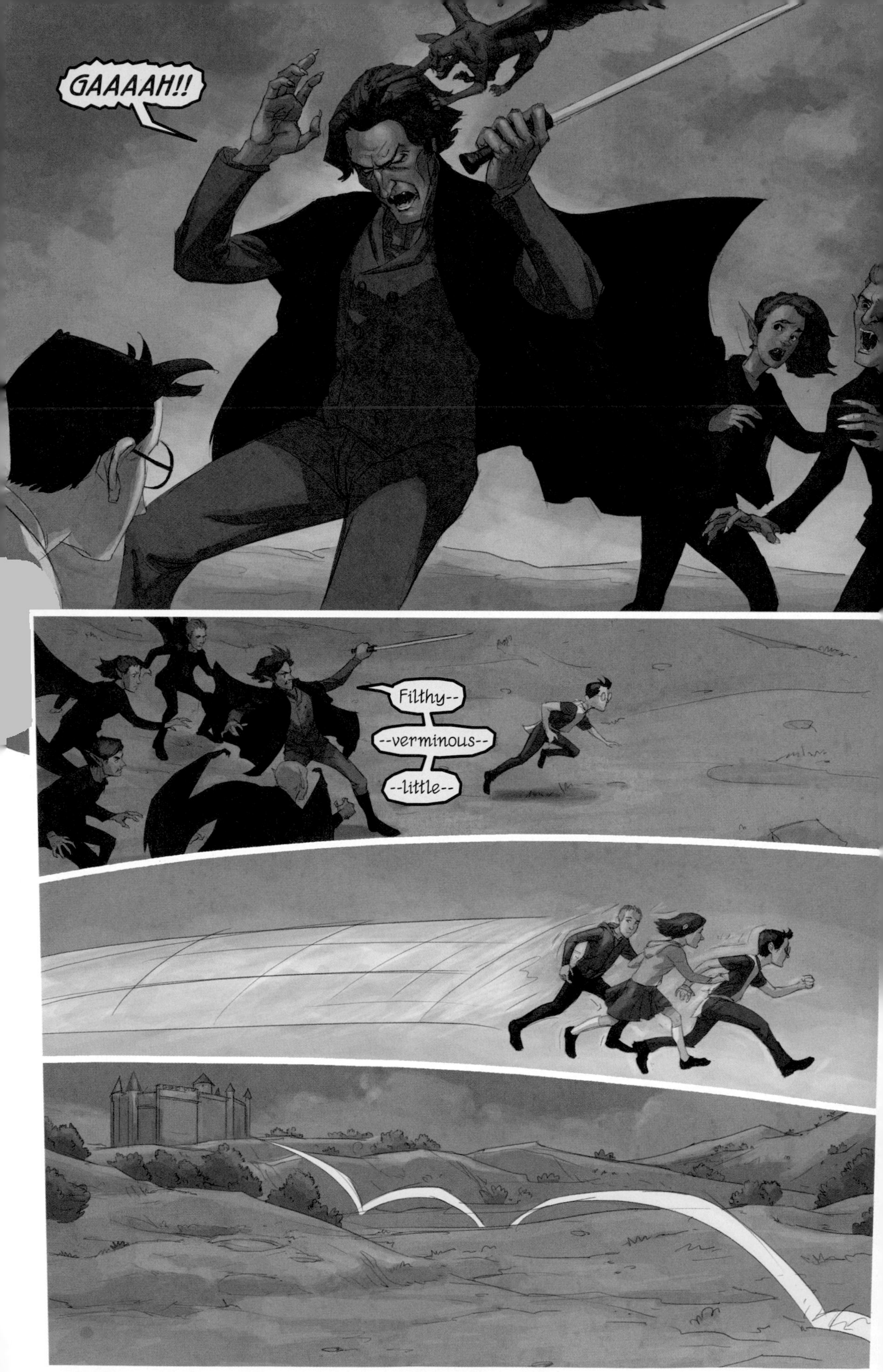
GAAAAH!!
Filthy--
--verminous--
--little--

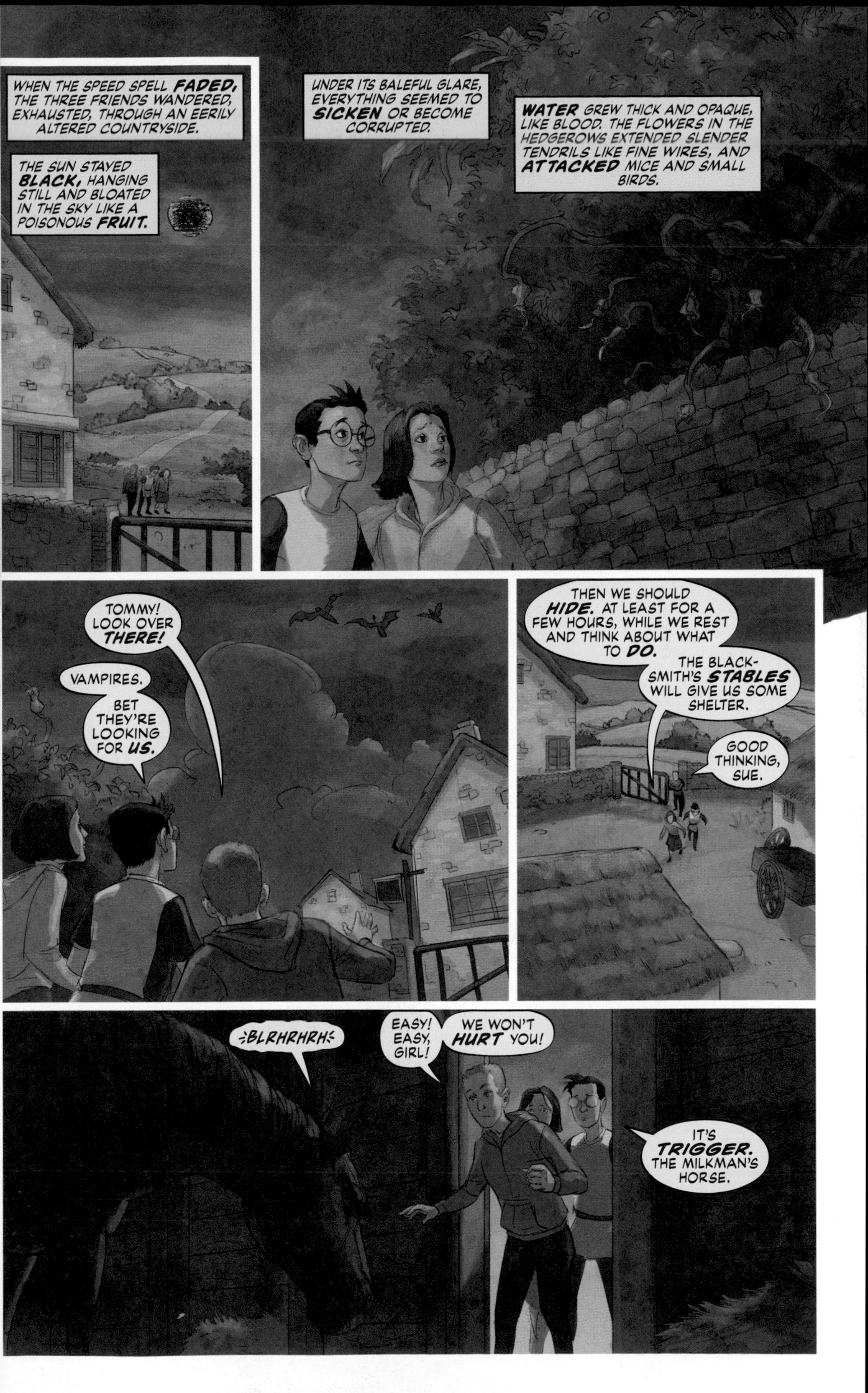
WHEN THE SPEED SPELL FADED, THE THREE FRIENDS WANDERED, EXHAUSTED, THROUGH AN EERILY ALTERED COUNTRYSIDE.
THE SUN STAYED BLACK, HANGING STILL AND BLOATED IN THE SKY LIKE A POISONOUS FRUIT.
UNDER ITS BALEFUL GLARE, EVERYTHING SEEMED TO SICKEN OR BECOME CORRUPTED.
WATER GREW THICK AND OPAQUE, LIKE BLOOD. THE FLOWERS IN THE HEDGEROWS EXTENDED SLENDER TENDRILS LIKE FINE WIRES, AND ATTACKED MICE AND SMALL BIRDS.
TOMMY! LOOK OVER THERE!
VAMPIRES.
BET THEY'RE LOOKING FOR US.
THEN WE SHOULD HIDE. AT LEAST FOR A FEW HOURS, WHILE WE REST AND THINK ABOUT WHAT TO DO.
THE BLACK-SMITH'S STABLES WILL GIVE US SOME SHELTER.
GOOD THINKING, SUE.
BLRHRHRH
EASY! EASY, GIRL!
WE WON'T HURT YOU!
IT'S TRIGGER. THE MILKMAN'S HORSE.

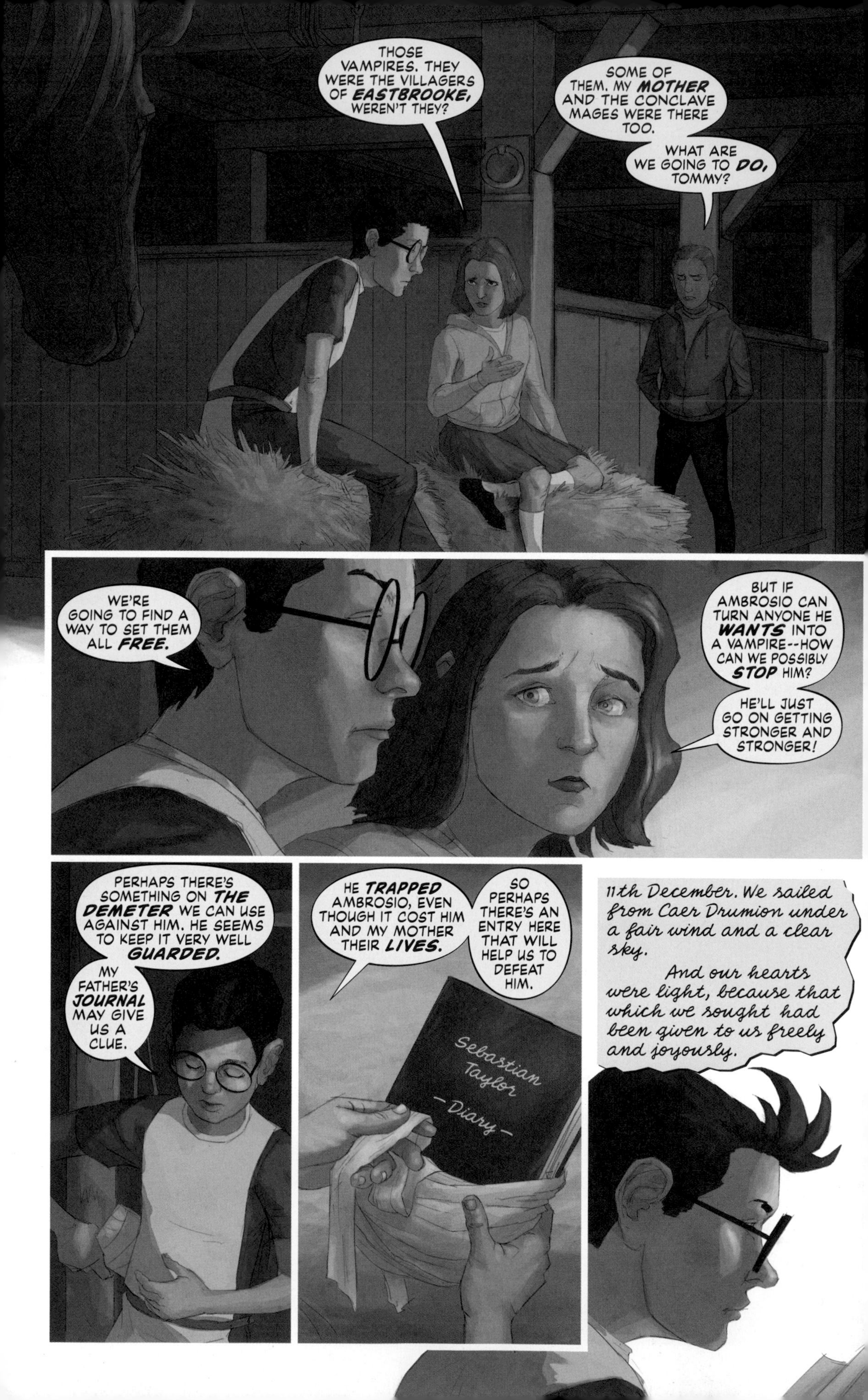
THOSE VAMPIRES. THEY WERE THE VILLAGERS OF EASTBROOKE, WEREN'T THEY?
SOME OF THEM. MY MOTHER AND THE CONCLAVE MAGES WERE THERE TOO.
WHAT ARE WE GOING TO DO, TOMMY?
WE'RE GOING TO FIND A WAY TO SET THEM ALL FREE.
BUT IF AMBROSIO CAN TURN ANYONE HE WANTS INTO A VAMPIRE--HOW CAN WE POSSIBLY STOP HIM?
HE'LL JUST GO ON GETTING STRONGER AND STRONGER!
PERHAPS THERE'S SOMETHING ON THE DEMETER WE CAN USE AGAINST HIM. HE SEEMS TO KEEP IT VERY WELL GUARDED.
MY FATHER'S JOURNAL MAY GIVE US A CLUE.
HE TRAPPED AMBROSIO, EVEN THOUGH IT COST HIM AND MY MOTHER THEIR LIVES.
SO PERHAPS THERE'S AN ENTRY HERE THAT WILL HELP US TO DEFEAT HIM.
Sebastian Taylor
-Diary-
11th December. We sailed from Caer Drumion under a fair wind and a clear sky.
And our hearts were light, because that which we sought had been given to us freely and joyously.

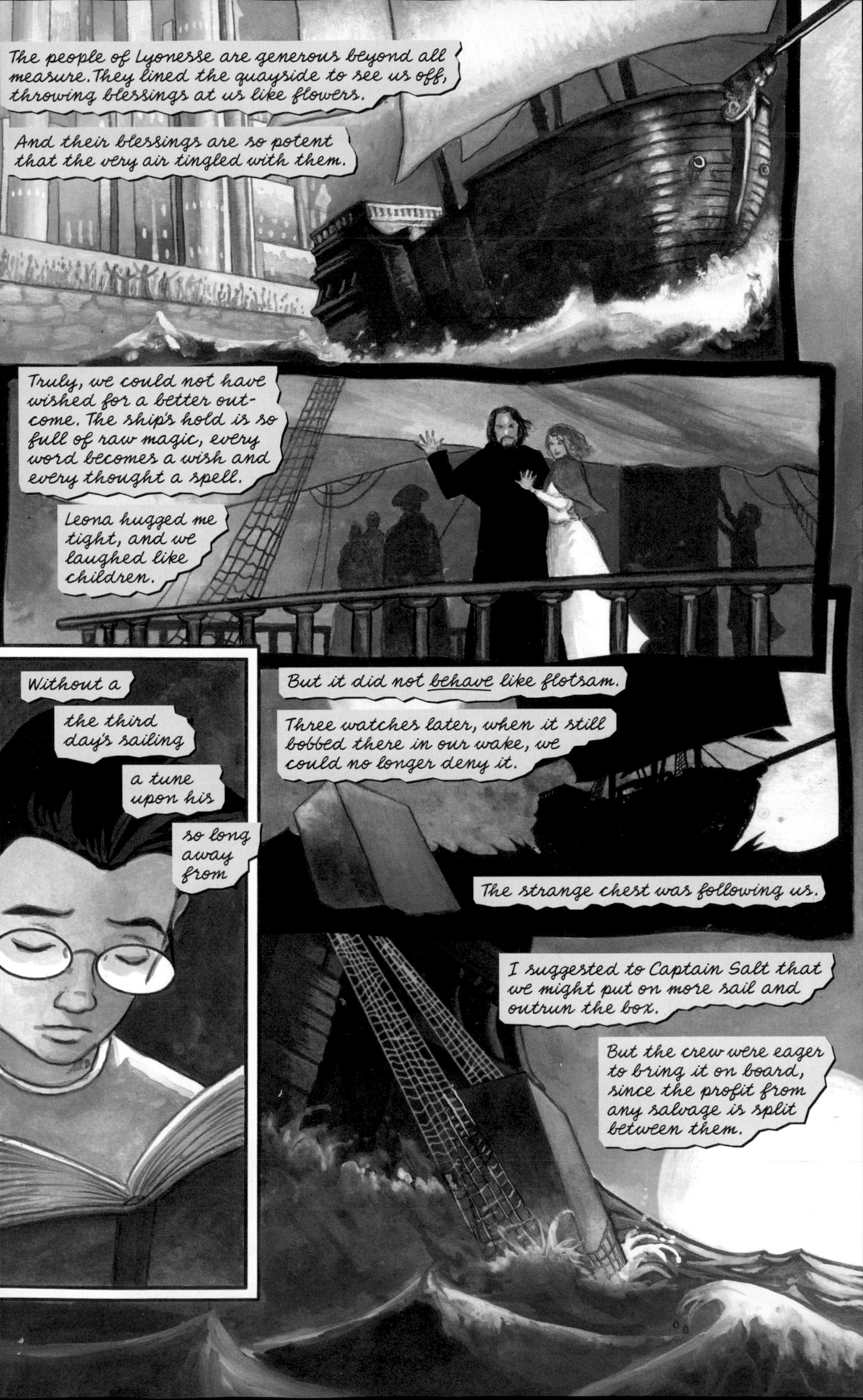
The people of Lyonesse are generous beyond all measure. They lined the quayside to see us off, throwing blessings at us like flowers.
And their blessings are so potent that the very air tingled with them.
Truly, we could not have wished for a better outcome. The ship's hold is so full of raw magic, every word becomes a wish and every thought a spell.
Leona hugged me tight, and we laughed like children.
Without a
the third day's sailing
a tune upon his
so long away from
But it did not behave like flotsam.
Three watches later, when it still bobbed there in our wake, we could no longer deny it.
The strange chest was following us.
I suggested to Captain Salt that we might put on more sail and outrun the box.
But the crew were eager to bring it on board, since the profit from any salvage is split between them.

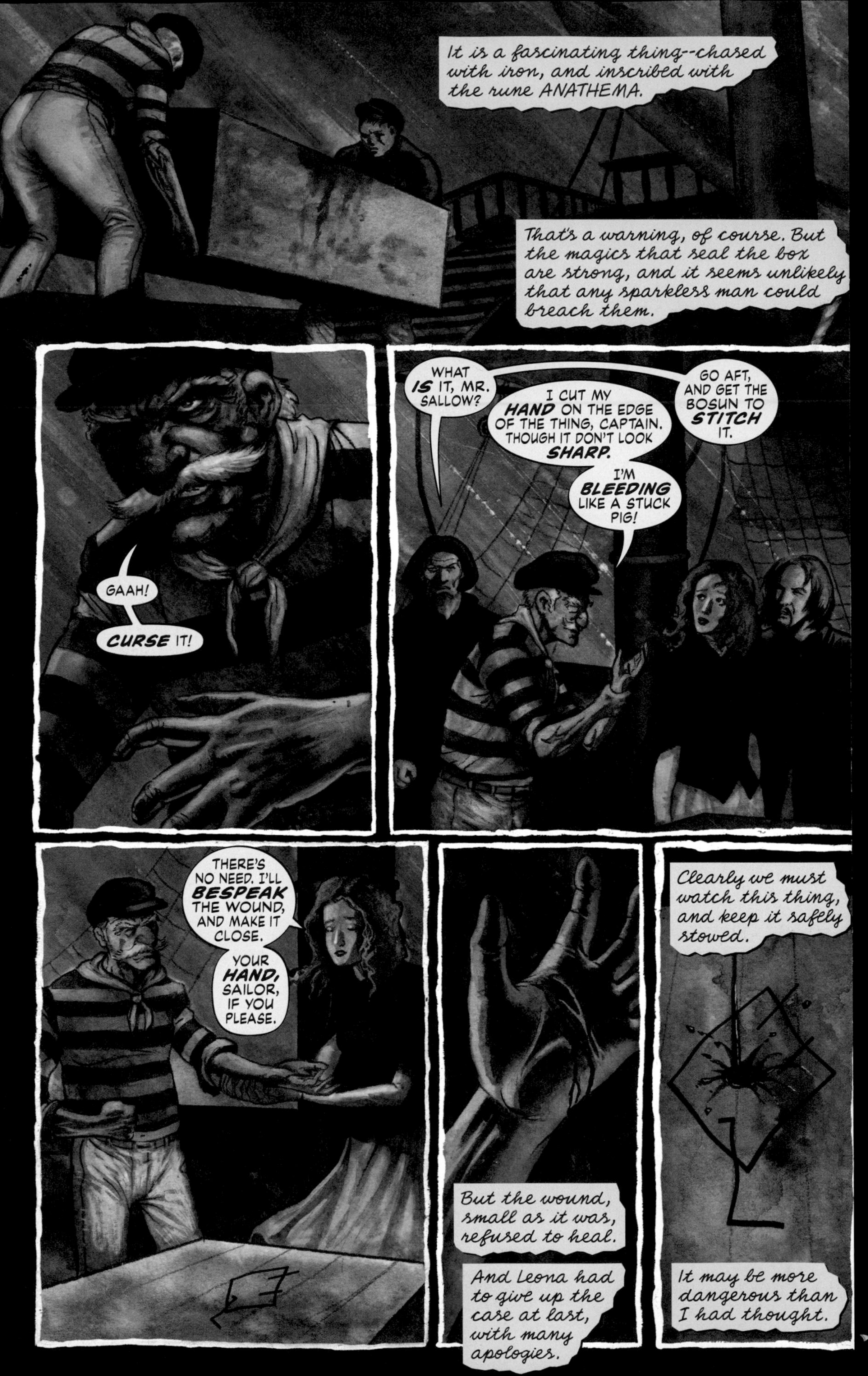
It is a fascinating thing--chased with iron, and inscribed with the rune ANATHEMA.
That's a warning, of course. But the magics that seal the box are strong, and it seems unlikely that any sparkless man could breach them.
GAAH!
CURSE IT!
WHAT IS IT, MR. SALLOW?
I CUT MY HAND ON THE EDGE OF THE THING, CAPTAIN. THOUGH IT DON'T LOOK SHARP.
I'M BLEEDING LIKE A STUCK PIG!
GO AFT, AND GET THE BOSUN TO STITCH IT.
THERE'S NO NEED. I'LL BESPEAK THE WOUND, AND MAKE IT CLOSE.
YOUR HAND, SAILOR, IF YOU PLEASE.
But the wound, small as it was, refused to heal.
And Leona had to give up the case at last, with many apologies.
Clearly we must watch this thing, and keep it safely stowed.
It may be more dangerous than I had thought.

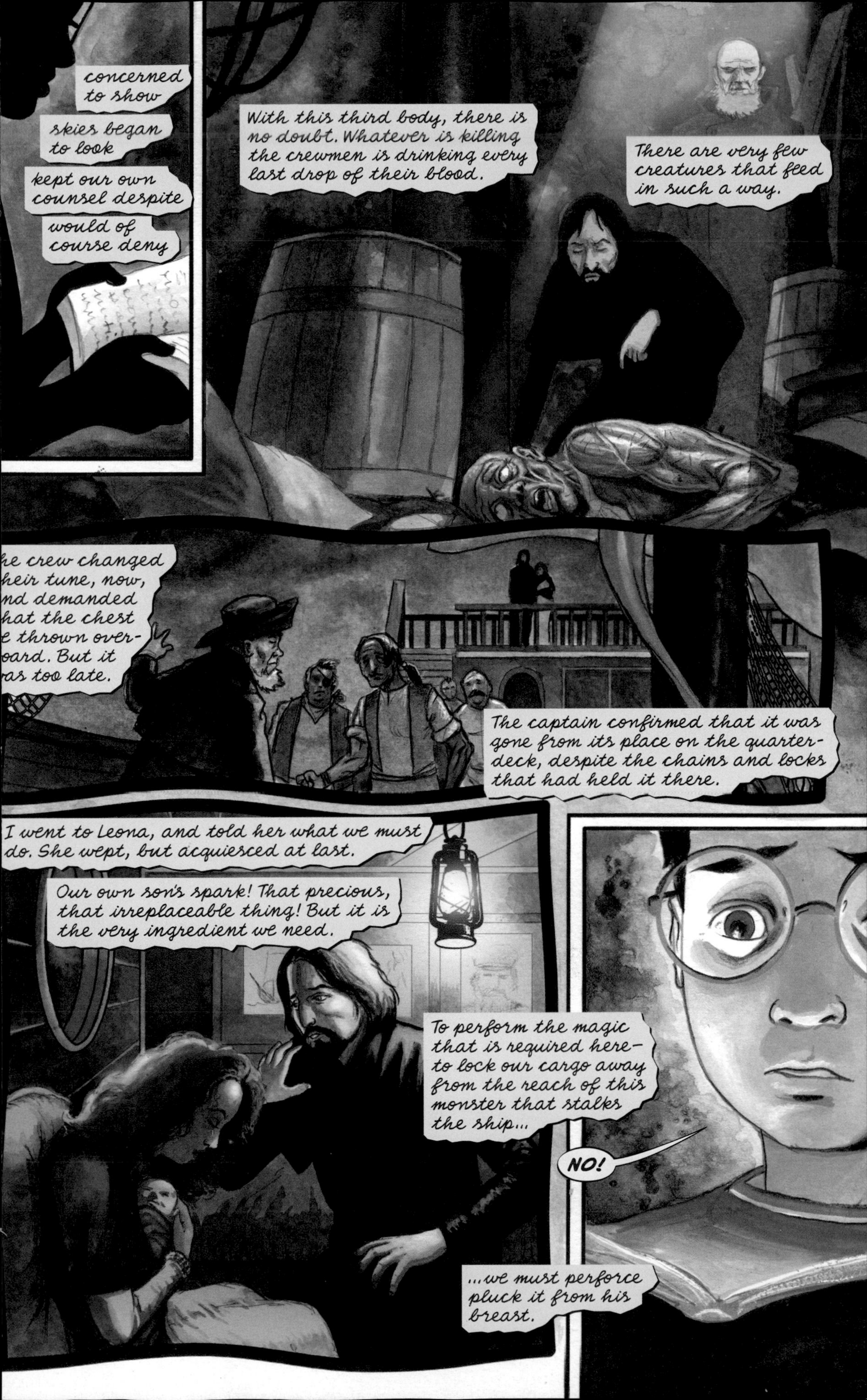
concerned to show
skies began to look
kept our own counsel despite
would of course deny
With this third body, there is no doubt. Whatever is killing the crewmen is drinking every last drop of their blood.
There are very few creatures that feed in such a way.
he crew changed heir tune, now, nd demanded hat the chest e thrown over- oard. But it as too late.
The captain confirmed that it was gone from its place on the quarter-deck, despite the chains and locks that had held it there.
I went to Leona, and told her what we must do. She wept, but acquiesced at last.
Our own son's spark! That precious, that irreplaceable thing! But it is the very ingredient we need.
To perform the magic that is required here- to lock our cargo away from the reach of this monster that stalks the ship...
NO!
...we must perforce pluck it from his breast.

NOOOOOO!

TOMMY, WHAT IS IT? WHAT'S THE *MATTER?*

MY--MY OWN *FATHER!* SEBASTIAN TAYLOR!

HE STOLE MY *SPARK!* HE DREW THE *MAGIC* OUT OF ME!

WHY? WHY WOULD HE *DO* THAT?

TO FIGHT *AMBROSIO.* WHEN THEY FIRST MET HIM, ON THE SHIP.

MY PARENTS DIDN'T HAVE ENOUGH MAGIC OF THEIR *OWN,* SO THEY TOOK MINE.

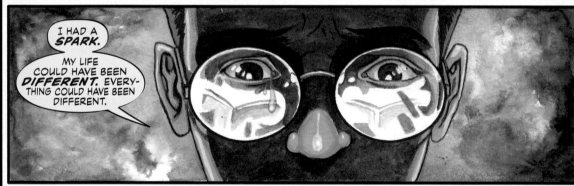

I HAD A *SPARK.*

MY LIFE COULD HAVE BEEN *DIFFERENT.* EVERYTHING COULD HAVE BEEN DIFFERENT.

OH, TOMMY!

DON'T SAY *ANYTHING,* SUE. PLEASE!

I...I DON'T WANT TO *TALK* RIGHT NOW.

SINCE WORDS WERE OF NO *USE* TO HER FRIEND, SUE HELD HIM CLOSE.

UNTIL THE WRENCHING *TEARS* STOPPED, AND HE WAS STILL AGAIN.

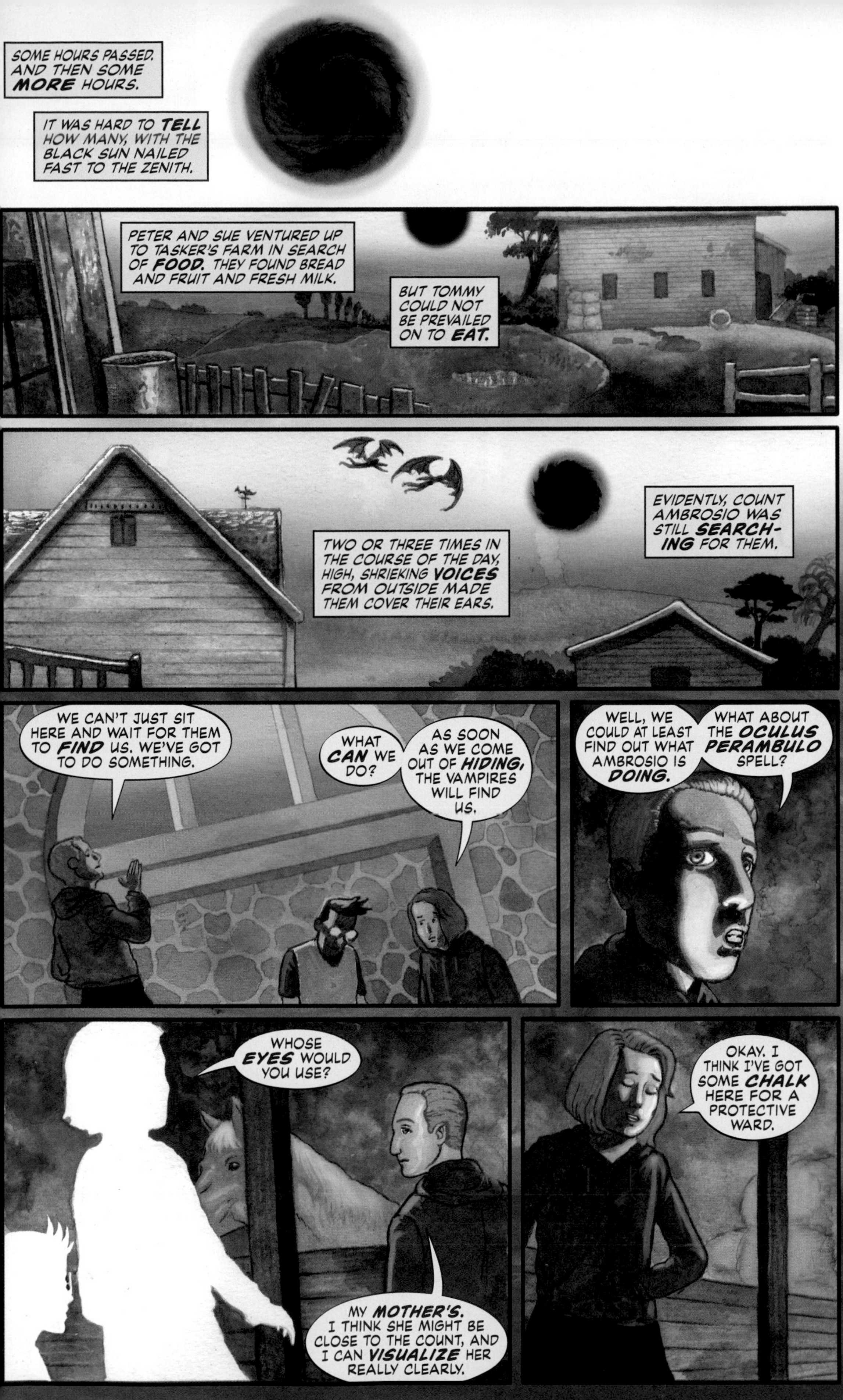
SOME HOURS PASSED. AND THEN SOME MORE HOURS.
IT WAS HARD TO TELL HOW MANY, WITH THE BLACK SUN NAILED FAST TO THE ZENITH.
PETER AND SUE VENTURED UP TO TASKER'S FARM IN SEARCH OF FOOD. THEY FOUND BREAD AND FRUIT AND FRESH MILK.
BUT TOMMY COULD NOT BE PREVAILED ON TO EAT.
TWO OR THREE TIMES IN THE COURSE OF THE DAY, HIGH, SHRIEKING VOICES FROM OUTSIDE MADE THEM COVER THEIR EARS.
EVIDENTLY, COUNT AMBROSIO WAS STILL SEARCHING FOR THEM.
WE CAN'T JUST SIT HERE AND WAIT FOR THEM TO FIND US. WE'VE GOT TO DO SOMETHING.
WHAT CAN WE DO?
AS SOON AS WE COME OUT OF HIDING, THE VAMPIRES WILL FIND US.
WELL, WE COULD AT LEAST FIND OUT WHAT AMBROSIO IS DOING.
WHAT ABOUT THE OCULUS PERAMBULO SPELL?
WHOSE EYES WOULD YOU USE?
MY MOTHER'S. I THINK SHE MIGHT BE CLOSE TO THE COUNT, AND I CAN VISUALIZE HER REALLY CLEARLY.
OKAY. I THINK I'VE GOT SOME CHALK HERE FOR A PROTECTIVE WARD.

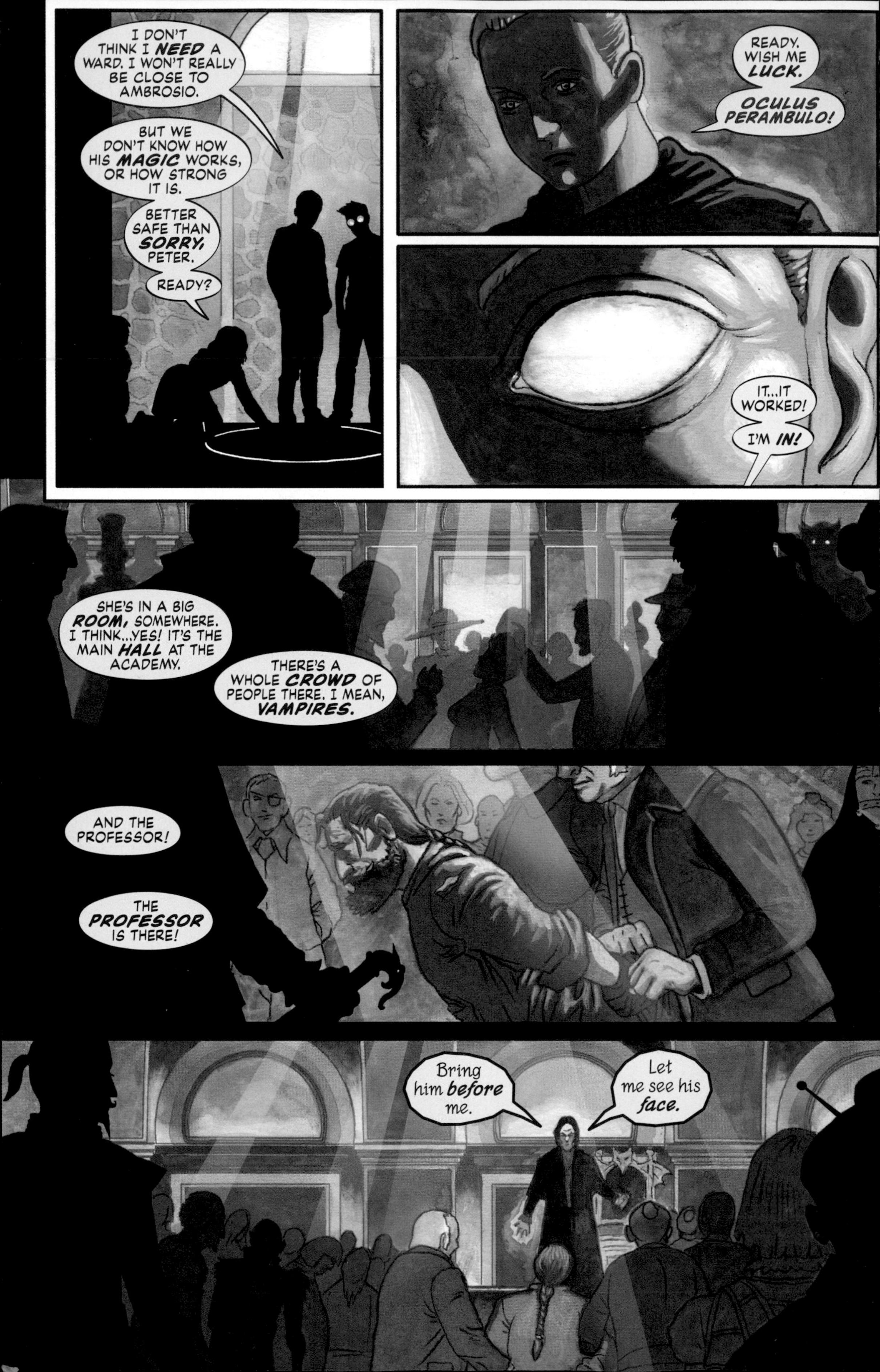
I DON'T THINK I NEED A WARD. I WON'T REALLY BE CLOSE TO AMBROSIO.
BUT WE DON'T KNOW HOW HIS MAGIC WORKS, OR HOW STRONG IT IS.
BETTER SAFE THAN SORRY, PETER.
READY?
READY. WISH ME LUCK.
OCULUS PERAMBULO!
IT...IT WORKED!
I'M IN!
SHE'S IN A BIG ROOM, SOMEWHERE. I THINK...YES! IT'S THE MAIN HALL AT THE ACADEMY.
THERE'S A WHOLE CROWD OF PEOPLE THERE. I MEAN, VAMPIRES.
AND THE PROFESSOR!
THE PROFESSOR IS THERE!
Bring him before me.
Let me see his face.

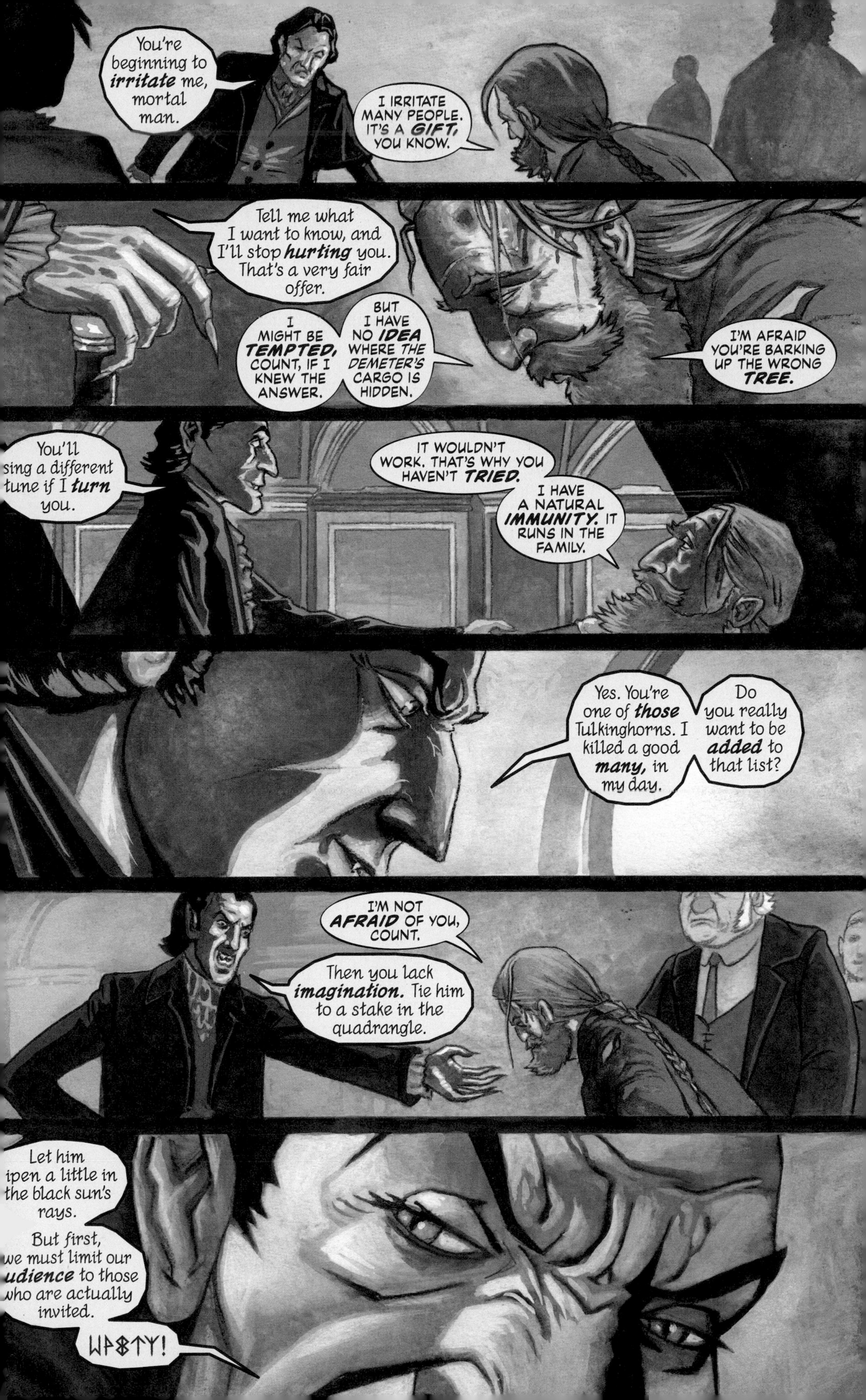
You're beginning to irritate me, mortal man.
I IRRITATE MANY PEOPLE. IT'S A GIFT, YOU KNOW.
Tell me what I want to know, and I'll stop hurting you. That's a very fair offer.
I MIGHT BE TEMPTED, COUNT, IF I KNEW THE ANSWER.
BUT I HAVE NO IDEA WHERE THE DEMETER'S CARGO IS HIDDEN.
I'M AFRAID YOU'RE BARKING UP THE WRONG TREE.
You'll sing a different tune if I turn you.
IT WOULDN'T WORK. THAT'S WHY YOU HAVEN'T TRIED.
I HAVE A NATURAL IMMUNITY. IT RUNS IN THE FAMILY.
Yes. You're one of those Tulkinghorns. I killed a good many, in my day.
Do you really want to be added to that list?
I'M NOT AFRAID OF YOU, COUNT.
Then you lack imagination. Tie him to a stake in the quadrangle.
Let him ipen a little in the black sun's rays.
But first, we must limit our udience to those who are actually invited.

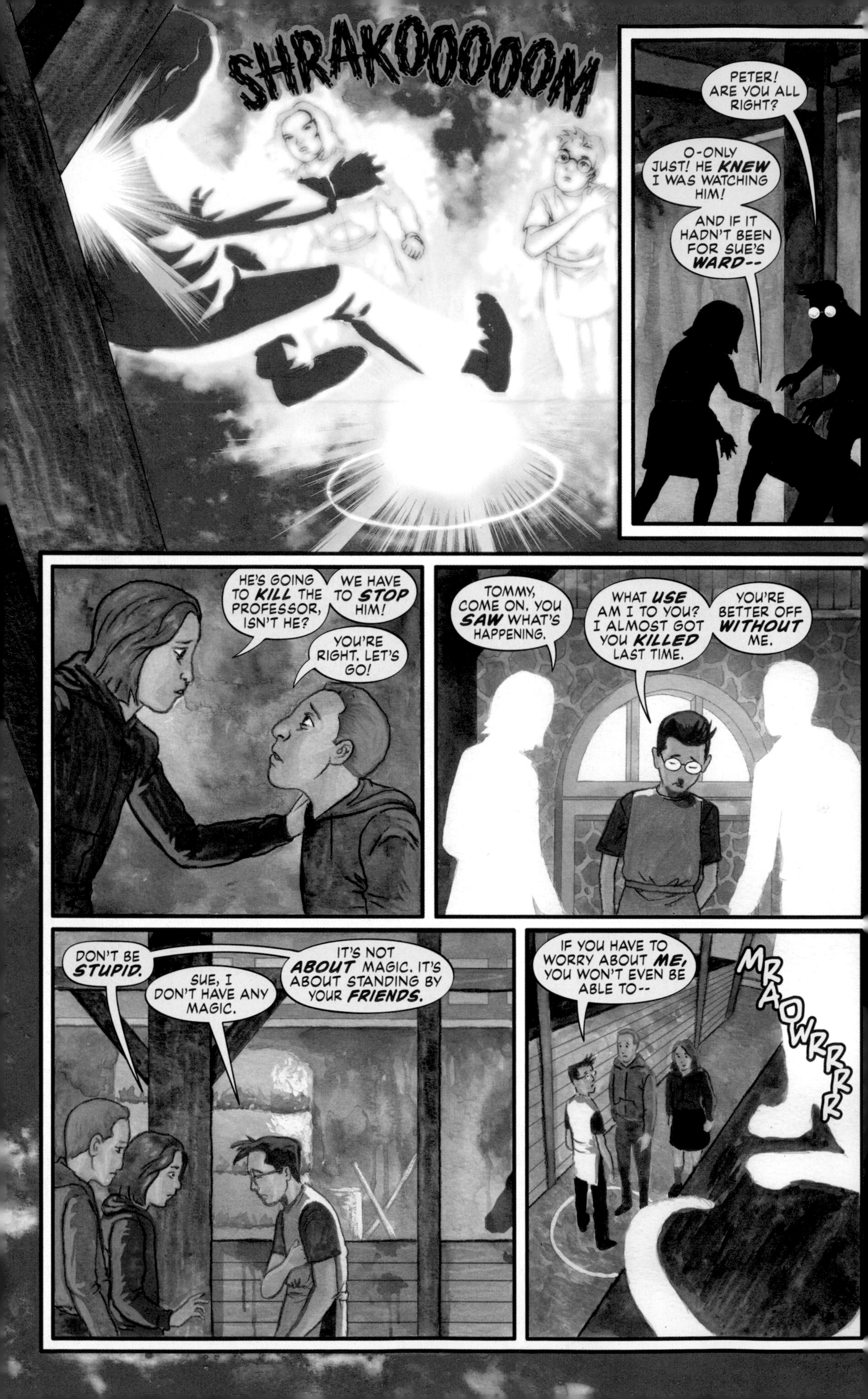
SHRAKOOOOOM
PETER! ARE YOU ALL RIGHT?
O-ONLY JUST! HE **KNEW** I WAS WATCHING HIM!
AND IF IT HADN'T BEEN FOR SUE'S ***WARD--***
HE'S GOING TO ***KILL*** THE PROFESSOR, ISN'T HE?
WE HAVE TO ***STOP*** HIM!
YOU'RE RIGHT. LET'S GO!
TOMMY, COME ON. YOU ***SAW*** WHAT'S HAPPENING.
WHAT ***USE*** AM I TO YOU? I ALMOST GOT YOU ***KILLED*** LAST TIME.
YOU'RE BETTER OFF ***WITHOUT*** ME.
DON'T BE ***STUPID.***
SUE, I DON'T HAVE ANY MAGIC.
IT'S NOT ***ABOUT*** MAGIC. IT'S ABOUT STANDING BY YOUR ***FRIENDS.***
IF YOU HAVE TO WORRY ABOUT ***ME,*** YOU WON'T EVEN BE ABLE TO--
MRAOWRRRR

IT'S *MINGUS!*

WHO?

MY FATHER'S *FAMILIAR.* SHE SAVED MY LIFE WHEN AMBROSIO ATTACKED ME.

HERE, GIRL!

MRAOWRR

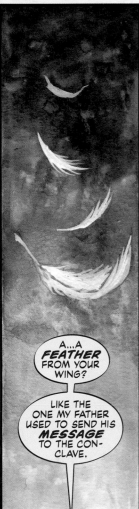

A...A *FEATHER* FROM YOUR WING?

LIKE THE ONE MY FATHER USED TO SEND HIS *MESSAGE* TO THE CONCLAVE.

IS THIS--?

ARE YOU TELLING ME--?

PENNA EXAUDI.

PENNA VOLENTI.

PENNA PERLOQUI.

AAAA!

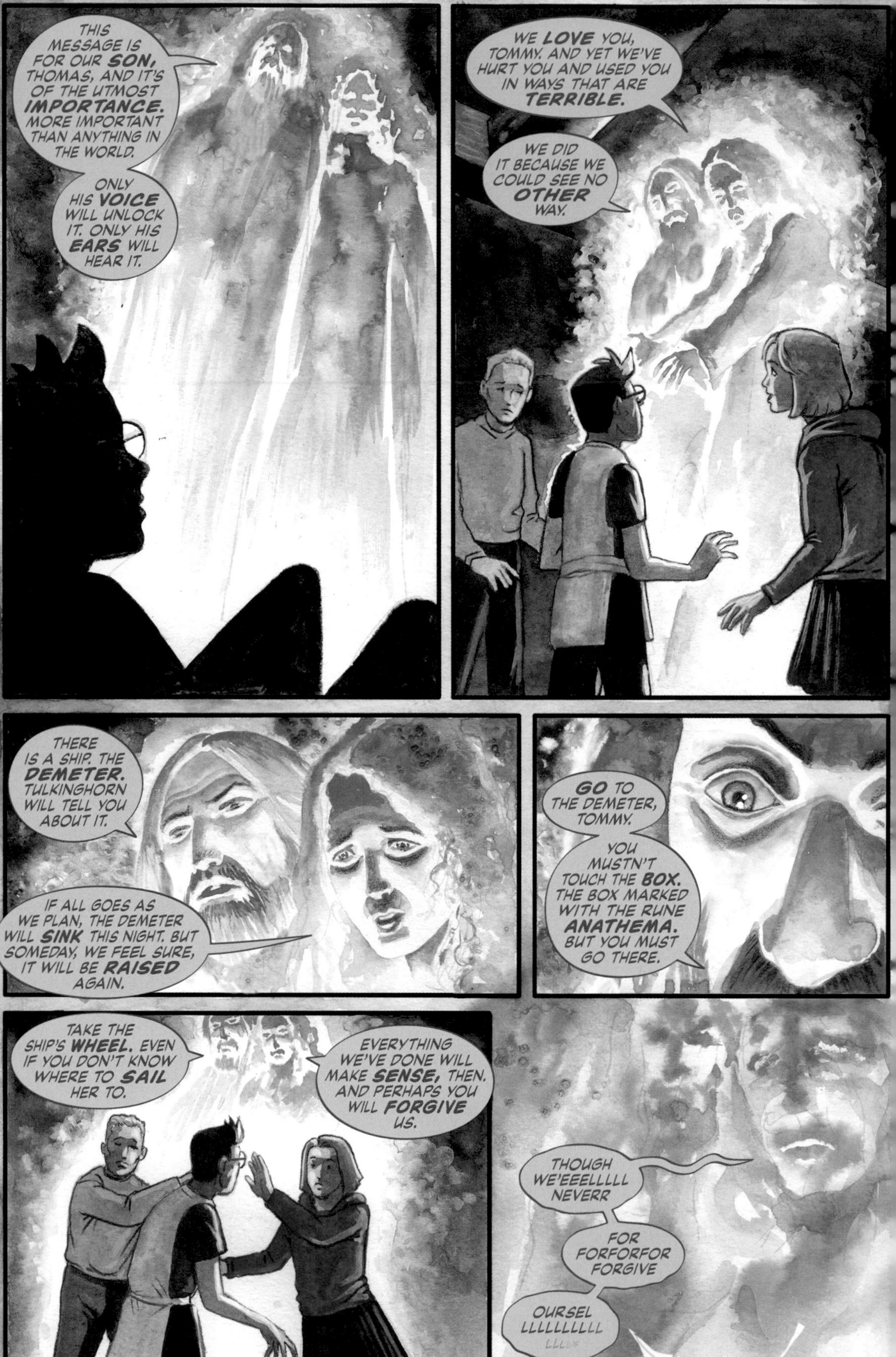
THIS MESSAGE IS FOR OUR SON, THOMAS, AND IT'S OF THE UTMOST IMPORTANCE. MORE IMPORTANT THAN ANYTHING IN THE WORLD.
ONLY HIS VOICE WILL UNLOCK IT. ONLY HIS EARS WILL HEAR IT.
WE LOVE YOU, TOMMY. AND YET WE'VE HURT YOU AND USED YOU IN WAYS THAT ARE TERRIBLE.
WE DID IT BECAUSE WE COULD SEE NO OTHER WAY.
THERE IS A SHIP. THE DEMETER. TULKINGHORN WILL TELL YOU ABOUT IT.
IF ALL GOES AS WE PLAN, THE DEMETER WILL SINK THIS NIGHT. BUT SOMEDAY, WE FEEL SURE, IT WILL BE RAISED AGAIN.
GO TO THE DEMETER, TOMMY.
YOU MUSTN'T TOUCH THE BOX. THE BOX MARKED WITH THE RUNE ANATHEMA. BUT YOU MUST GO THERE.
TAKE THE SHIP'S WHEEL. EVEN IF YOU DON'T KNOW WHERE TO SAIL HER TO.
EVERYTHING WE'VE DONE WILL MAKE SENSE, THEN. AND PERHAPS YOU WILL FORGIVE US.
THOUGH WE'EEELLLLL NEVERR
FOR FORFORFOR FORGIVE
OURSEL LLLLLLLLLL LLLL

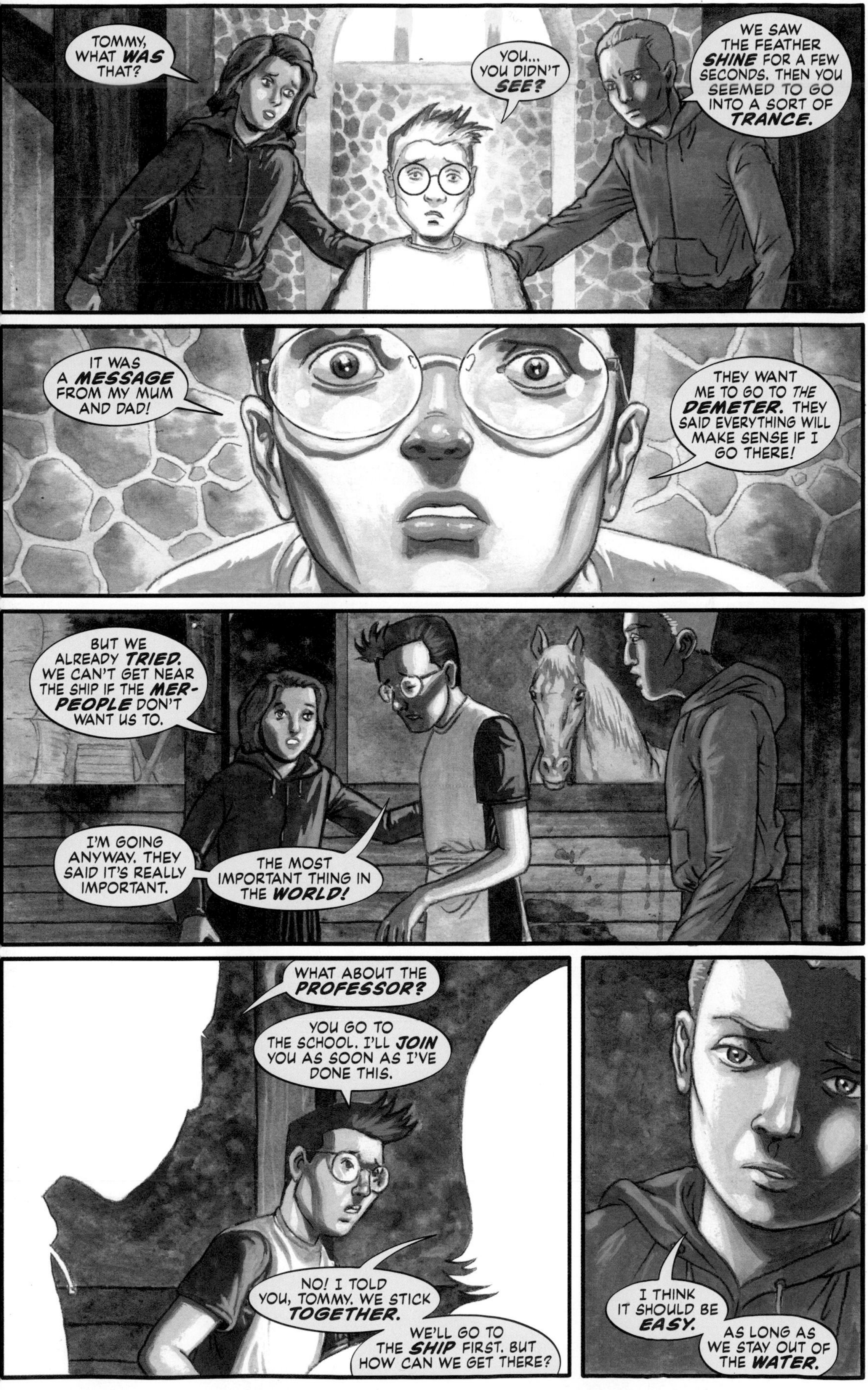
TOMMY, WHAT WAS THAT?
YOU... YOU DIDN'T SEE?
WE SAW THE FEATHER SHINE FOR A FEW SECONDS. THEN YOU SEEMED TO GO INTO A SORT OF TRANCE.
IT WAS A MESSAGE FROM MY MUM AND DAD!
THEY WANT ME TO GO TO THE DEMETER. THEY SAID EVERYTHING WILL MAKE SENSE IF I GO THERE!
BUT WE ALREADY TRIED. WE CAN'T GET NEAR THE SHIP IF THE MER-PEOPLE DON'T WANT US TO.
I'M GOING ANYWAY. THEY SAID IT'S REALLY IMPORTANT.
THE MOST IMPORTANT THING IN THE WORLD!
WHAT ABOUT THE PROFESSOR?
YOU GO TO THE SCHOOL. I'LL JOIN YOU AS SOON AS I'VE DONE THIS.
NO! I TOLD YOU, TOMMY. WE STICK TOGETHER.
WE'LL GO TO THE SHIP FIRST. BUT HOW CAN WE GET THERE?
I THINK IT SHOULD BE EASY.
AS LONG AS WE STAY OUT OF THE WATER.

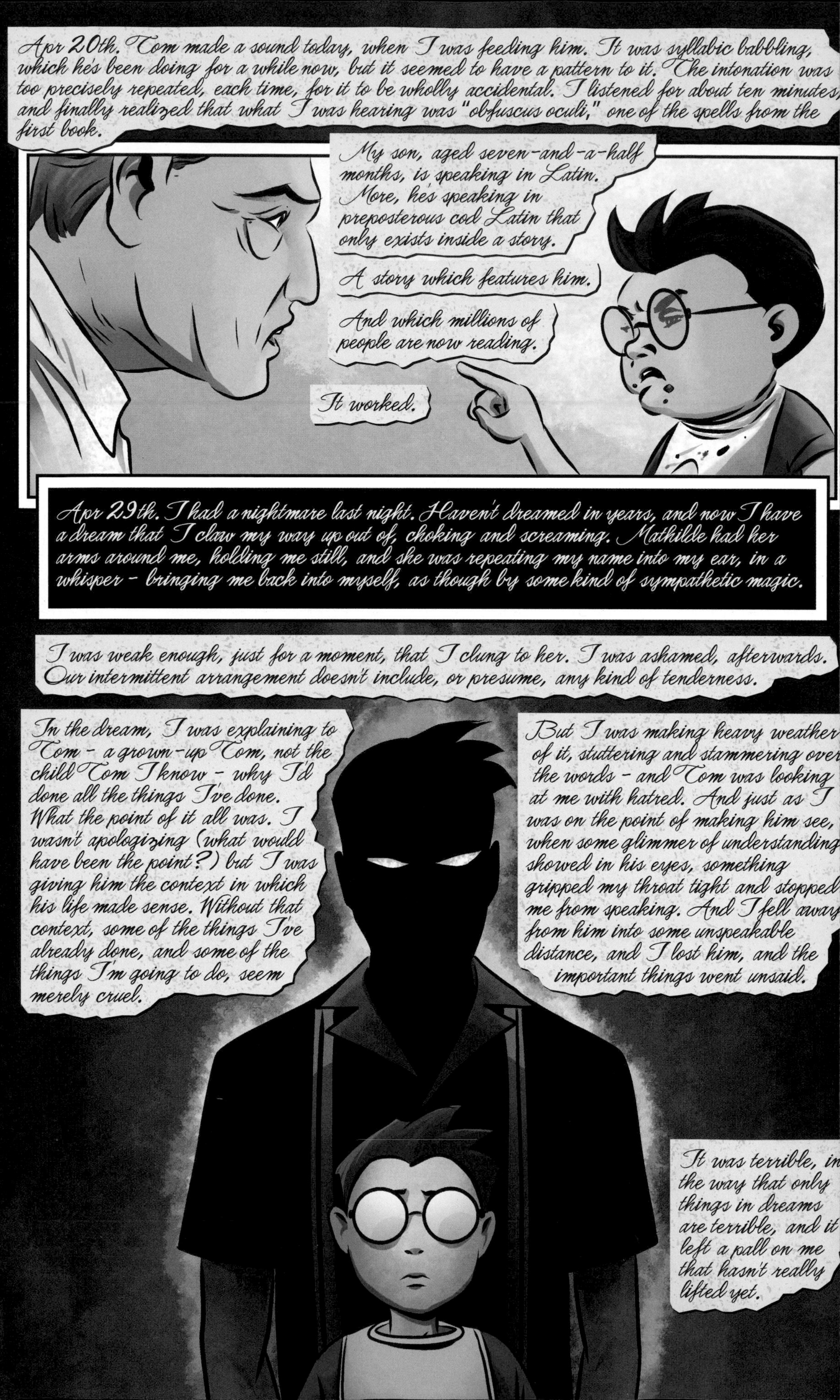
Apr 20th. Tom made a sound today, when I was feeding him. It was syllabic babbling, which he's been doing for a while now, but it seemed to have a pattern to it. The intonation was too precisely repeated, each time, for it to be wholly accidental. I listened for about ten minutes, and finally realized that what I was hearing was "obfuscus oculi," one of the spells from the first book.
My son, aged seven-and-a-half months, is speaking in Latin. More, he's speaking in preposterous cod Latin that only exists inside a story.
A story which features him.
And which millions of people are now reading.
It worked.
Apr 29th. I had a nightmare last night. Haven't dreamed in years, and now I have a dream that I claw my way up out of, choking and screaming. Mathilde had her arms around me, holding me still, and she was repeating my name into my ear, in a whisper - bringing me back into myself, as though by some kind of sympathetic magic.
I was weak enough, just for a moment, that I clung to her. I was ashamed, afterwards. Our intermittent arrangement doesn't include, or presume, any kind of tenderness.
In the dream, I was explaining to Tom - a grown-up Tom, not the child Tom I know - why I'd done all the things I've done. What the point of it all was. I wasn't apologizing (what would have been the point?) but I was giving him the context in which his life made sense. Without that context, some of the things I've already done, and some of the things I'm going to do, seem merely cruel.
But I was making heavy weather of it, stuttering and stammering over the words - and Tom was looking at me with hatred. And just as I was on the point of making him see, when some glimmer of understanding showed in his eyes, something gripped my throat tight and stopped me from speaking. And I fell away from him into some unspeakable distance, and I lost him, and the important things went unsaid.
It was terrible, in the way that only things in dreams are terrible, and it left a pall on me that hasn't really lifted yet.

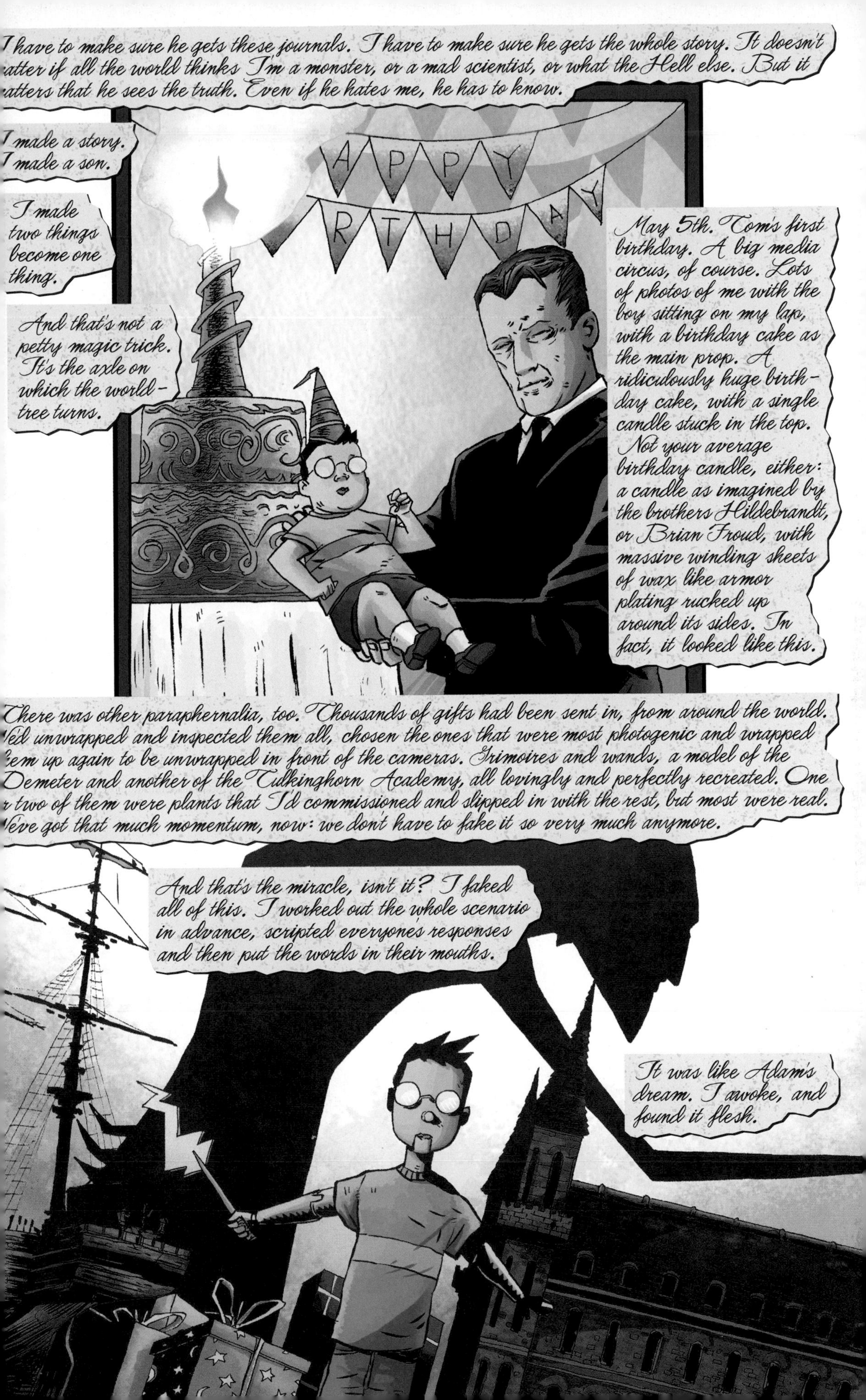
I have to make sure he gets these journals. I have to make sure he gets the whole story. It doesn't atter if all the world thinks I'm a monster, or a mad scientist, or what the Hell else. But it atters that he sees the truth. Even if he hates me, he has to know.
I made a story. I made a son.
I made two things become one thing.
And that's not a petty magic trick. It's the axle on which the world-tree turns.
APPY
RTHDAY
May 5th. Tom's first birthday. A big media circus, of course. Lots of photos of me with the boy sitting on my lap, with a birthday cake as the main prop. A ridiculously huge birth-day cake, with a single candle stuck in the top. Not your average birthday candle, either: a candle as imagined by the brothers Hildebrandt, or Brian Froud, with massive winding sheets of wax like armor plating rucked up around its sides. In fact, it looked like this.
There was other paraphernalia, too. Thousands of gifts had been sent in, from around the world. 'd unwrapped and inspected them all, chosen the ones that were most photogenic and wrapped em up again to be unwrapped in front of the cameras. Grimoires and wands, a model of the Demeter and another of the Tulkinghorn Academy, all lovingly and perfectly recreated. One r two of them were plants that I'd commissioned and slipped in with the rest, but most were real. 've got that much momentum, now: we don't have to fake it so very much anymore.
And that's the miracle, isn't it? I faked all of this. I worked out the whole scenario in advance, scripted everyone's responses and then put the words in their mouths.
It was like Adam's dream. I awoke, and found it flesh.

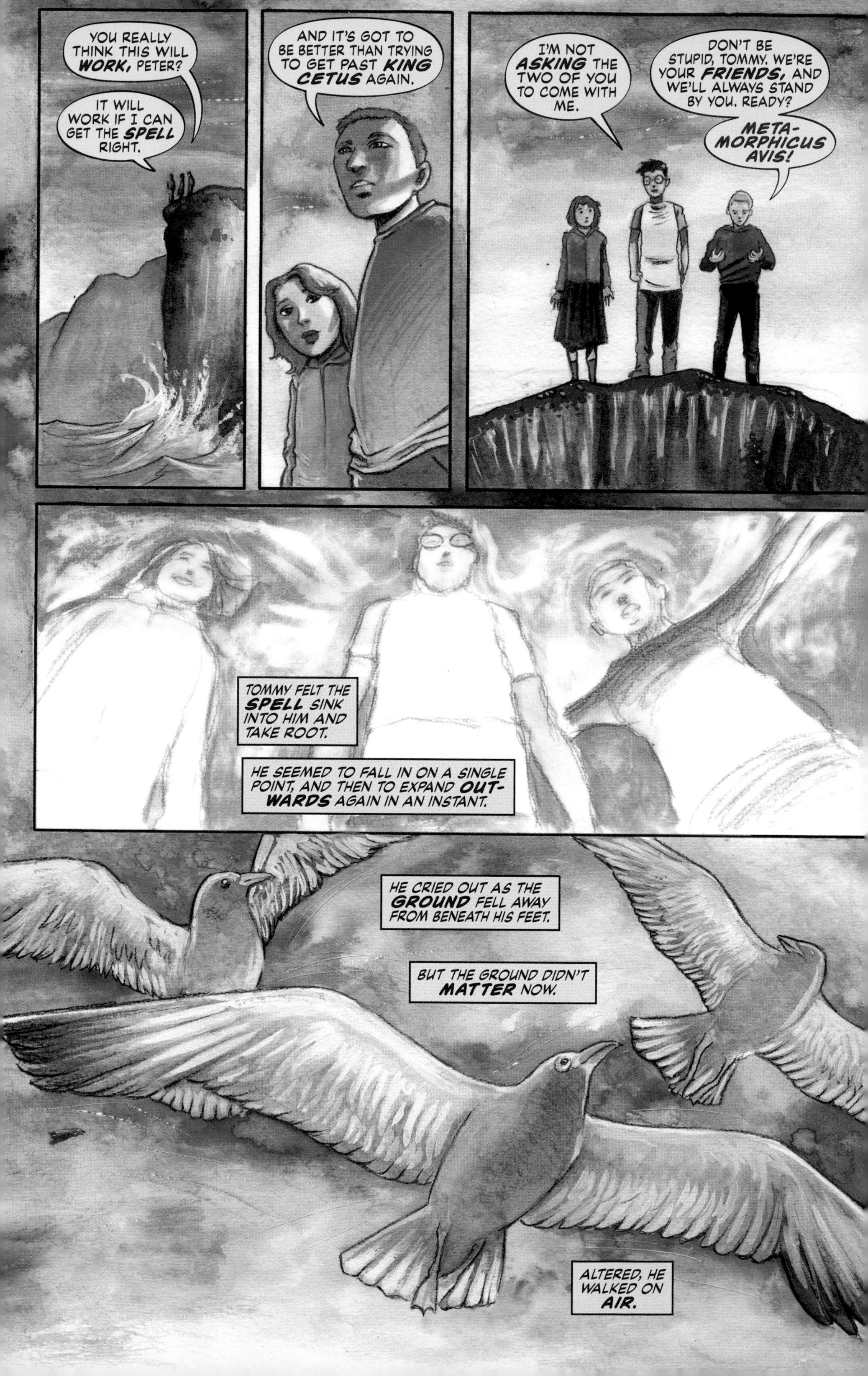
YOU REALLY THINK THIS WILL WORK, PETER?
IT WILL WORK IF I CAN GET THE SPELL RIGHT.
AND IT'S GOT TO BE BETTER THAN TRYING TO GET PAST KING CETUS AGAIN.
I'M NOT ASKING THE TWO OF YOU TO COME WITH ME.
DON'T BE STUPID, TOMMY. WE'RE YOUR FRIENDS, AND WE'LL ALWAYS STAND BY YOU. READY?
META-MORPHICUS AVIS!
TOMMY FELT THE SPELL SINK INTO HIM AND TAKE ROOT.
HE SEEMED TO FALL IN ON A SINGLE POINT, AND THEN TO EXPAND OUT-WARDS AGAIN IN AN INSTANT.
HE CRIED OUT AS THE GROUND FELL AWAY FROM BENEATH HIS FEET.
BUT THE GROUND DIDN'T MATTER NOW.
ALTERED, HE WALKED ON AIR.

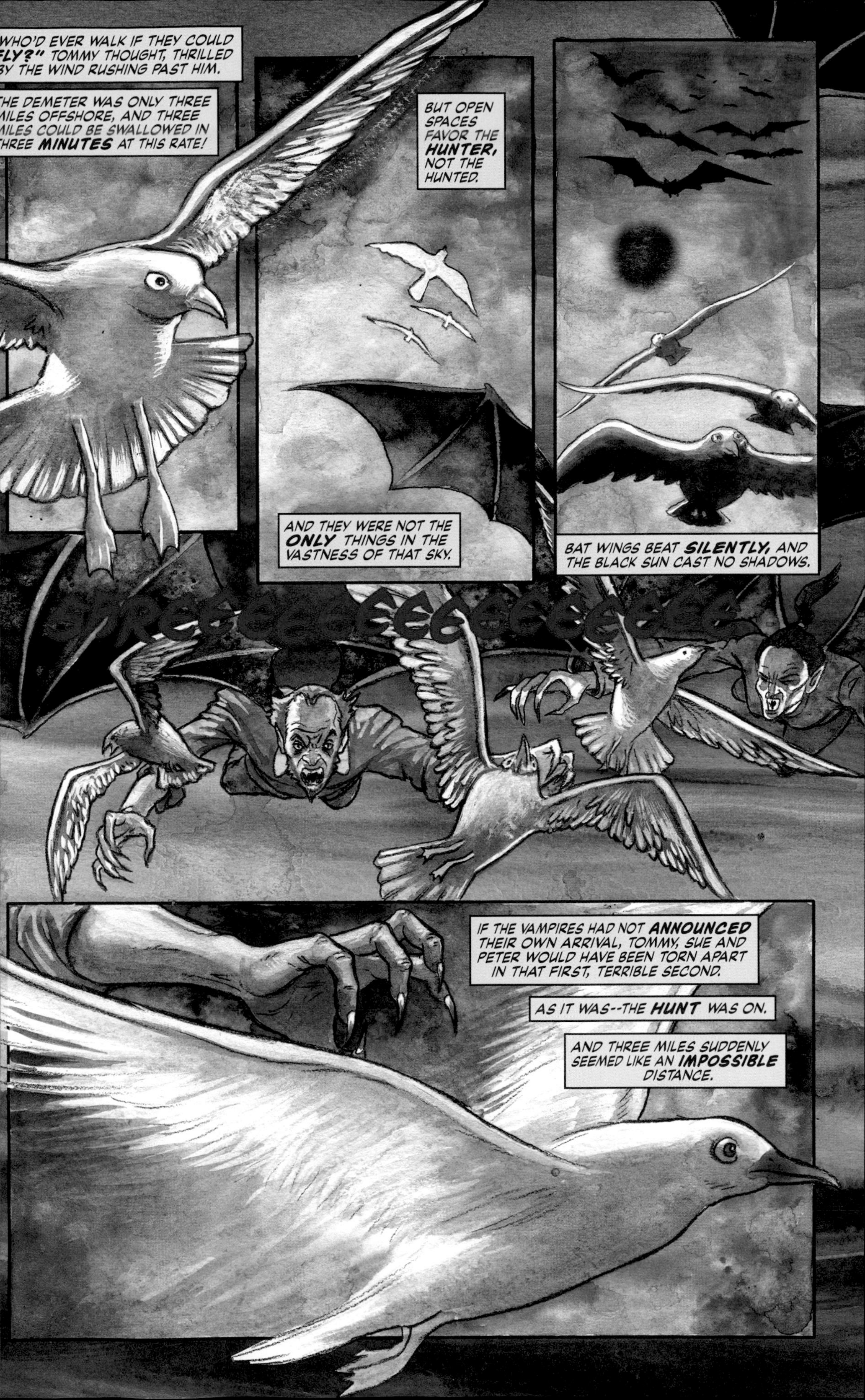
WHO'D EVER WALK IF THEY COULD FLY?" TOMMY THOUGHT, THRILLED BY THE WIND RUSHING PAST HIM.
THE DEMETER WAS ONLY THREE MILES OFFSHORE, AND THREE MILES COULD BE SWALLOWED IN THREE MINUTES AT THIS RATE!
BUT OPEN SPACES FAVOR THE HUNTER, NOT THE HUNTED.
AND THEY WERE NOT THE ONLY THINGS IN THE VASTNESS OF THAT SKY.
BAT WINGS BEAT SILENTLY, AND THE BLACK SUN CAST NO SHADOWS.
IF THE VAMPIRES HAD NOT ANNOUNCED THEIR OWN ARRIVAL, TOMMY, SUE AND PETER WOULD HAVE BEEN TORN APART IN THAT FIRST, TERRIBLE SECOND.
AS IT WAS--THE HUNT WAS ON.
AND THREE MILES SUDDENLY SEEMED LIKE AN IMPOSSIBLE DISTANCE.

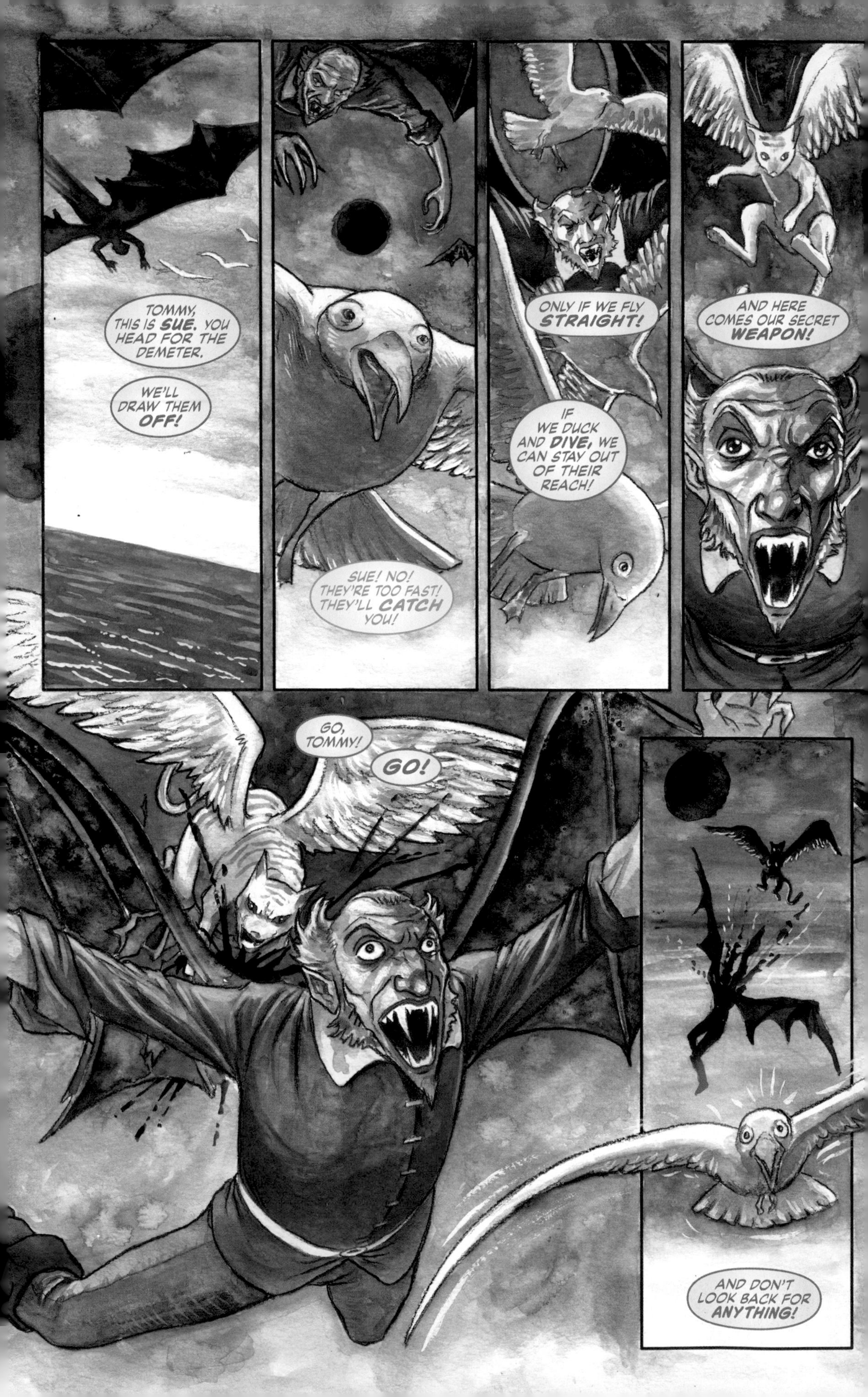
TOMMY, THIS IS SUE. YOU HEAD FOR THE DEMETER.
WE'LL DRAW THEM OFF!
SUE! NO! THEY'RE TOO FAST! THEY'LL CATCH YOU!
ONLY IF WE FLY STRAIGHT!
IF WE DUCK AND DIVE, WE CAN STAY OUT OF THEIR REACH!
AND HERE COMES OUR SECRET WEAPON!
GO, TOMMY!
GO!
AND DON'T LOOK BACK FOR ANYTHING!

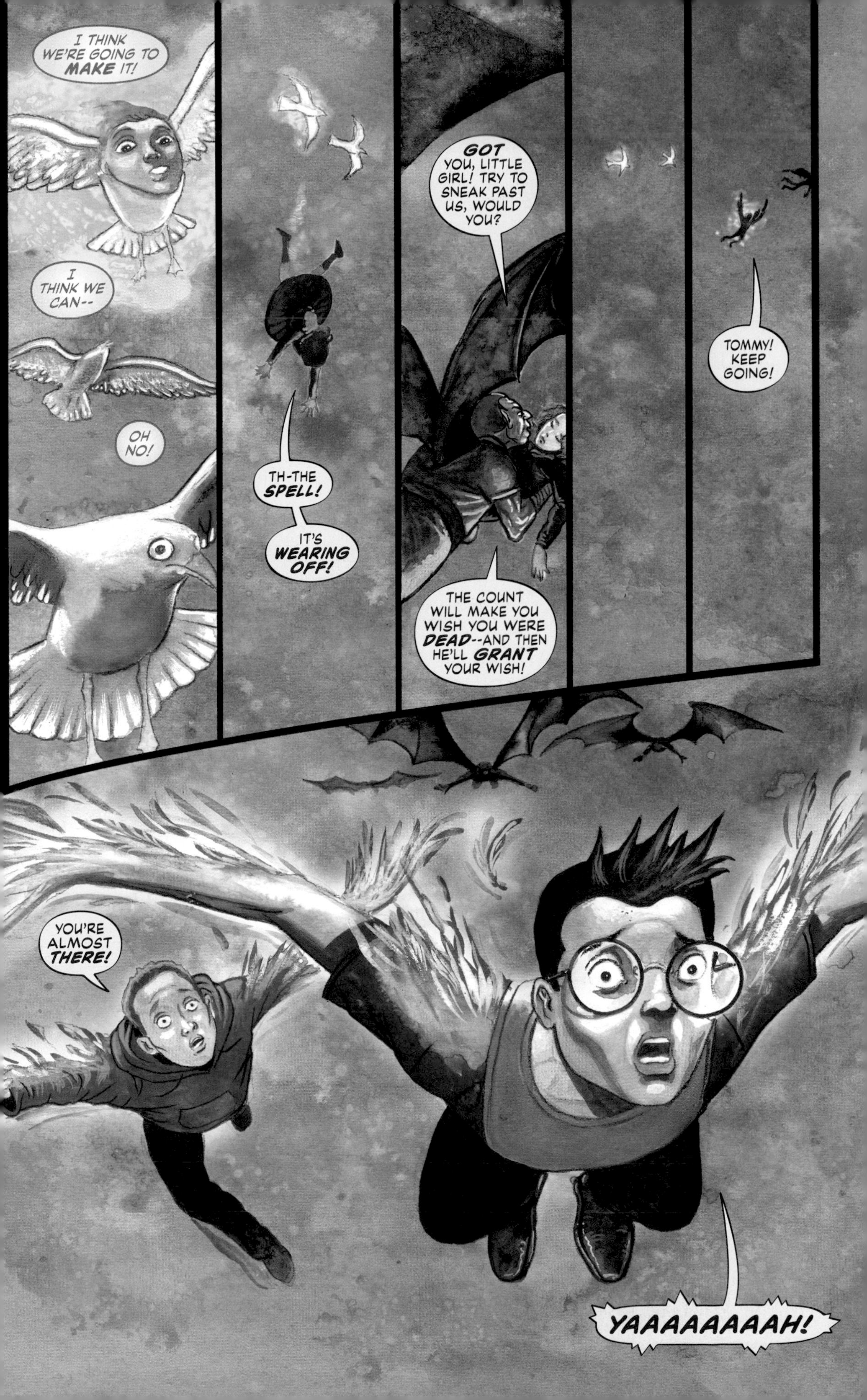
I THINK WE'RE GOING TO MAKE IT!
I THINK WE CAN--
OH NO!
TH-THE SPELL!
IT'S WEARING OFF!
GOT YOU, LITTLE GIRL! TRY TO SNEAK PAST US, WOULD YOU?
THE COUNT WILL MAKE YOU WISH YOU WERE DEAD--AND THEN HE'LL GRANT YOUR WISH!
TOMMY! KEEP GOING!
YOU'RE ALMOST THERE!
YAAAAAAAAH!

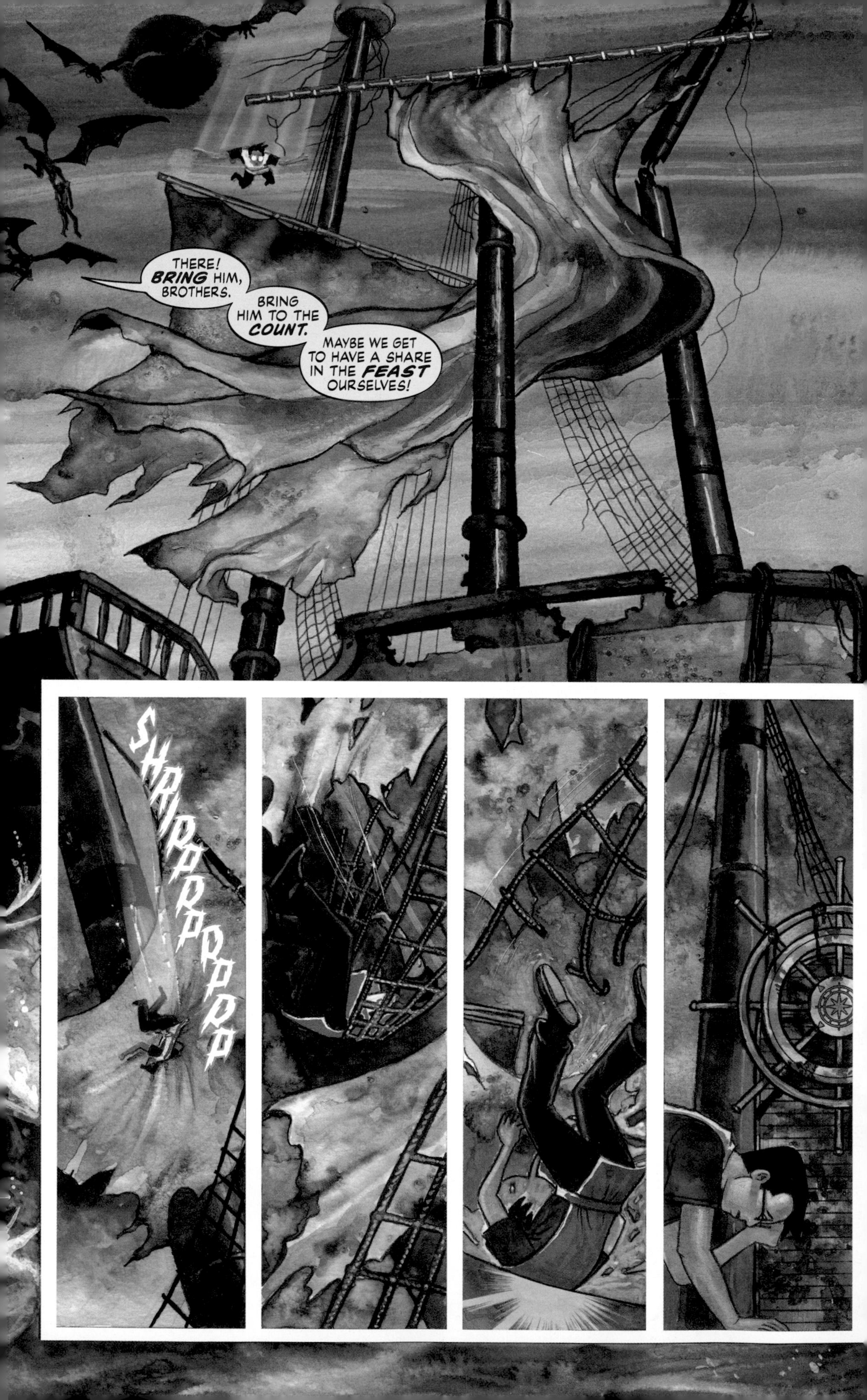
THERE! BRING HIM, BROTHERS.
BRING HIM TO THE COUNT.
MAYBE WE GET TO HAVE A SHARE IN THE FEAST OURSELVES!
SHRIPPPPPPP

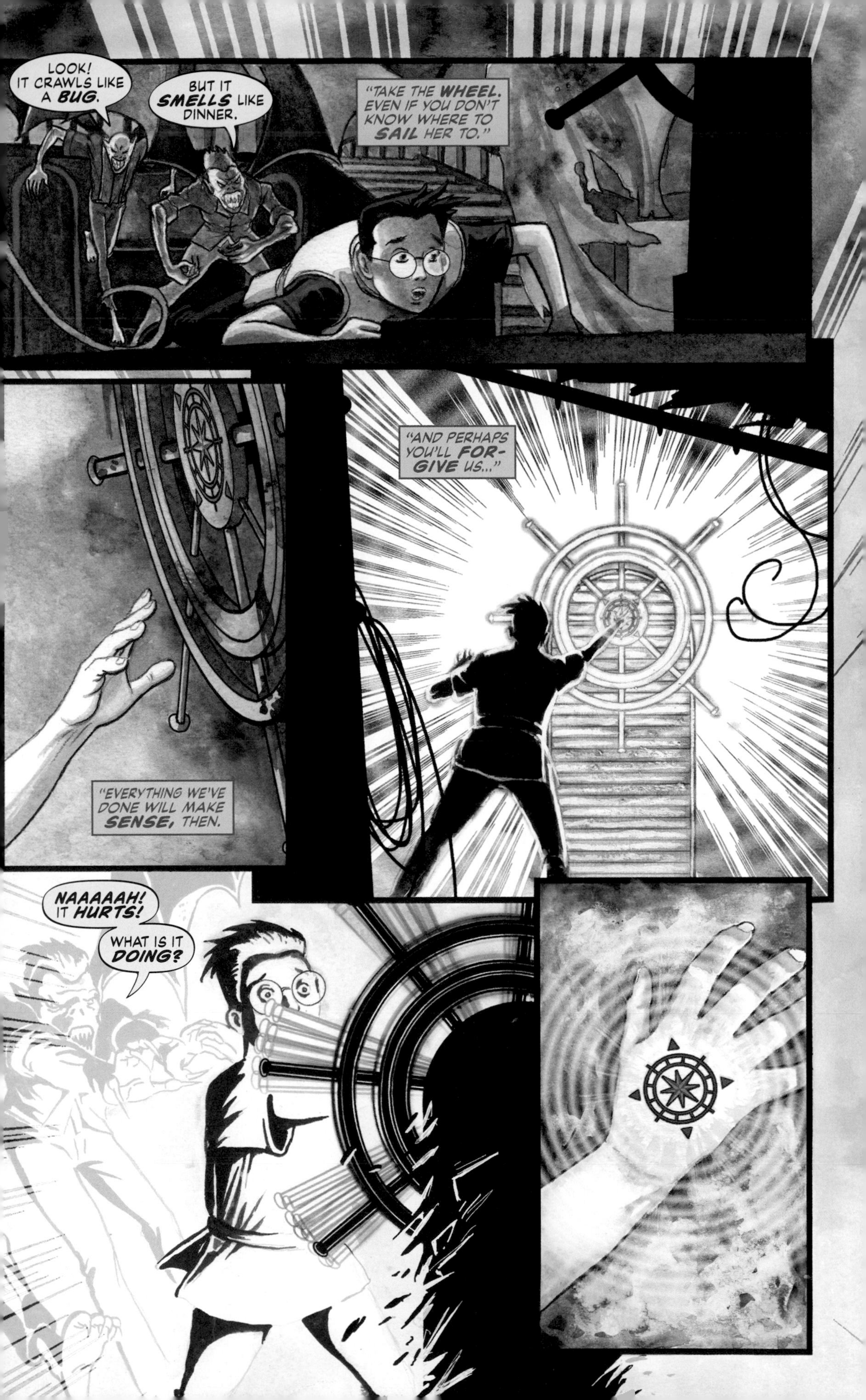
LOOK! IT CRAWLS LIKE A BUG.
BUT IT SMELLS LIKE DINNER.
"TAKE THE WHEEL. EVEN IF YOU DON'T KNOW WHERE TO SAIL HER TO."
"EVERYTHING WE'VE DONE WILL MAKE SENSE, THEN.
"AND PERHAPS YOU'LL FOR-GIVE US..."
NAAAAAH! IT HURTS!
WHAT IS IT DOING?

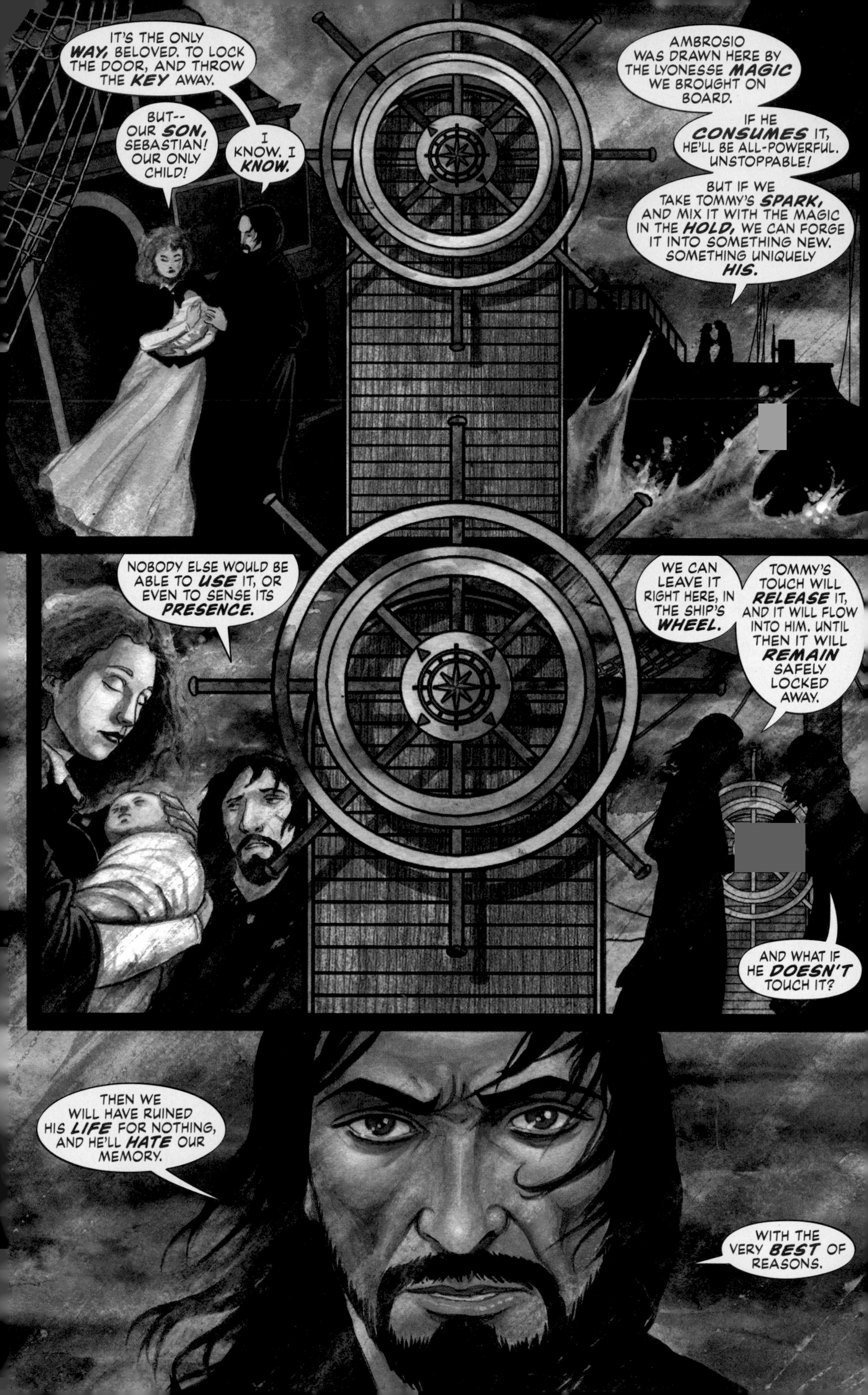

IT'S THE ONLY WAY, BELOVED. TO LOCK THE DOOR, AND THROW THE KEY AWAY.
BUT-- OUR SON, SEBASTIAN! OUR ONLY CHILD!
I KNOW. I KNOW.
AMBROSIO WAS DRAWN HERE BY THE LYONESSE MAGIC WE BROUGHT ON BOARD.
IF HE CONSUMES IT, HE'LL BE ALL-POWERFUL. UNSTOPPABLE!
BUT IF WE TAKE TOMMY'S SPARK, AND MIX IT WITH THE MAGIC IN THE HOLD, WE CAN FORGE IT INTO SOMETHING NEW. SOMETHING UNIQUELY HIS.
NOBODY ELSE WOULD BE ABLE TO USE IT, OR EVEN TO SENSE ITS PRESENCE.
WE CAN LEAVE IT RIGHT HERE, IN THE SHIP'S WHEEL.
TOMMY'S TOUCH WILL RELEASE IT, AND IT WILL FLOW INTO HIM. UNTIL THEN IT WILL REMAIN SAFELY LOCKED AWAY.
AND WHAT IF HE DOESN'T TOUCH IT?
THEN WE WILL HAVE RUINED HIS LIFE FOR NOTHING, AND HE'LL HATE OUR MEMORY.
WITH THE VERY BEST OF REASONS.

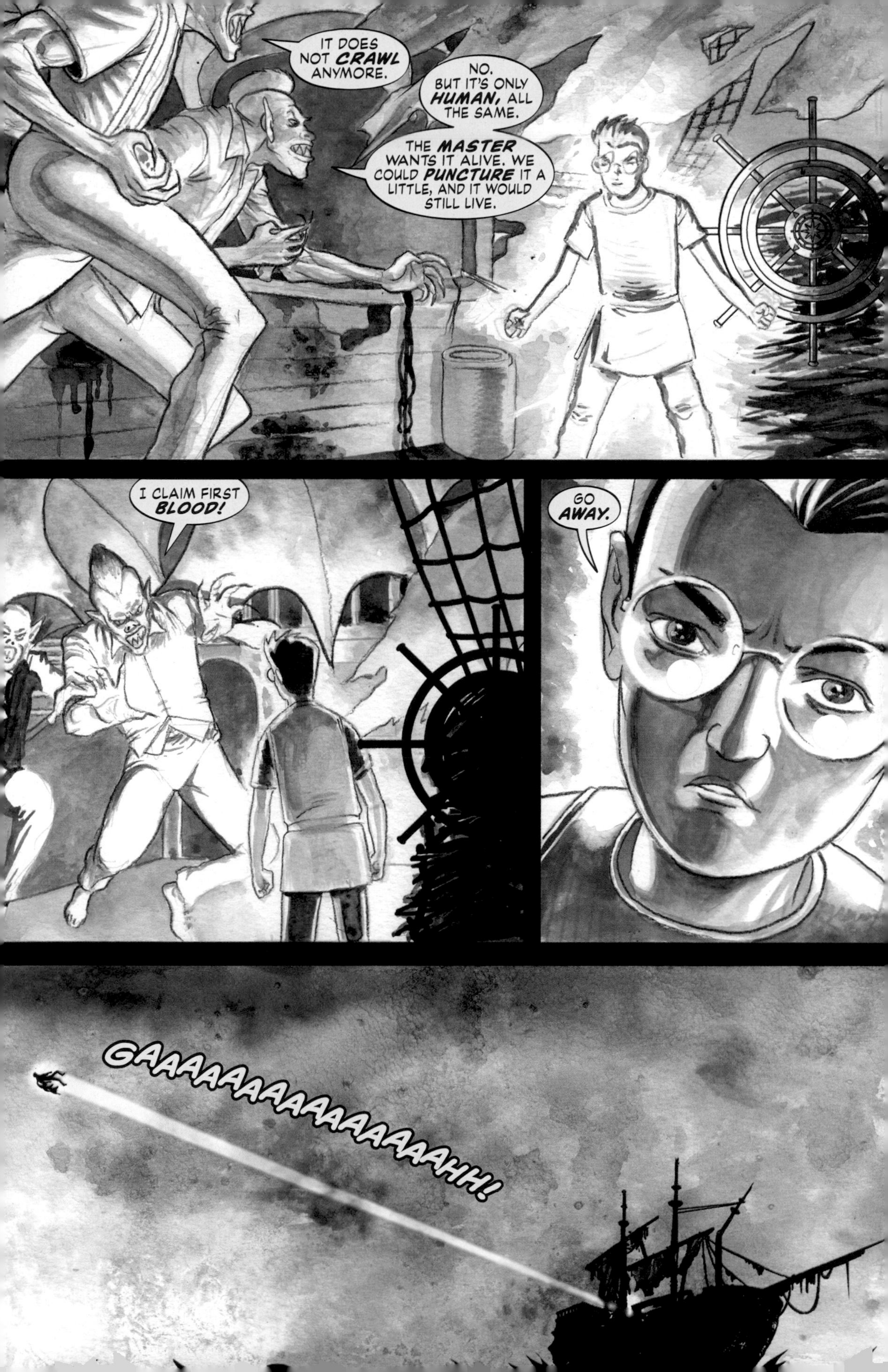
IT DOES NOT **CRAWL** ANYMORE.
NO. BUT IT'S ONLY **HUMAN,** ALL THE SAME.
THE **MASTER** WANTS IT ALIVE. WE COULD **PUNCTURE** IT A LITTLE, AND IT WOULD STILL LIVE.
I CLAIM FIRST **BLOOD!**
GO **AWAY.**
GAAAAAAAAAAAAAAAAAAHH!

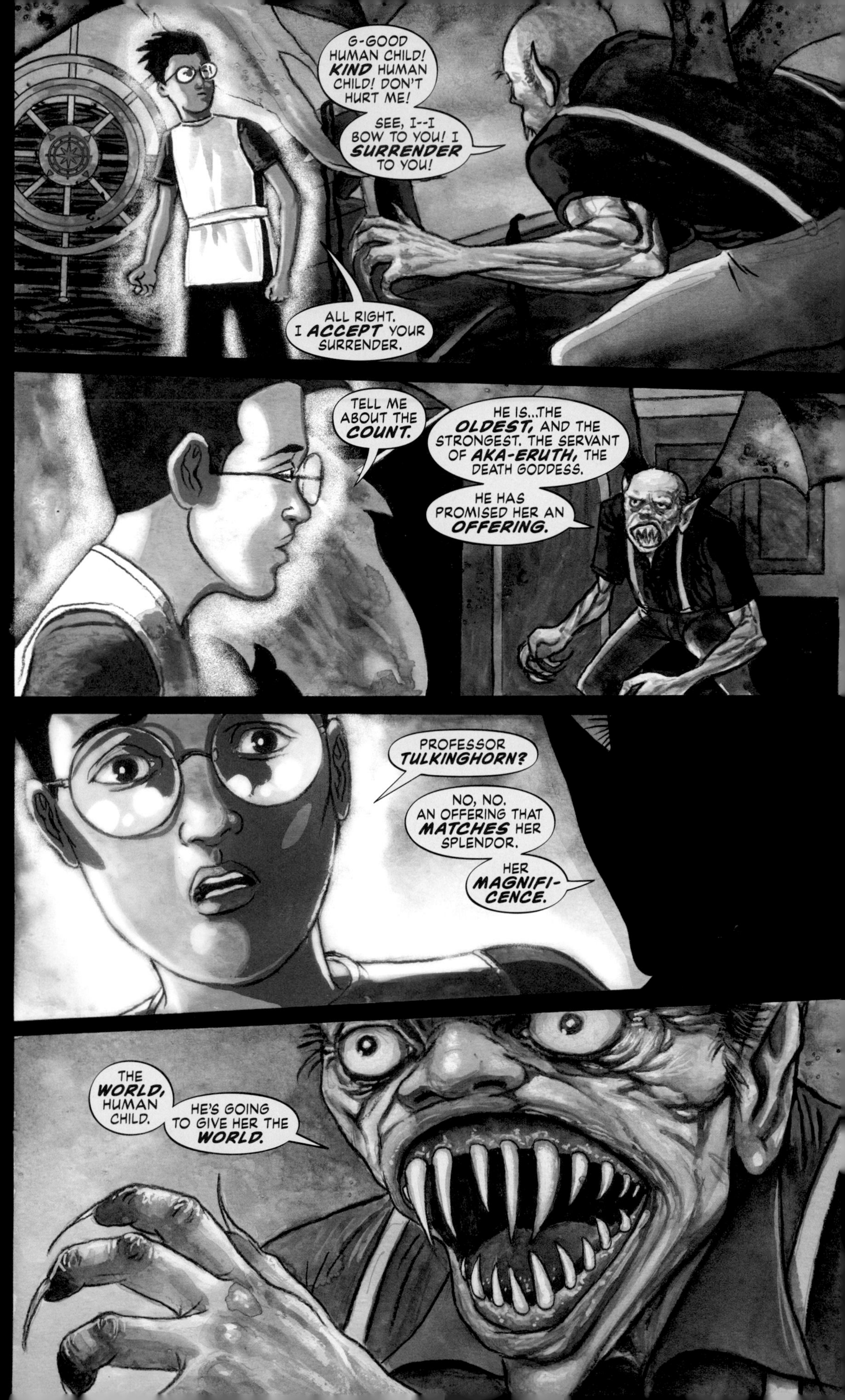
G-GOOD HUMAN CHILD! KIND HUMAN CHILD! DON'T HURT ME!
SEE, I--I BOW TO YOU! I SURRENDER TO YOU!
ALL RIGHT. I ACCEPT YOUR SURRENDER.
TELL ME ABOUT THE COUNT.
HE IS...THE OLDEST, AND THE STRONGEST. THE SERVANT OF AKA-ERUTH, THE DEATH GODDESS.
HE HAS PROMISED HER AN OFFERING.
PROFESSOR TULKINGHORN?
NO, NO. AN OFFERING THAT MATCHES HER SPLENDOR.
HER MAGNIFI-CENCE.
THE WORLD, HUMAN CHILD.
HE'S GOING TO GIVE HER THE WORLD.

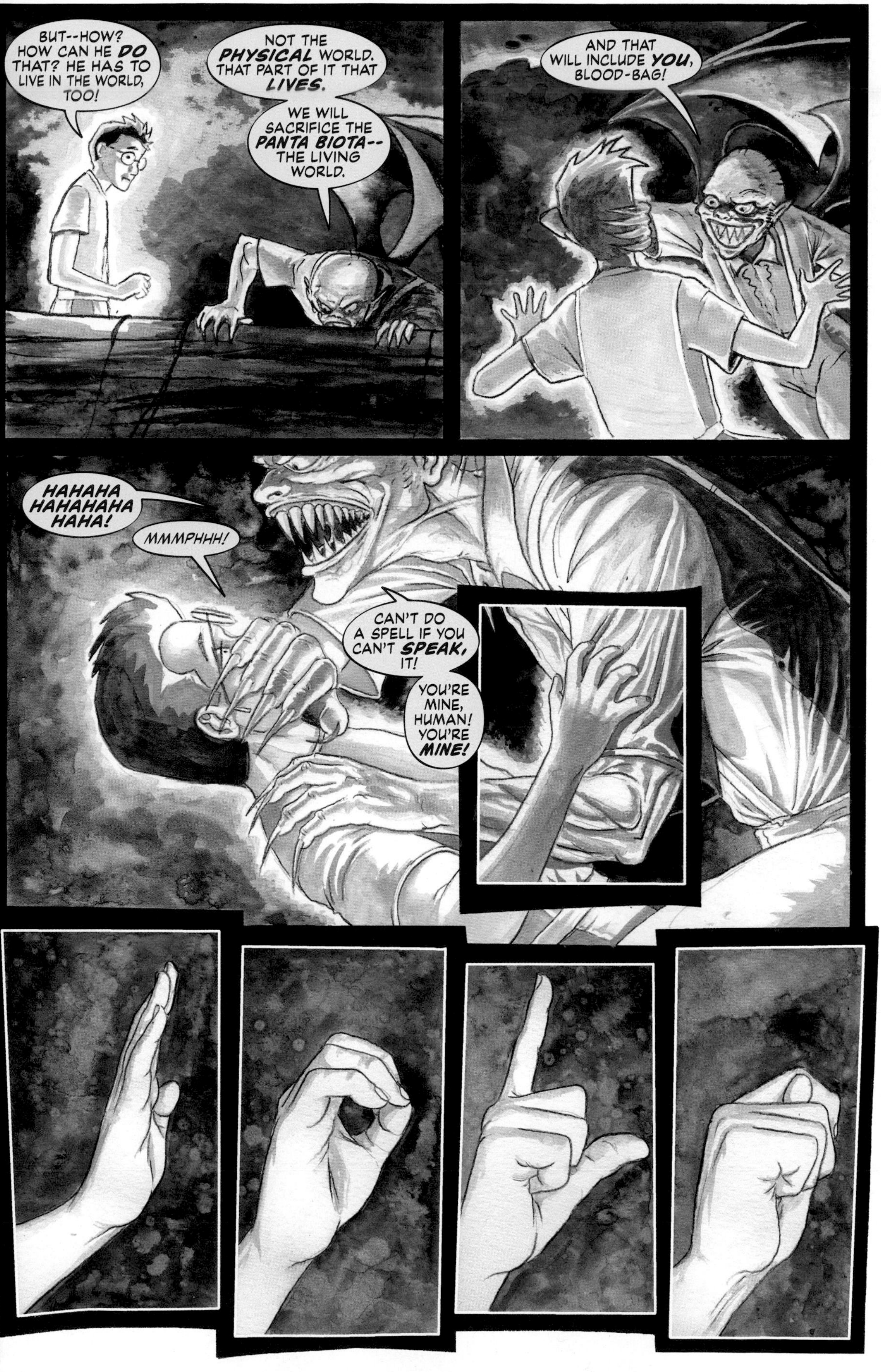
BUT--HOW? HOW CAN HE DO THAT? HE HAS TO LIVE IN THE WORLD, TOO!
NOT THE PHYSICAL WORLD. THAT PART OF IT THAT LIVES.
WE WILL SACRIFICE THE PANTA BIOTA-- THE LIVING WORLD.
AND THAT WILL INCLUDE YOU, BLOOD-BAG!
HAHAHA HAHAHAHA HAHA!
MMMPHHH!
CAN'T DO A SPELL IF YOU CAN'T SPEAK, IT!
YOU'RE MINE, HUMAN! YOU'RE MINE!

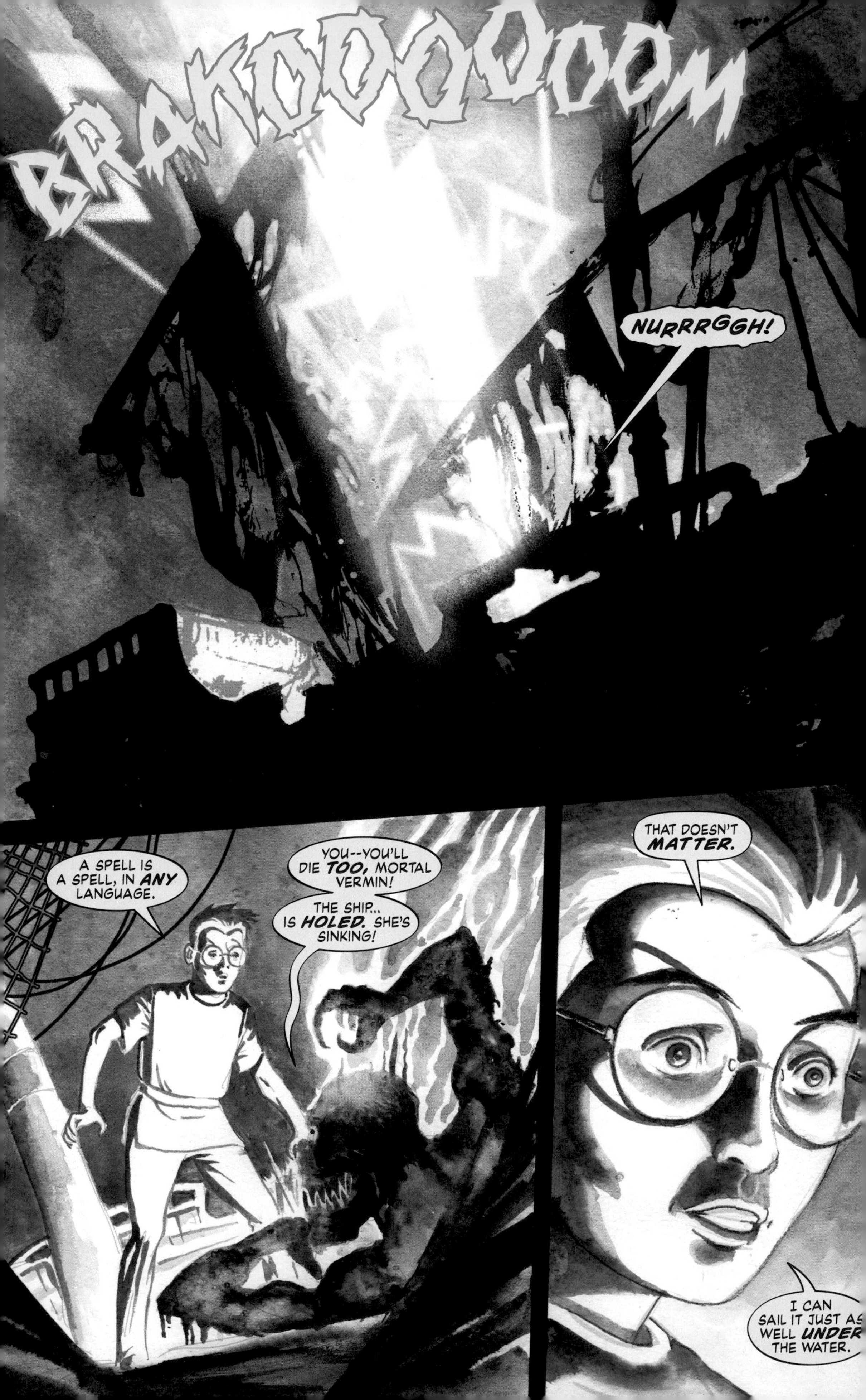
BRAKOOOOOOM
NURRRGGH!
A SPELL IS A SPELL, IN ANY LANGUAGE.
YOU--YOU'LL DIE TOO, MORTAL VERMIN!
THE SHIP.. IS HOLED. SHE'S SINKING!
THAT DOESN'T MATTER.
I CAN SAIL IT JUST AS WELL UNDER THE WATER.

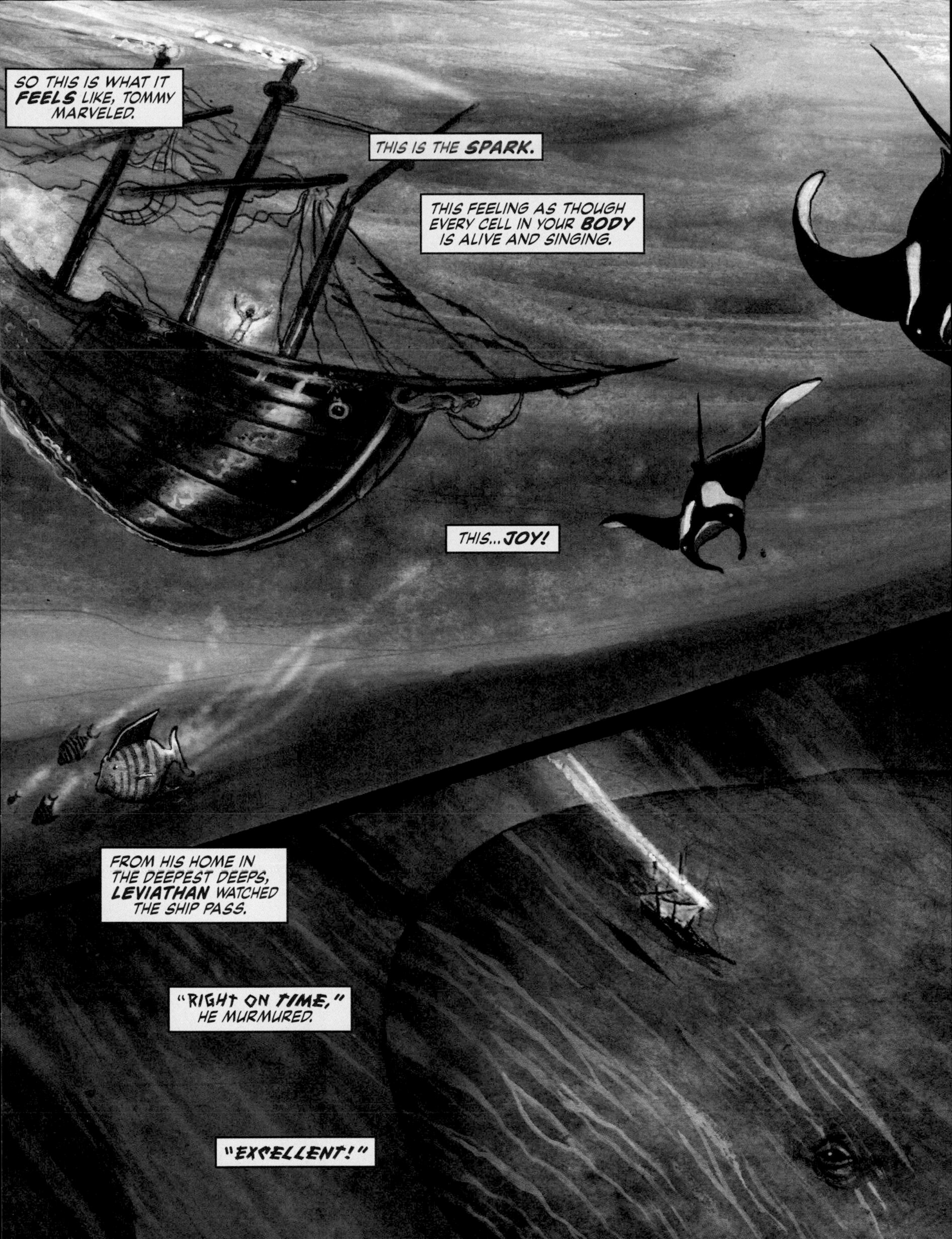
SO THIS IS WHAT IT FEELS LIKE, TOMMY MARVELED.
THIS IS THE SPARK.
THIS FEELING AS THOUGH EVERY CELL IN YOUR BODY IS ALIVE AND SINGING.
THIS...JOY!
FROM HIS HOME IN THE DEEPEST DEEPS, LEVIATHAN WATCHED THE SHIP PASS.
"RIGHT ON TIME," HE MURMURED.
"EXCELLENT!"

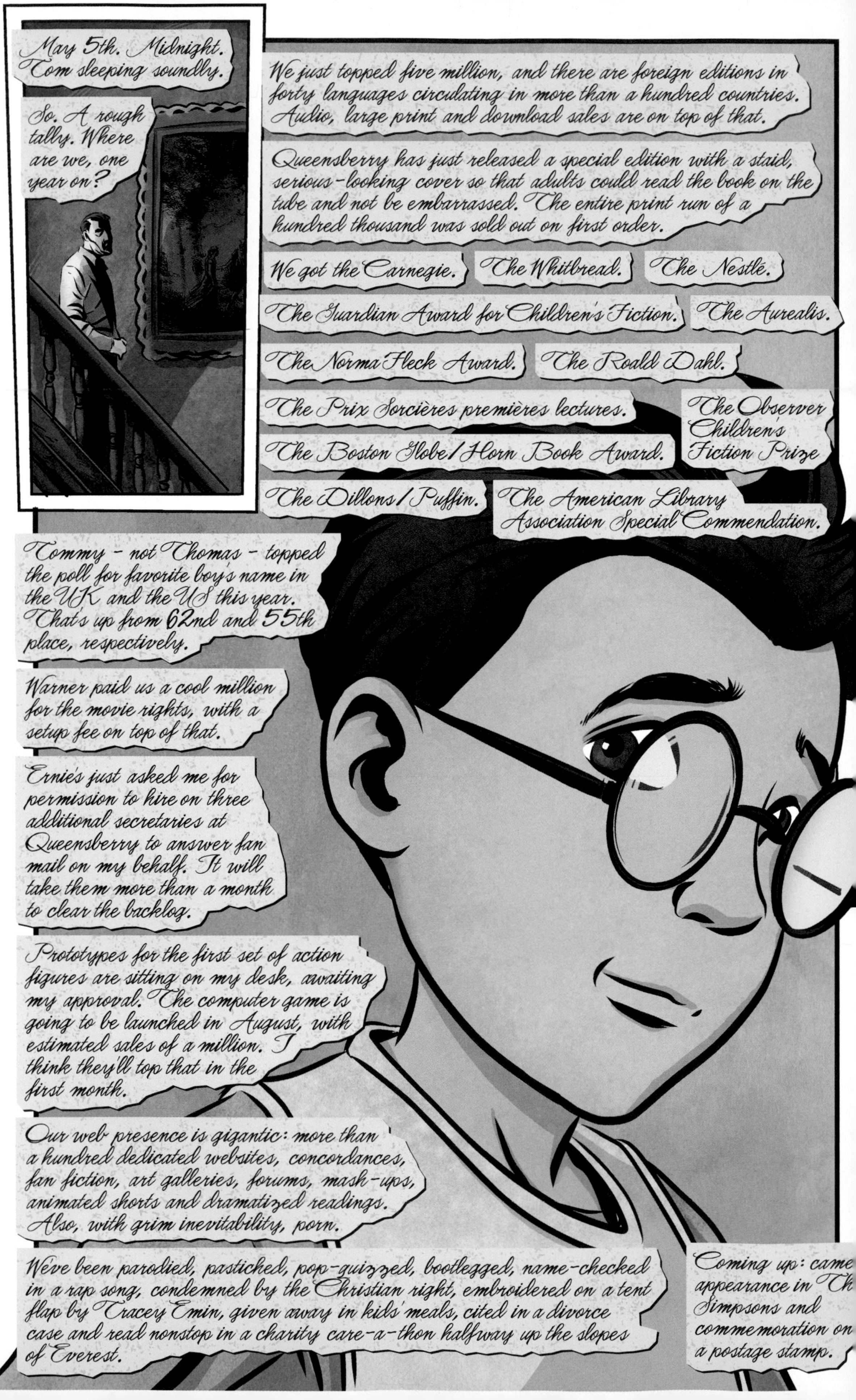
May 5th. Midnight. Tom sleeping soundly.
So. A rough tally. Where are we, one year on?
We just topped five million, and there are foreign editions in forty languages circulating in more than a hundred countries. Audio, large print and download sales are on top of that.
Queensberry has just released a special edition with a staid, serious-looking cover so that adults could read the book on the tube and not be embarrassed. The entire print run of a hundred thousand was sold out on first order.
We got the Carnegie.
The Whitbread.
The Nestlé.
The Guardian Award for Children's Fiction.
The Aurealis.
The Norma Fleck Award.
The Roald Dahl.
The Prix Sorcières premières lectures.
The Observer Children's Fiction Prize
The Boston Globe/Horn Book Award.
The Dillons/Puffin.
The American Library Association Special Commendation.
Tommy - not Thomas - topped the poll for favorite boy's name in the UK and the US this year. That's up from 62nd and 55th place, respectively.
Warner paid us a cool million for the movie rights, with a setup fee on top of that.
Ernie's just asked me for permission to hire on three additional secretaries at Queensberry to answer fan mail on my behalf. It will take them more than a month to clear the backlog.
Prototypes for the first set of action figures are sitting on my desk, awaiting my approval. The computer game is going to be launched in August, with estimated sales of a million. I think they'll top that in the first month.
Our web presence is gigantic: more than a hundred dedicated websites, concordances, fan fiction, art galleries, forums, mash-ups, animated shorts and dramatized readings. Also, with grim inevitability, porn.
We've been parodied, pastiched, pop-quizzed, bootlegged, name-checked in a rap song, condemned by the Christian right, embroidered on a tent flap by Tracey Emin, given away in kids' meals, cited in a divorce case and read nonstop in a charity care-a-thon halfway up the slopes of Everest.
Coming up: came appearance in Th Simpsons and commemoration on a postage stamp.

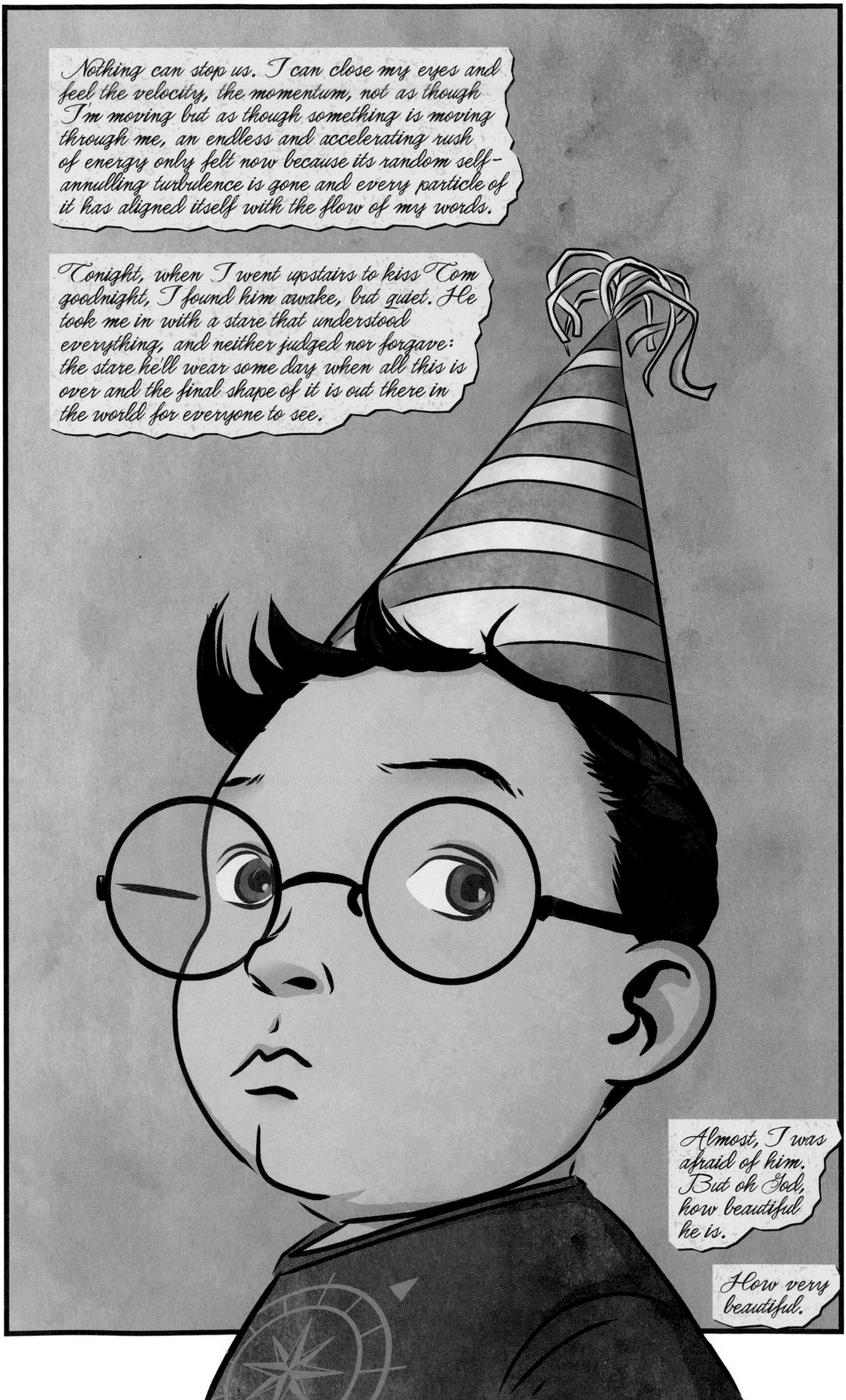
Nothing can stop us. I can close my eyes and feel the velocity, the momentum, not as though I'm moving but as though something is moving through me, an endless and accelerating rush of energy only felt now because its random self-annulling turbulence is gone and every particle of it has aligned itself with the flow of my words.
Tonight, when I went upstairs to kiss Tom goodnight, I found him awake, but quiet. He took me in with a stare that understood everything, and neither judged nor forgave: the stare he'll wear some day when all this is over and the final shape of it is out there in the world for everyone to see.
Almost, I was afraid of him. But oh God, how beautiful he is.
How very beautiful.

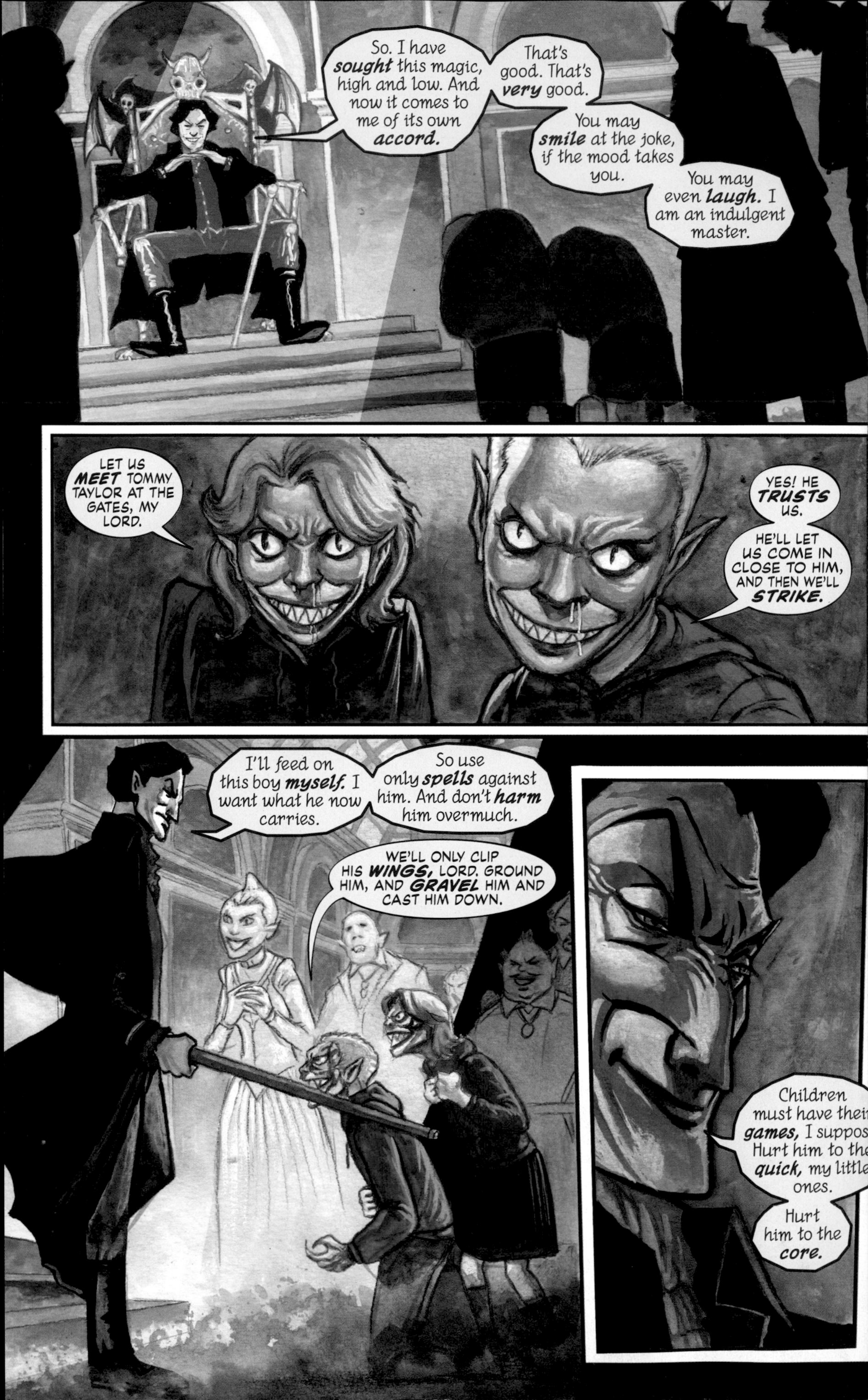

So. I have sought this magic, high and low. And now it comes to me of its own accord.
That's good. That's very good.
You may smile at the joke, if the mood takes you.
You may even laugh. I am an indulgent master.
LET US MEET TOMMY TAYLOR AT THE GATES, MY LORD.
YES! HE TRUSTS US.
HE'LL LET US COME IN CLOSE TO HIM, AND THEN WE'LL STRIKE.
I'll feed on this boy myself. I want what he now carries.
So use only spells against him. And don't harm him overmuch.
WE'LL ONLY CLIP HIS WINGS, LORD. GROUND HIM, AND GRAVEL HIM AND CAST HIM DOWN.
Children must have their games, I suppos
Hurt him to the quick, my little ones.
Hurt him to the core.

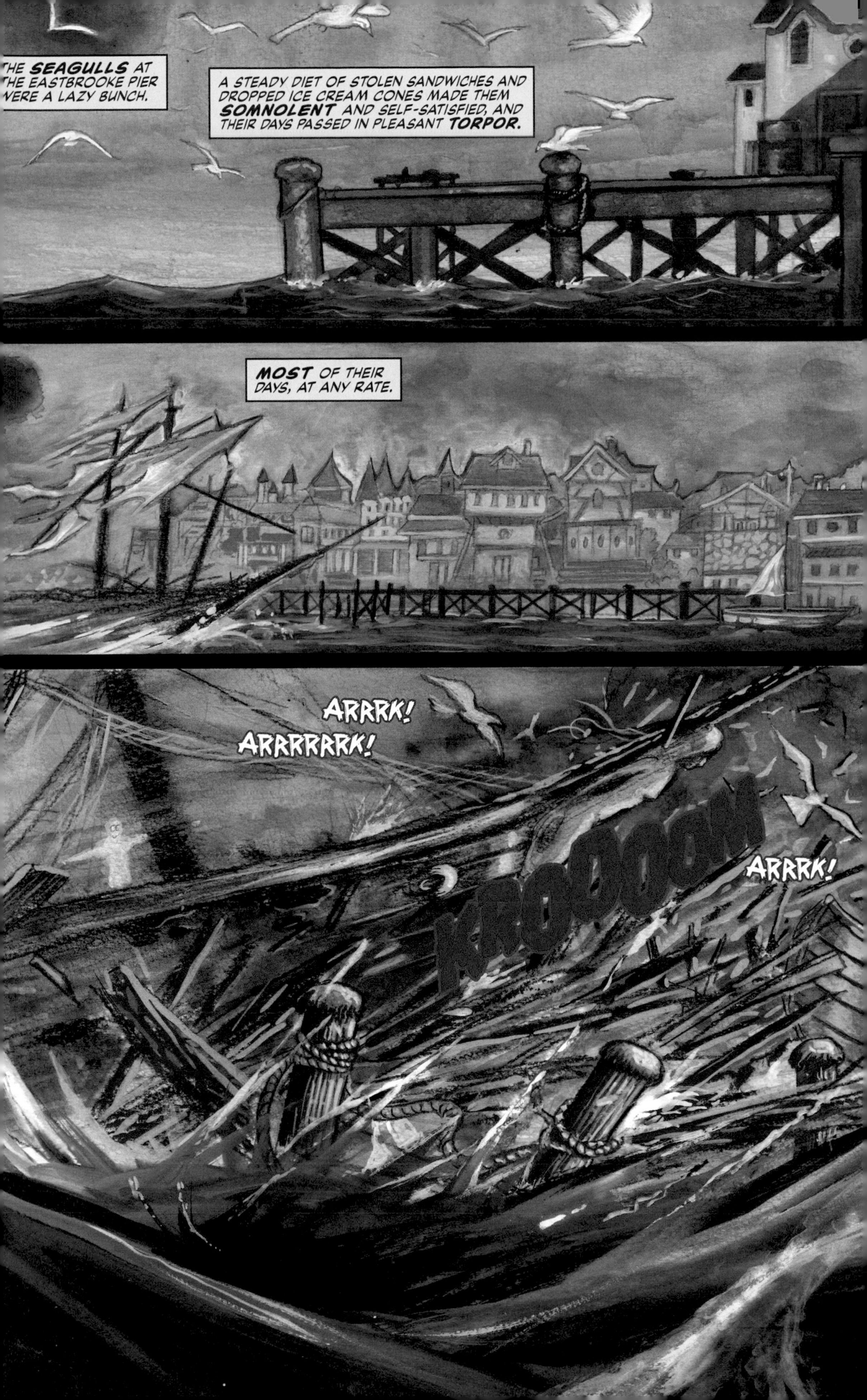
THE SEAGULLS AT THE EASTBROOKE PIER WERE A LAZY BUNCH.
A STEADY DIET OF STOLEN SANDWICHES AND DROPPED ICE CREAM CONES MADE THEM SOMNOLENT AND SELF-SATISFIED, AND THEIR DAYS PASSED IN PLEASANT TORPOR.
MOST OF THEIR DAYS, AT ANY RATE.
ARRRK!
ARRRRRRK!
KROOOOOM
ARRRK!

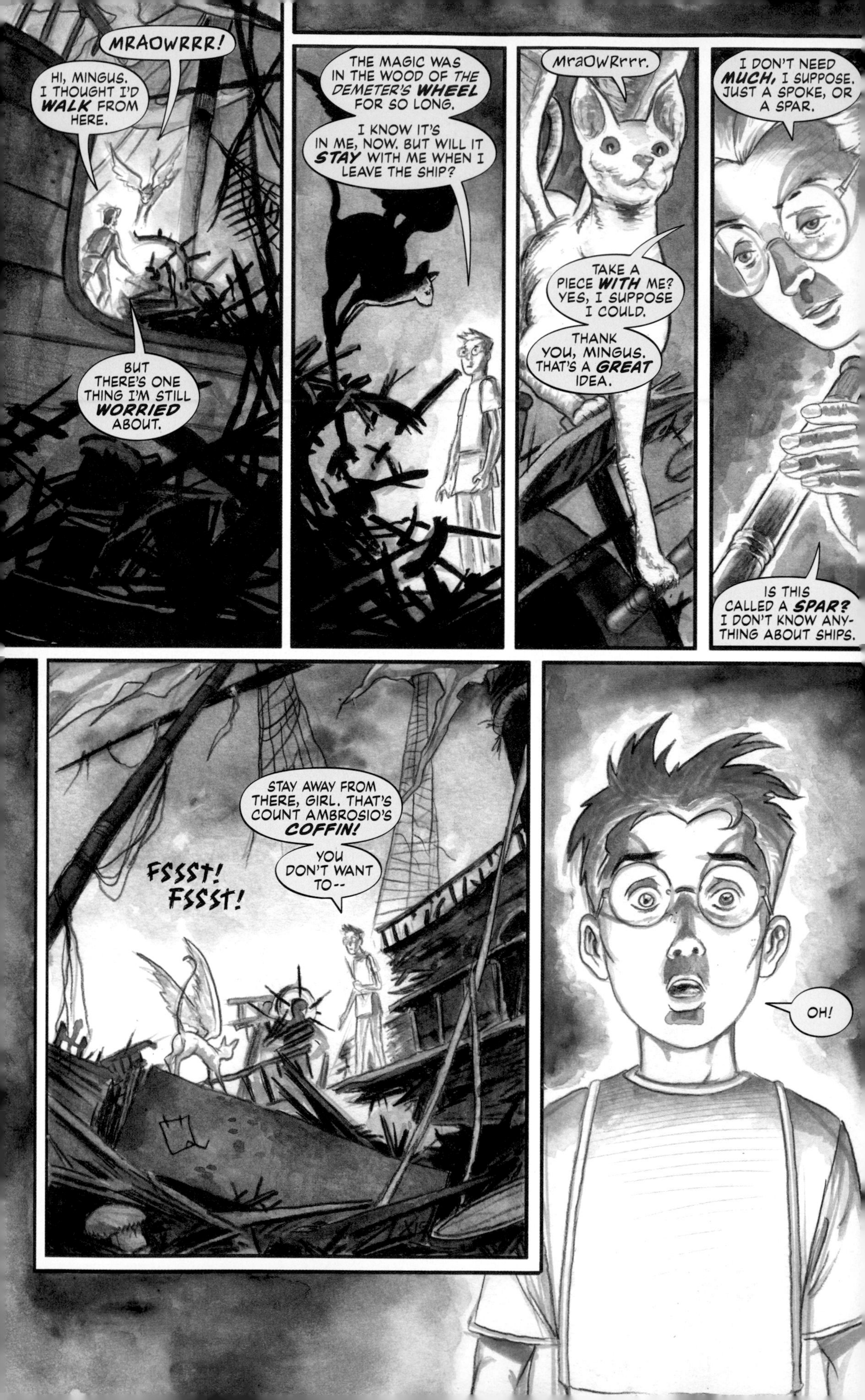
MRAOWRRR!
HI, MINGUS. I THOUGHT I'D WALK FROM HERE.
BUT THERE'S ONE THING I'M STILL WORRIED ABOUT.
THE MAGIC WAS IN THE WOOD OF THE DEMETER'S WHEEL FOR SO LONG.
I KNOW IT'S IN ME, NOW. BUT WILL IT STAY WITH ME WHEN I LEAVE THE SHIP?
MraOWRrrr.
TAKE A PIECE WITH ME? YES, I SUPPOSE I COULD.
THANK YOU, MINGUS. THAT'S A GREAT IDEA.
I DON'T NEED MUCH, I SUPPOSE. JUST A SPOKE, OR A SPAR.
IS THIS CALLED A SPAR? I DON'T KNOW ANYTHING ABOUT SHIPS.
STAY AWAY FROM THERE, GIRL. THAT'S COUNT AMBROSIO'S COFFIN!
YOU DON'T WANT TO--
FSSST! FSSST!
OH!

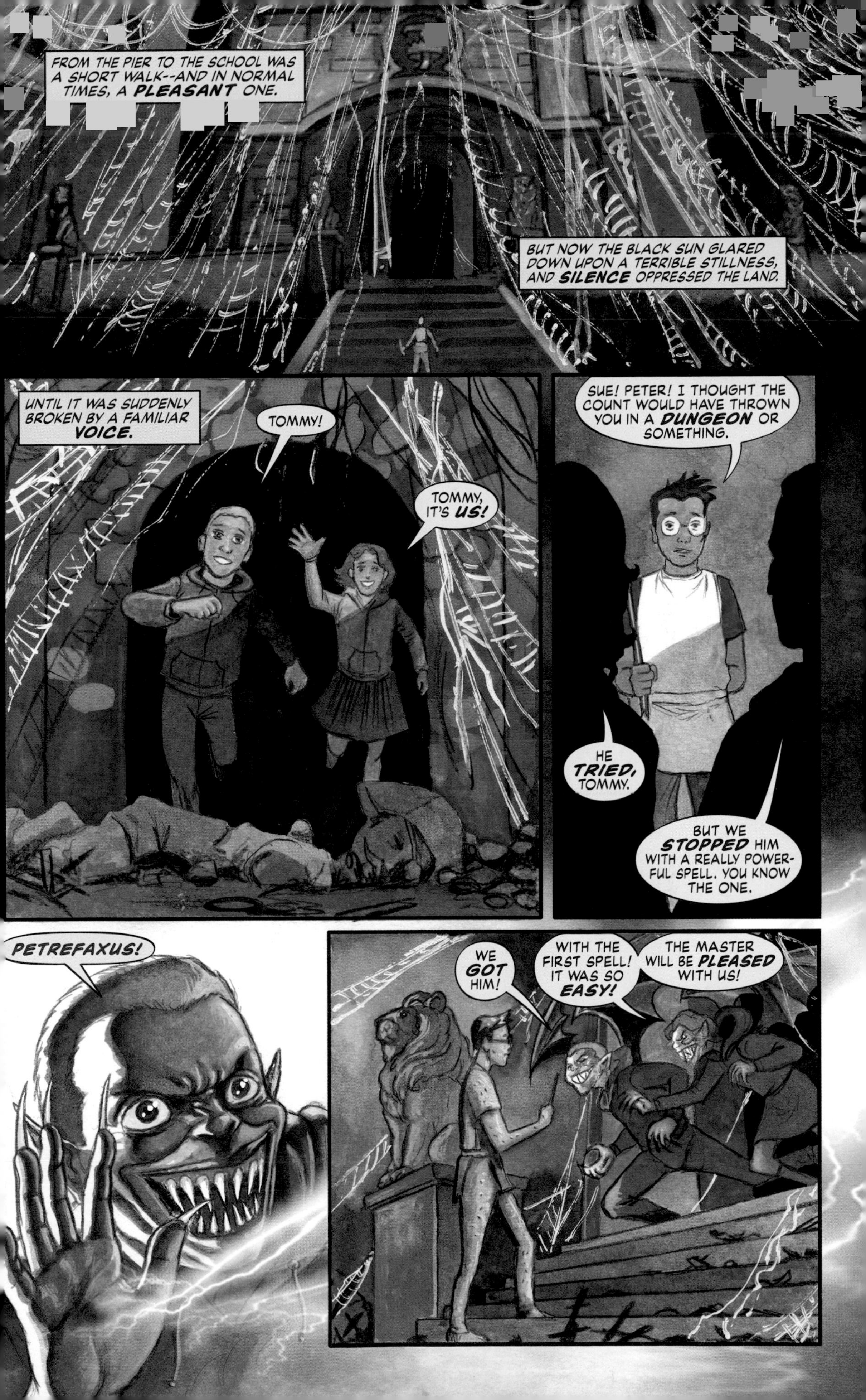
FROM THE PIER TO THE SCHOOL WAS A SHORT WALK--AND IN NORMAL TIMES, A PLEASANT ONE.
BUT NOW THE BLACK SUN GLARED DOWN UPON A TERRIBLE STILLNESS, AND SILENCE OPPRESSED THE LAND.
UNTIL IT WAS SUDDENLY BROKEN BY A FAMILIAR VOICE.
TOMMY!
TOMMY, IT'S US!
SUE! PETER! I THOUGHT THE COUNT WOULD HAVE THROWN YOU IN A DUNGEON OR SOMETHING.
HE TRIED, TOMMY.
BUT WE STOPPED HIM WITH A REALLY POWERFUL SPELL. YOU KNOW THE ONE.
PETREFAXUS!
WE GOT HIM!
WITH THE FIRST SPELL! IT WAS SO EASY!
THE MASTER WILL BE PLEASED WITH US!

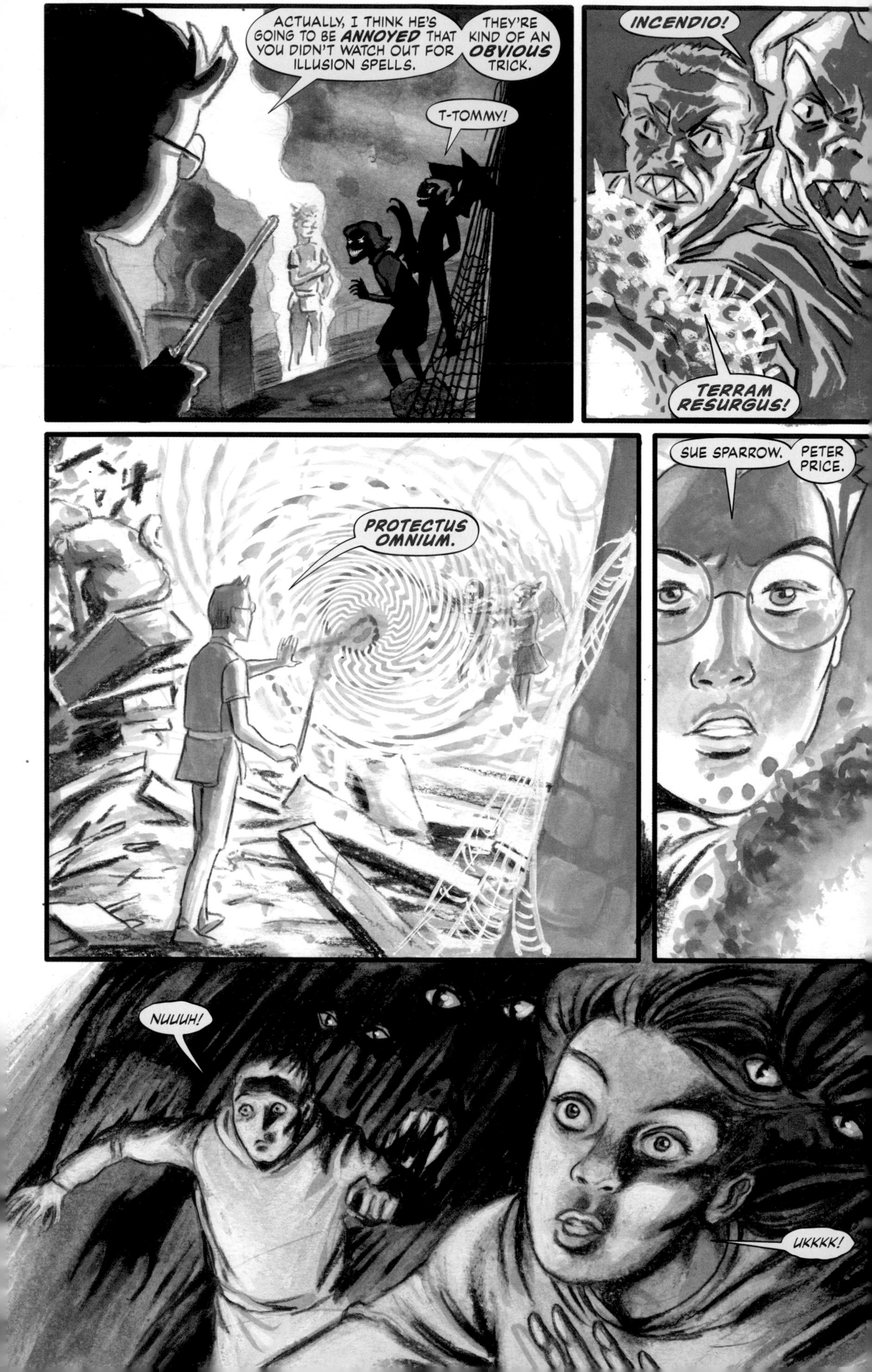

ACTUALLY, I THINK HE'S GOING TO BE ANNOYED THAT YOU DIDN'T WATCH OUT FOR ILLUSION SPELLS.
THEY'RE KIND OF AN OBVIOUS TRICK.
T-TOMMY!
INCENDIO!
TERRAM RESURGUS!
PROTECTUS OMNIUM.
SUE SPARROW.
PETER PRICE.
NUUUH!
UKKKK!

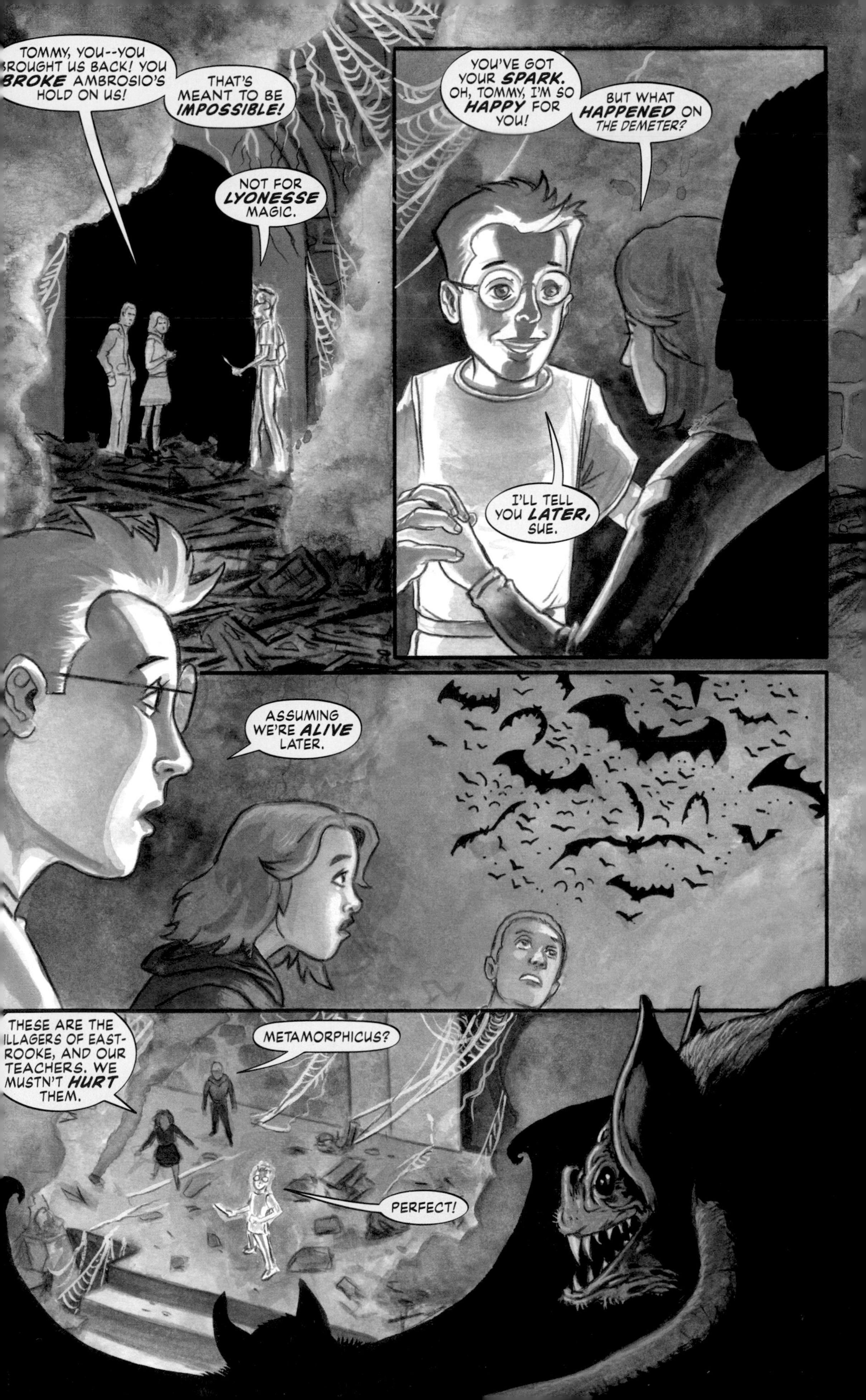
TOMMY, YOU--YOU BROUGHT US BACK! YOU BROKE AMBROSIO'S HOLD ON US!
THAT'S MEANT TO BE IMPOSSIBLE!
NOT FOR LYONESSE MAGIC.
YOU'VE GOT YOUR SPARK. OH, TOMMY, I'M SO HAPPY FOR YOU!
BUT WHAT HAPPENED ON THE DEMETER?
I'LL TELL YOU LATER, SUE.
ASSUMING WE'RE ALIVE LATER.
THESE ARE THE ILLAGERS OF EAST-ROOKE, AND OUR TEACHERS. WE MUSTN'T HURT THEM.
METAMORPHICUS?
PERFECT!

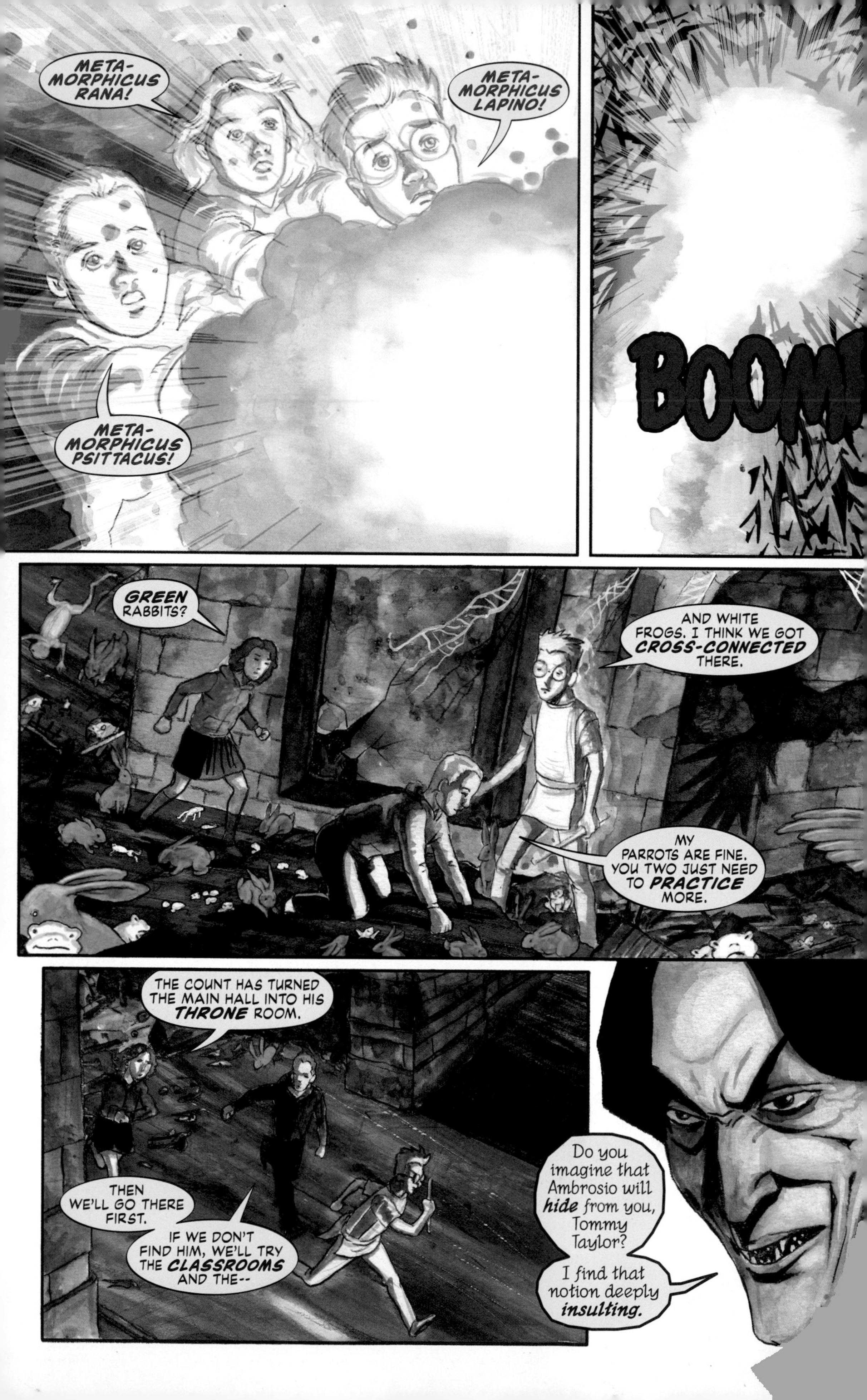
META-MORPHICUS RANA!
META-MORPHICUS LAPINO!
META-MORPHICUS PSITTACUS!
BOOM
GREEN RABBITS?
AND WHITE FROGS. I THINK WE GOT CROSS-CONNECTED THERE.
MY PARROTS ARE FINE. YOU TWO JUST NEED TO PRACTICE MORE.
THE COUNT HAS TURNED THE MAIN HALL INTO HIS THRONE ROOM.
THEN WE'LL GO THERE FIRST.
IF WE DON'T FIND HIM, WE'LL TRY THE CLASSROOMS AND THE--
Do you imagine that Ambrosio will hide from you, Tommy Taylor?
I find that notion deeply insulting.

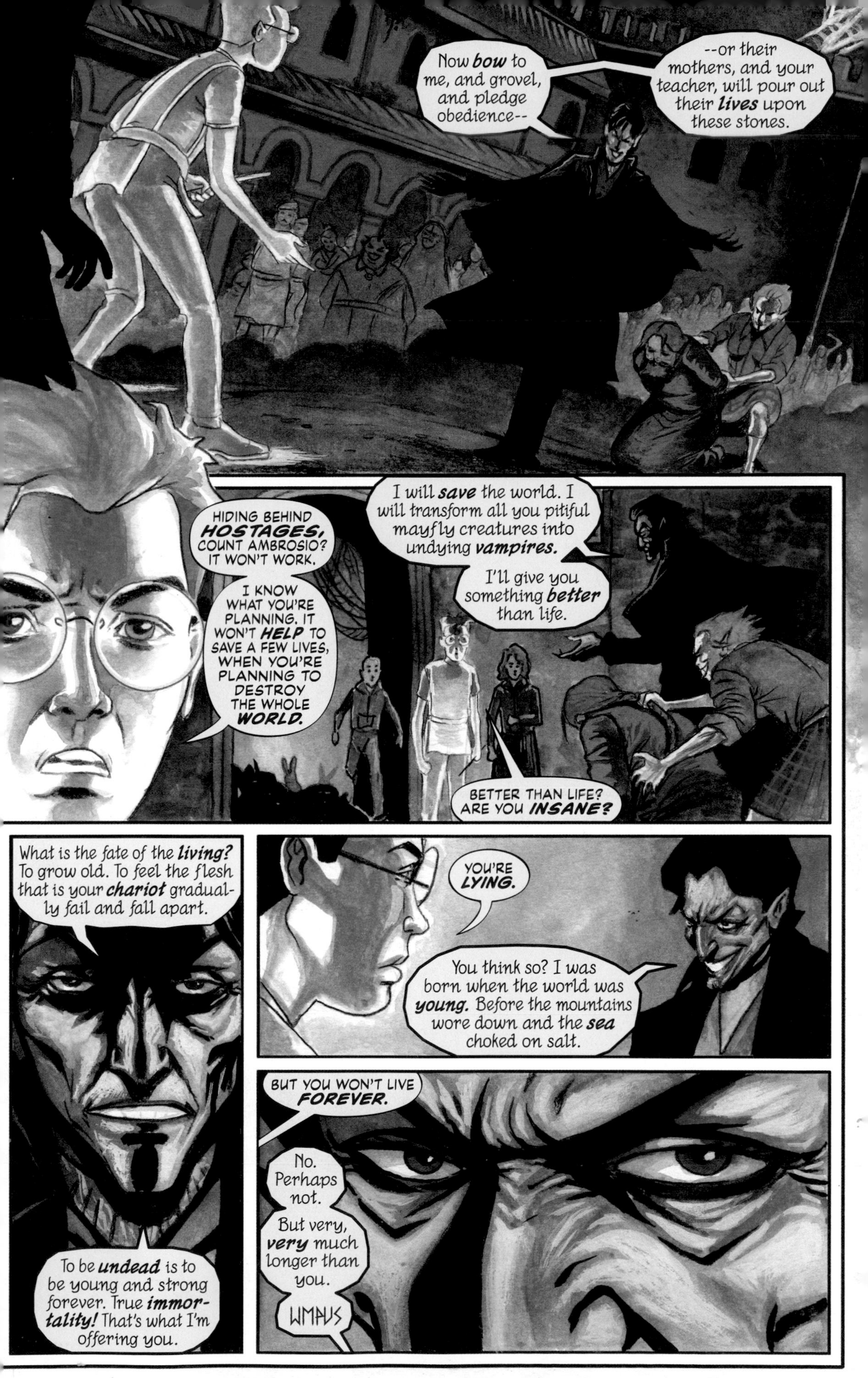
Now bow to me, and grovel, and pledge obedience--
--or their mothers, and your teacher, will pour out their lives upon these stones.
HIDING BEHIND HOSTAGES, COUNT AMBROSIO? IT WON'T WORK.
I KNOW WHAT YOU'RE PLANNING. IT WON'T HELP TO SAVE A FEW LIVES, WHEN YOU'RE PLANNING TO DESTROY THE WHOLE WORLD.
I will save the world. I will transform all you pitiful mayfly creatures into undying vampires.
I'll give you something better than life.
BETTER THAN LIFE? ARE YOU INSANE?
What is the fate of the living? To grow old. To feel the flesh that is your chariot gradually fail and fall apart.
To be undead is to be young and strong forever. True immortality! That's what I'm offering you.
YOU'RE LYING.
You think so? I was born when the world was young. Before the mountains wore down and the sea choked on salt.
BUT YOU WON'T LIVE FOREVER.
No. Perhaps not.
But very, very much longer than you.
WMAUS

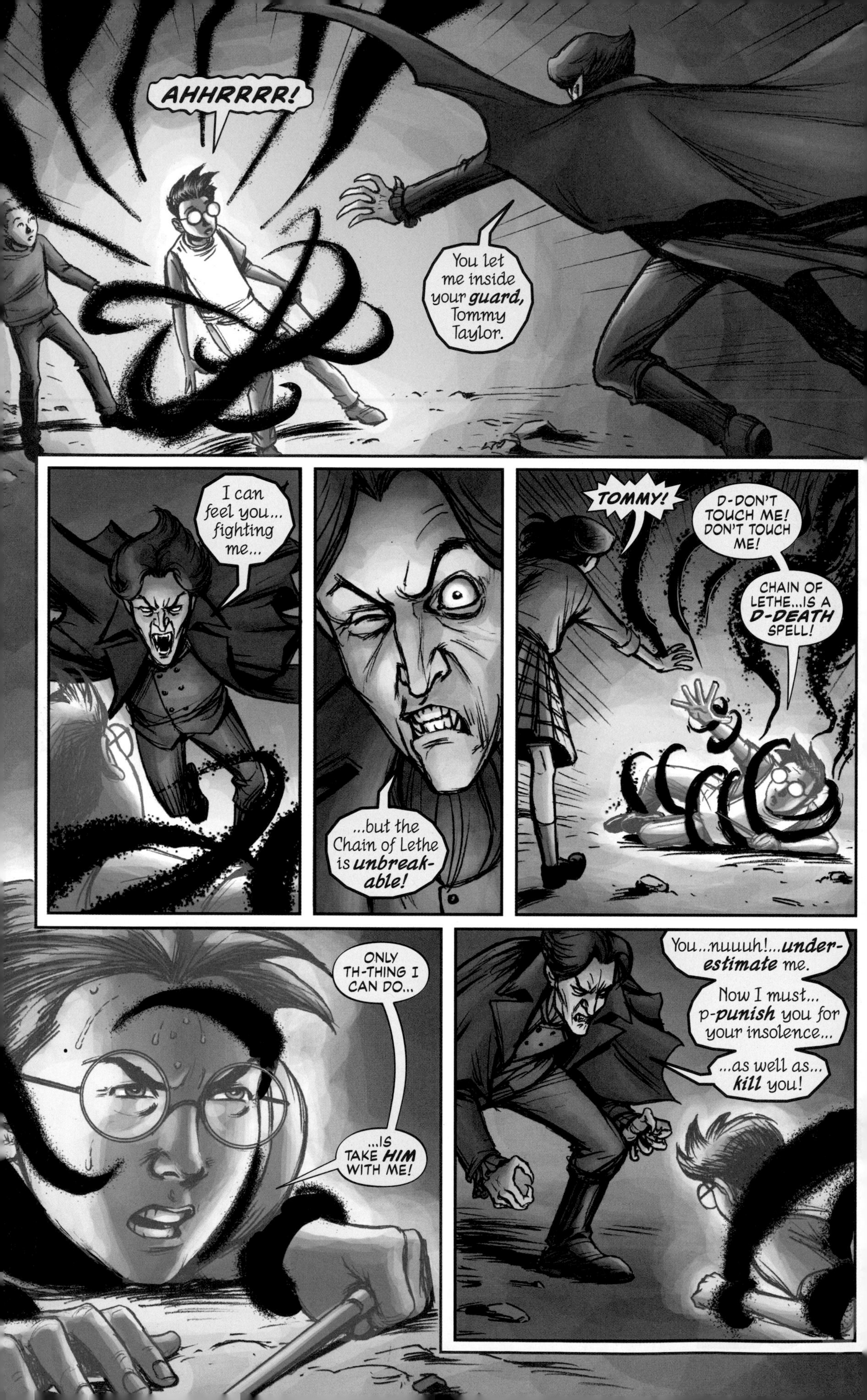
AHHRRRR!
You let me inside your ***guard,*** Tommy Taylor.
I can feel you... fighting me...
...but the Chain of Lethe is ***unbreak-able!***
TOMMY!
D-DON'T TOUCH ME! DON'T TOUCH ME!
CHAIN OF LETHE...IS A ***D-DEATH*** SPELL!
ONLY TH-THING I CAN DO...
...IS TAKE ***HIM*** WITH ME!
You...nuuuh!...***under-estimate*** me.
Now I must... p-***punish*** you for your insolence...
...as well as... ***kill*** you!

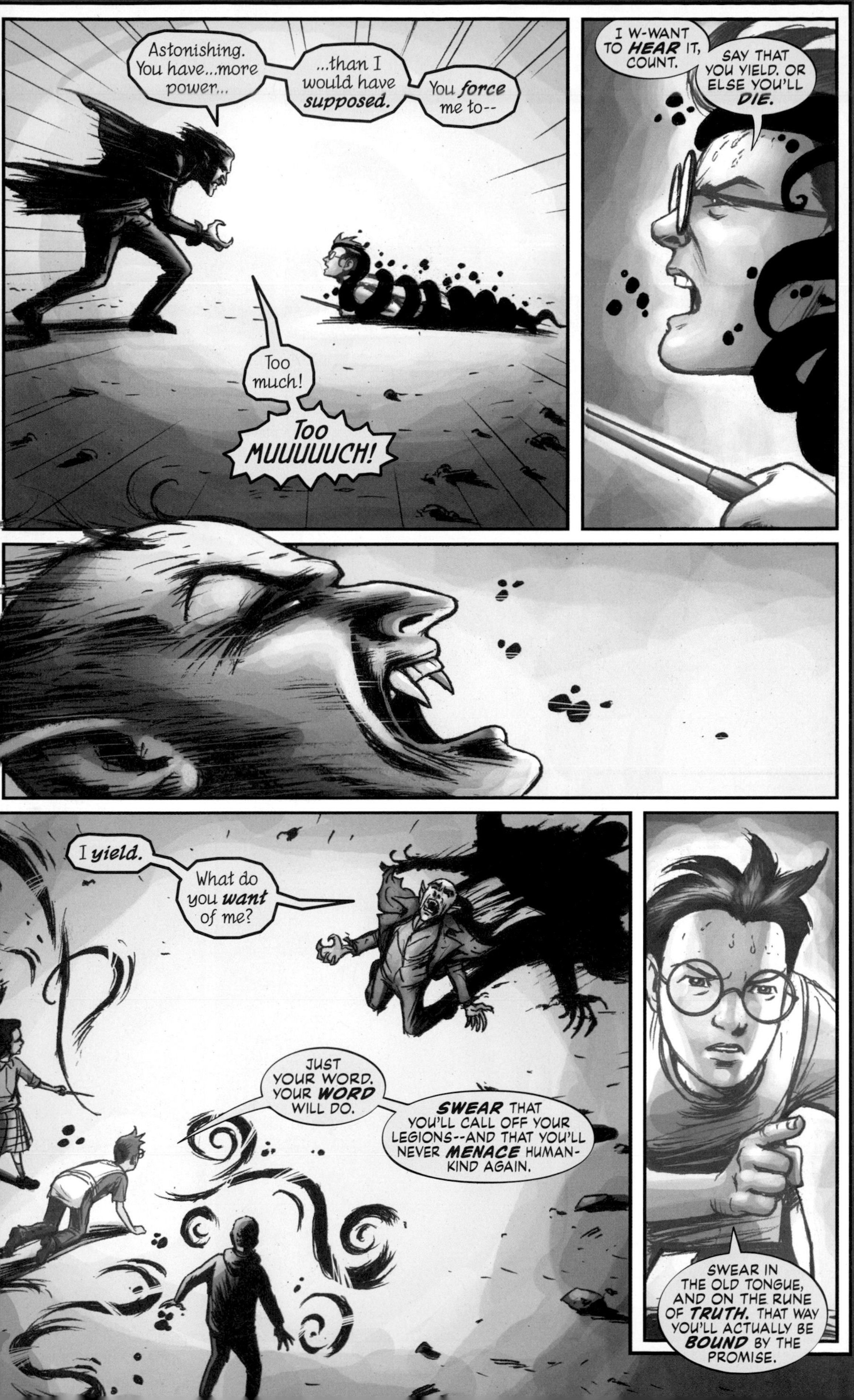
Astonishing. You have...more power...
...than I would have supposed.
You force me to--
I W-WANT TO HEAR IT, COUNT.
SAY THAT YOU YIELD. OR ELSE YOU'LL DIE.
Too much!
Too MUUUUUCH!
I yield.
What do you want of me?
JUST YOUR WORD. YOUR WORD WILL DO.
SWEAR THAT YOU'LL CALL OFF YOUR LEGIONS--AND THAT YOU'LL NEVER MENACE HUMAN-KIND AGAIN.
SWEAR IN THE OLD TONGUE, AND ON THE RUNE OF TRUTH. THAT WAY YOU'LL ACTUALLY BE BOUND BY THE PROMISE.

ᛕᚤᚥᚠᚻᛟᚤ

GOOD. NOW LIFT YOUR **CONTROL** FROM THESE PEOPLE.

TAKE YOUR FOOT FROM THEIR **SOULS,** AND LET THEM THINK AND ACT FOR THEMSELVES.

why? Autonomy is **wasted** on such cattle.

But this day is yours, Tommy Taylor. So be it. ᚠᛒᛏᛁᛃᛋᚷᚩᛟ

B- BLESS MY SOUL!

IT'S **OVER!**

THANK THE **SEVEN!** IT'S FINALLY OVER!

MUM! YOU'RE ALL RIGHT! IF YOU'RE **ALL RIGHT!**

I'M FINE, THANK YOU, SUZIE! BUT WHY AM I HOLDING A **KNIFE,** IF THERE'S NOTHING TO BE CHOPPED OR SLICED?

I MUST BE WANDERING IN MY **WITS!**

AN **ASTONISHING** PERFORMANCE, TOMMY. I SEE YOU FOUND YOUR **SPARK.**

THANK YOU, PROFESSOR. IT'S NOT JUST MY **OWN** SPARK. I'VE GOT ALL THE **MAGIC** FROM THE **DEMETER'S** HOLD.

AND YOU WEAR IT **WELL,** MY BOY. YOU WEAR IT **WELL.**

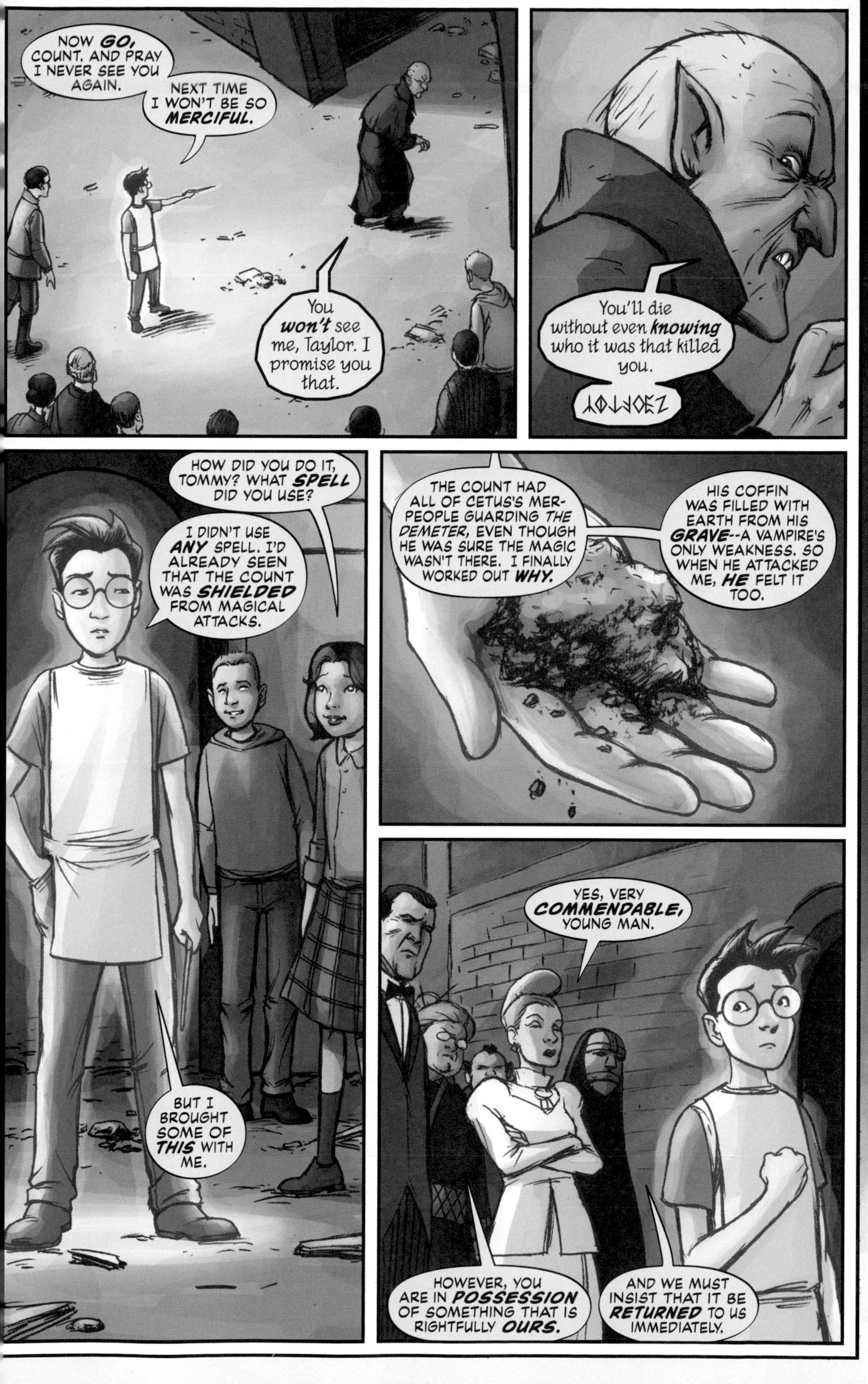

NOW GO, COUNT. AND PRAY I NEVER SEE YOU AGAIN.
NEXT TIME I WON'T BE SO MERCIFUL.
You won't see me, Taylor. I promise you that.
You'll die without even knowing who it was that killed you.
HOW DID YOU DO IT, TOMMY? WHAT SPELL DID YOU USE?
I DIDN'T USE ANY SPELL. I'D ALREADY SEEN THAT THE COUNT WAS SHIELDED FROM MAGICAL ATTACKS.
BUT I BROUGHT SOME OF THIS WITH ME.
THE COUNT HAD ALL OF CETUS'S MER-PEOPLE GUARDING THE DEMETER, EVEN THOUGH HE WAS SURE THE MAGIC WASN'T THERE. I FINALLY WORKED OUT WHY.
HIS COFFIN WAS FILLED WITH EARTH FROM HIS GRAVE--A VAMPIRE'S ONLY WEAKNESS. SO WHEN HE ATTACKED ME, HE FELT IT TOO.
YES, VERY COMMENDABLE, YOUNG MAN.
HOWEVER, YOU ARE IN POSSESSION OF SOMETHING THAT IS RIGHTFULLY OURS.
AND WE MUST INSIST THAT IT BE RETURNED TO US IMMEDIATELY.

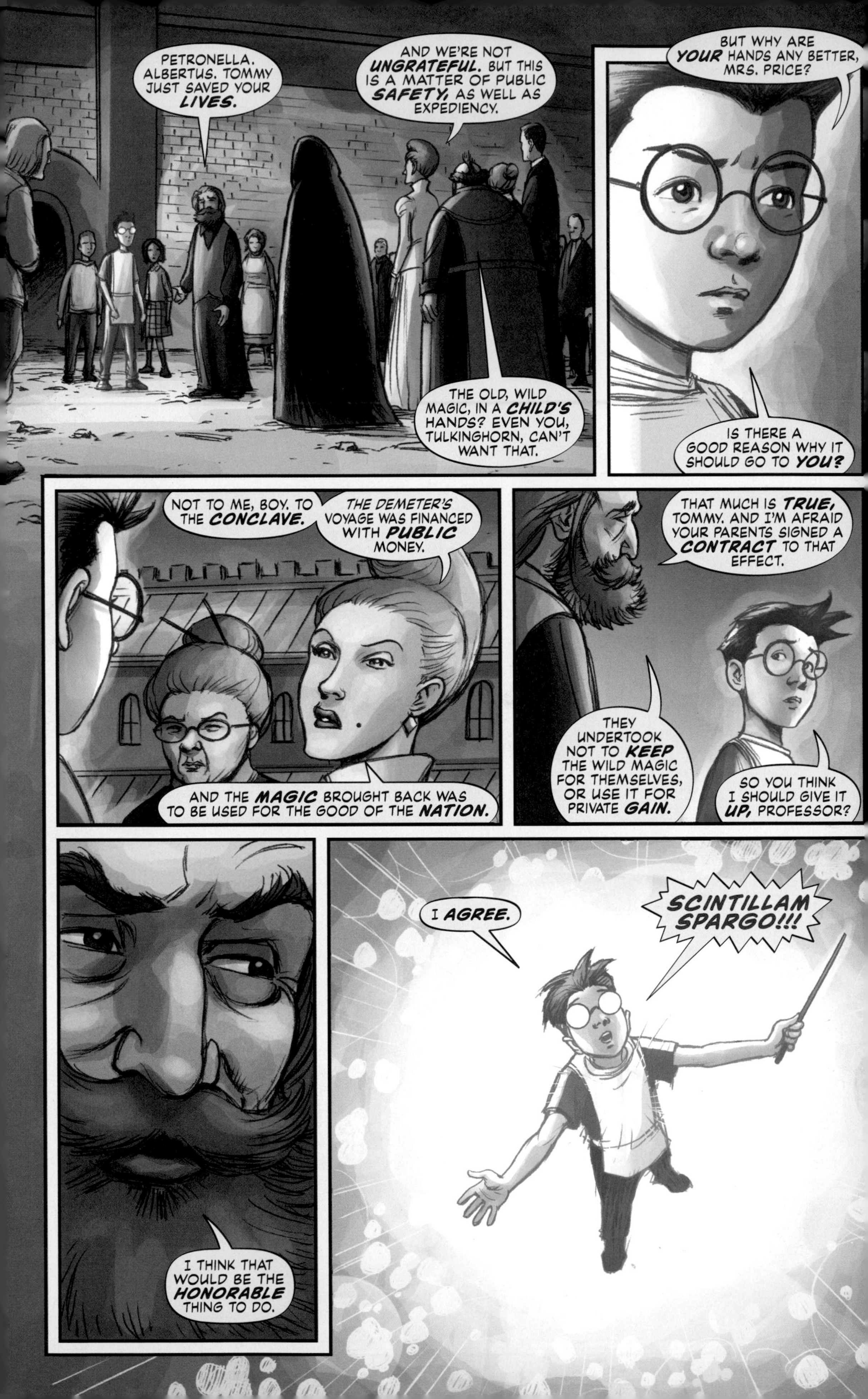
PETRONELLA. ALBERTUS. TOMMY JUST SAVED YOUR LIVES.
AND WE'RE NOT UNGRATEFUL. BUT THIS IS A MATTER OF PUBLIC SAFETY, AS WELL AS EXPEDIENCY.
THE OLD, WILD MAGIC, IN A CHILD'S HANDS? EVEN YOU, TULKINGHORN, CAN'T WANT THAT.
BUT WHY ARE YOUR HANDS ANY BETTER, MRS. PRICE?
IS THERE A GOOD REASON WHY IT SHOULD GO TO YOU?
NOT TO ME, BOY. TO THE CONCLAVE.
THE DEMETER'S VOYAGE WAS FINANCED WITH PUBLIC MONEY.
AND THE MAGIC BROUGHT BACK WAS TO BE USED FOR THE GOOD OF THE NATION.
THAT MUCH IS TRUE, TOMMY. AND I'M AFRAID YOUR PARENTS SIGNED A CONTRACT TO THAT EFFECT.
THEY UNDERTOOK NOT TO KEEP THE WILD MAGIC FOR THEMSELVES, OR USE IT FOR PRIVATE GAIN.
SO YOU THINK I SHOULD GIVE IT UP, PROFESSOR?
I THINK THAT WOULD BE THE HONORABLE THING TO DO.
I AGREE.
SCINTILLAM SPARGO!!!

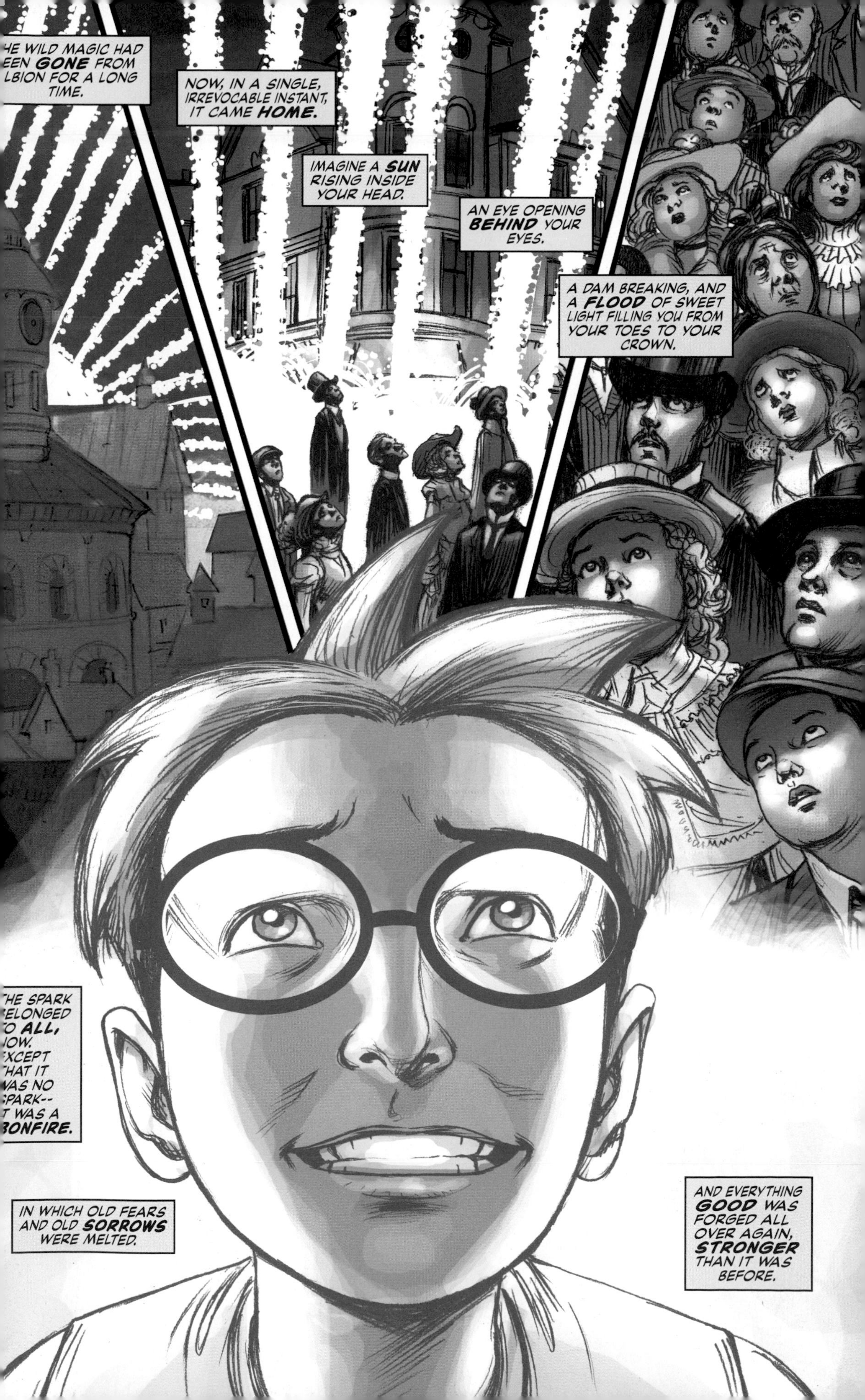
HE WILD MAGIC HAD EEN GONE FROM LBION FOR A LONG TIME.
NOW, IN A SINGLE, IRREVOCABLE INSTANT, IT CAME HOME.
IMAGINE A SUN RISING INSIDE YOUR HEAD.
AN EYE OPENING BEHIND YOUR EYES.
A DAM BREAKING, AND A FLOOD OF SWEET LIGHT FILLING YOU FROM YOUR TOES TO YOUR CROWN.
HE SPARK ELONGED O ALL, IOW. XCEPT HAT IT VAS NO PARK-- T WAS A ONFIRE.
IN WHICH OLD FEARS AND OLD SORROWS WERE MELTED.
AND EVERYTHING GOOD WAS FORGED ALL OVER AGAIN, STRONGER THAN IT WAS BEFORE.

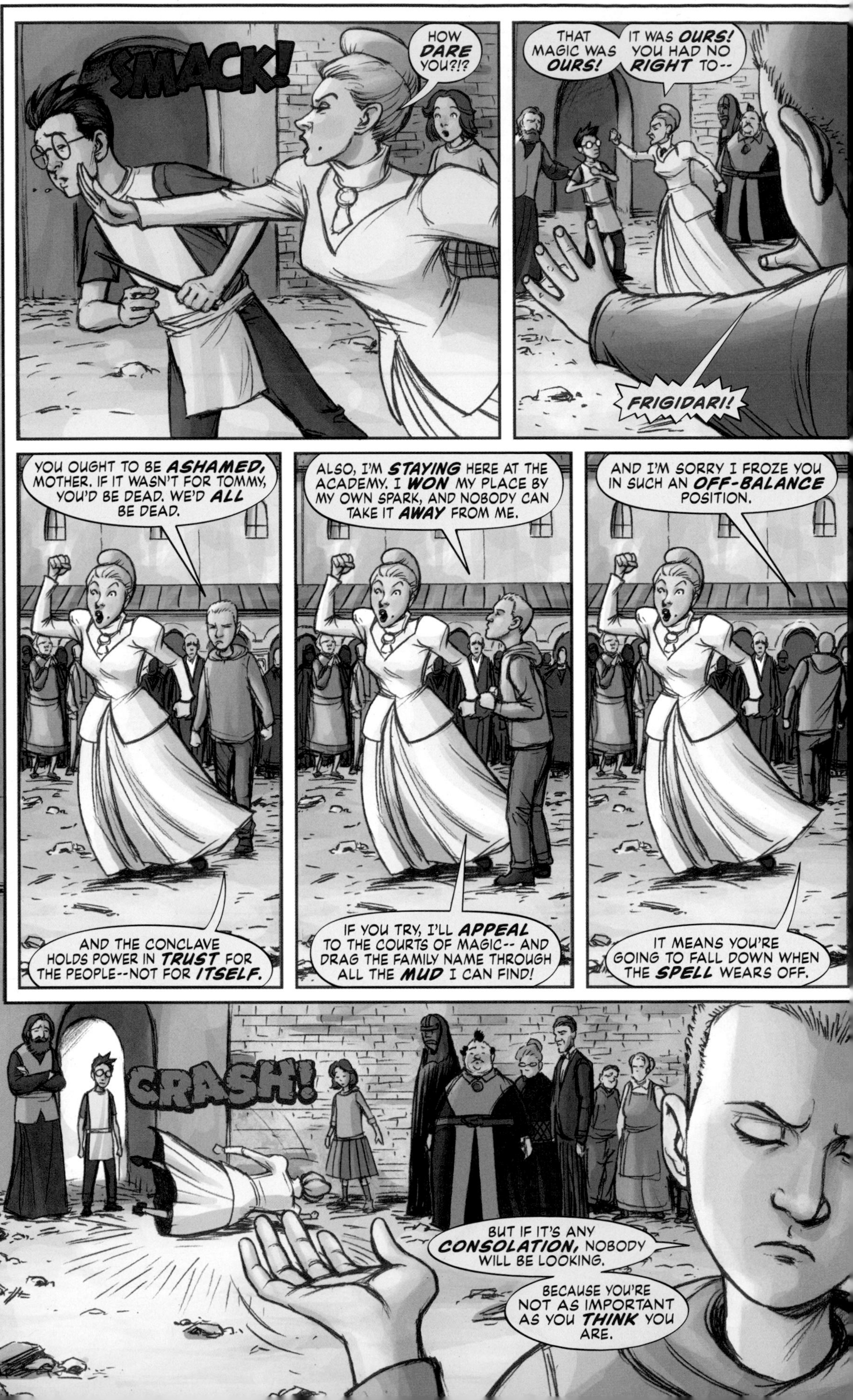
SMACK!
HOW DARE YOU?!?
THAT MAGIC WAS OURS!
IT WAS OURS! YOU HAD NO RIGHT TO--
FRIGIDARI!
YOU OUGHT TO BE ASHAMED, MOTHER. IF IT WASN'T FOR TOMMY, YOU'D BE DEAD. WE'D ALL BE DEAD.
AND THE CONCLAVE HOLDS POWER IN TRUST FOR THE PEOPLE--NOT FOR ITSELF.
ALSO, I'M STAYING HERE AT THE ACADEMY. I WON MY PLACE BY MY OWN SPARK, AND NOBODY CAN TAKE IT AWAY FROM ME.
IF YOU TRY, I'LL APPEAL TO THE COURTS OF MAGIC-- AND DRAG THE FAMILY NAME THROUGH ALL THE MUD I CAN FIND!
AND I'M SORRY I FROZE YOU IN SUCH AN OFF-BALANCE POSITION.
IT MEANS YOU'RE GOING TO FALL DOWN WHEN THE SPELL WEARS OFF.
CRASH!
BUT IF IT'S ANY CONSOLATION, NOBODY WILL BE LOOKING.
BECAUSE YOU'RE NOT AS IMPORTANT AS YOU THINK YOU ARE.

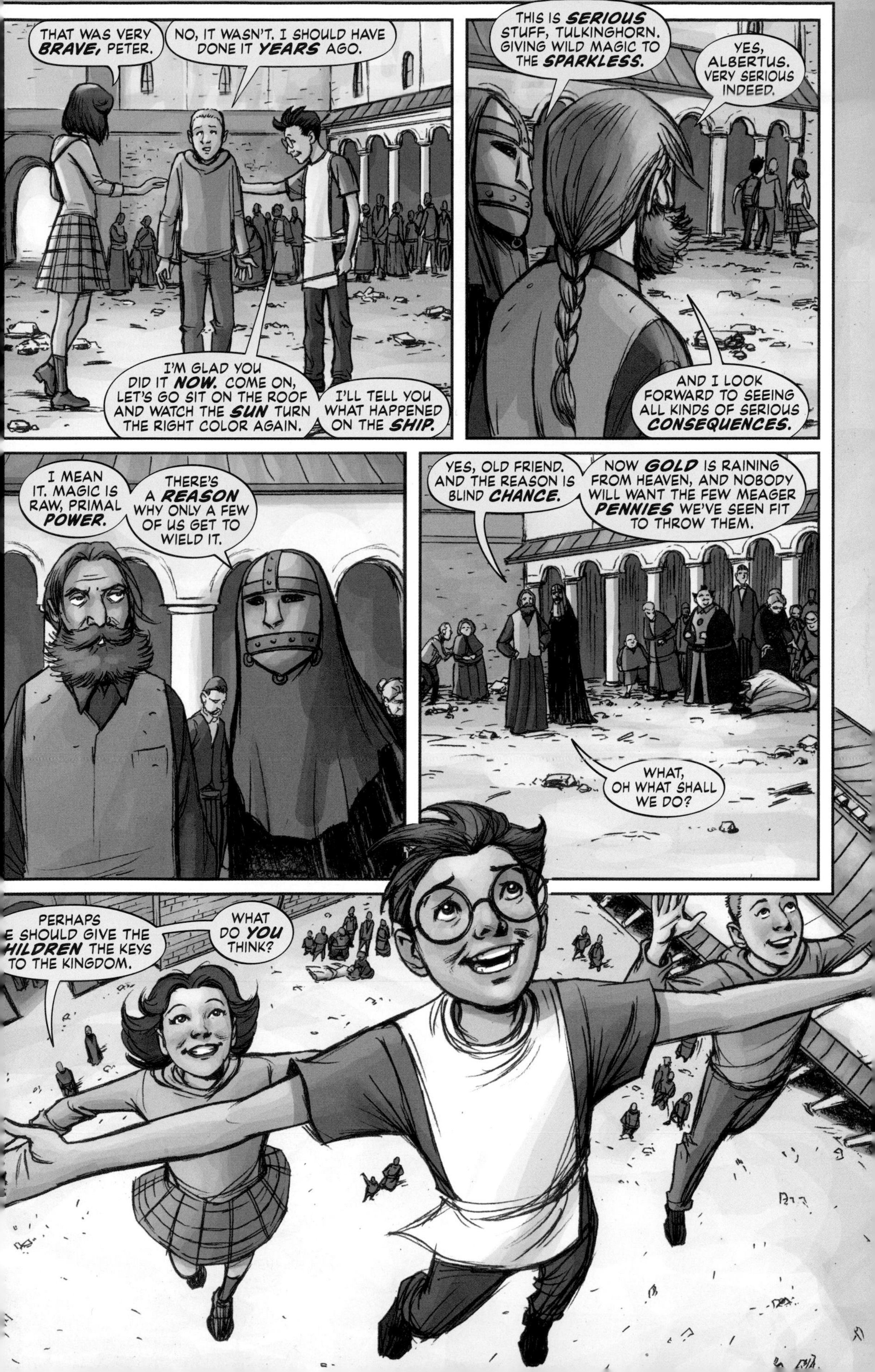
THAT WAS VERY BRAVE, PETER.
NO, IT WASN'T. I SHOULD HAVE DONE IT YEARS AGO.
I'M GLAD YOU DID IT NOW. COME ON, LET'S GO SIT ON THE ROOF AND WATCH THE SUN TURN THE RIGHT COLOR AGAIN.
I'LL TELL YOU WHAT HAPPENED ON THE SHIP.
THIS IS SERIOUS STUFF, TULKINGHORN. GIVING WILD MAGIC TO THE SPARKLESS.
YES, ALBERTUS. VERY SERIOUS INDEED.
AND I LOOK FORWARD TO SEEING ALL KINDS OF SERIOUS CONSEQUENCES.
I MEAN IT. MAGIC IS RAW, PRIMAL POWER.
THERE'S A REASON WHY ONLY A FEW OF US GET TO WIELD IT.
YES, OLD FRIEND. AND THE REASON IS BLIND CHANCE.
NOW GOLD IS RAINING FROM HEAVEN, AND NOBODY WILL WANT THE FEW MEAGER PENNIES WE'VE SEEN FIT TO THROW THEM.
WHAT, OH WHAT SHALL WE DO?
PERHAPS E SHOULD GIVE THE HILDREN THE KEYS TO THE KINGDOM.
WHAT DO YOU THINK?

WHAT MORE THERE IS TO TELL IS QUICKLY TOLD.

IN EASTBROOKE, AS EVERYWHERE ELSE, **MAGIC** NOW BECAME A FEATURE OF EVERYDAY LIFE.

THE CONCLAVE PROPHESIED THAT THIS WOULD BE THE END OF THE WORLD, BUT IT SEEMED THAT THIS **DOOM-MONGERING** WAS OVERLY PESSIMISTIC.

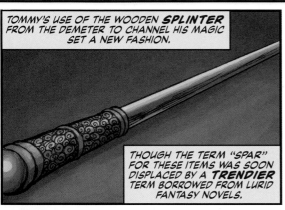

TOMMY'S USE OF THE WOODEN **SPLINTER** FROM THE DEMETER TO CHANNEL HIS MAGIC SET A NEW FASHION.

THOUGH THE TERM "SPAR" FOR THESE ITEMS WAS SOON DISPLACED BY A **TRENDIER** TERM BORROWED FROM LURID FANTASY NOVELS.

IN DUE COURSE, TOMMY TAYLOR WAS ENROLLED AS A **STUDENT** AT THE TULKINGHORN ACADEMY.

THE WINGED CAT, **MINGUS,** REMAINED WITH HIM AS HIS COMPANION AND HIS FRIEND.

AS CLOSE TO HIM, PERHAPS, AS THOSE **OTHER** FRIENDS, SUE AND PETER...

...WHOSE DESTINIES SEEMED TO BE CLOSELY **ENTWINED** WITH HIS OWN.

HIS **STUDIES** NOW CONSUMED MOST OF HIS TIME, BUT HE STILL CAME TWICE A WEEK TO TELL **STORIES** TO THE DEAF CHILD, ROSE COLLIER.

INCLUDING, NOW, THE STOR OF HOW LEARNING TO TAL TO HER HAD SAVED HIS LIFE AND PERHAPS THE **WORL**

THE DEMETER--THE SHIP THAT SANK **TWICE**--REMAINED EMBEDDED IN THE STRUCTURE OF THE EASTBROOKE **PIER.**

IT IS CURRENTLY A **COFFEE SHOP.**

The End

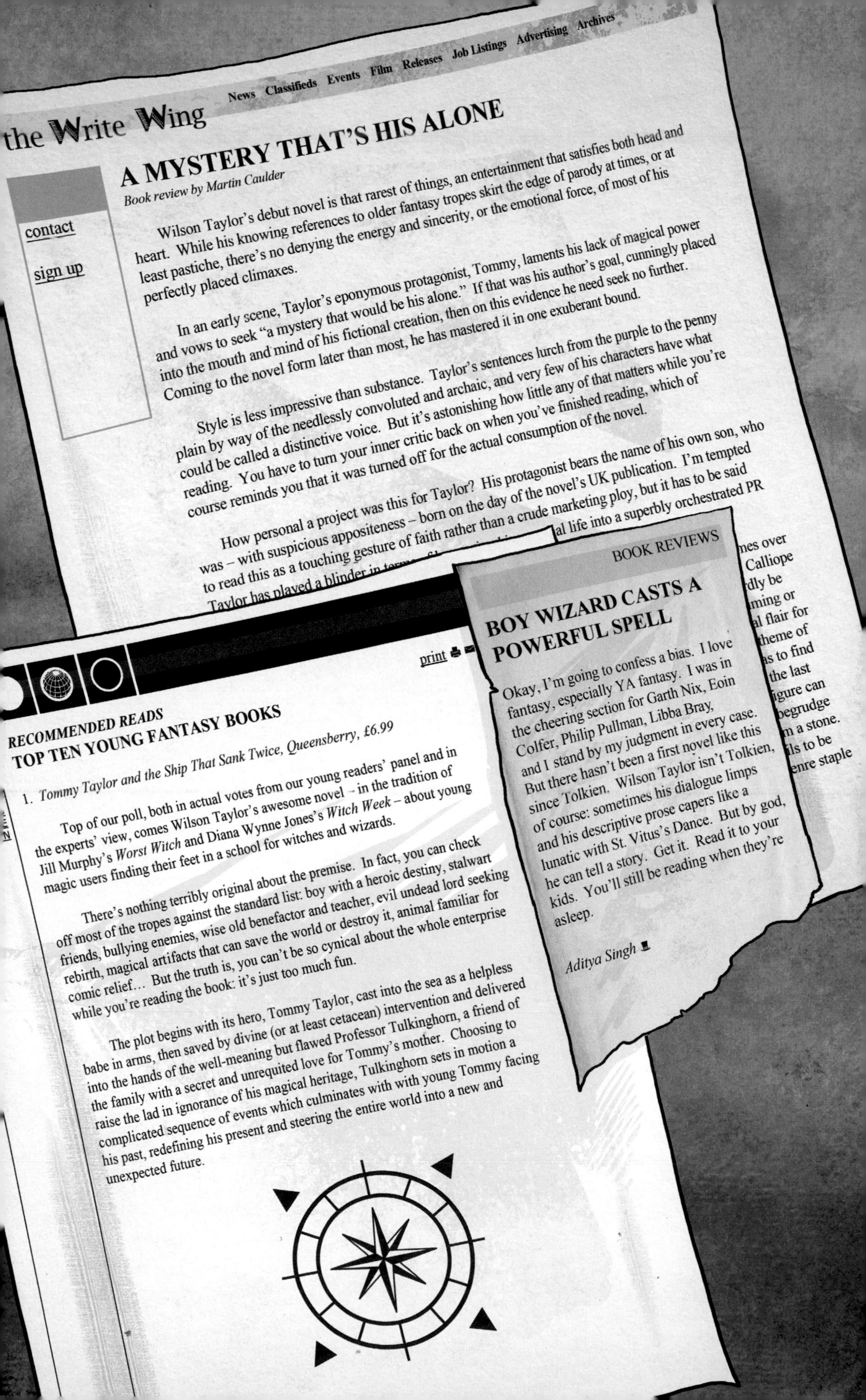

the Write Wing

News Classifieds Events Film Releases Job Listings Advertising Archives

contact

sign up

A MYSTERY THAT'S HIS ALONE

Book review by Martin Caulder

Wilson Taylor's debut novel is that rarest of things, an entertainment that satisfies both head and heart. While his knowing references to older fantasy tropes skirt the edge of parody at times, or at least pastiche, there's no denying the energy and sincerity, or the emotional force, of most of his perfectly placed climaxes.

In an early scene, Taylor's eponymous protagonist, Tommy, laments his lack of magical power and vows to seek "a mystery that would be his alone." If that was his author's goal, cunningly placed into the mouth and mind of his fictional creation, then on this evidence he need seek no further. Coming to the novel form later than most, he has mastered it in one exuberant bound.

Style is less impressive than substance. Taylor's sentences lurch from the purple to the penny plain by way of the needlessly convoluted and archaic, and very few of his characters have what could be called a distinctive voice. But it's astonishing how little any of that matters while you're reading. You have to turn your inner critic back on when you've finished reading, which of course reminds you that it was turned off for the actual consumption of the novel.

How personal a project was this for Taylor? His protagonist bears the name of his own son, who was – with suspicious appositeness – born on the day of the novel's UK publication. I'm tempted to read this as a touching gesture of faith rather than a crude marketing ploy, but it has to be said Taylor has played a blinder in term... al life into a superbly orchestrated PR

...mes over ... Calliope ... rdly be ... ming or ... al flair for ... theme of ... s to find ... the last ... figure can ... begrudge ... m a stone. ... ils to be ... enre staple

print

RECOMMENDED READS

TOP TEN YOUNG FANTASY BOOKS

1. *Tommy Taylor and the Ship That Sank Twice*, *Queensberry*, £6.99

Top of our poll, both in actual votes from our young readers' panel and in the experts' view, comes Wilson Taylor's awesome novel – in the tradition of Jill Murphy's *Worst Witch* and Diana Wynne Jones's *Witch Week* – about young magic users finding their feet in a school for witches and wizards.

There's nothing terribly original about the premise. In fact, you can check off most of the tropes against the standard list: boy with a heroic destiny, stalwart friends, bullying enemies, wise old benefactor and teacher, evil undead lord seeking rebirth, magical artifacts that can save the world or destroy it, animal familiar for comic relief... But the truth is, you can't be so cynical about the whole enterprise while you're reading the book: it's just too much fun.

The plot begins with its hero, Tommy Taylor, cast into the sea as a helpless babe in arms, then saved by divine (or at least cetacean) intervention and delivered into the hands of the well-meaning but flawed Professor Tulkinghorn, a friend of the family with a secret and unrequited love for Tommy's mother. Choosing to raise the lad in ignorance of his magical heritage, Tulkinghorn sets in motion a complicated sequence of events which culminates with with young Tommy facing his past, redefining his present and steering the entire world into a new and unexpected future.

BOOK REVIEWS

BOY WIZARD CASTS A POWERFUL SPELL

Okay, I'm going to confess a bias. I love fantasy, especially YA fantasy. I was in the cheering section for Garth Nix, Eoin Colfer, Philip Pullman, Libba Bray, and I stand by my judgment in every case. But there hasn't been a first novel like this since Tolkien. Wilson Taylor isn't Tolkien, of course: sometimes his dialogue limps and his descriptive prose capers like a lunatic with St. Vitus's Dance. But by god, he can tell a story. Get it. Read it to your kids. You'll still be reading when they're asleep.

Aditya Singh

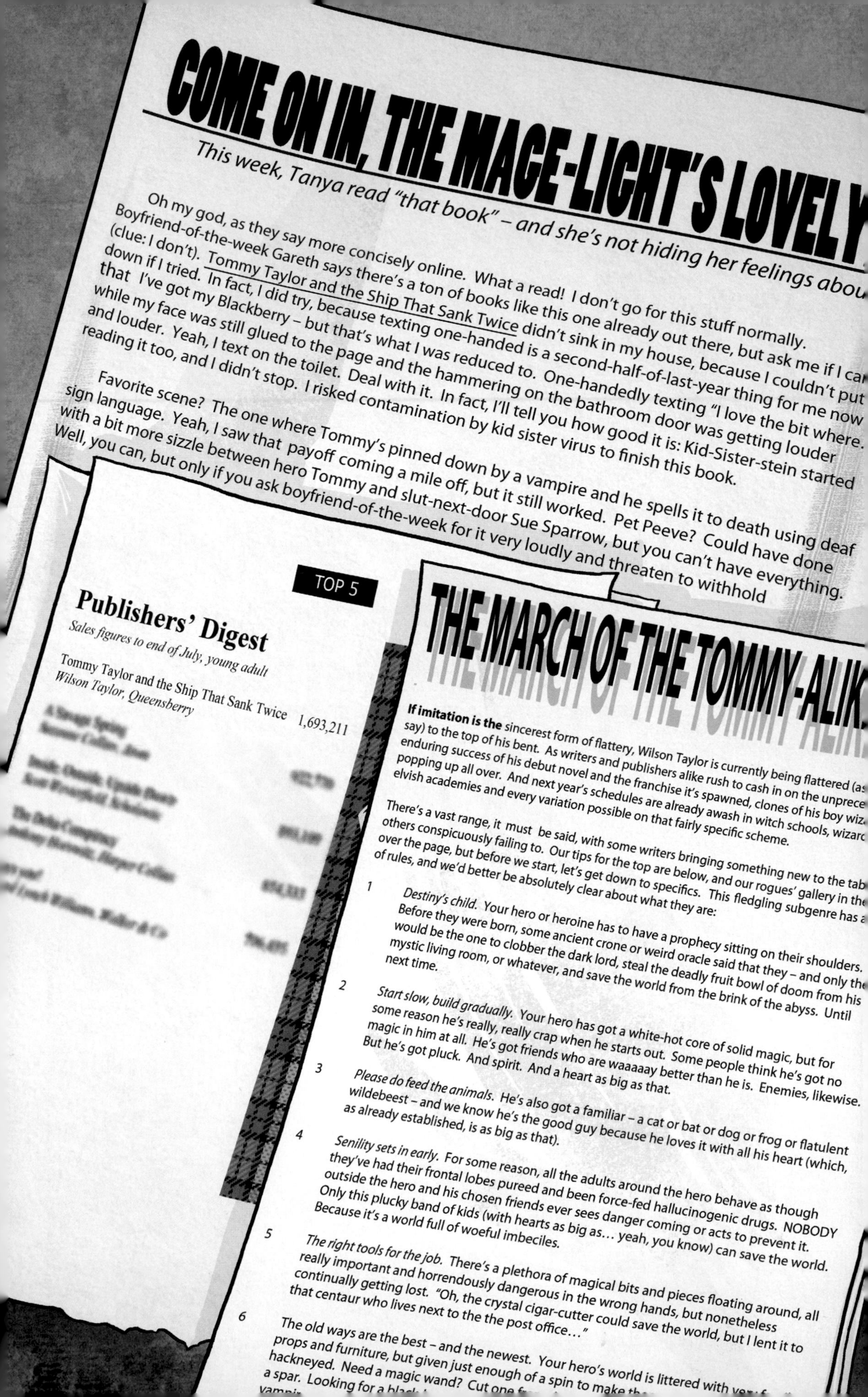

COME ON IN, THE MAGE-LIGHT'S LOVELY

This week, Tanya read "that book" – and she's not hiding her feelings abou[t]

Oh my god, as they say more concisely online. What a read! I don't go for this stuff normally. Boyfriend-of-the-week Gareth says there's a ton of books like this one already out there, but ask me if I car[e] (clue: I don't). Tommy Taylor and the Ship That Sank Twice didn't sink in my house, because I couldn't put that I've got my Blackberry – but that's what I was reduced to. One-handedly texting "I love the bit where[.] down if I tried. In fact, I did try, because texting one-handed is a second-half-of-last-year thing for me now while my face was still glued to the page and the hammering on the bathroom door was getting louder and louder. Yeah, I text on the toilet. Deal with it. In fact, I'll tell you how good it is: Kid-Sister-stein started reading it too, and I didn't stop. I risked contamination by kid sister virus to finish this book.

Favorite scene? The one where Tommy's pinned down by a vampire and he spells it to death using deaf sign language. Yeah, I saw that payoff coming a mile off, but it still worked. Pet Peeve? Could have done with a bit more sizzle between hero Tommy and slut-next-door Sue Sparrow, but you can't have everything. Well, you can, but only if you ask boyfriend-of-the-week for it very loudly and threaten to withhold

---

Publishers' Digest
Sales figures to end of July, young adult

TOP 5

Tommy Taylor and the Ship That Sank Twice *Wilson Taylor, Queensberry*	1,693,211
A Street Spray *Banner Colin, Ann*	
Inside Clouds, Upside Down *Kate Peopled, Scholastic*	422,79
The Dela Company *Anthony Horwall, Harper Collins*	995,199
... you! *... track William, Walter & Co*	654,333
The	706,691

THE MARCH OF THE TOMMY-ALIK[E]

If imitation is the sincerest form of flattery, Wilson Taylor is currently being flattered (as [they] say) to the top of his bent. As writers and publishers alike rush to cash in on the unprece[dented] enduring success of his debut novel and the franchise it's spawned, clones of his boy wiz[ard are] popping up all over. And next year's schedules are already awash in witch schools, wizard[...] elvish academies and every variation possible on that fairly specific scheme.

There's a vast range, it must be said, with some writers bringing something new to the tab[le and] others conspicuously failing to. Our tips for the top are below, and our rogues' gallery in the [...] over the page, but before we start, let's get down to specifics. This fledgling subgenre has a[...] of rules, and we'd better be absolutely clear about what they are:

1 *Destiny's child.* Your hero or heroine has to have a prophecy sitting on their shoulders. Before they were born, some ancient crone or weird oracle said that they – and only the[y] would be the one to clobber the dark lord, steal the deadly fruit bowl of doom from his mystic living room, or whatever, and save the world from the brink of the abyss. Until next time.

2 *Start slow, build gradually.* Your hero has got a white-hot core of solid magic, but for some reason he's really, really crap when he starts out. Some people think he's got no magic in him at all. He's got friends who are waaaaay better than he is. Enemies, likewise. But he's got pluck. And spirit. And a heart as big as that.

3 *Please do feed the animals.* He's also got a familiar – a cat or bat or dog or frog or flatulent wildebeest – and we know he's the good guy because he loves it with all his heart (which, as already established, is as big as that).

4 *Senility sets in early.* For some reason, all the adults around the hero behave as though they've had their frontal lobes pureed and been force-fed hallucinogenic drugs. NOBODY outside the hero and his chosen friends ever sees danger coming or acts to prevent it. Only this plucky band of kids (with hearts as big as… yeah, you know) can save the world. Because it's a world full of woeful imbeciles.

5 *The right tools for the job.* There's a plethora of magical bits and pieces floating around, all really important and horrendously dangerous in the wrong hands, but nonetheless continually getting lost. "Oh, the crystal cigar-cutter could save the world, but I lent it to that centaur who lives next to the the post office…"

6 *The old ways are the best – and the newest.* Your hero's world is littered with ver[y f...] props and furniture, but given just enough of a spin to make th[...] hackneyed. Need a magic wand? Cut one f[...] a spar. Looking for a black[...] vampir[...]

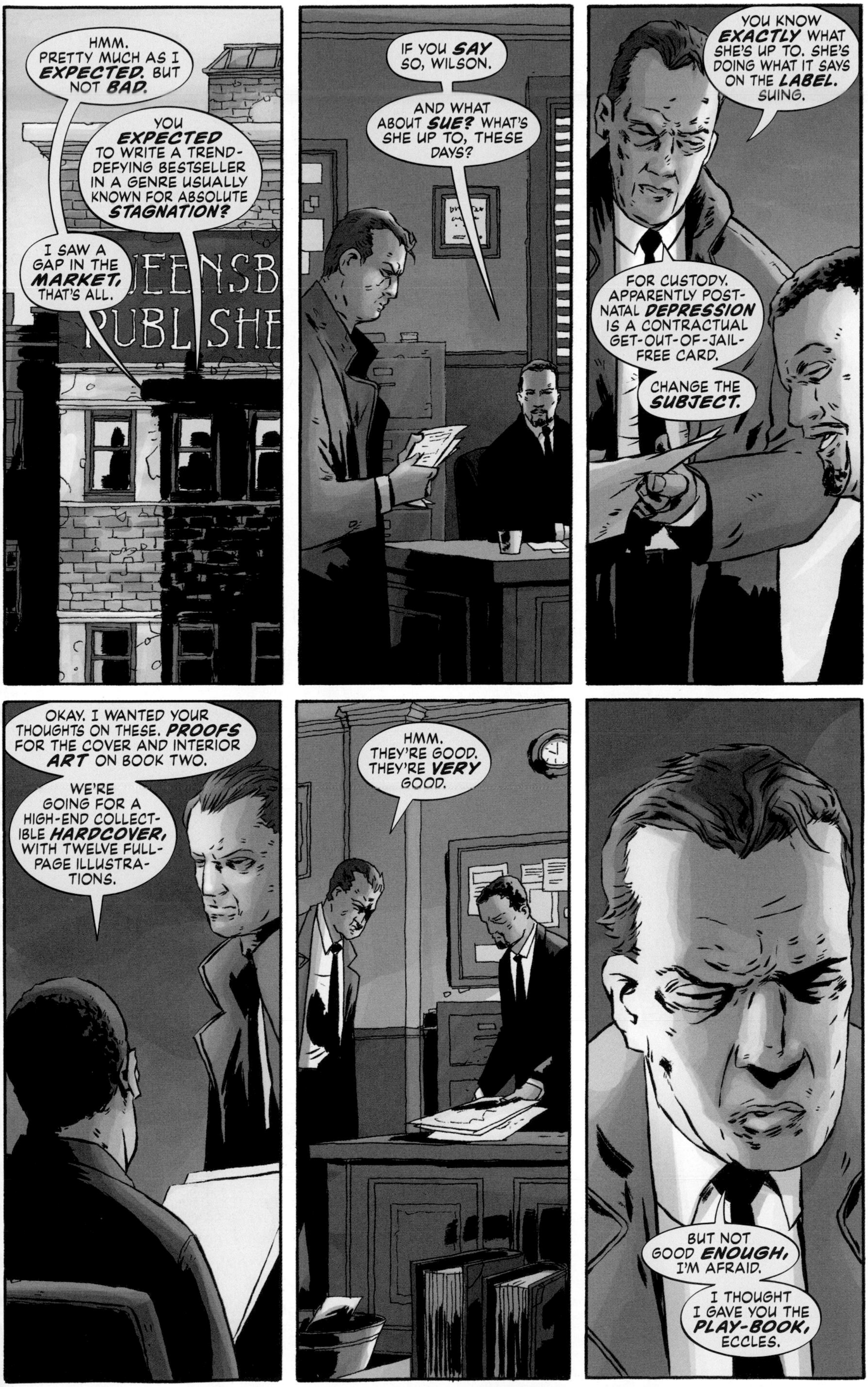
HMM. PRETTY MUCH AS I EXPECTED. BUT NOT BAD.
YOU EXPECTED TO WRITE A TREND-DEFYING BESTSELLER IN A GENRE USUALLY KNOWN FOR ABSOLUTE STAGNATION?
I SAW A GAP IN THE MARKET, THAT'S ALL.
IF YOU SAY SO, WILSON.
AND WHAT ABOUT SUE? WHAT'S SHE UP TO, THESE DAYS?
YOU KNOW EXACTLY WHAT SHE'S UP TO. SHE'S DOING WHAT IT SAYS ON THE LABEL. SUING.
FOR CUSTODY. APPARENTLY POST-NATAL DEPRESSION IS A CONTRACTUAL GET-OUT-OF-JAIL-FREE CARD.
CHANGE THE SUBJECT.
OKAY. I WANTED YOUR THOUGHTS ON THESE. PROOFS FOR THE COVER AND INTERIOR ART ON BOOK TWO.
WE'RE GOING FOR A HIGH-END COLLECTIBLE HARDCOVER, WITH TWELVE FULL-PAGE ILLUSTRATIONS.
HMM. THEY'RE GOOD. THEY'RE VERY GOOD.
BUT NOT GOOD ENOUGH, I'M AFRAID.
I THOUGHT I GAVE YOU THE PLAY-BOOK, ECCLES.

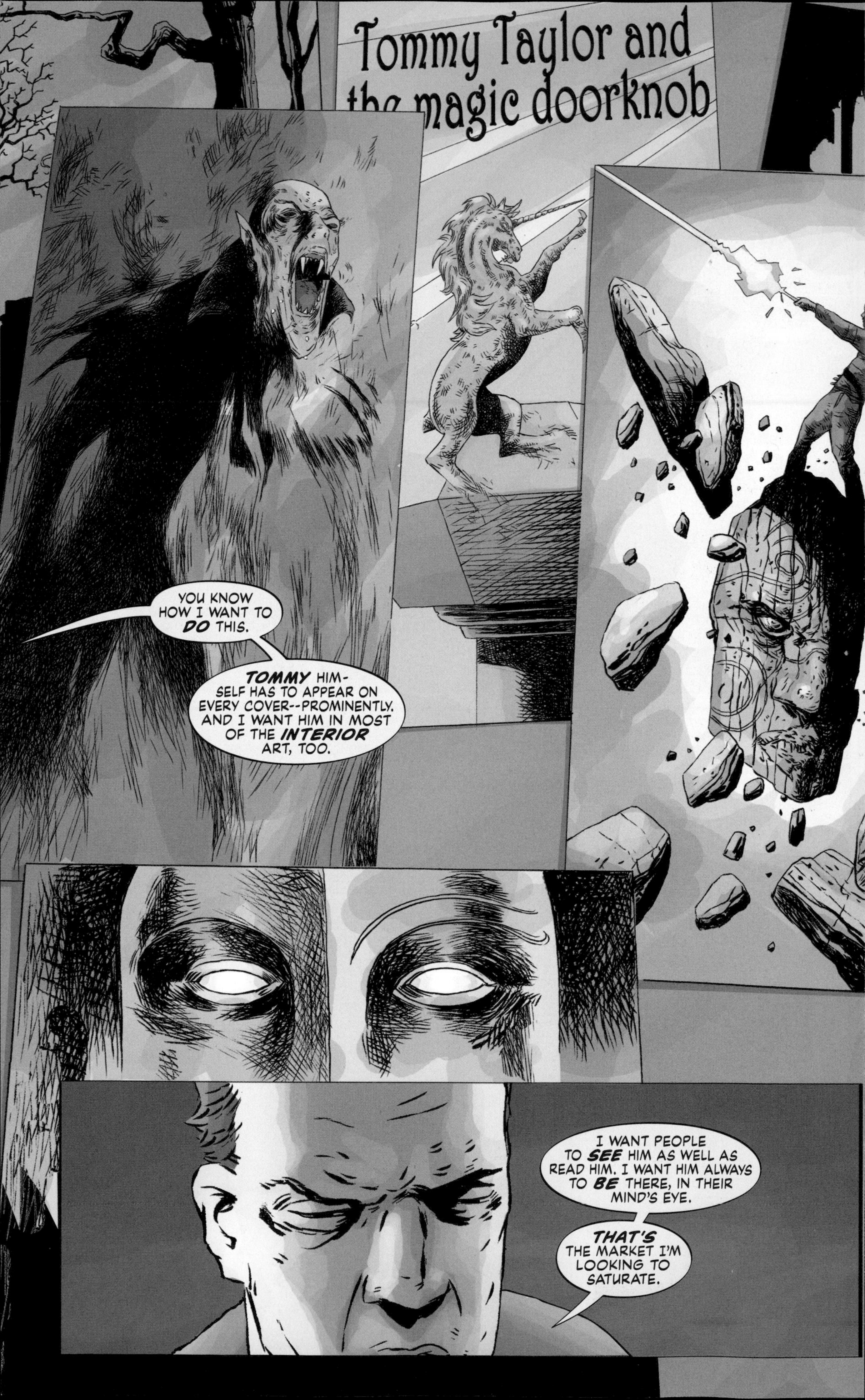
Tommy Taylor and the magic doorknob
YOU KNOW HOW I WANT TO DO THIS.
TOMMY HIMSELF HAS TO APPEAR ON EVERY COVER--PROMINENTLY. AND I WANT HIM IN MOST OF THE INTERIOR ART, TOO.
I WANT PEOPLE TO SEE HIM AS WELL AS READ HIM. I WANT HIM ALWAYS TO BE THERE, IN THEIR MIND'S EYE.
THAT'S THE MARKET I'M LOOKING TO SATURATE.

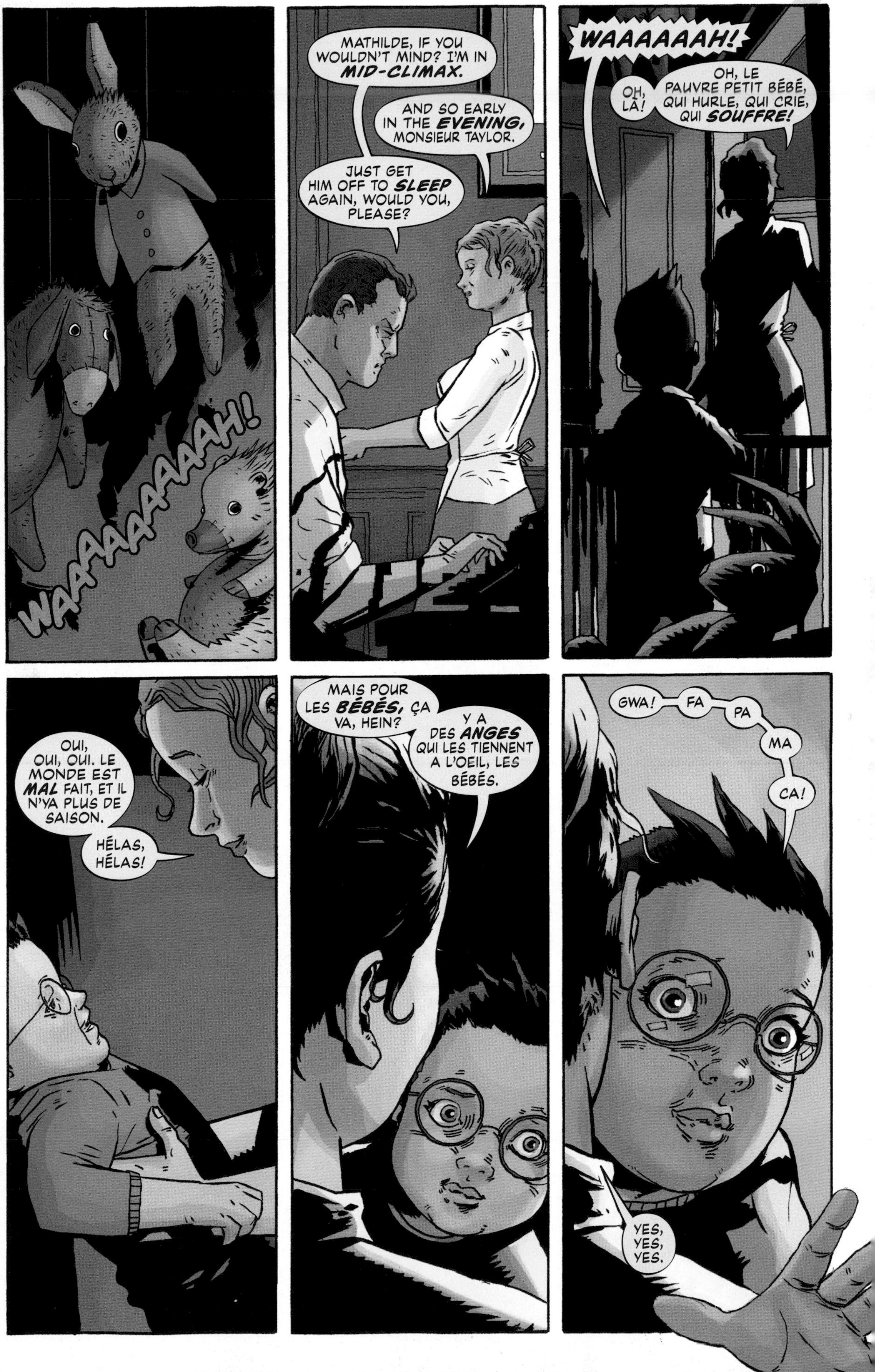

WAAAAAAAAAH!
MATHILDE, IF YOU WOULDN'T MIND? I'M IN MID-CLIMAX.
AND SO EARLY IN THE EVENING, MONSIEUR TAYLOR.
JUST GET HIM OFF TO SLEEP AGAIN, WOULD YOU, PLEASE?
WAAAAAAH!
OH, LÀ!
OH, LE PAUVRE PETIT BÉBÉ, QUI HURLE, QUI CRIE, QUI SOUFFRE!
OUI, OUI, OUI. LE MONDE EST MAL FAIT, ET IL N'YA PLUS DE SAISON.
HÉLAS, HÉLAS!
MAIS POUR LES BÉBÉS, ÇA VA, HEIN?
Y A DES ANGES QUI LES TIENNENT A L'OEIL, LES BÉBÉS.
GWA!
FA
PA
MA
CA!
YES, YES, YES.

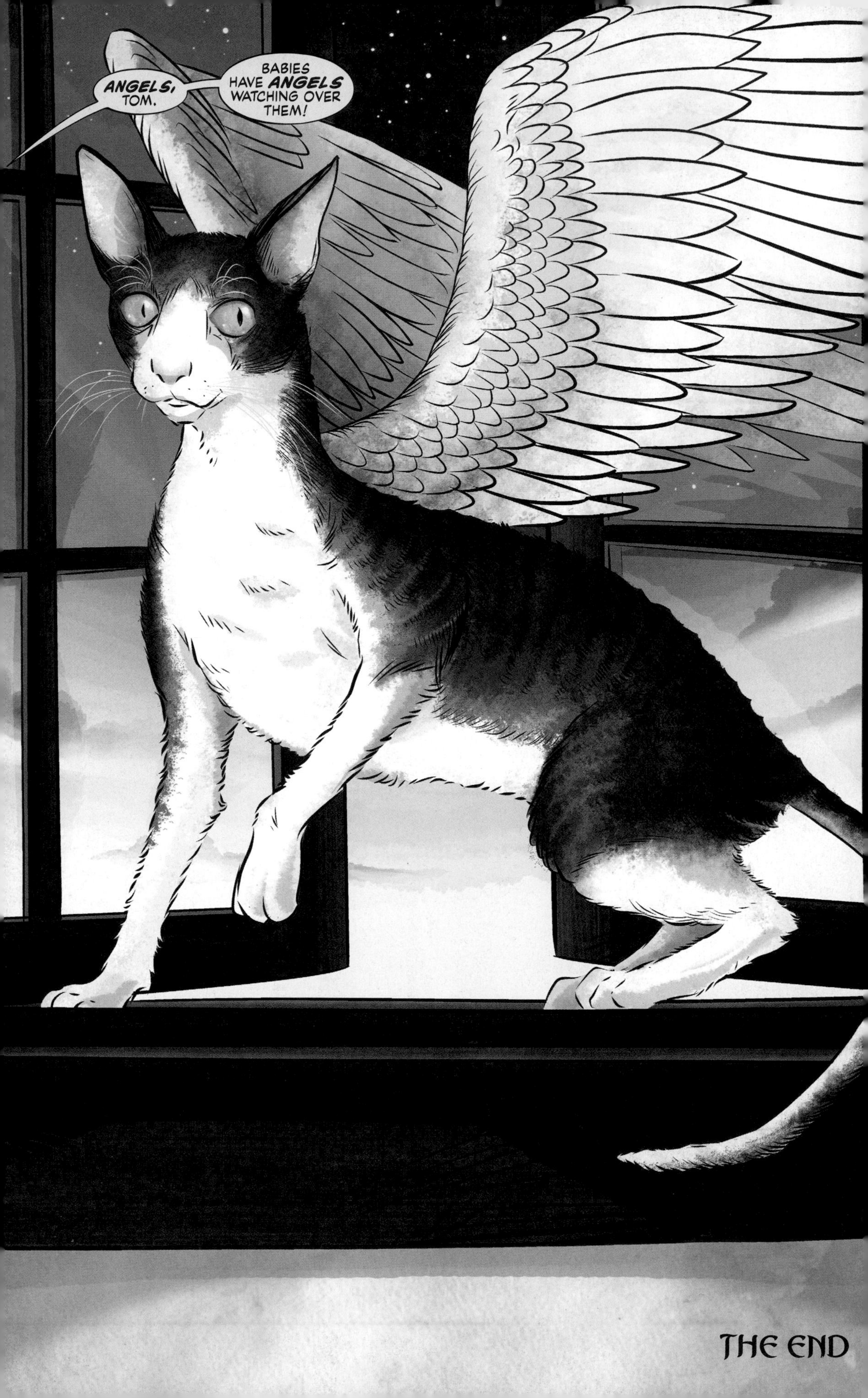
BABIES HAVE ANGELS WATCHING OVER THEM!
ANGELS, TOM.
THE END

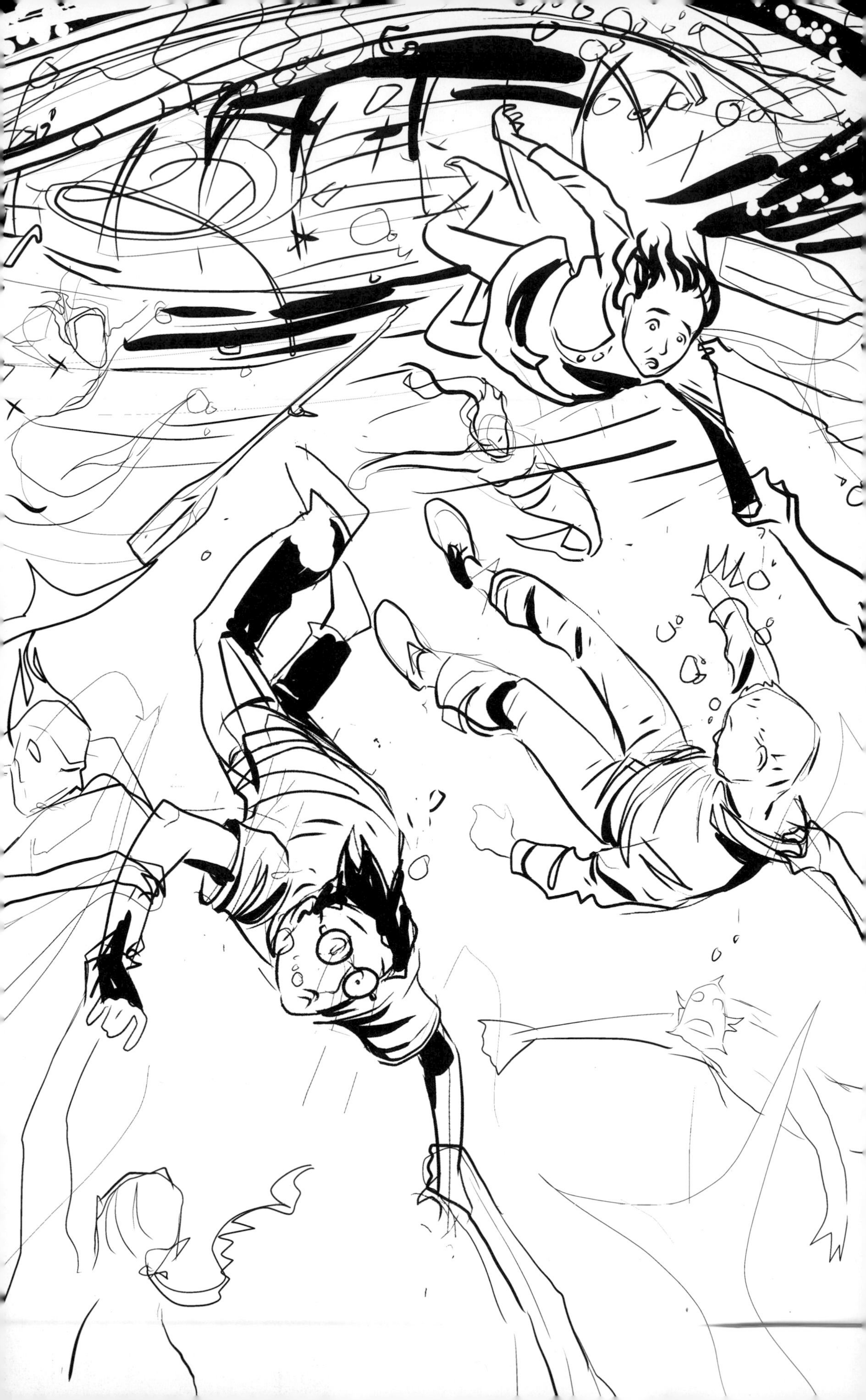

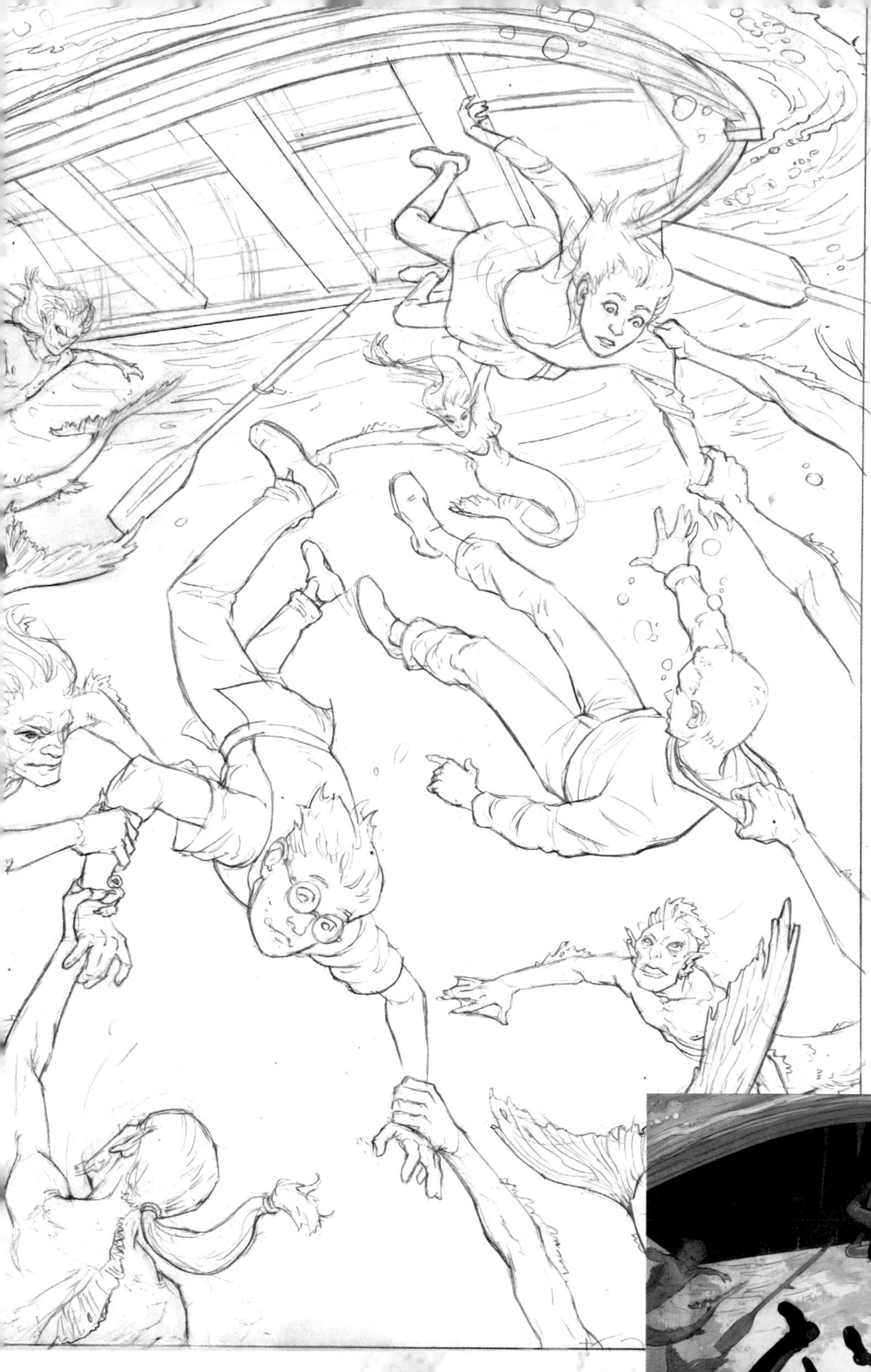

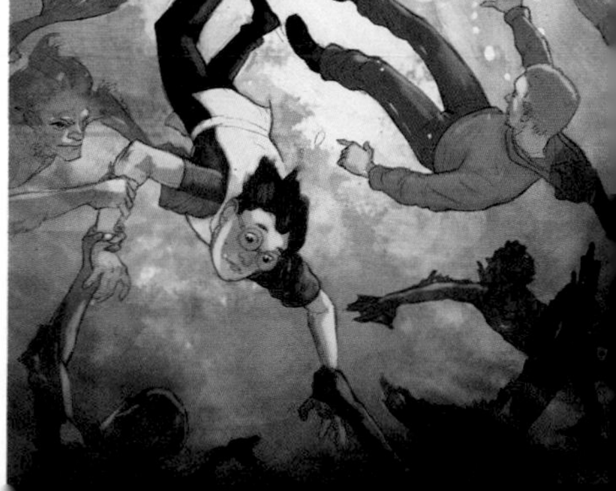

PROCESS: INTERIORS

From Peter Gross's layout of page 76 to Kurt Huggins' pencils and Zelda Devon's final color

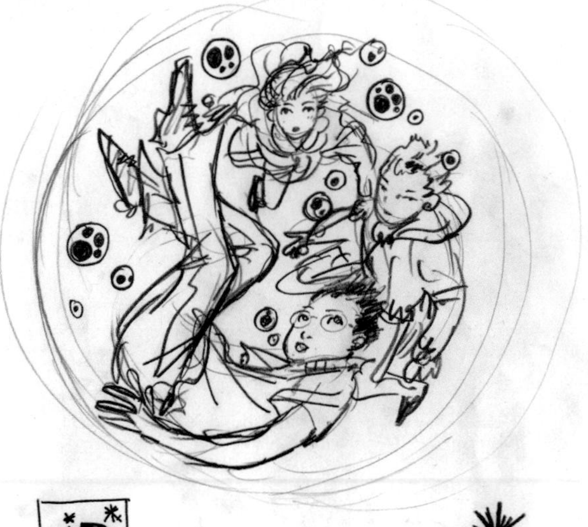

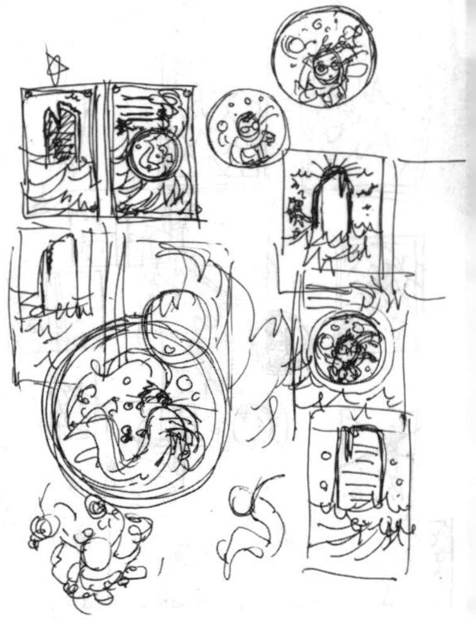

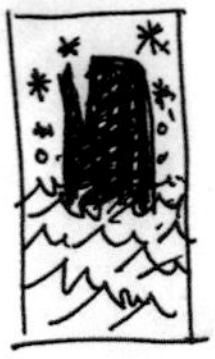

PROCESS: COVER

From Yuko Shimizu's cover roughs to inspired design.

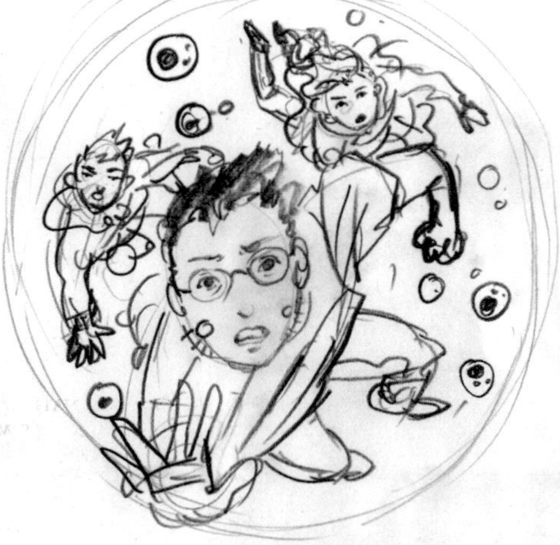

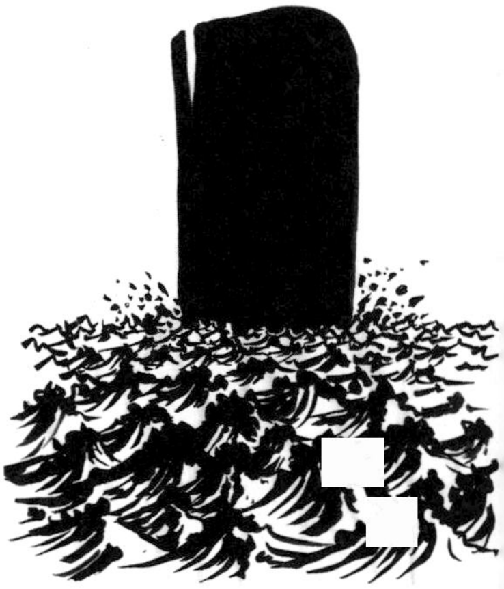

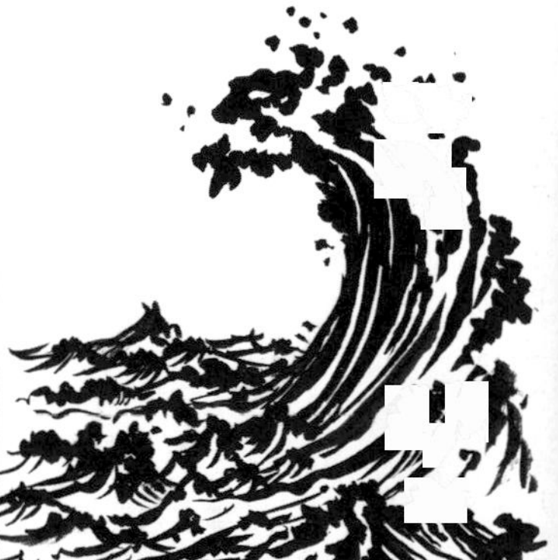

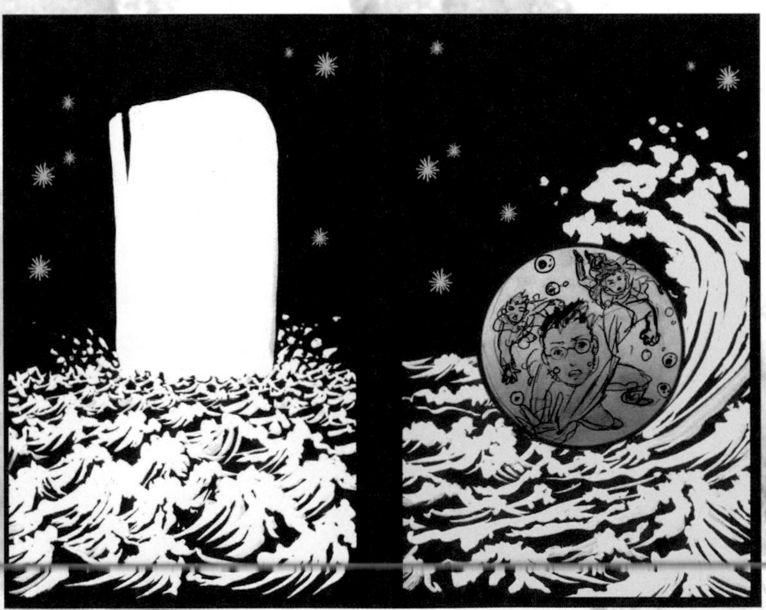

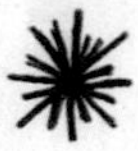

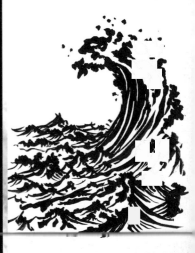

VERTIGO

"Incredibly fun and ridiculously addictive."
—USA TODAY.COM

"Ambitious, exciting. Grade A-."
— THE ONION/THE A.V. CLUB

"A wish-I'd-thought-of-it premise, beautifully executed. Highly recommended for anyone who thinks that fantasy can do more than just help you escape the real world."
—BRIAN K. VAUGHAN, Y: THE LAST MAN

FROM THE WRITER OF *LUCIFER* AND *HELLBLAZER*

MIKE CAREY

with PETER GROSS

THE UNWRITTEN VOL. 3: DEAD MAN'S KNOCK

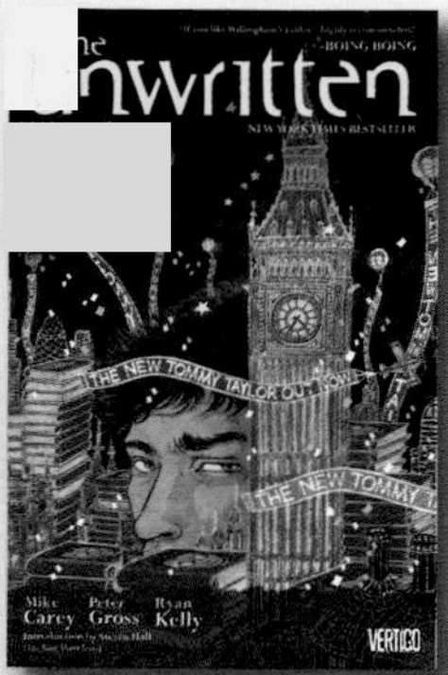

the unwritten
NEW YORK TIMES BESTSELLER
THE NEW TOMMY TAYLOR
Mike Carey
Peter Gross
Ryan Kelly
VERTIGO

THE UNWRITTEN VOL. 4: LEVIATHAN

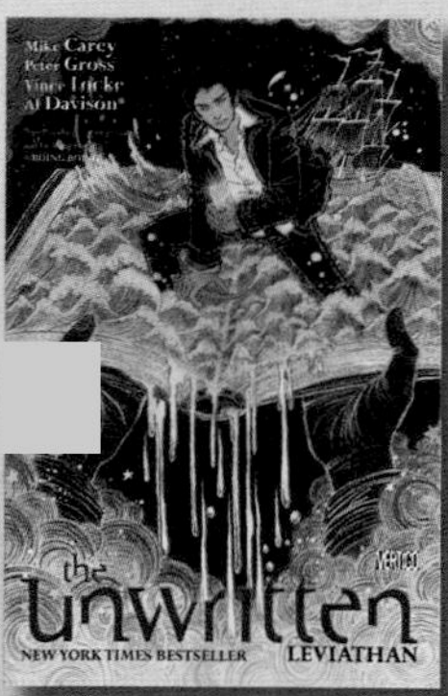

Mike Carey
Peter Gross
the unwritten
NEW YORK TIMES BESTSELLER
LEVIATHAN

THE UNWRITTEN VOL. 1: TOMMY TAYLOR AND THE BOGUS IDENTITY

THE UNWRITTEN VOL. 2: INSIDE MAN

THE UNWRITTEN VOL. 3: DEAD MAN'S KNOCK

THE UNWRITTEN VOL. 4: LEVIATHAN

THE UNWRITTEN VOL. 5: ON TO GENESIS

THE UNWRITTEN VOL. 6: TOMMY TAYLOR AND THE WAR OF WORDS

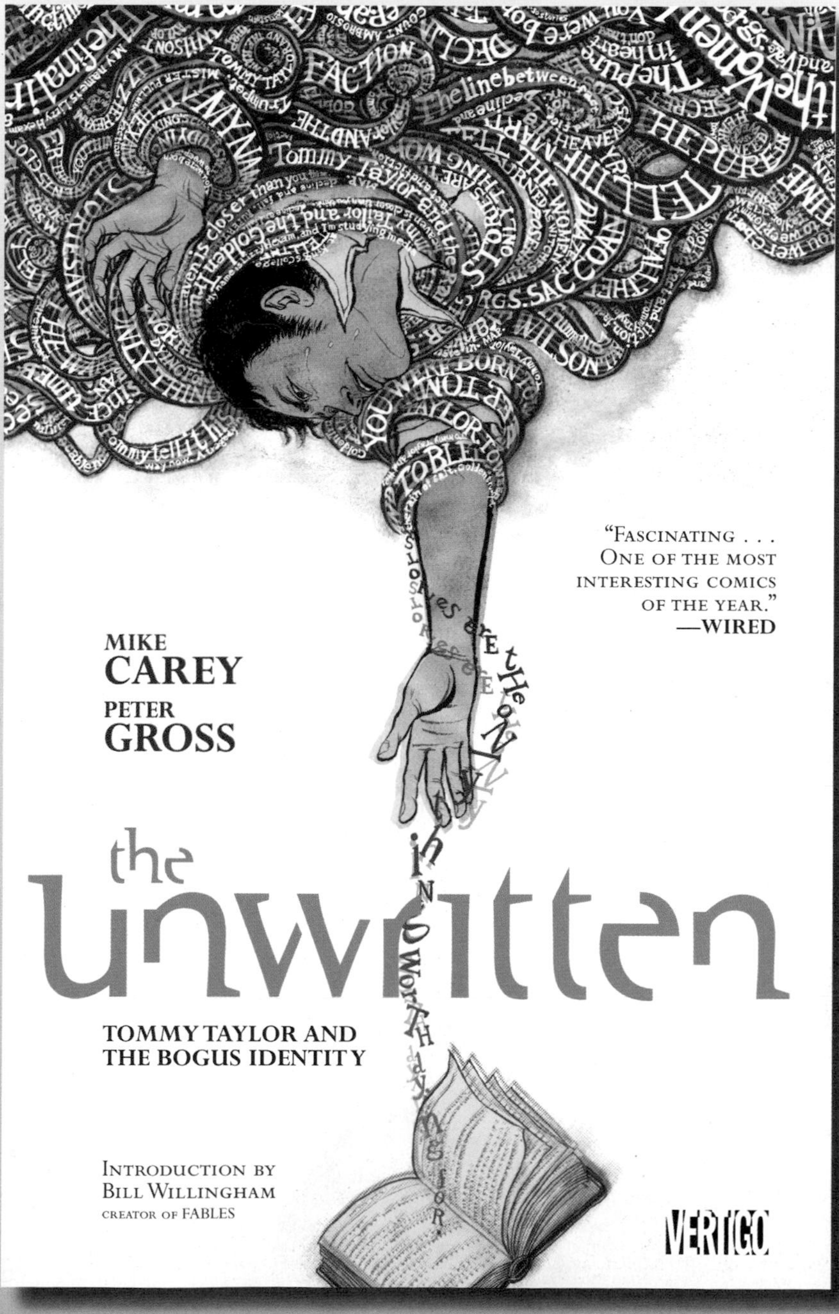

"FASCINATING . . . ONE OF THE MOST INTERESTING COMICS OF THE YEAR." —WIRED
MIKE CAREY
PETER GROSS
the unwritten
TOMMY TAYLOR AND THE BOGUS IDENTITY
INTRODUCTION BY BILL WILLINGHAM
CREATOR OF FABLES
VERTIGO

Mike Carey is a British writer of comic books and prose fiction. He
began his career at US independent publisher Caliber with *Inferno* and
Doctor Faustus before making his Vertigo debut with two stories in THE
SANDMAN PRESENTS series. He's remained a Vertigo writer ever since,
co-creating the Eisner-nominated LUCIFER, CROSSING MIDNIGHT and
THE UNWRITTEN along with many graphic novels and miniseries and a
four-year run on HELLBLAZER. His novels include the *Felix Castor* series,
The Dead Sea Deception (as Adam Blake), *The Steel Seraglio* (with Linda and
Louise Carey) and the forthcoming *The Girl with All the Gifts*.

Peter Gross is the co-creator of Vertigo's multi-Eisner-nominated
series THE UNWRITTEN, and co-creator and artist of *American Jesus*
with Mark Millar. He also illustrated two of Vertigo's longest-running
series, LUCIFER, and THE BOOKS OF MAGIC and he suspects that he
might be the only artist/writer who has had work published for Vertigo
every year of the imprint's existence. He lives in Minneapolis, Minnesota,
with his wife, Jeanne McGee, their daughter Alice and a cat who looks
suspiciously like Tommy Taylor's cat, Mingus.

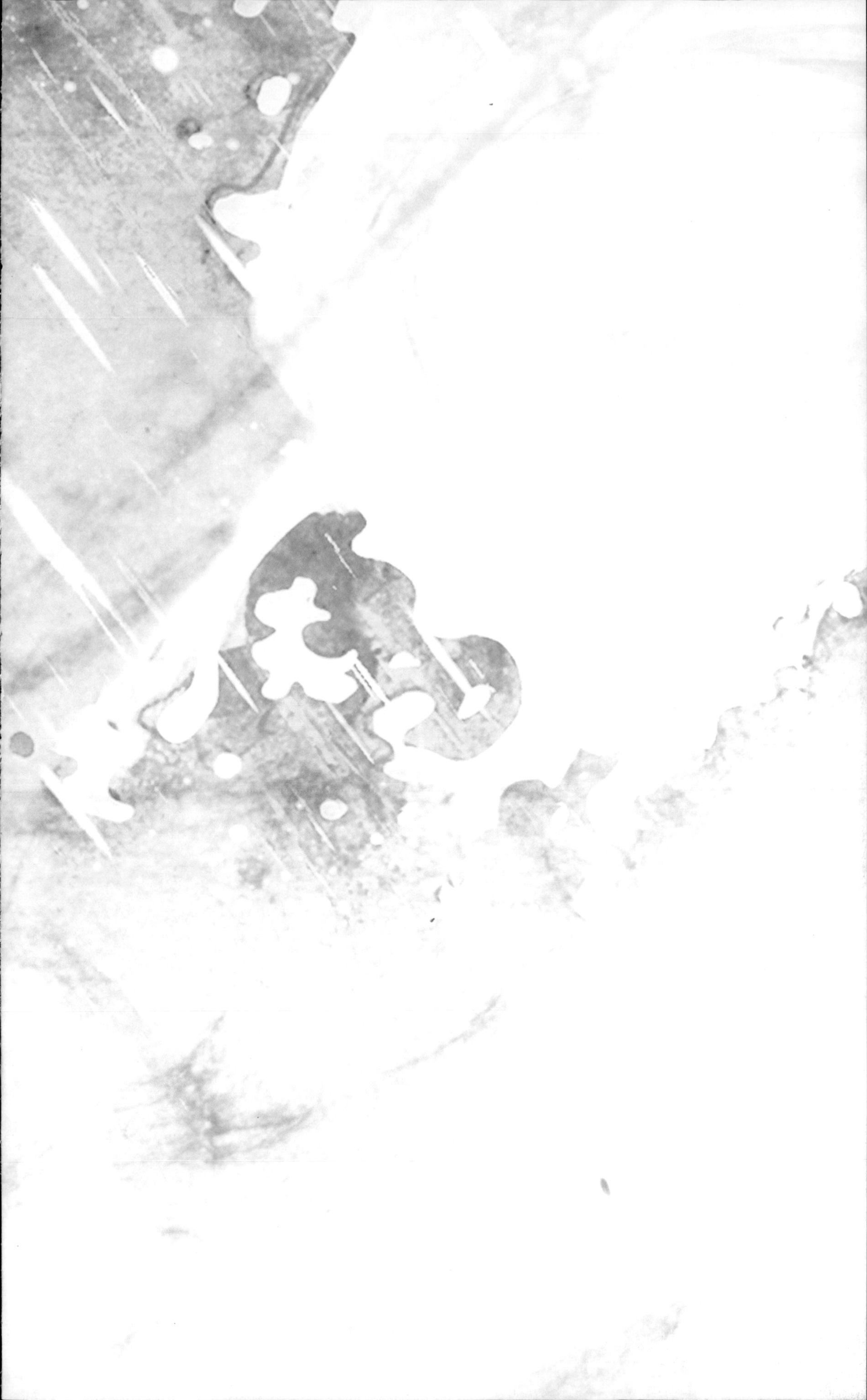